WHEN Minor League Baseball Almost WENT Bust

1946-1963

Edited by George Pawlush

Associate editors Marshall Adesman, Mike Huber, Len Levin, and Bill Nowlin

Society for American Baseball Research, Inc.
Phoenix, AZ

When Minor League Baseball Almost Went Bust: 1946-1963

Edited by George Pawlush
Associate editors Marshall Adesman, Mike Huber, Len Levin, and Bill Nowlin

Design: Rachael Sullivan
Front cover photographs: Artillery Park in Kingston, Pennsylvania, was the home of Wilkes-Barre minor-league baseball from 1925 to 1955. Shown are fans and players at a Wilkes-Barre Barons game in 1947. The team was a Class-A Eastern League affiliate of the Cleveland Indians. Collection of George Pawlush.
Vintage ball and bat photograph by Nisit Rawo | Dreamstime.com
The Carbondale Pioneers were members of the Class-D North Atlantic League from 1946 to 1950. They played at Russell Park, which was the largest venue in the league and could accommodate 5000 fans. During their five-year existence, Carbondale was an affiliate of the Philadelphia Phillies. The photo was taken in 1946. Collection of George Pawlush.

ISBN 978-1-960819-29-1 paper
ISBN 978-1-960819-28-4 ebook

Library of Congress Control Number: 2024922267

Cronkite School at ASU
555 N. Central Ave. #406-C
Phoenix, AZ 85004
Phone: (602) 496-1460
Web: www.sabr.org
Facebook: Society for American Baseball Research
Twitter: @SABR

CONTENTS

THE MINOR LEAGUES OF MY YOUTH

When Minor League Baseball Almost Went Bust looks at the highs and lows of an era that was driven by new technology and the emergence of alternate ways for baseball fans to spend their leisure time. It was also a time when I discovered minor-league baseball and *The Sporting News.*

Interest in minor-league baseball was extremely high in the post-World War II United States and Canada. It seemed as if every town wanted to get into the game. In 1949 the minor leagues reached their zenith with 59 leagues, 448 teams, and an estimated 10,000 players. Just 14 years later, in 1963, minor-league baseball had shrunken to 18 leagues and 129 teams, and was on life support until rescued by the major leagues.

This book includes articles about the many leagues and teams that didn't survive this era,and shows the grit of the owners and fans in these towns and cities who fought to keep baseball alive in their communities. Ultimately, most of the teams succumbed to forces beyond their control. The book captures some historic baseball events such as Jackie Robinson breaking the minor-league color barrier, joining the Montreal Royals in 1946, and the adoption of the major leagues' 1963 Player Development Contract, which stabilized minor-league baseball.

A major issue for many minor-league teams in the late 1940s and 1950s was a lack of major-league support. In 1949 just 235 teams were affiliated with major-league organizations, while 213 were independently operated. Sufficient financing was always an issue for the independent teams, which had to recruit players. Their primary source of income came from selling their top prospects to major-league organizations. Very few independent teams ever made money. They survived year-to-year based on their attendance and the willingness of their local governments to support them, especially with the rental of their baseball facilities.

By the early 1950s minor-league baseball began a rapid decline. Clubs not affiliated with a major-league organization were the first to go out of business. Factors that fueled this decline included the growth of television and the affordability of home air conditioners, giving fans more incentives to stay at home and watch TV rather than go to games. Recreational sports like golf, tennis, and bowling offered additional outlets for fans to spend their free time. In addition, the steady growth of professional and college football, professional basketball, Little League baseball, and horseracing drew people away from ballparks.

By 1963 major-league owners realized that something had to be done to stem the downward spiral of the minor leagues. The minor-league system was too important to player development. The major leagues responded with the Player Development Contract, which gave the minors a new life as it began to cover minor-league affiliates' operating expenses. This opened a new era for minor-league baseball that remains true to today.

It has been said that "it takes a village" to get the job done. And this book, which took almost three years to accomplish, wouldn't have happened without the dedicated efforts of the 39 people who served as authors, editors, and fact-checkers. We came together as a team to complete the project. (You can see who they are by checking the list of contributors in this volume.)

This is the first publication of SABR's Minor Leagues Research Committee in over 25 years and, hopefully, will the first of a series in the years ahead.

—George Pawlush, editor and chairman of the SABR Minor Leagues Research Committee

A SAVE FOR MINOR-LEAGUE BASEBALL: THE 1963 PLAYER DEVELOPMENT PLAN

By Michael Rinehart Jr.

Prior to the complete overhaul in 2020, the biggest shakeup of the minor-league baseball structure came in 1963 with the introduction of the Player Development Plan. Considering the downward trend in the popularity and sustainability of minor-league teams throughout the 1950s, Commissioner Ford Frick assembled a committee of baseball minds to address the issue.[1] What came from it was a lifeline thrown to minor-league baseball in the form of the Player Development Plan. The plan called for each major-league team to essentially take over much of the financial burden of five minor-league teams in order to save minor-league baseball.[2] The minor leagues and the major leagues have had a longstanding relationship with one another and play an important role in each other's success.

In 1901 the consensus across all the minor leagues was the necessity to unify and protect themselves from the feuding major leagues. The brand-new American League was attempting to join the major-league ranks, and was doing so by stealing players, including some of the game's biggest stars, from the National League, using the promise of higher salaries and a more professional style of play.[3] Minor-league owners, who had protection with the National League through the National Agreement, now feared that this feud would negatively affect them. On September 5, 1901, the Leland Hotel in Chicago hosted a meeting of minor-league presidents and executives who decided to unify as one solid organization, independent from the majors.[4] The National Association of Professional Baseball Leagues (NAPBL) was thus born and provided a solid backing and voice for minor-league baseball.

SABR: The Rucker Archive.

John Galbreath, left, and his fellow Pittsburgh Pirate co-owners, Frank McKinney and Thomas Johnson, shown in 1959, were adamant that minor-league baseball had to be stabilized.

The NAPBL set guidelines and cemented the initial structure of the minor-league baseball system, with clearly defined classifications for leagues. The first NAPBL season in 1902 included four levels, from Class A (the highest) to Class D, the lowest.[5] The classification system stood for decades with a handful of minor adjustments over the years. The first modification came in 1912, when the AA classification was added and thus became the highest level of the minors, a structure that lasted through the 1945 season. In 1936 the A1 classification was introduced, adding a level between AA and A. After the 1937 season, the NAPBL saw the need for an additional classification below Class D, so an E level was added, although it wound up being utilized for part of just one season, 1943.[6]

The first major restructuring took effect for the 1946 season. Minor-league teams and leagues struggled throughout the first half of the 1940s due to World War II, but the end of the war in the summer of 1945 signaled a huge return for baseball as part of renewed nationwide interest in recreation and getting back to a sense of normalcy. In 1946 the AAA classification became the new highest level of the minors, with the A1 level essentially being renamed AA. Classes A through E remained in effect as well.[7] Minor-league baseball reached its peak of popularity and success in 1949, with 59 leagues and 448 teams.[8] But the 1950s proved to be a different story for minor-league baseball, with a sharp decline in attendance, leading to the rapid disappearance of teams and leagues. Many contributing factors are cited in the blame game for this sudden decline, including the introduction of television, home air-conditioning, the Korean War, and the improvement in transportation that saw the creation of the interstate highway system, as well as a shift from city life to the suburbs.

However, perhaps the simplest reason for the decline is that minor-league baseball arguably expanded too aggressively to be sustained. When soldiers returned home, league and team owners cashed in on the available players and the desire of fans to get out to the ballpark. This led to a plethora of teams in small towns that ultimately were unable to support a club for the long haul. As attendance across the minor-league landscape declined and operating costs rose, many teams and leagues simply folded, sometimes in mid-season. Knowing the significance of the minors in the success of major-league baseball, Commissioner Frick knew that action needed to be taken to right the ship and get the minor leagues back on track. A Player Development Fund of up to $1 million was approved in 1959 as a temporary solution to saving the minor leagues.[9] The majors sent payments to minor-league teams, ranging from $2,000 in the lower levels up to $20,000 in AAA, to help subsidize rising operating costs.[10] Although this was a very welcome financial addition, it was clear that it wouldn't be enough. Commissioner Frick then created what became known as the Major-Minor League Committee to find a more permanent solution.[11]

Often referred to as the "Save the Minors Committee," it was led by Pittsburgh Pirates owner John Galbreath and consisted of three representatives from the American League, three from the National League, and six from the minor leagues, with one representative from each of the six class designations (AAA to D).[12] This group of 12 men with decades of experience in baseball was given the task of stabilizing the minors with a comprehensive plan that would be mutually beneficial to all parties.

Some of the key points the committee addressed included creating a steady flow of prospects from the minors to the majors; a financial-stability blueprint for the minors to keep teams and leagues from folding; and an overall balanced and organized system of teams and leagues.

After more than a year of working on viable solutions for this overhaul of the minor-league structure, the Major-Minor League Committee met on Friday, April 20, 1962, in Chicago to finalize a report for Commissioner Frick. What became known as the Player Development Plan called for the complete overhaul of the minor-league baseball structure.[13] The specifics still needed to be ironed out, but the initial outline of the plan was as follows: There would be a guaranteed operation of at least 100 minor-league clubs (five franchises for each of the 20 National League and American League teams). Classifications would be merged into AAA, AA, and A; this would eliminate B, C, D, and E classifications; the breakdowns would be 20 AAA teams, 20 AA teams, and 60 A teams. Further, each major-league team would be responsible for taking a larger financial burden of their minor-league affiliates, providing a full roster and paying most of their salaries. Minor-league owners would be responsible for the ballpark rental and some other financial responsibilities. Lastly, Player Development Fund payments to minor-league teams would end.[14]

SABR: The Rucker Archive.

Ford Frick.

Commissioner Frick gave his full support to the broad general plan presented to him by the committee and called a special meeting of major-league owners to share the details.[15] The Player Development Plan was approved unanimously and was to begin with the 1963 season, with the full plan set to be in effect by 1965.[16] The Major-Minor League Committee would continue to fine-tune the plan and fill in more specific detail for a smooth rollout. More than four months after the approval of the general plan, these specific details were added and scheduled to be voted on at the coming 1962 Winter Meetings:[17]

1. Major-league teams would provide a full roster to at least five minor-league teams, including coaching staff. The major-league team was to provide 21 players in AAA, 19 players in AA, and 18 players in A. Minor-league teams were allowed to independently sign three free agents; if the contracts any of these players were subsequently sold, all revenue would stay with the minor-league club.
2. The major-league team would pay the salaries of managers.
3. Major-league teams would pay for most of the players' salaries over a set monthly limit: $800 per month for Class-AAA players, $150 per month for Class-AA players, $50 per month for Class-A players and full salaries paid for former Class-D teams.
4. Major-league teams would cover all expenses related to spring training, including transportation to the minor-league city afterward.
5. Minor-league teams would cover park rental, traveling expenses, lodging for away games, and meals.
6. Minor-league teams would give their major-league affiliate the right to select player contracts and move them during the season.
7. Any player whose contract a minor-league club owned outright could be purchased by their major-league affiliate for a fee ranging from $5,000 to $20,000, before being offered to another team.
8. The realignment of minor-league classifications would be as follows: International League, American Association, and Pacific Coast League to remain AAA, while Texas League and Mexican League remain AA and are joined by Eastern League and South Atlantic League.
9. All leagues that were in Class B, C, and D would be reclassified to Class A.

The Player Development Plan had the support from NAPBL President George Trautman, but it still needed to be voted on at the Minor League Winter Meetings, which were being held November 26 to 29 in Rochester, New York. Although some minor-league officials voiced concerns regarding this plan as a permanent solution, it was seen as at least a step in the right direction and a necessity to successfully operate a sound minor-league system. However, there were still a few details to be worked out before an approval vote, one of which was that the plan allowed for 20 AAA teams (one for each major-league team), but in 1962 there had been 22 AAA teams split between the three leagues. The Vancouver Mounties of the Pacific Coast League were dropped due to their inability to reach an agreement with a major-league club, leaving the league with seven teams. Meanwhile, the Omaha Dodgers folded, leaving the American Association with only five teams.

The PCL was ready to absorb Denver to round out to eight clubs, but that would leave the American Association with only four teams. From there, a plan emerged to combine the four-team American Association with the International League to create a 12-team league with two divisions. However, the International League rejected the proposal. With each minor league responsible for the expenses of travel, it would be unfavorable for either the PCL or International League to take on more than eight clubs and broaden the distance of travel.

Another plan thrown into discussion was shifting Salt Lake City to the American Association to give them and the Pacific Coast League each six teams. The PCL was understandably unwilling to lose one of its most successful franchises and downsize itself, so it was back to the drawing board. It took the full four days of the Winter Meetings, but with the promise of financial help from the major leagues to cover added transportation costs, the American Association was dissolved and the PCL and International League each became a 10-team league. From the American Association, the PCL took on Denver, Oklahoma City, and Dallas/Fort Worth, while the International League acquired Indianapolis and Little Rock.[18]

With the AAA problem solved, the Minor League Winter Meetings concluded with approval of the Player Development Plan. The next and final step was getting a green light from the major leagues at their Winter Meetings, and since the plan had been initiated by the major leagues, it was no surprise that it passed unanimously. After many months of working out all the details for a restructured minor-league system, the Player Development Plan was finally enacted. It came at the expense of the American Association, but Commissioner Frick appointed its president, Jim Burris, to oversee the Player Development Program to ensure a smooth rollout for the 1963 season. A new chapter of baseball was opened.

The Player Development Plan of 1963 provided much-needed relief to the minors' outdated structure. Although there was still some doubt and opposition to the plan, ultimately it proved to be an overall success. Minor-league teams now had full rosters of players, due to either signing a working Player Development Contract with a major-league team or, in a few cases, being owned outright by the big-league club. The restructuring organized the system and created a clear path for major-league teams to move their prospects up the ladder through the minors. Possibly the most important result of the Player Development Plan was the stability it brought to minor-league team owners and minor-league baseball as a whole. The big-league "parents" had now taken on a greater portion of the financial burden from their minor-league affiliates, which resulted in the success of leagues and clubs finishing out full seasons and avoiding crippling financial losses.

There were a couple leagues in organized baseball to note that fell outside the Player Development Plan. The Appalachian League, which had been a short-season Class D league, was given the new distinction of a Rookie League. The Appalachian League primarily only included players who had no prior experience in affiliated baseball and played a shorter 70-game season that began in late June. All teams in the Appalachian League were operated by major league clubs. Additionally, the Mexican League was granted admission to the National Association of Professional Baseball Leagues in 1955 as a Class AA league and continued that designation through the 1963 restructuring. Although the Mexican League retained the Class AA status, it was not included as part of the Player Development Plan.

The Player Development Plan created a system that, with some fine-tuning over the years, remained in place until 2020 as a staple in the relationship between minor- and major-league baseball. The minors survived the dark days of low interest and sparse attendance and came out on the other side thriving, going on to unprecedented attendance numbers and popularity. Minor- and major-league baseball go hand in hand and are integral to each other's success. Their relationship over the years has played an important role for communities across the country, connecting generations of families to America's greatest game.

This article was edited by Marshall Adesman and fact-checked by Mike Huber.

SOURCES

In addition to those listed in the Notes, information was provided by the following:

Cooper, J.J. "A Complete Working History of the Working Agreement Between Major and Minor Leagues," https://www.baseballamerica.com/stories/a-complete-history-of-the-working-agreement-between-major-and-minor-leagues/, October 18, 2019.

Kahan, Oscar. "22 Clubs, Only 20 Tieups, Add Up to Headache," *The Sporting News*, December 8, 1962: 2.

Miller, Norman (United Press International). "Distressed American Association Gives Minors a Splitting Headache," *Passaic* (New Jersey) *Herald-News*, November 29, 1962.

NOTES

1. "'Save the Minors' Committee Named; Cronin Included," *Boston Globe*, August 3, 1956: 7.
2. Clifford Kachline, "Majors Pick Up $10 Million Tab in Minors," *The Sporting News*, December 15, 1962: 5.
3. David Hill, "MLB History: American League Organizes as Major League," *Call to the Pen*, January 28, 2017, found online at https://calltothepen.com/2017/01/28/mlb-history-american-league-organizes-major-league/.
4. "Minor Leagues in Union: Baseball Organizations Combine for Protection," *Chicago Tribune*, September 6, 1901: 6.
5. "Minor League Meeting Closed," *Buffalo Courier*, October 27, 1901: 28.
6. Baseball-Reference.com, https://www.baseball-reference.com/register/league.cgi. "Major, Minor League Doings in a Nutshell," *Chicago Tribune*, December 3, 1937: 27.
7. John Cronin, "Truth in the Minor League Class Restructure: The Case for the Reclassification of the Minors," *SABR Baseball Research Journal*, Spring 2013, found online at https://sabr.org/journal/article/truth-in-the-minor-league-class-structure-the-case-for-the-reclassification-of-the-minors/.
8. Lloyd Johnson and Miles Wolff, *The Encyclopedia of Minor League Baseball*, 2nd edition (Durham, North Carolina: Baseball America, 1997), 347.
9. "Fund Set for Minor Program," *Raleigh* (North Carolina) *News and Observer*, May 22, 1959: 19.
10. "Majors Vote In New Bonus Rule," *St. Lucie* (Florida) *News Tribune*, December 3, 1961: 15.
11. "Frick to Call Player Development Meet," *Oakland Tribune*, April 24, 1962: 41.
12. "Majors Earmark Million $ in 'Save Minor' Program," *New York Daily News*, October 31, 1962: 42. The 12 members of the Major-Minor League Committee were John Galbreath (owner of the Pittsburgh Pirates, chairman of the major-league half), Buzzie Bavasi (general manager of the Los Angeles Dodgers, key figure in integrating the minor leagues in the late 1940s), Chub Feeney (general manager of the San Francisco Giants, went on to be president of the National League, 1970-1986), George Medinger (vice president of the Cleveland Indians), Dick O'Connell (executive vice president of the Boston Red Sox), Ed Doherty (general manager of the Washington Senators, president of the American Association, 1953-1960), George Sisler Jr. (general manager of the Rochester Red Wings of the Class AAA International League, chairman of minor-league half), Dick Butler (president of the Class-AA Texas League), Sam Smith (president of the Class-A South Atlantic League), Jim Fleishman (president of the Class-B Northwest League), Herman White (president of the Class-C Northern League), and Herb Smith (president of the St. Petersburg Saints of the Class-D Florida State League).

13 "Frick to Call Player Development Meet."

14 "Minor Loop Plan Okayed," *Tampa Tribune,* May 19, 1962: 21.

15 Jack Hand (Associated Press), "Majors Vote Changes for Minor Loops," *Bangor* (Maine) *Daily News,* May 19, 1962: 13.

16 Associated Press, "Three Class Minors Seen," *Fort Worth* (Texas) *Star-Telegram,* May 19, 1962: 16.

17 Chris Jones, "1962 Winter Meetings: Addition by Subtraction," in Steve Weingarten and Bill Nowlin, eds., *Baseball's Business: The Winter Meetings: 1958-2016*, Vol. 2, found online at https://sabr.org/journal/article/1962-winter-meetings-addition-by-subtraction/.

18 "Leagues Absorb Old Association," *Edmonton* (Alberta) *Journal*, December 1, 1962: 43.

PROFESSIONAL BASEBALL AND AMUSEMENT PARKS

By Vince Guerrieri

Many amusement parks had seen their fortunes intertwined with minor-league baseball, and both faced hard times in the post-World War II era. The amusement parks that had survived to the 1950s – many of which started life at the turn of the century as "trolley parks," built at the end of a streetcar line – were starting to look old and shabby. Many were in urban areas, which made them not only landlocked for future development, but prone to decline as the cities themselves were being abandoned by residents for the suburbs.

New technologies also contributed to the decline of amusement parks and minor-league baseball in the postwar era. The trolley lines that transported revelers to the parks had gradually been replaced, first by buses and then by personal automobiles. And radio and television in postwar America were major factors that led to minor-league baseball's decline, only halting after the market was effectively restructured with the 1963 Professional Baseball Agreement.

The 1950s were difficult times for both minor-league baseball and amusement parks. The New England League folded after the 1949 season, the Colonial League did the same after the 1950 season, and the Mid-Atlantic League, with franchises in Canton and Youngstown that played home games at amusement parks, folded after the 1951 season. Throughout the decade, leagues faltered and in some instances disappeared, victims of suburbanization, TV and radio broadcasts of the major leagues, and the minor leagues' own overextension.

Concurrently, many of the trolley parks that had survived the Great Depression fell victim to suburbanization and urban unrest in the 1950s and 1960s. Chicago's Riverview Park, Palisades Park in New Jersey, and Euclid Beach in Cleveland all closed.

By the 1960s, many urban amusement parks and independent minor-league teams faced the same unappealing choice of fate: closure or conglomeration.

The rise of professional baseball in the late nineteenth and early twentieth centuries coincided with the rise of the amusement park.

In the era of horse-drawn streetcars, there might be a picnic ground at the end of the line, maybe including a bandstand and a dance pavilion. The parks were built to encourage ridership during off-peak hours.

But as those lines became electrified, many of the companies paid a flat rate for power, and started setting up large amusement parks at the end of the line, most of which included similar features like rides, games, and a dance hall.[1]

These trolley parks also in many instances had a field. When they hosted company picnics or gatherings of fraternal organizations, the fields might host a pickup baseball game. (In the Great Lakes region, it was not uncommon for a lot of factories to have an amateur baseball team – or an amateur basketball team; there are still NBA teams today that can trace their roots back to amateur company teams in the days before World War II.) The fields would also host barnstorming teams, both of major leaguers and of Negro League players, and in some instances, become the home field for independent minor-league teams.

The history of baseball at amusement parks goes back almost as far as the game itself. In 1885 John B. Day owned two teams under the auspices of the Metropolitan Exhibition Company. The Gothams (later Giants) were the more popular team, and after that season Day sold off the other team that called the Polo Grounds home. The new owner of the Metropolitans was Erastus Wiman, who moved the team to Staten Island's St. George Grounds. Wiman had visions of a grand resort near a ferry/railroad terminal, but they did not come to pass, and the Metropolitans played at St. George Grounds for two years before being bought and merged with the Brooklyn Greys.

Because most trolley lines ended at the outskirts of a city or even outside the city limits, they were sometimes used by major-league teams to skirt local blue laws prohibiting Sunday baseball. In fact, the Cleveland Spiders played two games at Geauga Lake, a lakeside recreation area, in 1888,[2] and Euclid Beach Park, an amusement park, in 1898.[3] League Park – built for the Spiders but eventually home to the Indians as well – was built at its location at Lexington Avenue and East 66th Street because it was a trolley stop for a line owned by brothers Frank and Stanley Robison, who also owned the team.

Sometimes, the rides were added to the ballpark. Chris Von Der Ahe, owner of the St. Louis Brown Stockings, installed a shoot-the-chutes water slide in his ballpark, known variously as Sportsman's Park, League Park, and finally Robison Field after Von Der Ahe went bankrupt and the team was bought by the Robison brothers.[4]

In 1903 the Los Angeles Angels made their debut in the new Pacific Coast League. Their initial home was Chutes Park, a trolley park that included a variety of rides as well as a ballfield and a wooden grandstand. Chutes Park was dismantled in 1910, and the Angels moved on to Washington Park.[5] In 1906 a lake was filled in near Ponce de Leon amusement park, owned by the Georgia Railway and Electric Company, and a new wooden grandstand was built for the Atlanta Crackers, a minor-league team also owned by the railroad. Ponce de Leon Park was the Crackers' home for the remainder of their existence, until the Braves relocated to Atlanta from Milwaukee in 1966. The amusement park had disappeared decades earlier.[6]

In 1913 the Federal League began play as a minor league. (The next year it signed some American and National League players in an ultimately quixotic effort to compete with the two leagues.) The first game in Federal League history occurred in Cleveland, as the Green Sox, managed by Cy Young, hosted the Covington Blue Sox at Luna Park, an amusement park on Cleveland's East Side.[7] Both the team and the park were owned by asphalt magnate M.F. "Fred" Bramley.[8] He'd bought the park in 1910 from its founder, Frederick Ingersoll, and bought into the league to use a team as one more entertainment option for visitors.

By 1910, every city with a population of at least 20,000 had some kind of trolley park.[9] But the seeds for their demise were already growing. That year, a total of 458,377 autos were on the road, a far cry from the 8,000 a decade earlier. Once viewed as playthings for the rich, autos had become consumer goods for working people, thanks largely to Henry Ford. Ford's Model T also made the internal combustion engine the dominant power plant for autos, which to that point had also been powered by electric batteries or in some cases by steam boilers.[10] The availability of autos and the ease and availability of gasoline suddenly made electric trolleys archaic, supplanted by gas-powered buses (which didn't have to stay on tracks and could change routes more nimbly) or personal cars.

In the 1930s, as lower-level minor-league teams shifted, many found quick places to put down roots at local amusement parks. After the Mid-Atlantic League team in Beckley, West Virginia, folded following the 1935 season, league operators drummed up enough interest in Canton, Ohio, which had minor-league teams off and on since the turn of the century. The newly renamed Terriers would begin play in Lakeside Park, a ballpark at Meyers Lake amusement park. Lakeside had been used in the early twentieth century as a minor-league venue but was more prominent in the preceding 15 years as a home for pro football, most notably Jim Thorpe and the Canton Bulldogs.[11] And three years later, when the Johnstown Mid-Atlantic team moved to Youngstown, it found a welcome home at Idora Park, the amusement park on the city's southern outskirts, already a frequent stop for barnstorming teams.[12] Although both the Canton and Youngstown teams were able to start play reasonably quickly, both ballparks needed a lot of renovation.

Minor-league baseball reached its zenith in the postwar era, with 448 teams in 59 leagues in 1949, drawing 39.8 million fans.[13] But within a decade, it had all collapsed. By 1960 there were just 22 minor leagues operating.[14] Changes were attributable to major-league expansion and broadcasting games on television and radio.

But even years after many trolley parks met their demise (in 2010, it was estimated that just 11 trolley parks were still operating[15]), minor-league baseball and amusement parks remain inextricably linked. In 1997 a central Pennsylvania group began pursuit of a minor-league baseball team. A year later, ground was broken for a new ballpark, and in 1999 the Altoona Curve began play in the Eastern League, in a ballpark in the shadow of the Skyliner, a roller coaster at Lakemont Park, one of the few remaining trolley parks.[16]

In 1998 New York Mayor Rudy Giuliani lured a pair of New York-Penn League teams to the city, to begin play three years later. One, a Yankees affiliate named for its parent club, played on Staten Island. The other, a Mets affiliate, returned pro baseball to

Brooklyn for the first time in 40 years. It was named by its fans, in honor of the Cyclone, a landmark roller coaster at Coney Island.

Its new field was nearby – on the former site of Steeplechase Park, at one point the most popular amusement park on Coney Island.[17]

This article was edited by Cathy Kreyche and fact-checked by Mike Huber.

NOTES

1 It should be noted that trolleys indirectly provided the namesake for a major-league team: The name Dodgers was shortened from "Trolley Dodgers," from a task that residents in Brooklyn had to do in the late 1800. Further reading: https://gizmodo.com/the-la-dodgers-got-their-name-from-brooklyns-deadly-str-1687077696.

2 John Thorn, "Neutral Sites," *Our Game*, July 1, 2016. Found online at https://ourgame.mlblogs.com/neutral-sites-6ecd92b9e375.

3 David Fleitz, *Rowdy Patsy Tebeau and the Cleveland Spiders* (Jefferson, North Carolina: McFarland & Co., 2017), 157.

4 The Robisons also owned the Spiders, but were more limited by Blue Laws in Cleveland. They took players from their Cleveland team to St. Louis, leaving the Spiders to put together the worst record in major-league history, 20-134 in 1899. The team was contracted by the National League after the season.

5 Ron Selter, "The Pacific Coast League Ballparks of Los Angeles," *The National Pastime*, 2011. Found online at https://sabr.org/journal/article/the-pacific-coast-league-ballparks-of-los-angeles/.

6 Andrew Mearns, "Atlanta's First Famous Baseball Park Was Also Home to a Giant Magnolia Tree in Center Field," Cut4, May 23, 2018. Found online at https://www.mlb.com/cut4/history-of-ponce-de-leon-park-in-atlanta-c277672886.

7 At one point, there were dozens of amusement parks name Luna Park, many started or operated by Frederick Ingersoll. Luna Park's stadium also hosted early NFL teams. "Luna Park: A Sliver of Coney Island in Cleveland," *Cleveland Historical*. https://clevelandhistorical.org/items/show/259.

8 Robert Wiggins, *The Federal League of Base Ball Clubs: The History of an Outlaw Major League* (Jefferson, North Carolina: McFarland & Co., 2009), 9.

9 Katie Thornton, "How the Amusement Park Conquered America," *Bloomberg CityLab*, July 9, 2022. Found online at https://www.bloomberg.com/news/features/2022-07-09/the-american-amusement-park-s-wild-ride.

10 The main advantage electric cars had was that unlike the Model T, they didn't have to be cranked to start the engine. But the electric starter was patented in 1911 and introduced the next year, ensuring that the internal combustion engine was here to stay.

11 William E. Akin, *The Middle-Atlantic League, 1925-1952: A Baseball History* (Jefferson, North Carolina: MacFarland & Company, 2015), 125.

12 Akin, 178.

13 https://milb.com/milb/history/presidents.jsp?mc=_trautman. Some sources have attendance over 41 million that season.

14 Steve Treder, "Dig the 1950s," *The Hardball Times*. Found online at https://tht.fangraphs.com/dig_the_1950s/#:~:text=In%201950%20there%20were%2058,baseball%20had%20largely%20become%20extinct.

15 Beth J. Harpaz, "TrolleyPparks: Survivors of an Earlier Era," NBCNews.com. Found online at https://www.nbcnews.com/id/wbna38349493.

16 Mark Leberfinger, "Baseball Stadium Project Commences," *Tyrone* (Pennsylvania) *Daily Herald*, March 9, 1998:

17 Nicholas Dawidoff, "The House That Rudy Built," *New York Times Magazine*. August 12, 2001: 40.

BACK TO THE FARM: IN-SEASON MINOR-MAJOR EXHIBITION GAMES

By Kurt Blumenau

Fans in Montreal and Toronto watched major-league baseball teams years before the Expos or Blue Jays came to town. Same thing with Milwaukee and the Braves or Brewers. For that matter, fans in relatively obscure outposts like Cranston, Rhode Island; Gloversville, New York; and Wisconsin Rapids, Wisconsin, also got to see big leaguers take the field between 1946 and 1963.

The institution that made it happen was the in-season exhibition game. In the twenty-first century, these games are as extinct as the emery ball. But in decades past, major-league teams used offdays during the regular season to play minor-league teams, college teams, and even semipro and company-sponsored outfits. This article will focus exclusively on matchups between major- and minor-league teams – although the faceoffs between the St. Louis Browns and the Belleville Kiwanis, or the Pittsburgh Pirates and the Waterbury Brasscos, are worth exploring in some other setting.[1]

In-season exhibitions were played long before 1946 – researchers have identified them as far back as 1871 – and they continued long after 1963. Still, they merit discussion in a minor-league history of these years. They were a familiar aspect of the baseball calendar and a distinctive experience for fans outside major-league cities. Despite their noncompetitive nature, they were also, from time to time, the settings for interesting or noteworthy gameplay.

BY THE NUMBERS

Between 1946 and 1963, major- and minor-league teams faced off during the major-league season roughly 228 times, for an average of about 13 times per season.[2] The majority of these games involved a single minor-league team – the Albany (New York) Senators, the Denver Bears, the Toronto Maple Leafs – though it also became common later in the period for big-league teams to face minor-league all-star squads.

Research led by SABR's Walter LeConte, which identified 5,000 in-season exhibition games of all types from 1871 to 2012, found that the International League accounted for 467 of them – about 9 percent of the total,[3] more than any other minor league. Since the IL traditionally operated at the highest level of the minors,[4] this confirms that big-league teams were most likely to face off against their top minor-league affiliate. The Eastern League, which most frequently operated at the second-highest level of the minors,[5] ranks second on LeConte's list with 314 in-season exhibitions.

Did the minor leaguers – in theory, the inferior team in every matchup – ever win? A scan through the list of games indicates that the minor leaguers won about 70 games in this period, or about 30 percent of the time.

Of course, the big leaguers didn't always play at 100 percent intensity, since no one wanted to get hurt in a game that didn't count. It happened from time to time anyway. Milwaukee Braves catcher Paul Burris suffered a broken and dislocated elbow in a home-plate collision during a June 22, 1953, exhibition game against the Eau Claire (Wisconsin) Bears of the Class-C Northern League. Burris, who had last played a regular-season game on June 4, never appeared again in the big leagues, although he continued to play in the minors through the 1956 season.[6]

It was also typical for major-league managers to remove their starters after a few innings, sometimes with bitter results. In July 1948, disappointed Montreal Royals fans booed and threw seat cushions when the parent Brooklyn Dodgers pulled local hero Jackie Robinson out of the game after his first-inning at-bat.[7] Robinson had been a Montreal fan favorite two seasons earlier, when he hit .349 for the pennant- and playoff-winning Royals of the Triple-A International League en route to integrating the White major leagues.

Major-league managers often used the games as warm-ups for players coming off injury, and as informal tryouts for minor-league players. To cite one example: On June 27, 1955, Baltimore Orioles manager Paul Richards started the injured Joe Coleman against the York (Pennsylvania) White Roses of the Class-B Piedmont League. When Coleman was ineffective, Richards replaced him with Jack Moreland, a semi-pro player on tryout, and then with Dick Fitzgerald, a barely 20-year-old rookie formerly of Lafayette College in Pennsylvania. The White Roses stomped their parent club 13-1.[8]

Moreland got his picture in a local newspaper, wearing an Orioles uniform and talking to Richards on the bench, but that seems to have been the highlight of his career. A search of Baseball-Reference in December 2022 found no record that he ever played in a regular-season professional game. Fitzgerald pitched in six pro seasons, including three at Triple A, but never reached the majors.

Even if the big-leaguers were easing up on the throttle, the occasional minor-league victory provided a thrill and a source of pride to fans in those communities. The language used by a sportswriter in Scranton, Pennsylvania, in 1948 captures the sentiment: "The Scranton Miners turned giant killers at the Stadium last night where they defeated the Boston Red Sox, 2-1, before a near record attendance of 12,165. … Nine Boston scribes accompanied the team here and were mighty impressed with the local setup."[9]

Fourteen seasons later, a sportswriter in Williamsport, Pennsylvania, sounded the same tone after the local Grays beat the Philadelphia Phillies: "The superb five-hit pitching of Ray Culp, Richie Allen's three-run homer and the 12 hits the Grays collected off three Philadelphia pitchers presented Eastern League class at its best against the big leaguers last night at Bowman Field."[10]

THE WHYS AND WHENS

Major-league teams played in-season exhibitions for a number of reasons. Some have faded as the sport has changed, while others remain familiar today.

Big-league schedules included open days – often, but not always, on Mondays – that could be used for exhibitions.[11] The All-Star break also offered an opportunity to squeeze in an exhibition or two, though the top star or stars from the major-league team might be absent. On July 10, 1951, while Philadelphia Phillies outfielder Richie Ashburn was making a dazzling catch at the All-Star Game at Detroit's Briggs Stadium, his

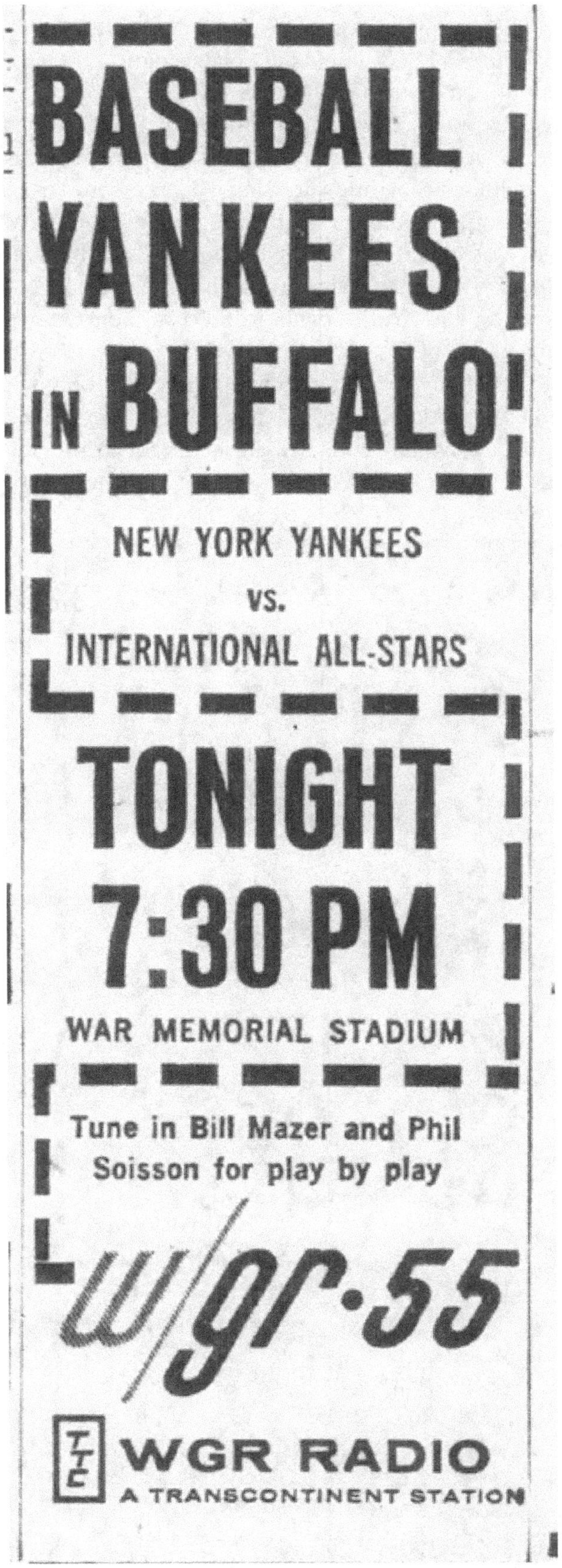

Buffalo Courier-Express, August 19, 1963

Advertisement for August 19, 1963 exhibition game featuring the New York Yankees against the International League All-Stars at Buffalo's War Memorial Stadium.

Phillies teammates were in Schenectady, New York, dropping a 2-1 decision to the Schenectady Blue Jays, their affiliate in the Class-A Eastern League.[12]

Unless rain kept the attendance down, exhibitions in minor-league towns served as major money-makers for the home team, often drawing the largest crowds of the season. Sometimes they were the largest in local history, as on July 9, 1951, when a city-record crowd of 10,077 in Ottawa, Ontario, watched the eventual NL champion New York Giants lose 4-1 to their Ottawa farmhands.[13] Willie Mays and the Giants drew a crowd of 21,832 five years later to brand-new Metropolitan Stadium in Bloomington, Minnesota; the Giants' game against the Minneapolis Millers was, at the time, the largest baseball crowd in the history of the Upper Midwest.[14]

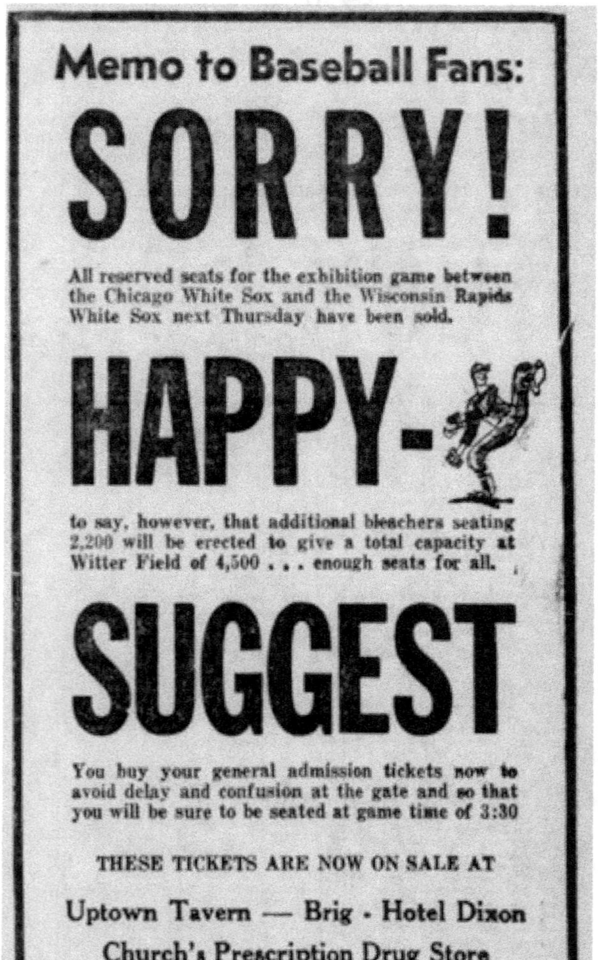

Wisconsin Daily Tribune, July 26, 1948.

Wisconsin Rapids advertisement.

Rochester (New York) Community Baseball, the community ownership group of the Triple-A Red Wings, might have lost money in 1959 if not for an exhibition with the parent St. Louis Cardinals. According to the local newspaper, the Red Wings cleared more than $4,000 from the exhibition while posting a year-end profit of $3,935.[15] The May 4 game drew 7,850 fans, and gate receipts were split evenly between the teams, with the Cardinals paying all their own expenses.[16]

The division of gate receipts mentioned above confirms that big-league teams benefited from exhibitions as well, collecting money from what otherwise would have been open dates. Another example: The New York Yankees collected $17,040 from a net gate of $42,601 in August 1963, when a local record crowd of 28,524 at Buffalo, New York's War Memorial Stadium watched the IL All-Stars shut out the Yanks on two hits, 5-0.[17]

Big-league players, in contrast, are not known to have gained financially from in-season exhibitions on a regular basis. Players' contracts typically required them to appear in games at the club's discretion from Opening Day until the season's end, in exchange for regular salary payments. Players received side benefits from in-season exhibitions – such as being wined and dined at banquets or receiving gifts, like the pair of pants and electric razor given to Washington Senators pitcher Dick Welteroth when he returned to Bridgeport, Connecticut, for a 1948 exhibition.[18] But there's no indication that they regularly received extra money for playing.[19]

(Exceptions existed. Connie Mack reportedly divided the Philadelphia A's share of money from two July 1948 exhibition games among the team's players. It was a generous act, and was greeted with incredulity by the newspaper that reported it.[20])

The games also offered public-relations opportunities for the major-league team. Players mingled with starstruck fans and signed autographs – or risked a public chastising, like the tut-tutting Mickey Mantle and Whitey Ford got from the Binghamton, New York, newspaper in June 1954 after making themselves scarce for signatures. "The Yankees may be world champions but to a lot of young Triple Cities fans they are far from that," a scribe wrote.[21]

Sometimes, a pregame home-run-hitting contest gave the big leaguers a chance to flex their muscles in a risk-free setting for the minor-league fans. In June 1950 Scranton fans got to see Ted Williams and former local hero Walt Dropo tee off before the game

– though their lighter-hitting teammates Bobby Doerr and Al Zarilla pulled off an upset tie for victory in the home-run derby.[22]

All the while, managers and front-office officials from the big-league team ingratiated themselves with the locals – thanking the fans for their support and praising the local facilities. Even the New York Giants' vinegary Leo Durocher was on his best behavior during his team's visit to Ottawa in 1951. "Yesterday, Durocher was the polished operator, the goodwill ambassador ... affable, all smiles, co-operative, dapper," one scribe in the Canadian capital reported.[23]

While it might seem surprising, the major- and minor-league teams that played these exhibitions were not always affiliated. As rumors of Milwaukee's major-league future circulated in the summer of 1952, the minor-league Brewers hosted the Chicago Cubs, St. Louis Browns, Chicago White Sox, and their parent Boston Braves – who made Milwaukee a major-league city for real when they moved there the following season.

Three years earlier, the St. Louis Cardinals' Interstate League farm team in Allentown, Pennsylvania, hosted the Philadelphia Phillies, giving Allentown fans a chance to watch area native Curt Simmons pitch for the Phillies. That same season, the Montreal Royals hosted the New York Giants, crosstown rivals of their parent Dodgers, and beat them, 4-2.

And in 1947, the unaffiliated Waterbury (Connecticut) Timers of the Class-B Colonial League lured the New York Yankees and Phillies to town, both while traveling to series in Boston. The eventual World Series champion Yankees played in the rain to about 9,000 fans; the Phillies, to fewer than 1,000.[24]

Some exhibitions were about much more than making money for the home team or scoring public-relations points with local fans. One such game occurred in Rome, New York – population: about 40,000 – on July 9, 1946, during that season's All-Star break.[25] Billy Southworth, son of the Boston Braves' manager of the same name, had starred in the outfield for the Rome Colonels in 1939 before entering the military during World War II. After serving in Europe, the younger Southworth was killed in a plane crash in Flushing, New York, in February 1945. With the elder Southworth in attendance, the Colonels dedicated monuments to his son and two other former players who died in military service. The Braves then defeated the Colonels 15-7.[26]

Exhibition games have also sometimes raised money for worthy charitable causes. This noble tradition continued on June 26, 1952, when the Cincinnati Reds and the IL's Buffalo Bisons – a Detroit Tigers farm club – played an exhibition to raise money for former St. Louis Cardinals infielder George "Specs" Toporcer. Toporcer, who had settled not far away in Rochester, was struggling with encroaching blindness; the game raised nearly $13,000 for his medical expenses.[27] The Reds happened to be traveling from New York to Chicago that day, in between series with the Giants and Cubs.

As major-league baseball expanded in the early 1960s, the new franchises joined the exhibition parade. The Los Angeles Angels, second Washington Senators, Houston Colt .45s, and New York Mets all played minor-league exhibitions in their earliest years.

The Angels lost their first two ventures into the arena, being dropped 3-0 by the Toronto Maple Leafs in 1961 and 6-5 by a team of Pacific Coast League all-stars in 1962. Similarly, the Colts – in the telling of one Texas newspaper – got "drygulched" by a team of all-stars from the Double-A Texas League in 1963, losing 7-3.[28] Outfielder Jim Beauchamp, then a Cardinals farmhand, hit a ninth-inning grand slam off Houston's Dick Drott to win it. Perhaps not coincidentally, Houston traded for Beauchamp in the subsequent offseason, and he was a Colt in 1964.

WHAT HAPPENED NEXT?

In-season exhibitions involving major- and minor-league teams remained a part of professional baseball's fabric after 1963. In fact, they became slightly more frequent for a time. LeConte's research indicates that 169 exhibition games of this type were played from 1964 through 1974, or more than 15 per season.[29]

Several factors – some already at work in 1963 – combined to bring an end to major-minor exhibitions, as well as other types of in-season exhibitions.

The longer 162-game season adopted in 1962 left fewer open dates on the schedule. Collective-bargaining agreements between players and owners also limited the number of in-season exhibitions to three in 1970, then reduced it to two for most teams in 1977.[30] For context, the 1952 St. Louis Browns played five in-season exhibitions against minor-league teams – plus a sixth against a company-sponsored team – while the '53 Browns and 1952 Boston Braves each played four.[31]

As relationships between major-league players and owners – once lopsided in favor of the latter – became

SABR: *The Rucker Archive.*

Former St. Louis Cardinals player George "Specs" Toporcer was the beneficiary of proceeds to cover his medical expenses, from an exhibition game in Buffalo on June 26, 1952.

more balanced, the players began to stick up for their preference of days off and rest during the season. And, as teams invested more money in players, they became more wary of injuries, and less willing to trot out their starters in Ottawa or Tacoma for games that didn't count.

In one incident near the end of the exhibition era, truculent Baltimore Orioles outfielder Albert Belle posted a petition in his locker in 1999, encouraging his teammates to boycott that season's exhibition game against the Rochester Red Wings.[32] The Orioles and Wings played that season for the last time, ending a tradition that began in 1961.

The list of in-season exhibitions compiled by LeConte – which runs through 2013 – includes four major-minor games in 2001, three in 2002, and none since. The final major-minor matchup on the list took place in Buffalo on July 1, 2002, when the Indians beat the Bisons 4-3 in seven innings. The game fulfilled the terms of the teams' then-current player-development contract, which called on the parent club to make a visit to Buffalo. "It was Cleveland's first visit to Buffalo since 1996 and could be the last for a long time," one newspaper reported presciently.[33]

In baseball and life, trends swing back and forth. (Consider the shifts in ballpark design from jewel boxes to symmetrical multi-use stadia, and then back to jewel box-influenced retro facilities.) With that in mind, it seems inadvisable to say firmly that minor-major exhibitions will never make a comeback.

At the time of this writing in 2024, the thrills of these exhibitions seemed particularly remote. A major-league team's stop in a minor-league city no longer seems like a visit from distant gods, now that the Internet brings game highlights and athletes' social media posts directly to fans. Also, minor-league teams have diversified their money-making approach, focusing on colorful merchandise and a full calendar of promotions rather than isolated big paydays.

AUTHOR'S NOTE AND ACKNOWLEDGMENTS

The author is massively indebted to Walter LeConte, as well as to other SABR members who assisted him in compiling listings of in-season exhibition games involving major-league teams between 1879 and 2012. These lists, as well as an accompanying article by LeConte, were available as of fall 2022 in the Special Features section of the Retrosheet website.

While the lists are impressive, they might not be definitively complete. In researching this story, the author discovered an in-season minor-major exhibition that was not listed there – namely, the May 4, 1959, matchup between the St. Louis Cardinals and Rochester Red Wings. The author submitted this information to Retrosheet for consideration.

This article was edited by Thomas Rathkamp and fact-checked by George Pawlush.

SOURCES

In addition to the specific sources cited in the Notes, the author used Baseball-Reference and Retrosheet websites for general player, team, and season data. Walter LeConte's list of in-season exhibition games and accompanying article, mentioned above, was also a primary source.

NOTES

1 The Browns beat the Belleville (Illinois) Kiwanis 6-3 in Belleville on July 10, 1950. It took the Pirates 11 innings to beat the Waterbury (Connecticut) Brasscos 8-5 in Waterbury on July 29, 1946. While Waterbury had fielded a minor-league team called the Brasscos in the 1920s, the team that played the Pirates in 1946 was semipro. "Pirates Defeat Semi-Pros, 8-5," *Pittsburgh Press,* July 30, 1946: 20.

2 A note on methodology: The author started with Retrosheet's list of in-season exhibitions compiled by Walter LeConte and others (see Author's Note.) The author cut and pasted all the games from 1946 through 1963 into

a spreadsheet. He then deleted any games that involved two major-league teams; semipro teams; college teams; military teams; and teams backed by community organizations such as police and Kiwanis. The author also deleted several games in which the local team could not be identified as belonging to a specific league.

3 For clarity, the 5,000 number represents *all* in-season exhibition games, not just the ones pitting minor- and major-league teams against each other. The IL's percentage of the total would be even higher if other types of exhibitions were filtered out.

4 Before 1946, Double A was the highest level of the minors; the IL operated at that level from 1912 to 1945. In 1946, the Triple-A level replaced Double A as the highest level of the minors, and the IL became a Triple-A circuit. Walter LeConte, "ISEG Update," Retrosheet. Posted February 12, 2013; accessed September 23, 2022.

5 The Eastern League operated at Class A from 1919 through 1962, then moved to Double A in 1963.

6 "Milwaukee Takes 13-11 Decision Over Eau Claire," *Eau Claire* (Wisconsin) *Daily Telegram,* June 23, 1953: 9; Jay Hurd, "Paul Burris," SABR Biography Project, accessed September 23, 2022.

7 Dink Carroll, "17,809 Fans Denounce Dodger Club as Robinson Is Pulled Out of Game," *Montreal Gazette,* July 13, 1948: 14. The Dodgers were jointly managed that night by coaches Clyde Sukeforth and Jake Pitler, as manager Leo Durocher was in St. Louis for the All-Star Game.

8 "Orioles Jolted by York Farmhands, 13-1," *York* (Pennsylvania) *Dispatch,* June 28, 1955: 15.

9 Jimmy Calpin, "Miners Beat Red Sox in Ninth, 2-1, Before 12,165 Fans," *Scranton* (Pennsylvania) *Tribune,* June 15, 1948: 17. The Miners were a Red Sox affiliate in the Class-A Eastern League.

10 "Ray Culp's 5-Hitter Beats Phils, 5-1," *Williamsport* (Pennsylvania) *Sun-Gazette,* August 1, 1962: 9. The Eastern League was a Class-A loop at that time. Culp pitched four seasons with the Phillies and made an All-Star appearance in his rookie year, 1963, placing third in National League Rookie of the Year voting. Allen went on to play parts of nine seasons with the Phillies, in which he made three All-Star appearances and won the 1964 NL Rookie of the Year Award.

11 Of the 228 major-vs.-minor exhibitions listed in LeConte's spreadsheet, 124 – or about 54 percent – took place on Mondays; 34 on Tuesdays; 19 on Wednesdays; 43 on Thursdays; 6 on Fridays; and 2 on Saturdays.

12 Phillies manager Eddie Sawyer was also in Detroit managing the National League team, an honor traditionally given to the manager of the league's champion team in the preceding season. "Ashburn Leaping into Air to Spear Near-Homer in All-Star Game" (photo and caption), *Philadelphia Inquirer,* July 11, 1951: 34; Associated Press, "Phillies Lose, 2-1 to Schenectady," *Philadelphia Inquirer,* July 11, 1951: 34.

13 Jack Koffman, "Over 10,000 See Ottawa Giants Whip Durocher's Gang, 4-1," *Ottawa* (Ontario) *Evening Citizen,* July 10, 1951: 14.

14 T.S. Flynn, "June 7, 1956: Willie Mays Homers Twice in Giants' Exhibition Win at Metropolitan Stadium," SABR Games Project. Accessed online December 27, 2022.

15 George Beahon, "Wings Report Profit of $3,935 for 1959," *Rochester* (New York) *Democrat and Chronicle,* November 21, 1959: 14.

16 George Beahon, "Cards Rally for 6 Runs in 12th Inning, Trip Wings, 10-4, Before 7,850 Fans," *Rochester Democrat and Chronicle,* May 5, 1959: 32.

17 Cy Kritzer, "An Authentic Team of All-Stars Shocks Yankees Before 28,524," *Buffalo Evening News,* August 20, 1963: 12.

18 The Senators played the Bridgeport Bees on August 23, 1948. Welteroth, a former Bridgeport player, received $100 from the Bees' owners and an additional $50 from fans, as well as the pair of pants and electric razor donated by businesses. John Johansen, "Senators Connect for 17 Hits and Trounce Bees 15-5," *Bridgeport* (Connecticut) *Telegram,* August 24, 1948: 12.

19 Postseason barnstorming tours offered players a chance to make extra money from exhibitions *outside* the regular season, as extensively detailed in SABR member Thomas Barthel's *Baseball Barnstorming and Exhibition Games, 1901-1962: A History of Off-Season Major League Play* (Jefferson, North Carolina: McFarland, 2007). However, player contracts strictly dictated the relationship between player and team *during* the season.

20 Al Cartwright, "A La Carte," *Wilmington* (Delaware) *Journal,* July 14, 1948: 28. Cartwright's words: "The heat must have Connie Mack. … He cut up the Athletics' share from the exhibition games here Monday night and in Harrisburg last night among the players." The *Philadelphia Inquirer* also reported that Mack shared some proceeds from an August 1948 exhibition in Meriden, Connecticut, with A's players. That game is not mentioned in this article because the opposition was an independent squad of local players, not a minor-league team. Art Morrow, "Mack Feted with Team at Meriden," *Philadelphia Inquirer,* August 17, 1948: 24.

21 Charley Peet, "Some Yanks Were Really Tough (To Get Along With, That Is)," *Binghamton* (New York) *Press,* June 29, 1954: 19. The Yankees were in Binghamton to play their Eastern League affiliate, the Binghamton Triplets. The name Triple Cities (and Triplets) refers to the three neighboring communities of Binghamton, Endicott, and Johnson City, New York.

22 Jimmy Calpin, "Red Sox Outslug Scranton Before 9,342 Fans, 9 to 3," *Scranton Tribune,* July 13, 1950: 17. Dropo had played for the Scranton team three seasons earlier, earning attention for his raw power.

23 Edward MacCabe, "The Sportspiel," *Ottawa* (Ontario) *Journal,* July 10, 1951: 13.

24 Associated Press, "New London Bows to Stamford in Colonial League," *Meriden* (Connecticut) *Journal,* August 8, 1947: 4; Associated Press, "Phillies Defeat Waterbury, 7 to 2," *Bridgeport* (Connecticut) *Telegram,* September 4, 1947: 16. The Yankees' strong turnout in Waterbury might have been owed, in part, to a pitching appearance by Spec Shea, a native of the nearby town of Naugatuck.

25 Rome's population was measured at 34,224 in the 1940 US Census and 41,682 in the 1950 Census. The entire population of Rome could have just about fit into the Braves' home park of Braves Field, which had a capacity of 37,746 in 1946, according to the Seamheads.com ballpark database, accessed October 23, 2022.

26 Associated Press, "Braves Win, 15-7, at Ceremony for Southworth's Son," *Boston Globe,* July 10, 1946: 11.

27 Cy Kritzer, "Herd May Obtain Kazak, Howell from Cincy Reds," *Buffalo Evening News,* June 27, 1952: 35. The Reds won the game, 5-3, behind homers by Ted Kluszewski and Cal Abrams.

28 United Press International, "Texas Leaguers Drygulch Colts in Exhibition," *McAllen* (Texas) *Valley Evening Monitor,* August 2, 1963: 13.

29 To prepare a list of major-minor exhibitions from 1964 through 1974, the author copied games from the LeConte list into a spreadsheet, and again deleted games not involving minor-league teams – such as those involving college or military teams. It should be noted that, while in-season exhibitions against minor-league teams became slightly more common during this period, other types of exhibitions -- those against company-sponsored and semipro teams – disappeared from the major-league agenda.

30 Author's review of 1970, 1976, and 1990-93 collective-bargaining agreements made available through SABR's Business of Baseball site. Accessed October 28, 2022. The 1976 agreement allowed the president of each league to grant special permission for up to three additional in-season exhibitions; each team was limited to no more than two unless given permission for a third. By the 1990-93 agreement, the number of in-season exhibitions had been reduced still further, to no more than one unless a team was allowed a second by its league president.

31 In addition to their five exhibitions against minor-league teams, the 1952 Browns played against a team in Moraine, Ohio, sponsored by a business called Moraine Products, according to LeConte's research and contemporary news accounts. Similarly, the '53 Browns also played semipro teams in Hartford, Connecticut, and Fort Wayne, Indiana, on top of their four games against minor-league teams. In still another example of a heavy exhibition workload, the 1948 Philadelphia A's played minor-league teams three times, and also played in-season exhibitions against the Pittsburgh Pirates and Philadelphia Phillies of the National League.

32 Bob Matthews, "Wings Should Ask the Orioles to Leave Belle Behind," *Rochester Democrat and Chronicle,* June 24, 1999: 3D.

33 Bob Matthews, "Fans Selecting All-Star Starters a Hit," *Rochester Democrat and Chronicle,* July 2, 2002: 2D.

THE SAGA OF PLAYERS WHO HIT HOME RUNS IN THE SAME PARK AS BOTH MINOR AND MAJOR LEAGUERS

By Alan Cohen

Who homered in the same ballpark in the minors and majors?

R.C. Stevens of the 1960 Pirates made several stops in the minors and majors from 1952 through 1963. In an article in the *Quad City Times*, he remembered a homer against the Giants at Seals Stadium on May 5, 1958.[1] He had also hit home runs at Seals Stadium as a member of the Hollywood Stars, for whom he played during the 1955, 1956, and 1957 seasons. The first of his homers at Seals Stadium came on April 24, 1955, and he also homered there on July 15, 1956, a year in which he hit 27 home runs, good for third in the Pacific Coast League.

More than 60 players, including five Hall of Famers, homered in the same ballpark in the minors and majors during the years from 1954 through 1962, as the number of teams, cities, and stadiums grew substantially.

Major-league baseball, as it was defined prior to 1953, was confined to 10 cities, but aging ballparks, dwindling crowds, and the moving of the country's population resulted in owners looking to make changes. By 1962, franchise shifts and expansion resulted in a completely new major-league landscape, and five ballparks that had been minor-league venues were being used by major-league teams. They were Memorial Stadium (Baltimore), Roosevelt Stadium (Jersey City), Seals Stadium (San Francisco), Metropolitan Stadium (Minneapolis), and Wrigley Field (Los Angeles).

Brooklyn had won six of 10 National League pennants going into the 1957 season. They were drawing well at Ebbets Field, attracting 1,213,562 fans in 1956. But owner Walter O'Malley was determined to get a new facility. During 1956 and 1957, his Dodgers played 15 games at Roosevelt Stadium in Jersey City, New Jersey. O'Malley set his sights farther west, and in Los Angeles he found his pot of gold. Our story first takes us to Roosevelt Stadium, where three players homered in both the minors and majors.

ROOSEVELT STADIUM

On April 18, 1946, Montreal played the Jersey City Giants before a crowd of more than 25,500 on Opening Day at Roosevelt Stadium,[2] and Jackie Robinson played his first game in Organized Baseball.

He observed "that watching this minor league game would be more sports writers than would be watching

SABR: The Rucker Archive.

Ted Kluszewski measures up Earl Averill Jr., 1961.

SABR: The Rucker Archive.

Dale Long, with catcher's glove

any opening day major league game – sports writers present because they knew that unfolding here on this diamond was a story much bigger than baseball, a story as far-reaching in essence as the very idea of democracy and the equality of men."[3] After grounding out in the first inning, he came to bat in the third with runners on base. It was a bunting situation, but manager Clay Hopper ordered Robinson to swing away, and Robinson slammed a three-run homer over the left-field fence. In 1956, Robinson was in his 10th year with Brooklyn, and seven games were played at Roosevelt Stadium. Robinson homered there on July 31, with his second-inning two-run blast putting the Dodgers ahead 2-1, as Brooklyn defeated the Braves, 3-2.

Another Hall of Famer homered there in both the minors and majors. Duke Snider first appeared with the Brooklyn Dodgers in 1947 and started 1948 in Brooklyn. He got off to a bad start and was sent to Montreal on May 22. He first played in Jersey City on June 10, and he went 3-for-5, scored three runs, drove in six, and homered in the process. As an established major-league All-Star, he hit two homers at Roosevelt Stadium in 1956, with the first coming on July 25 against Cincinnati. The score was tied in the bottom of the ninth. Snider came up with one out, and his walk-off homer gave the Dodgers a 2-1 win.

Hank Sauer was the third player to accomplish the "deed." His first homer at Roosevelt Stadium came on May 20, 1946, when he hit one out in a 4-2 Syracuse win over Jersey City. In 1947 he hit 50 homers, including four at Roosevelt Stadium. He had the next-to-last major-league home run hit during the brief tenure of Roosevelt Stadium as a major-league site. Sauer had been acquired by the New York Giants in a trade with the Cardinals, and his Roosevelt Stadium home run came on August 7, 1957. With the Dodgers leading 5-3 in the top of the ninth, the Giants got the first two men on base. Sauer was called on to pinch-hit, and his three-run homer put the Giants in the lead in an 8-5 victory.

SEALS STADIUM AND WRIGLEY FIELD OF LOS ANGELES

In their championship year of 1954, the New York Giants' home attendance was 1,155,067. From 1955 on, it went downhill, and owner Horace Stoneham was looking to move. His eyes were initially set on Minneapolis and the new ballpark in nearby Bloomington. However, Minneapolis wasn't the destination for the Giants, and Metropolitan Stadium did not see major-league baseball until 1961. The Dodgers' O'Malley encouraged Stoneham to set his eyes west, and San Francisco embraced the Giants with open arms. San Francisco had long been the home of the Seals in the Pacific Coast League, and they had been playing in Seals Stadium since 1931. For two years the Giants played at Seals Stadium, and in the 1958 season 1,272,625 fans came to see major-league baseball in the "City by the Bay."

Los Angeles had two minor-league teams in 1957. The Hollywood Stars played at Gilmore Field and the Los Angeles Angels played at Wrigley Field, their home since it opened in 1925. Prior to the 1957 season, O'Malley bought Wrigley Field and affiliated with the Angels. But Wrigley Field, even as a temporary home, was too small for O'Malley in 1958, and the Dodgers played their first four seasons at the cavernous Los Angeles Coliseum. The seating capacity at the Coliseum exceeded 90,000. The Dodgers drew 1,845,556 fans in their first season, including 78,682 for their home opener. When the Dodgers advanced to the World Series in 1959, crowds exceeded 92.000 for each of the three games played in Los Angeles. Wrigley Field was unoccupied until 1961 when expansion delivered the big-league Angels to the facility. The Angels used Wrigley Field for one season before moving to Dodger Stadium.

Seals Stadium was not a home-run hitter's paradise. The Seals homered in only 38 of the 84 games played at home in 1957, while the opposition homered in only 30 games. Eight players homered there in the minors and in the majors. Wrigley Field, with its power alleys being only 345 feet from home plate, was far more hospitable, and 242 homers were struck there in 1961.

On May 21, 1949, infielder Orestes "Minnie" Miñoso was optioned by the Cleveland Indians to San Diego of the PCL. He had spent three years with the

Negro League New York Cubans. Late in 1948 he was signed by the Indians and played 11 games for Dayton of the Class A Central League. He started 1949 with Cleveland, but the Indians wanted their new Cuban third baseman to learn to play the outfield, and he was sent to the PCL. In his first game with San Diego, he was charged with two errors. By the time he made it back to the majors, however, nobody questioned his ability in the outfield. He became the preeminent left fielder in the American League, leading the league in games played at that position for six consecutive seasons and earning three Gold Gloves.

In the second game of a PCL doubleheader on August 7, 1949, Miñoso went 4-for-5 with a homer and five RBIs as the San Diego Padres defeated the homestanding Angels, 7-4. On May 1, 1951, he became the first player of color to play in Chicago for either major-league team. By the time major-league baseball came to Wrigley Field in 1961, Miñoso was in the second year of his second go-round with the White Sox. On September 8, 1961, he homered at Wrigley Field.

Jackie Jensen was the Golden Boy, complete with as good a signing bonus as the Oakland Oaks could deliver in 1949. He started off slowly with Oakland, in the field and at the plate. When Oakland visited Wrigley Field on August 30, he homered in a 10-3 win over the Angels. For the season, Jensen batted .261. Jensen was then sold to the Yankees. He played with the Yankees and Senators before arriving in Boston in 1954 for his best years, highlighted by winning the American League MVP Award in 1958. With the Red Sox, he returned to Wrigley Field and homered on May 8, 1961.

In 1949 the Hollywood Stars won their first pennant since 1930. Their center fielder, Irv Noren, was chosen the league's MVP. The Stars were not affiliated, and Noren was on loan from Brooklyn. He slugged 29 homers to go along with a .330 batting average. On April 22 the Stars played the second game of a series at Seals Stadium, and in the third inning Noren homered to give the Stars a 3-0 lead in a game they won, 6-4. His bat came alive with the Yankees in 1954. He had his best season, batting .319 and getting named to the All-Star team. By 1958, he was in the National League and returned to the West Coast to face the Giants as a member of the Cardinals, when he homered at Seals Stadium on July 6.

San Diego had an informal arrangement with Cleveland. The Indians were on the lookout for young Black talent, and Bill Veeck signed 20-year-old Al Smith off the roster of the Cleveland Buckeyes of the Negro American League in 1948. On April 8, 1950, with the Padres, Smith homered at Wrigley Field. In the majors, Smith's best season for homers was 1961 with the White Sox. Of his 28 homers that year, three were hit at Wrigley Field in Los Angeles, with the first coming on May 19.

Dale Long hit home runs in eight consecutive games for the Pirates in 1956. In 1944, at the age of 18, he signed with the Milwaukee Brewers of the American Association. He spent the next seven years with no fewer than 11 minor-league teams before getting his first crack at the big time in 1951. It was a brief stay. After being selected off waivers by the St. Louis Browns and being subsequently released, Long signed on with the Seals, and found his stroke in Seals Stadium. The first of two 1951 Seals Stadium homers came on July 27, 1951, as the team shut out the Angels, 4-0.

In 1953, Long joined the Stars. Long's first minor-league Wrigley Field blast came on May 28, 1953, and was followed by others on May 30 and May 31. On the Stars' second trip to Wrigley, Long slammed four round-trippers in the eight-game series. He won both the home-run (35) and RBI (116) crowns. The first of his Seals Stadium minor-league homers with the Stars left the premises on June 12, 1953. He banged another two days later. He hit two more in July. In 1954, it was more of the same. Long hit another two homers at Wrigley Field and complemented these with a pair of two-homer games at Seals Stadium. Total minor-league damage: Wrigley Field – nine homers; Seals Stadium – 10 homers.

With the Cubs on April 27, 1958, Long slugged the first of his Seals Stadium major-league homers. It came off Rubén Gómez as the Cubs defeated the Giants 5-4. He had three homers at Seals Stadium in 1958, and another one in 1959. With the expansion Washington Senators in 1961, he had three home runs at Wrigley Field, the first coming on May 21.

Earl Averill Jr. played for San Diego in 1957, blasting one out of LA's Wrigley Field on May 29. In 1958 he batted .347 with 24 homers and 87 RBIs and was named the PCL Most Valuable Player. After the 1960 season, Averill was placed in the pool for the major-league expansion draft and was selected by the Angels. On April 27 the Angels played their home opener at Wrigley Field against the Twins. Angels manager Bill Rigney felt that Averill would hit well at Wrigley and put him in the starting lineup. In the bottom of the second inning, Averill hit a two-run homer, which was all the Angels would score in a 4-2 loss.[4] It was the first Angels homer at Wrigley. Of his career-high 21 major-league home runs that year, 16 came at Wrigley Field.

Among those to accomplish the deed, however, none stands out more than the one-and-only Steve Bilko.

The LA legend hit 313 minor-league home runs, including 148 in three years (1955-57) with the PCL Angels, 97 of which were at Wrigley Field and four of which soared out of Seals Stadium. His first Wrigley blast came on April 20, 1955. His first Seals Stadium round-tripper came on May 21, 1955.

Bilko started 1950 with the Cardinals, but he was not ready for the big time. He was batting .182 when he was sent to Rochester in early May. By then the International League Orioles were playing in Memorial Stadium, and Bilko hit the first of his two minor-league Memorial Stadium home runs on June 23, 1950.

After three phenomenal PCL seasons (during which he slammed more than 50 home runs in both 1956 and 1957), Bilko returned to the majors in 1958 and hit homers at each of the three former minor-league venues. On June 9, 1958, with Cincinnati, he homered off Johnny Antonelli of the San Francisco Giants at Seals Stadium. On June 7, 1960, with Detroit, he homered off Hoyt Wilhelm at Memorial Stadium in a 5-2 Tigers win.

With the expansion Angels, Bilko hit 11 homers at Wrigley Field. The first came off Herb Score, who was then pitching for the White Sox, on May 19, 1961. The last of Bilko's home runs at Wrigley was the last home run ever hit at the facility. It came on October 1, in the last inning of the last game played there. The solo homer came with two outs, but was too little, too late in an 8-5 loss.

Rocky Colavito was sent to San Diego of the PCL on June 25, 1956, and spent about five weeks with the Padres. During a July 4 doubleheader, there were 10 home runs, including three by Bilko. It was in the second game that Colavito slammed his first homer at Wrigley Field. On July 14, after hitting a total of 12 home runs and batting .368 in 35 games, he was recalled by Cleveland. In 1961, with Detroit, he returned to Wrigley Field and bashed the first of his Wrigley Field major-league homers on May 26. He had four home runs at Wrigley Field during the 1961 season.

Earl Battey spent the latter part of 1957 with the PCL Angels, going deep for the first time at Wrigley Field on August 13. On September 8 he sent three balls flying out of Wrigley, accounting for all three of his team's runs in a 14-inning 3-2 win over Sacramento. Battey was traded to Washington prior to the 1960 season and moved with the team to the Twin Cities for the 1961 season. Returning to Los Angeles in 1961, he homered on April 27 in the first major-league game played at Wrigley Field. His three-run-homer in the sixth inning put the Twins in the lead as they spoiled the Angels' home opener with a 4-2 win.

MEMORIAL STADIUM

The St. Louis Browns had long been one of the doormats of the American League, and by 1953 it was clear that the franchise could not survive in St. Louis. In hopes of attracting major-league baseball, Baltimore had completely renovated a facility then known as Babe Ruth Field. Memorial Stadium saw its first action in 1950, and for four seasons the Baltimore Orioles of the International League, a Phillies affiliate, called Memorial Stadium home. Eleven ballplayers homered there in the minors and majors during the time-period of this story.[5]

The first was Andy Carey, playing for Syracuse on September 7, 1952, who homered with one on at Memorial Stadium in a 5-0 win over the Orioles. Carey's third-inning homer put the Chiefs in front to stay. He played for the great Yankees teams of the 1950s, hitting 47 homers before being traded to Kansas City and finishing his career with the Dodgers. He became the first player to hit homers at the same ballpark in the minors and majors in the migration/expansion era when, in his second full year with the Yankees, he homered on May 16, 1954, as the Yankees defeated Baltimore, 2-0. He homered four times at Memorial Stadium as a major leaguer.

METROPOLITAN STADIUM

Minneapolis, in pursuit of a major-league team, replaced its minor-league facility, Nicollet Field, with Metropolitan Stadium in Bloomington in 1956. The ballpark was built to be expandable to major-league size when major-league ball came to the Twin Cities. The minor-league Minneapolis Millers occupied the facility for five years. The Washington Senators, perennially at or near the bottom of the American League standings, moved to Minneapolis in 1961, became the Minnesota Twins, and took up residence at Metropolitan Stadium. Of the 29 players who homered at this ballpark in the minors and majors, two future Hall of Famers stand out.[6]

Carl Yastrzemski signed with Boston in 1958. With the Millers in 1960, he was among the league leaders in batting all season. Toward the end of the season, he went on a 30-game hitting streak that raised his average to .339, good for second in the league. Early in his career, the homers came slowly. His first homer of 1960 did not come until June 5, and it was on the road at Indianapolis. He connected at home for the first time on June 11, once again victimizing Indianapolis. He joined the Red Sox in 1961, and he hit 18 at the Minnesota locale, the first coming on May 29, 1962.

Harmon Killebrew hit 246 homers at Metropolitan Stadium during his career. He signed with Washington and spent parts of the next five seasons in the nation's capital from 1954 through 1958, hitting 11 homers with 30 RBIs. In 1958 the Senators shipped him out to Indianapolis in the American Association where, in 38 games, he hit two homers and batted .215. The second of those two homers came at Metropolitan Stadium, on June 15. In 1959 he banged out an American League-leading 42 homers. He went to Minnesota when the Senators became the Twins in 1961, and his first big-league Metropolitan Stadium blast came on April 30, 1961.

This article was edited by Marshall Adesman and fact checked by Carl Riechers.

SOURCES

In addition to the sources shown in the Notes, the author used Baseball-Reference.com, Retrosheet.org, and, for minor-league box scores, *The Sporting News*.

NOTES

1 Eric Page, "Davenport's Stevens Made Big Splash in Majors Debut 50 Years Ago This Week," *Quad-City Times* (Davenport, Iowa), April 13, 2008: B1, B3.

2 Cy Kritzer, "Robinson Steals Int Show; Bears Off to Fast Getaway," *The Sporting News*, April 25, 1946: 18.

3 Jackie Robinson (with Carl Rowan), *Wait till Next Year: The Story of Jackie Robinson* (New York: Random House, 1960), 151-152.

4 "Compact Wrigley Field Made to Order for LA's Young Backstop, Earl Averill," *Bridgeport* (Connecticut) *Sunday Herald*, May 14, 1961: 6.

5 The following players hit home runs at Memorial Stadium in the minors and majors:

Player	Minors	Majors
Andy Carey	9/7/1952 (Syracuse)	4 - First on 5/16/1954 (w NYY) off Dave Koslo
Bill Tuttle	4/22/1953 (Buffalo)	3 - first on 6/18/1955 (w DET) off Fritz Dorish
Harry Chiti	5/24/1952 (Springfield)	6/06/1958 (w KCA) off Connie Johnson
Steve Bilko	6/23/1950 (Rochester)	2 - first on 6/7/1960 (w DET) off Hoyt Wilhelm
Tom Burgess	6/17/1953 (Rochester)	5/15/1961 (w LAA) off Milt Pappas
Smoky Burgess	5/22/1950 (Springfield)	6/26/1967 (w CHW) off Pete Rickert
Chico Fernández	7/17/1953 (Montreal)	7/23/1960 (w DET) off Hal Brown
Bubba Phillips	5/6/1952 (Buffalo)	2- first on 4/24/1961 (w CLE) off Milt Pappas
Vic Power	7/14/1951 (Syracuse)	3 - first on 6/10/1956 (w KCA) off Fritz Dorish
Don Bollweg	4/20/1950 (Rochester)	8/4/1954 (w PHA) off Duane Pillette
Jim Brideweser	6/13/1953 (Syracuse)	5/24/1957 off Frank Sullivan (BOS)
Hank Foiles	9/08/1951 (Syracuse)	9/29/1961 off Warren Hacker (CHW)
Glenn Davis	9/4/1993 (Bowie)	3 - first on 4/19/1991 off Kenny Rogers (TEX)

Henry Aaron hit his first Memorial Stadium home runs while with the Indianapolis Clowns on May 18, 1952. After spending the first 21 years of his major-league career in the National League, he returned to Memorial Stadium, as a member of the Milwaukee Brewers, and hit his first Memorial Stadium AL/NL major-league homer on May 19, 1976.

6 The following players hit home runs at Metropolitan Stadium in the minors and majors:

Player	Minors	Majors
Harmon Killebrew	6/15/1958 (Indianapolis)	246 – first on 4/30/1961 off Bob Shaw (CHW)
Julio Becquer	6/26/1956 (Louisville)	3 – first on 6/20/1961 off Jack Fisher (BAL)
Zoilo Versalles	6/26/1960 (Charleston)	57 – first on 5/10/1961 off Dick Hall (BAL)
Sandy Valdespino	8/17/1960 (Charleston)	3 – first on 4/13/1966 off Rollie Sheldon (KCA)
Johnny Goryl	8/06/1959 (Minneapolis)	2 – first on 7/21/1963 off Don Rudolph (WSA)
Joe Altobelli	6/13/1958 (Indianapolis)	2 – first on 9/11/1961 off Tom Morgan (LAA)
Marv Throneberry	6/27/1957 (Denver)	5/18/1961 (w KCA) off Jim Kaat
Johnny Callison	6/15/1958 (Indianapolis)	5/8/1972 (w NYY) off Bert Blyleven
Joe Koppe	7/28/1958 (Wichita)	6/24/1962 (w LAA) off Ray Moore
Willie Tasby	8/11/1958 (Louisville)	2 – first on 4/22/1961 (w WSA) off Pedro Ramos
John Romano	6/22/1957 (Indianapolis)	11 – first on 5/9/1962 (w CLE) off Jack Kralick
Lou Clinton	5/17/1958 (Minneapolis)	12 – first on 8/17/1962 (w BOS) off Jack Kralick
Charley Lau	8/16/1957 (Charleston, WV)	5/08/1964 (w KCA) off Bill Dailey
Bob Schmidt	5/09/1957 (Minneapolis)	6/01/1962 (w WAS) off Jim Kaat
Eddie Bressoud	6/27/1957 (Minneapolis)	4 – first on 8/17/1962 (w BOS) off Georges Maranda
Don Demeter	5/04/1957 (St. Paul)	7 – first on 4/26/1964 (w DET) off Jim Kaat
Johnny Blanchard	6/26/1957 (Denver)	3 – first on 6/24/1961 (w NYY) off Bert 9/Cueto
Woodie Held	5/27/1956 (Denver)	11 - first on 5/22/1961 (w CLE) off Ed Palmquist
Willie Kirkland	4/25/1956 (Minneapolis)	2 - first on 9/28/1961 (w CLE) off Don Lee
Bob Tillman	4/23/1960 (Minneapolis)	5 - first on 5/29/1962 (w BOS) off Lee Strange
Steve Boros	5/25/1960 (Denver)	3 - first on 5/23/1961 (w DET) off Ray Moore
Earl Wilson	5/28/1960 (Minneapolis)	8/17/1962 (w BOS) off Georges Maranda
Carl Yastrzemski	6/11/1960 (Minneapolis)	18 - first on 5/29/1962 (w BOS) off Lee Strange
Ed Charles	7/31/1960 (Louisville)	2 - first on 6/7/1966 (w KCA) off Jim Kaat

Chuck Schilling	7/07/1960 (Minneapolis)	4 - first on 5/7/1961 (w BOS) off Camilo Pascual
Camilo Carreón	8/15/1959 (Indianapolis)	3 - first on May 1, 1961 (w CHW) off Chuck Stobbs
Donald G. Leppert	4/26/1956 (Wichita)	8/18/1963 (w WSA) off Garry Roggenburk
Jim Gentile	5/30/1959 (St. Paul)	7 - first on 5/9/1961 (w BAL) off Pedro Ramos
Jerry Kindall	9/29/1959 (Fort Worth)	5 - first on 9/16/1962 (w CLE) off Camilo Pascual

THE BOOM AND BUST OF HOPE:

The Pacific Coast League and What Might Have Been

By John Bauer

Perhaps the Pacific Coast League never had a chance.

For decades, the PCL was baseball to fans along the Pacific Coast, the closest thing to the major leagues recognized in the East and Midwest. The league thrived before the age of air travel, but as modernization shrank the country, the PCL came into closer contact with the Eastern major leagues. To be sure, there were plenty of examples of players like Ted Williams and Joe DiMaggio, who made their way from California to the big cities of the East, but plenty more simply stayed and made careers out West. With the American League and National League jealously guarding their major-league status and the PCL increasingly defending what it had built, the Eastern establishment and the Western pretenders seemed destined to collide. Would the established major leagues claim the West Coast for themselves or would the PCL force the AL and NL to recognize the West Coast circuit as an equal?

The resolution to this question is key to understanding the structure of major-league baseball that emerged in the postwar era. Despite the efforts of the Western upstarts, they never really had a chance. Several factors conspired against the PCL's pretensions to major-league status. First, the boom of postwar attendance may have heightened expectations about the size of the PCL fan base, but the subsequent inability to sustain the surge of fan interest held the league back. Second, most PCL cities lacked ballparks that would have provided a potential major-league foundation. Outside of a few league cities, the facilities were generally substandard and kept fans away. Third, the television age was beginning. Baseball had a new competitor for people's leisure time, and the national and regional broadcasting of ballgames lessened the incentive to attend in person. Fourth, government officials, crucially in Los Angeles and San Francisco, made no mistake about their preference to lure major-league baseball rather than strengthen local PCL teams. Civic leaders were seduced by big-league ball from afar and made offers to strangers that were never extended to locals. Finally, the preceding factors left the PCL unable to take advantage of the Open classification it was granted in late 1951. Open classification suggested a path to major-league status, but the PCL proved unable to take advantage. Instead of growing into a major league, the PCL's largest cities became colonized and co-opted into the existing major-league order.

The major leagues had seriously eyed the West Coast since 1941. The American League planned to vote on December 8, 1941, to approve the transfer of the St. Louis Browns to Los Angeles. The bombing of Pearl Harbor on December 7 drew the United States

SABR: The Rucker Archive.

Ted Williams.

into World War II and scuppered any talk of relocation for the foreseeable future. After the war fans flocked to major- and minor-league games, and the PCL shared in the attendance increase. In 1945 the league broke its attendance record with almost 3 million fans. One year later, admissions exceeded 3.7 million, and the San Francisco Seals set a minor-league record with 670,563 patrons.[1] The good times continued into 1947 as the PCL crossed the 4 million mark in attendance for the first time; five teams exceeded a half-million, with both San Francisco and Los Angeles drawing in excess of 600,000.[2] In fact, every team in the league outdrew the American League's "poor sister," the St. Louis Browns.

Amid this business boom, PCL President Clarence "Pants" Rowland requested recognition from the American League and National League as a major league.[3] The majors denied the initial request in 1946 and, although there was some thought to "going outlaw," the PCL stayed within the system of Organized Baseball.[4] Flagship clubs like the San Francisco Seals and Los Angeles Angels conducted business on a footing similar to major-league teams; moreover, the Angels had a direct connection to the majors as they were part of the Chicago Cubs system through owner Philip Wrigley. Their ballparks, Seals Stadium and Wrigley Field respectively, were among the best facilities on the West Coast but they were atypical of the league. In general, however, playing facilities played a significant role in holding back the league. Most ballparks were small and decrepit in comparison to major-league ballparks. When he made his push for major status, Rowland believed the ballparks could be brought to big-league standards within three years.[5] That assessment was hopelessly optimistic.

Sales of television sets exploded after the war, and baseball provided programming potential. Just as the majors began taking advantage of the new medium, so did the PCL. While there was money to be made, there was a knock-on effect for in-person attendance. Los Angeles and the Hollywood Stars were early adapters to television, consistently airing games as early as 1947 (the Stars actually experimented with televising games in the prewar years),[6] but as telecasts increased in 1948 and 1949, attendance figures declined. Plus, major-league teams started broadcasting games nationwide, cannibalizing their own gates but devastating minor-league teams with a better product available to fans without leaving their homes. By 1950, PCL attendance fell to around 3 million, a decline of more than 25 percent from just three years earlier.[7] More exposure to major-league baseball undermined the PCL's position; after all, "[i]f you could listen to the big boys on the box at home, why go out to the park to see the local Minor Leaguers play?"[8] Even when clubs reduced the number of broadcasts, attendance failed to rebound.

In 1951 the PCL pressed again for major-league recognition, and this time the league appeared ready for a fight. The major-league draft was increasingly a point of contention. The draft, which allowed major-league teams to purchase the rights to a minor-league player, meant that major-league clubs could claim PCL players for a mere $10,000; clubs complained that they invested more to develop a player than they received in return. Seals owner Paul Fagan said, "I'm just convinced that San Francisco deserves baseball of the highest caliber, and that is impossible to acquire with the draft annually taking our best players and forcing us to sell others or suffer great financial loss."[9] The Seals proposed to go outlaw, but the league deadlocked on their motion.[10] Fagan had reason to be concerned. In San Francisco alone, attendance fell with the Seals' fortunes, with the gate slipping below 200,000 in 1951, just four years removed from their record-setting season.

The major leagues relented, but only to a point. With Congress taking an interest in the majors' antitrust exemption amid television's negative effect on the minors, the majors created the "Open" classification to appease the restless PCL. The new classification was intended to provide the league with room to grow toward major-league status but offered no guarantee.

With Open classification, the majors extended the period before which a player could be drafted from four years to five, and allowed PCL players to opt out of the draft. The price for players drafted out of the PCL jumped to $15,000. As Oakland Oaks owner Clarence "Brick" Laws noted, "Draft relief will be our first step toward becoming a major league. [With relief] we can reach major league standards in a few years."[11] At first, draft relief seemed to work. Ahead of the 1952 season, 19 of 20 draft-eligible PCL players opted for contracts that exempted them from being claimed.[12] Fagan observed, "Now we no longer have to serve as a fish hatchery for the majors, by developing players for them."[13] Intending to establish its independence of operations, the PCL voted not to take optioned players starting with the 1953 season, and operating agreements with major-league clubs were restricted.

Attendance declined once again in 1952 despite a general decrease in the number of games broadcast both by PCL teams and from Eastern major-league cities.[14] Fagan and Sacramento Solons owner Charles Graham believed fans remained more focused on major-league teams than local PCL clubs.[15] Claims to major-league status were also undermined by the actions of the PCL's own clubs. In January 1952 the Pittsburgh Pirates purchased a minority interest in the Hollywood Stars. Fagan protested, "The 'Coast League must divorce itself 100 percent from the majors!"[16] The deal was approved ultimately, and it proved a harbinger rather than an exception. In a few years, the Stars were effectively converted into a Pirates farm team, and more followed.

League attendance continued to plunge, with the 1953 gate almost 20 percent lower than the prior year, down to about 1.7 million, the lowest level since 1943. Rowland sought to tamp down rumors of a failing league, stating, "The financial structure of the league is sound as a bell of brass."[17] The decision to refrain from taking optioned players caused short-term pain as clubs scrambled to fill the talent gap while maintaining their purported major-league standard of play. Going their own way would require expansion of scouting operations, which squeezed already strained finances. With every club outside of Los Angeles and Hollywood supposedly losing large sums, several clubs planned to sell players to major-league clubs to stem the red ink. It was a turn from the potential of Open classification; instead of developing players free from major-league draft interference, clubs hawked those players to counter the losses caused by declining fan interest. The forbearance on optioned players was dropped after one season.

The big leagues began to remake their own map beginning in 1953. In the majors' first franchise shift in a half-century, the Braves left Boston, their home since 1871, for Milwaukee. In 1954 the St. Louis Browns moved to Baltimore; the next year the Athletics departed Philadelphia for Kansas City. Expansion was now an additional outlet for the majors; each league had amended its constitution – the NL in 1947, the AL in 1953 – to permit expansion to 10 clubs. Yankees co-owner Del Webb stated, "[Baseball] must study the fact that the Pacific Coast cannot be held off very much longer in its demand for major league baseball." He specifically mentioned Los Angeles and San Francisco. The PCL promised to fight attempts to crowd them out of their own cities. Rowland asserted, "We merely demand the right to try life as a major league with the eight cities which now are in the Pacific Coast League."[18]

The relocation era heightened a sense of the possible in the league's largest cities, and their aspirations had nothing to do with the PCL. Los Angeles Mayor Norris Poulson formed a task force in 1953 dedicated to enticing an existing major-league team to move west, and local oilman Edwin Pauley agreed to fund a study into whether the Los Angeles Coliseum could be retrofitted for baseball.[19] Pauley wrote to Brooklyn Dodgers owner Walter O'Malley to gauge his interest but the response was, "Nothing doing."[20] Francis McCarty, head of the San Francisco Board of Supervisors, claimed, "San Francisco is a major league town. … If we have to spend money to bring it here, it will be money well spent. We have to get off the dime."[21] There was no interest in spending money to elevate the status of their local PCL teams.

Abandonment was now on the table for the owners of the two Bay Area PCL teams. Claiming losses of $500,000 over the previous eight years, Fagan sold the team and its players to the league for $100,000 on September 24, 1953. With the league's blessing, Seals GM Damon Miller cobbled together the so-called Little Corporation of investors to maintain the team. The group was seriously undercapitalized and interest continued to swoon. Brick Laws considered the same strategy in Oakland; while he did not pull the trigger, his days at the decaying Emeryville Park were numbered. In November 1954 San Francisco voters approved a $5 million bond measure by more than 2 to 1 for a new ballpark as soon as the city acquired a major-league team. There was nothing for the Seals in that measure. Commissioner Ford Frick gloated to Curley Grieve, sports editor of *San Francisco Examiner*, "This vote of your people leaves no doubt as to how the citizens of San Francisco feel about big league baseball. They want it!"[22]

The PCL appeared to be resigning itself to a potential takeover at the league meetings in October 1953. Rowland appeared to be among the converted as he stated, "The Pacific Coast League has adapted itself to the inevitable."[23] Seattle Rainiers owner Emil Sick said, "Henceforth, the Coast League will welcome anyone with the courage and money to bring major league ball to any Coast League city – Seattle included."[24] Rowland somehow saw signs of an attendance rebound in 1954. He opined, "I feel the Coast League will have one whale of a year both attendance-wise and on the field," and projected replicating the record-setting 1947 season.[25] In the end, attendance fell short of 2 million once again, with a modest increase over 1953. In November 1954, Rowland resigned the league presidency in order to take the same title with the Chicago Cubs; he had left the Cubs in 1944 to take the helm of the PCL. He continued to believe the PCL could have been a major league in the 1940s. Although he questioned whether all eight cities could have supported major-league baseball, he explained, "My hope was that [major-league recognition] would be granted and then we could let nature take its course. Some would drop by the wayside and several cities from outside the territory could be substituted."[26] Perhaps a version of the PCL that involved other Western cities starved for big-league ball, such as Dallas, Denver, or Houston, could have made it.

The PCL named Claire Goodwin as its president on January 12, 1955. Recognized as a sportsman and business executive around Oakland, Goodwin arrived full of enthusiasm and ideas to reverse the league's fortunes. He observed, "The horizon is unlimited. I don't regard this job as an interim one until the majors come to the Coast. The PCL is here to stay."[27] He identified the issues of pressing concern, and targeted ballpark rehabilitation, admission prices, "hustle" to quicken game pace, and cooperation with the major leagues as primary initiatives. Goodwin also came out swinging about the conduct of the major leagues and its detrimental effect on the PCL: "When the majors leave us alone we'll have the stability, confidence and security to get the right kind of ball parks and launch a broad, long range program for development of young talent."[28] He telegrammed complaints to NL President Warren Giles over information that the senior circuit had prepared a 10-team schedule for 1955 that included Los Angeles and San Francisco. Goodwin protested, "Your statements are extremely detrimental to baseball in the Pacific Coast, whose territory you are theoretically taking over."[29]

Commissioner Frick stepped in to quell chatter about major-league teams muscling minor-league teams out of their home cities. In a memo sent to all 16 clubs in February 1955, Frick said, "[Minor league cities] are being definitely harmed by this loose talk on the part of their major league brothers."[30] Hollywood's Bob Cobb complained, "The Coast league has been crucified by such talk. It creates dissension, destroys the loyalty of our fans."[31] Still, Goodwin and Cobb were among those voices that acknowledged the PCL needed to take care of its own issues. The condition of its ballparks was a paramount issue. Cobb referred to league stadiums as "old" and "dirty";[32] and indeed, many were. Cobb had his own eye on Chavez Ravine, where he believed the Hollywood Stars could draw one million fans in a modern, 30,000-seat ballpark.[33] The San Diego Padres hoped to build a 20,000-seat ballpark – Lane Field could hold only 7,500 with a termite infestation condemning the bleachers section – and the league voted a $100,000 grant as seed money. The Portland Beavers planned a move of their own, with plans to trade the near-condemnation Vaughn Street Park for the larger but 30-year-old Multnomah Stadium. The latter's 22,000 capacity had room for expansion to around 33,000.

PCL President Goodwin targeted 3 million fans for 1955, and there were auspicious signs in the early days of the season. Attendance figures were up and game times were down, but rain and cold weather arrived to conspire against Goodwin's plans. After eight weeks, league attendance was down, with notable decreases in Hollywood, Oakland, and Sacramento. In San Francisco, the Little Corporation was on the verge of forfeiting the Seals to the league. The PCL amended its constitution to allow it to run the Seals, which happened after the collapse of a rescue bid from Hank Greenberg and the Cleveland Indians. Cobb labeled the Seals' situation a "debacle," noting that "[t]he people here (Los Angeles) and in San Francisco have shown they want baseball with a major league label."[34] The saga reached a conclusion in December 1955 with the announcement that the Boston Red Sox were acquiring the Seals for $150,000. Red Sox GM Joe Cronin promised that the Seals would not serve just as an appendage to the Boston farm system. Rather, Cronin noted, "This area is too big and too important to be represented by a farm club."[35] It was an embarrassing turnaround since 1947 for one of the PCL's signature franchises. Goodwin, in office for less than a year, saw the handwriting on the wall for his tenure. He remarked, "There's a gentlemanly way to do everything and all the Coast League has to do is tell me I'm through. I won't even ask why."[36] The league accepted his resignation at its December meeting. Leslie O'Connor, counsel to the PCL for several years and a former aide to former Commissioner Kenesaw Mountain Landis, succeeded Goodwin.

PCL baseball was truly at a crossroads in the Bay Area. The Seals could not be run as an independent entity and now required a bailout by a major-league team in order to survive. As their status diminished, the Seals found they had the Bay Area to themselves.

With the lease expiring on their ancient Emeryville Park home, the Oakland Oaks fled the country to Vancouver, British Columbia, to play the 1956 season as the Mounties. Any pretense toward independence was damaged by further dependence on the major leagues for players. In addition to the Seals' integration into the Red Sox structure, and accounting for the existing Stars-Pirates and Angels-Cubs arrangements, four more PCL teams opted for working agreements with major-league teams. The Rainiers teamed up with the Reds, the Beavers with the Dodgers, the Padres with the Indians, and the Mounties with the Orioles. Only the Solons entered the 1956 season as a completely independent entity.

O'Connor seemed realistic about the challenges facing the league. Like his predecessors, he praised the caliber of baseball, asserting that the PCL "is only a very minute step behind the majors insofar as quality of play is concerned."[37] But O'Connor also observed, "Merely putting a major league label on it won't make it big league. It must have the revenue."[38] As O'Connor was trying to ensure the viability of PCL baseball, the league's Open classification was under attack from International League President Frank Shaughnessy, who asserted that the PCL was in violation of criteria associated with the Open classification. With all but one club possessing a working agreement with a major-league team and PCL attendance slipping below expected standards, Shaughnessy argued that the PCL "is occupying open classification status under false pretenses"[39] and said he expected National Association President George Trautman to do something about it. O'Connor defended his league and, despite perhaps most evidence to the contrary, maintained that the PCL had not surrendered its major-league dream. That dream, according to O'Connor, was "not dead at all. Several of our club owners are still actively thinking of it, but we all realize we have a harder row to hoe now."[40] That row looked even harder when attendance figures showed the PCL falling behind both the IL and American Association when the final numbers were counted. The PCL held onto the Open classification for the 1957 season, but it would be the last.

On February 21, 1957, O'Malley made his play for the Coast. Using proceeds from the sale of Ebbets Field just months before, he purchased the Angels and Wrigley Field from the Cubs, surrendering the Dodgers' Texas League farm team in Fort Worth as part of the exchange. When the PCL considered approval of the purchase, O'Malley made no secret of his interest in securing territorial rights to Los Angeles should he move west, but he also claimed that the Angels would remain PCL members, albeit as a Dodgers farm club.[41] (Hollywood had no territorial claim to the region, a condition of their 1938 relocation from the Mission District of San Francisco.) While he made no commitments about moving the Dodgers, O'Malley was not behaving like a man content with a new minor-league toy 3,000 miles from his home base. In March Poulson and other civic leaders called upon O'Malley at the Dodgers' spring-training base in Vero Beach, Florida, and the Dodgers supremo knew the strength of his position. Poulson remarked, "One of our officials promised O'Malley the moon, and O'Malley asked for more."[42] In early May O'Malley spent several days in Los Angeles scouting potential stadium locations and meeting with local officials. Poulson proclaimed, "If the Dodgers come, it'll be next year."[43] City and county leaders placed before O'Malley a substantial proposal to sell Chavez Ravine, buy Wrigley Field, and handle infrastructure projects like freeway access.

Poulson and San Francisco Mayor George Christopher teamed up their efforts to secure major-league baseball. Poulson declared, "We intend to petition the major leagues for franchises for our cities at their next meeting. ... Yes, both leagues – the National and the American."[44] There had been a rumor,

SABR: The Rucker Archive.

Joe DiMaggio.

widely circulated in the *San Francisco Chronicle*, suggesting that the Red Sox would finance a new team in San Francisco and Yankees owner Del Webb would divest his interest in the Yankees in order to claim Los Angeles for the American League.[45] Cronin also quashed discussion about the Red Sox pulling up their stakes for the Bay Area.[46] After a three-game exhibition series at Seals Stadium in March 1957 between the Seals and Red Sox attracted 57,000 fans, Christopher's argument was strengthened. He stated, "We are happy to join hands with Los Angeles. In my opinion, major league baseball is coming to both our cities."[47] There was no mention of the existing PCL teams. With the New York Giants assumed to be leaving Manhattan – originally for Minneapolis before San Francisco entered the picture – and the Dodgers clearly considering their options, the NL authorized the two teams to move together in a May 28 vote. The opportunity to transport their ancient interborough New York rivalry to rival California cities was very seductive. Giles explained, "They are free to carry on discussions and negotiations with the knowledge that they have the sanction of the league for such a shift."[48]

O'Connor and the PCL could see that their ability to affect events was nil. While O'Connor said the PCL would attempt to oppose the moves, he asserted that his league would demand compensation (some suggested a figure as high as $10 million), and lashed out at local politicians and the NL. He pointed out that the "action of politicians and the major league involved in the proposed move has been brutal."[49] O'Connor directed particular opprobrium to Christopher, who "didn't have the courtesy to even consult us, [never offered the PCL any help, and] then he hands a bunch of Easterners $10,000,000 on a silver platter."[50] Interest in the Seals was not dead, as shown by a late Save the Seals campaign, but the Giants appeared to be coming. PCL owners directed O'Connor to reach out to Frick, Giles, and AL President Will Harridge for assistance in finding replacement cities and asking for a cut of TV and radio revenue. With the PCL's existence threatened by the loss of its two major cities, O'Connor argued, "We think part of that money belongs to us. … We're neither begging nor threatening. … We're telling them they're going to destroy this league, unless they can come up with something."[51]

On August 19 Giants owner Horace Stoneham confirmed plans to move to San Francisco, and the following day's *Chronicle* hailed the news in large type: "Say Hey! They're S.F. Giants Now." Days later, Stoneham purchased the Seals, in effect swapping his Minneapolis farm team with the Red Sox to smooth his path to San Francisco. O'Malley's move was held up briefly by politics within the Los Angeles City Council. Proponents of the city's package struggled to muster the necessary two-thirds vote, but the additional votes were found and the Dodgers confirmed their relocation plans on October 8.

O'Connor continued to complain, saying, "Nobody has had the decency or courtesy to contact me or any of our independent owners."[52] Defending his league, he added, "[We] have five franchises owned by independent people, who are practically told to step down a few grades in their baseball business."[53] With the Dodgers and Giants coming and nothing to stop them, it was left to the league to pick up the pieces and strike its best deal for indemnification. Initially, it was unclear if there would be a PCL in 1958. There was ample talk of lawsuits. O'Connor asserted, "Some of the clubs in our league are mad enough to sue anybody."[54] The Pacific Northwest teams and San Diego faced the possibility of being geographically marooned. At the 1957 Winter Meetings, the remaining six teams ultimately settled for $900,000 to be paid by the invaders over three years, a comparatively paltry sum in light of the riches that awaited. With no option to stay in Los Angeles, Cobb sold the Stars to Utah oilman Nicholas Morgan, who moved the team to Salt Lake City. Stoneham would place a team in Phoenix, and Spokane planned to build a stadium for a Dodgers farm team to replace the Angels. The PCL surrendered its Open status to the inevitable, and reverted to Triple-A status for the 1958 season. The major-league dream was truly over.

This article was edited by Marshall Adesman and fact-checked by Mark Richard.

SOURCES

In addition to the sources cited in the Notes, the author also consulted:

Dobbins, Dick. *The Grand Minor League* (Emeryville, California: Woodford Press, 1999).

Raley, Dan. *Pitchers of Beer: The Story of the Seattle Rainiers* (Lincoln: University of Nebraska Press, 2011).

NOTES

1 Dennis Snelling, *The Greatest Minor League: A History of the Pacific Coast League* (Jefferson, North Carolina: McFarland & Company, Inc., 2012), 212.

2 Bill O'Neal, *The Pacific Coast League: 1903-1988* (Austin, Texas: Eakin Press, 1990), 92.

3 O'Neal, 89.

4 O'Neal, 96.

5 Dan Taylor, *Lights, Camera, Fastball: How the Hollywood Stars Changed Baseball* (Lanham, Maryland: Rowman & Littlefield, 2021), 237.

6 Taylor, 250.

7 Snelling, 238.

8 Kevin Nelson, *The Golden Game: The Story of California Baseball* (Lincoln: University of Nebraska Press, 2004), 315.

9 Snelling, 243.

10 Snelling, 243.

11 Taylor, 245.

12 Taylor, 256.

13 Jack McDonald, "Coasters Sizzling Over Lane's Roasting," *The Sporting News*, April 15, 1953: 13.

14 Richard Beverage, *The Los Angeles Angels of the Pacific Coast League: A History, 1903-1957* (Jefferson, North Carolina: McFarland & Company, Inc., 2011), 160.

15 Jack McDonald, "Coast Slices Player Limit to 21, Views TV Picture," *The Sporting News*, January 28, 1953: 12.

16 Taylor, 265.

17 Jack McDonald, "Find Buyer for Seals, Fagan Tells Rowland at Coasters' Meeting," *The Sporting News*, May 20, 1953: 15.

18 J.G. Taylor Spink, „Webb Sees K.C. as Major League Entry," *The Sporting News*, July 22, 1953: 1, 2.

19 Taylor, 281.

20 Dan Daniel, "Over the Fence," *The Sporting News*, November 10, 1954: 10.

21 Walter Addiego, "Frisco Planning to Send 'Envoy' in Bid to Majors," *The Sporting News*, July 29, 1953: 6.

22 "Frick Enthused Over 'Frisco Approval of Major Stadium," *The Sporting News*, November 17, 1954: 8.

23 John B. Old, "Coast League Reverses Its Policy, Agrees to Aid Move for Major Ball," *The Sporting News*, November 4, 1953: 15.

24 "Coast League Reverses Its Policy, Agrees to Aid Move for Major Ball."

25 Old, "Coast Officials See Four-Million Gate Total in '54," *The Sporting News*, February 10, 1954: 26.

26 Edgar Munzel, "'Slash'" Major Rosters To 21' – Rowland," *The Sporting News*, December 29, 1954: 1.

27 Jack McDonald, "PCL Picks Goodwin as President, Votes Budget of $100,025," *The Sporting News*, January 19, 1955: 22.

28 "PCL Picks Goodwin as President."

29 "PCL Prexy Protests Talk of Coast Move by Majors," *The Sporting News*, February 9, 1955: 31.

30 Spink , "Coasters Given Shot in Arm by Invasion Curb," *The Sporting News*, February 16, 1955: 1, 4.

31 "Coasters Given Shot in Arm by Invasion Curb."

32 "Coasters Given Shot in Arm by Invasion Curb."

33 "Coasters Given Shot in Arm by Invasion Curb."

34 Sid Ziff, "Bob Cobb Invites Majors to Coast – 'Doors Wide Open,'" *The Sporting News*, August 31, 1955: 4.

35 "'Seals Won't Be Riddled to Help Bosox' – Cronin,'" *The Sporting News*, December 21, 1955: 20.

36 Jack McDonald, "Goodwin Picks Up Hat as PCL Keeps Hunting Seal Buyer," *The Sporting News*, November 23, 1955: 17.

37 Munzel, "O'Connor Sees Bright Era for Coast," *The Sporting News*, December 28, 1955: 1.

38 "O'Connor Sees Bright Era for Coast."

39 Cy Kritzer, "Shaughnessy Hits Majors' 'Shipment' of Players to Coast," *The Sporting News*, June 6, 1956: 16.

40 Jack McDonald, "O'Connor Answers Shag, Insists PCL Not Guilty of Violating Agreement," *The Sporting News*, September 19, 1956: 33.

41 P.J. Dragseth, *The 1957 San Francisco Seals: End of an Era in the Pacific Coast League* (Jefferson, North Carolina: McFarland & Company, Inc., 2013), 53.

42 Nelson, "The Golden Game," 313.

43 Taylor, "Lights, Camera, Fastball," 329.

44 "L.A., 'Frisco Mayors Plan Joint Action in Major Bids," *The Sporting News*, April 3, 1957: 2.

45 Dragseth, 48.

46 Dragseth, 137.

47 "L.A., 'Frisco Mayors Plan Joint Action in Major Bids."

48 Edgar Munzel, "Hurdles Looming for '58 Coast Shifts," *The Sporting News*, June 5, 1957: 5.

49 "PCL to Ask for 'Just Compensation,'" *The Sporting News*, June 5, 1957: 6.

50 "PCL to Ask for 'Just Compensation.'"

51 Jack McDonald, "'Throw Us a Life Preserver,' PCL Plea to Majors," *The Sporting News*, June 12, 1957: 6.

52 Harry Grayson, "Coast League Doing a Slow Burn on Shifts," *The Sporting News*, September 11, 1957: 10.

53 Grayson.

54 Jack McDonald, "Angry Coast Leaguers Talk of 'Big Lawsuits,'" *The Sporting News*, September 18, 1957: 8.

JACKIE ROBINSON AND THE 1946 INTERNATIONAL LEAGUE MVP AWARD

By C. Paul Rogers III

The 1946 Montreal Royals of the International League have received much attention over the years because Jackie Robinson broke Organized Baseball's historic and shameful color line by playing second base for the Royals.[1] But little consideration has been given to that season's MVP race, and the fact that Robinson did not win it, even though he had a truly exceptional season for one of the best minor-league teams in baseball history. Indeed, Robinson had such a tremendous season that several writers have incorrectly reported that Jackie did win the league Most Valuable Player Award.[2]

Those 1946 Royals were a juggernaut, winning 100 of 154 games and sweeping to the International League pennant by 18½ games. They dominated the league playoffs by defeating the fourth-place Newark Bears four games to two in the semifinals before dispatching the second-place Syracuse Chiefs in five games for the league championship. The Royals then defeated the Louisville Colonels, champions of the American Association, in six games to win the Little World Series.

The 27-year-old Jackie Robinson led the Royals, as he batted .349 to lead the league in batting average. Robinson's slash line was .349/.468/.462/.930 but of course little attention was paid to anything but batting average and, to a lesser extent, slugging average in those days. His 113 runs scored tied for tops in the league and his fielding was superb as he led the league in fielding percentage for second basemen. He stole 40 bases, second in the league only to his teammate, the speedster Marv Rackley. Robinson hit .357 in the league playoffs, "fielding his position spectacularly."[3] In the Little World Series against the Louisville Colonels, he remained a force, batting .333 despite constant and virulent racial abuse in Louisville for the three games played there.[4]

SABR: The Rucker Archive.

Jackie Robinson coming to home after hitting his first home run, as a member of the 1946 Montreal Royals.

But Robinson did not win the MVP Award or even finish second. The actual results for the league's MVP voting appear, in hindsight, surprising.[5] In the International League Baseball Writers Association voting, Robinson finished in fifth place, behind Eddie Robinson, the slugging first baseman for the Baltimore Orioles; Bobby Brown, the bonus-baby shortstop for the Newark Bears; Jackie's Montreal teammate Tommy Tatum; and Eddie Joost of Rochester.[6] *The Sporting News* also named Eddie Robinson the league MVP, followed by Brown in second place and Jackie Robinson third.[7]

THE MVP VOTING

Eddie Robinson was certainly a worthy MVP; he batted .318, smashed 34 home runs, and led the league with 121 RBIs in 143 games.[8] Bobby Brown, dubbed the "Golden Boy" by the press,[9] also had an impressive season in his first year in professional baseball, batting .341, second in the league behind Jackie Robinson, and tying for the most hits in the circuit with 174.[10] Jackie's Montreal teammate Tommy Tatum who finished third in the writers' voting, batted .319 and was a jack-of-all-trades who played six different positions for the Royals.[11]

The obvious question is: How could Jackie Robinson have finished third and fifth in the voting for the two International League MVP Awards given his performance in 1946, which one writer has asserted was "perhaps the best single season of any player ever in the International League"?[12] In the voting by the writers, Eddie Robinson was the runaway winner with 250 points. Second-place Brown had 135 points, followed closely by Tatum with 127 points, Joost with 120 points, and Jackie Robinson, in fifth place with 89 points.[13] Thus, according to the writers, Robinson was not even the most valuable player on his own team.

The voting for *The Sporting News* version of the MVP was conducted by its eight league correspondents, one for each International League entry.[14] That voting was tighter, with Eddie Robinson finishing on top with 51 votes, including three first-place votes, three seconds, and one third. Bobby Brown's runner-up total was 42 points, including one first-place vote, while Jackie Robinson finished with 30 points and two first-place votes.[15]

Although Branch Rickey's signing of Jackie Robinson and his season with the Royals have been well-documented,[16] the paths to the International League and beyond of the other MVP candidates have not and provide interesting context to the 1946 MVP race. While Tatum's subsequent big-league career was limited, both Eddie Robinson and Bobby Brown, who was in medical school at Tulane, had substantial major-league careers. Their routes to the International League, however, and then on to the major leagues differed significantly.

EDDIE ROBINSON

Eddie Robinson, from Paris, Texas, was 25 years old in 1946 and returning from three years of service in the Navy. While stationed in Hawaii he had undergone surgery to remove a bone tumor in his leg. The Navy surgeon, however, inadvertently damaged the peroneal nerve, which controls one's ability to lift one's foot. The damaged nerve threatened Robinson's baseball career and necessitated a second operation by a specialist in Bethesda, Maryland, to repair the damage and enable the nerve to grow back.

Robinson had appeared in eight games for the Cleveland Indians at the end of the 1942 season before joining the military and upon his discharge from the Navy reported to the Indians' 1946 spring training in Clearwater, Florida. When he reported he still had a brace on his leg and was not sure that his damaged leg would allow him to play. But the nerve had regenerated and grown over the previous six months, alleviating his drop foot and enabling him to discard the brace on the first day.[17]

After his long layoff from baseball, Robinson did not hit much during spring training, prompting the Indians to award the first-base job to Les Fleming and send Eddie to Baltimore so that he could play every day. But more hardship awaited Eddie when the season began. His daughter Robby Ann, who was born in late 1943, became seriously ill and was hospitalized at Johns Hopkins in Baltimore with an inoperable brain tumor. She lapsed into a coma while in intensive care and died before her third birthday. Eddie was understandably grief-stricken and missed several games before returning to the Orioles lineup.[18]

One of the highlights of Robinson's 1946 season came against the Newark Bears in a game in Baltimore. The Orioles played their games in Baltimore Stadium, which was a football stadium, since Oriole Park, the team's baseball park, had burned down during the 1944 season.[19] The baseball field was configured like the Los Angeles Coliseum later was when the Dodgers moved to the West Coast, with a high fence at a very short left field and no fence at all in right, just the other end of the football field. Thus, the only way to hit a home run to straightaway right field was to run around the bases while the ball was in play.

As Bobby Brown remembered years later, Eddie Robinson hit a ball about 40 feet over the head of Bears right fielder Hal Douglas. The ball rolled all the way to the steps of a temporary clubhouse in deep, deep right field. Robinson was always a slow runner, made even slower due to his damaged leg, but he circled the bases and was sitting in the dugout by the time Douglas retrieved the ball.[20]

Led by Robinson and Howie Moss, who hit 38 homers and drove in 112 runs,[21] the Orioles finished in a tie for third place in 1946 with an 80-73 record, 19 games behind Montreal, before losing to the second-place Syracuse Chiefs in six games in the first round of the playoffs.[22]

Robinson became the regular first baseman for the Cleveland Indians in 1947 until mid-August, when he fouled a pitch by Allie Reynolds off his ankle and fractured a bone, sidelining him for the season.[23] But he was back at first for the Indians' magical run to the pennant and World Series championship in 1948, batting .300 in the Series.

Robinson went on to play 13 big-league seasons with seven American League teams, making four All-Star teams, and playing in another World Series with the 1955 New York Yankees.[24] After his playing career, he successfully made the transition to the front office, eventually serving as general manager of the Atlanta Braves and of the Texas Rangers.

BOBBY BROWN

The 21-year-old Bobby Brown also had a unique path to the International League, straight from the Tulane Medical School, where, as he put it, he was "the best hitter in his medical school class."[25] He had begun his collegiate career at Stanford but enlisted in the Navy's wartime V12 program as a pre-med student when he turned 18. During his freshman year at Stanford, he hit .405 for the varsity[26] and caught the eye of Ty Cobb, who sometimes attended Stanford games. When Brown was called to active duty on July 1, 1943, the Navy sent him to UCLA to finish his pre-med studies. Brown played on the UCLA Bruins baseball team, where Jackie Robinson had starred a few years earlier, during his year there and batted close to .500.

With his pre-med studies complete, the Navy sent Brown to Tulane for medical school. There, seemingly against all odds, he managed to play for Tulane's baseball team during his first year in med school, again batting over .450.[27] Thus, due to the vagaries caused by World War II, Brown played and starred for three universities in three years.[28] He was later elected to the Sports Halls of Fame for all three schools.

With the war over, Brown was discharged from the Navy in January 1946. The Yankees then outbid several other teams and signed him to a record $52,000 bonus that spring while he was in his second year of medical school. The Tulane administration, after much deliberation, agreed to allow Brown to continue in medical school even after he signed a professional baseball contract.[29]

After signing, Brown reported to Yankees spring training in St. Petersburg, Florida, where the manager was Joe McCarthy. The 1946 camp was a very large one with all the war veteran players returning to baseball. Brown played exceptionally well, with one highlight a grand slam against the Norfolk minor-league outfit.

Near the end of camp, Yankees general manager George Weiss told Brown that he was going to start the season with the Binghamton (New York) Triplets of the Double-A Eastern League. Brown balked, however, and said he wanted to start at a higher classification and that he would not report to the Triplets. Weiss relented and said, "Okay, we will send you to Newark."[30]

Brown knew that breaking in directly with the Yankees infield would be difficult, since they had Phil Rizzuto at shortstop, George Stirnweiss, who had won the 1945 American League batting title, at second, and Billy Johnson, who was returning from the service after a strong rookie year in 1943, at third base. Brown also had worked out in the Newark ballpark when he was 14 years old and living in New Jersey, and so was familiar with the surroundings.

Brown appeared in 148 games, all but a handful at shortstop, for the 1946 Bears while no other player played in more than 117 games for Newark. At the end of the International League campaign, the Yankees sent a late-season call for Brown, along with Yogi Berra, pitcher Vic Raschi, and outfielder Frank Colman. With New York, Brown batted .333 in eight games and 29 plate appearances.[31] His minor-league days, like those of the two Robinsons, were at an end.

Brown continued to both attend medical school and play for the Yankees until he graduated in April 1950. He typically was not able to go to spring training and in at least two seasons showed up from Tulane on Opening Day. He showed his ability to come through in the clutch in the four World Series he played in with the Yankees, batting a cumulative .439 in 41 at-bats with five doubles, three triples, and nine runs batted in.

After the Korean Conflict broke out in 1950, the military began seeking doctors from the old V12 program who had gone to medical school during World War II but had not been deployed. Early in 1952, the now Dr. Brown was told that he had to reenlist as a medical officer or that he would be drafted as a private. He chose the Army, which required a two-year commitment, and on July 1, 1952, he reported to Fort Sam Houston in San Antonio, thus ending his season with the Yankees prematurely.

Brown was then deployed to Korea and arrived there on October 1, 1952, the day his Yankees opened the World Series against the Brooklyn Dodgers. He served in a MASH unit and with a field artillery battalion for 10 months before being transferred to the US military hospital in Tokyo for the rest of his deployment.[32]

Dr. Brown was honorably discharged in April 1954, having missed more than half of the 1952 and all of the 1953 seasons. He had an internal medicine residency lined up to begin July 1, 1954, at Stanford but was able to play for the Yankees for a couple of months, appearing in 29 games. Then on June 30, Brown played his last major-league game, manning third base and going 2-for-4 against Willard Nixon in a 6-1 Yankees loss to the Boston Red Sox in Fenway Park.[33] After the game he boarded a red-eye flight to San Francisco so he could begin his residency on July 1.[34] At 29 years of age, Brown walked away from baseball to pursue his medical career.

After his three-year residency program at Stanford, Brown returned to Tulane for a one-year cardiology fellowship. He then practiced cardiology for 25 years in Fort Worth before major-league baseball came calling again; he was named president of the American League, an office he filled from 1984 to 1994.[35] Later Dr. Brown's only regret would be that as a player he was not able to go to spring training and give baseball his undivided attention for a few years. But he had no regrets about becoming a doctor and practicing medicine.[36]

TOMMY TATUM

As mentioned, Tommy Tatum, who finished third in the writers' voting for MVP, had a stellar year for Montreal in 1946. After growing up in Oklahoma City, he broke into professional baseball in 1938 at 18 and had an eight-game cup of coffee with the Dodgers in 1941. In 1946 he was coming off three years in the US Army Signal Corps and, at 26, had one of the best seasons of his 15-year playing career. In addition to his .319 batting average, he stole 28 bases and made the International League All-Star team. Tatum made the Dodgers roster out of spring training in 1947 but ran into a very crowded Brooklyn outfield. After appearing in just six games for the Dodgers, mostly as a pinch-hitter, he was sold to the Cincinnati Reds on May 13. With the Reds he hit .273 in 69 games in his major-league swan song before returning to the minor leagues. He served as player-manager for the Oklahoma City Indians in the Texas League from 1951 through 1955 before retiring from baseball.

In his brief time with the 1947 Dodgers, Tatum did have a moment important for the annals of baseball history. On April 18 he had his only start for Brooklyn, batting third between Jackie Robinson, who was second in the lineup, and Dixie Walker against the New York Giants in the Polo Grounds. In the top of the third inning, Robinson led off with a home run to deep left field off Dave Koslo and was greeted with outstretched arms at home plate by Tatum. A photo taken at that moment captured the racial integration of the major leagues and was published in newspapers throughout the country.[37]

JACKIE ROBINSON

In his first year with the Brooklyn Dodgers, 1947, Jackie Robinson faced a torrent of racism and vitriol.[38] He somehow persevered as he batted .297 while playing first base, another new position, helping lead Brooklyn to the pennant. He went on to a storied 10-year Hall of Fame career for the Dodgers, who won six pennants and one World Series championship during his tenure.

Robinson's difficult rookie year with the Dodgers has rightfully received much attention.[39] However, Robinson's first major challenge, with his wife, Rachel, by his side, was to survive a month of spring training in 1946 with the Montreal Royals in the Jim Crow South.[40] The Royals were supposed to train in Sanford, Florida, but were forced to move their camp to Daytona Beach, near the parent Dodgers, because of threatened mob violence in Sanford.[41] The Royals also had to cancel games in Jacksonville, where the local authorities padlocked the field,[42] and Deland because of local segregation laws forbidding Whites from playing against Blacks.[43]

Robinson and fellow African American Johnny Wright were also subject to constant racial abuse when the Royals did play spring-training games. Robinson, who had relatively little baseball-playing experience,[44] struggled hitting against the curveball. He was also troubled by a sore arm,[45] necessitating a shift from shortstop, his former position, to second base.[46]

He also faced challenges from the opposition, such as the time in an exhibition game against Indianapolis when veteran pitcher Paul Derringer knocked Robinson down not once, but twice. Robinson then smashed the next pitch past third for a hit. Later in the game, Derringer again threw at Robinson's head. This time Robinson retaliated by smashing a triple to deep left field.[47]

Robinson's less-than-stellar spring training created some skepticism in Montreal about the impact he would have on the playing field. Some believed that the much more experienced Johnny Wright was the more likely of the two to eventually crack the Brooklyn Dodgers lineup.[48]

It didn't take long for Robinson to dispel that doubt as he had a spectacular debut on April 18 against the Jersey City Giants in their Roosevelt Stadium. After grounding out to shortstop in his first at-bat, Robinson came up again in the third inning with two men on base and nobody out. He smashed the first pitch from Jersey City's Warren Sandel over the left-field fence for a three-run home run.[49] He finished a memorable first game with four hits, two on bunts, three RBIs, and two stolen bases. For the day he also scored four runs, two improbably on balks he induced when dancing off third base.[50] The Royals won 14-1 to start the season with a bang. By the time of the Royals' home opener two weeks later, Robinson was hitting .362 with no sign of slowing down.

The season was not without its travails, however. Robinson missed some games in June with a leg issue. Later in the summer when he slumped and grew visibly tired and listless, a doctor ordered him to take 10 days off to relax and recharge his batteries. He did spend four days away from the team and the respite did indeed help get him back on track.[51]

For the most part, Robinson was treated well by the fans at home and away. The Montreal fans loved him, but he did encounter some racial taunting during his first trip to Baltimore.[52] Also, Syracuse Chiefs fans and players hurled invective at him early in the season.[53]

The worst treatment, however, occurred in Louisville in the Little World Series, which pitted the champions of the International League against the champions of the American Association, the Louisville Colonels. The first three games of the series were in Louisville and the verbal barrage from the fans there was abusive and constant. Robinson was only 1-for-10 as Louisville won two of the three games.

When the series moved to Montreal, the Royals fans showed their displeasure with the way Louisville had treated Robinson and, starting with leadoff man Johnny Welaj, booed every move a Colonels player made.[54] Once before hometown fans, Robinson quickly regained his form, driving in the winning run in the 10th inning of game four with a two-out line single to left. In the fifth game, he doubled, tripled, and had a key bunt single to drive in the decisive run, while in the final game he had two more hits and made several key plays in the field as the Royals beat Louisville 2-0 to wrap up the series.[55]

Robinson was 7-for-14 in the three games in Montreal and afterward was carried around the field by the jubilant fans, who chanted in French "[H]e has earned his stripes."[56] When he left the ballpark in his street clothes to rush to the airport to fly to Detroit, where he was to begin a barnstorming tour, he was again mobbed by thousands of fans, leading to the famous line about a White mob chasing a Black man out of love and not hatred.[57]

Robinson would describe the people of Montreal generally as being "warm and wonderful" to Rachel and himself. In fact, the citizenry was so attentive to them as a couple that he felt they had little privacy. But he would remember his time in Montreal with real fondness.[58]

Although Robinson was under intense scrutiny when he broke into the National League in 1947 with the Dodgers, he also played under tremendous pressure in 1946 with Montreal. It is difficult to underestimate the attention he drew. Robin Roberts, who was pitching in the semipro Northern League in Vermont that summer, remembered driving up to Montreal on an offday with a couple of teammates just to watch Robinson play. He came away very impressed; Robinson went 3-for-4 with a steal of home and played errorless ball at second base.[59]

Although Jackie Robinson did not win the International League MVP in 1946, he was named the National League Rookie of the Year the next year when he broke major-league baseball's unofficial color ban. In 1949 the 30-year-old Robinson led the National League in hitting with a .342 average and was named Most Valuable Player by the baseball writers, outdistancing Stan Musial 264 points to 226.[60]

AN ANALYSIS OF THE VOTING

The question remains, however, whether the voting for the 1946 International League Most Valuable Player Awards was racially biased. Viewed in hindsight over three-quarters of a century later, it is difficult to know for certain, but one cannot help but be suspicious.

Although it is unclear if the voting was based only on the regular season and not the playoffs,[61] either way Jackie Robinson's performance was exceptional. At a minimum, Robinson was the best player on the best team in the league, indeed on one of the best teams in minor-league history. But Eddie Robinson and Bobby Brown also had outstanding years for first-division ballclubs. Certainly, actual MVP Eddie Robinson had the best combination of power and average, resulting in a .983 OPS, second to Montreal's Lew Riggs, who appeared in only 90 games, and considerably better than Jackie's OPS of .930. Of the statistics that were considered paramount at the time, Eddie's 123 runs batted in, which led the league by a wide margin, coupled with his 34 home runs, certainly would have attracted widespread attention. His .578 slugging percentage, well above Jackie's .462, also led the league and would have been considered a major plus factor. Thus, Eddie was most deserving of the MVP.

Bobby Brown, who finished second in the MVP voting with 135 points to Jackie Robinson's 89-point total, had in many ways similar statistics to Jackie. Brown was second in hitting at .341 to Jackie's .349 and neither hit many home runs.[62] Robinson's .930 OPS was higher than Brown's .870. Both were very difficult to strike out; Robinson fanned 27 times in 553 plate appearances while Brown was even tougher, with only 19 punchouts in 597 times at the plate.[63] And most impressively, both were playing their first seasons in Organized Baseball.

It is also worth noting that Jackie Robinson did not mention the International League MVP Award in either of his two autobiographies.[64] Perhaps there is no reason that he should have, given that he did not win. However, he might well have mentioned it if he felt that he had been the victim of racial prejudice.[65] He was certainly not shy about later alluding to the racial injustices that confronted him.

The fact, however, that Jackie finished *fifth* in the voting by the sportswriters, well behind Eddie Joost, strongly smacks of discrimination. The 30-year-old Joost, who spent 17 years in the big leagues, had a fine year as the shortstop for the seventh-place Rochester Red Wings, with 19 home runs and 101 runs batted in. He batted a pedestrian .276, however – 73 points below Robinson – and did not come close to leading the league in any category. Yet he polled 120 points in the voting by the writers, well ahead of Jackie Robinson's 89-point total.

CONCLUSION

Thus, there is certainly circumstantial evidence of bias in that long-ago MVP voting. If we just look at the first-place votes in the writers' poll, Eddie Robinson received 16 of them, followed by Tommy Tatum with 10. Jackie Robinson garnered seven top votes while Jack Wallaesa of Toronto had the other.[66] While the author could not locate the votes of the individual sportswriters, it is likely that some left Jackie off their ballots entirely, considering that even with seven first-place votes, his 89-point total was far behind the four in front of him.

Both Jackie and Eddie Robinson overcame significant obstacles to get to the International League and endured a great deal of hardship in 1946, albeit of a very different nature. Whether the absence of prejudice in the MVP voting would have swapped them and made Jackie the winner is unlikely given Eddie's power numbers and .318 batting average. But it would certainly have made for a closer race and would have bumped Jackie Robinson well up from fifth place. How far up, we will never know.

This article was edited by David Siegel and fact-checked by Laura Peebles.

NOTES

1. Jack Anderson, "A Great Leap Forward: Jackie Robinsson and the View from Montreal," https://sabr.org/journal/article/a-great-leap-forward-jackie-robinson-and-the-view-from-montreal/.
2. Scott Simon, *Jackie Robinson and the Integration of Baseball* (Hoboken: John Wiley & Sons, Inc., 2002), 97; David Falkner, *Great Time Coming: The Life of Jackie Robinson from Baseball to Birmingham* (New York: Simon & Schuster, 1995), 138; Tommy Holmes, *Dodger Daze and Knights* (New York: David McKay Company, Inc., 1953), 200.
3. "Robinson's Bidding for Berths in Baseball Majors Next Spring," *Eau Claire* (Wisconsin) *Leader-Telegram*, October 23, 1946: 10.
4. Jules Tygiel, *Baseball's Great Experiment: Jackie Robinson and His Legacy* (New York: Oxford University Press, 1983), 141-42; Arnold Rampersad, *Jackie Robinson: A Biography* (New York: Alfred A. Knopf, 1997), 156-157; Maury Allen, *Jackie Robinson: A Life Remembered* (New York: Franklin Watts, 1987), 83.
5. According to one historian, at the time some believed Jackie Robinson should have received the MVP Award. Bill O'Neal, *The International League: A Baseball History 1884-1991* (Austin, Texas: Eakin Press, 1992), 141.
6. "Robinson Most Valuable in International Loop," *Elmira* (New York) *Star-Gazette*, October 17, 1946: 27.
7. "Robinson Third Oriole Honored in as Many Years," *The Sporting News*, October 16, 1946: 13.
8. Eddie Robinson was the third Baltimore Oriole in a row to win the International League MVP, following Howie Moss in 1944 and Sherm Lollar in 1945. The streak was broken in 1947 when Hank Sauer of Syracuse won the award.
9. Tom Meany, *The Magnificent Yankees* (New York: A.S Barnes & Company, 1952), 153; Arthur Daley, "Baseball's Golden Boy: Bobby Brown Keeps his Medical Career in Mind as He Hits Away for the Yanks," *Sportfolio Magazine*, October 1948: 49.
10. Danny Murtaugh, future manager of the Pittsburgh Pirates World Series winner in 1960, also had 174 hits for the Rochester Red Wings.
11. "Eddie Robinson International League V-Man, *Montreal Star*, October 5, 1946: 24.
12. Simon, 97.
13. "Robinson of Baltimore Named Most Valuable Man," *North Bay* (Ontario) *Nugget*, October 5, 1946:21.
14. "Robinson Third Oriole Honored in as Many Years," *The Sporting News*, October 16, 1946: 13. It is quite likely that those eight scribes also voted in the writers' balloting.
15. Montreal's Tatum and Baltimore's John Podgajny also received single first-place votes. Larry Berra of Newark, not yet referred to as Yogi by the baseball world, was far down the list with six total points. *The Sporting News*, October 16, 1946: 13. Berra had hit .314 in 77 games before his late season call-up to the Yankees.
16. Tygiel; Rampersad; Falkner.
17. Eddie Robinson with C. Paul Rogers III, *Lucky Me – My Sixty-Five Years in Baseball* (Dallas: SMU Press, 2011), 31-35.
18. Robinson with Rogers, 28-29.
19. O'Neal, 142.
20. Robinson with Rogers, xv.

21 After failed trials with the Indians and Cincinnati Reds late in 1946, the right-handed Moss returned to Baltimore for the 1947 season and took full advantage of the short-left field porch, smacking 53 homers to again lead the league. In all, "Howitzer Howie" led the International League in home runs four times, the only person in the history of the league to do so. O'Neal, 243. But in 76 major-league plate appearances over parts of three seasons, Moss failed to hit a home run, recorded no extra-base hits, and drove in only a single run.

22 The Orioles actually finished the regular season tied with the Newark Bears for third place, one game behind the second-place Chiefs. Baltimore then defeated Newark in a one-game playoff for third place, with the loser having to face first-place Montreal in the first round of the league playoffs.

23 Robinson with Rogers, 42.

24 Within months of his retirement as a player in 1957, Robinson's foot-drop issue recurred, an issue he dealt with the rest of his life. https://sabr.org/bioproj/person/Eddie-Robinson/.

25 William Clifford Roberts, MD, "Robert William ("Bobby") Brown, MD, Cardiologist, Major League Baseball Player (New York Yankee) and American League President: A Conversation with the Editor," *American Journal of Cardiology* (2008): 725.

26 Daley, 54.

27 According to Dr. Brown, if Tulane had an away game, typically against a service team, the Tulane team bus would wait for him outside his afternoon lab or class, and then leave. For home games, the Tulane coach would tell the opposition that "we can't start the game until the shortstop arrives and he is in med school." C. Paul Rogers III, "Wartime Baseball, Medicine, and the New York Yankees: A Conversation with Dr. Bobby Brown," *Elysian Fields Quarterly* (vol. 16, no. 3, 1999): 62-63.

28 "Wartime Baseball, Medicine, and the New York Yankees: A Conversation with Dr. Bobby Brown," *Elysian Fields Quarterly* (vol. 16, no. 3, 1999): 60-61.

29 Roberts, 725.

30 Roberts, 726.

31 In contrast, Yogi Berra batted .364 in 23 plate appearances.

32 Roberts, 733-734.

33 Eddie Robinson was Brown's teammate with the Yankees in 1954 and appeared as a pinch-hitter in Brown's last game.

34 Dr. Brown reported to the San Francisco County Hospital (which was part of the Stanford residency program) around noon on July 1. According to Brown, "They said report July 1. They didn't say what time." Rogers, 73.

35 Dr. Brown took a six-month hiatus from his practice in 1974 to serve as interim president of the Texas Rangers after Brad Corbett bought the team. Rogers, 74.

36 Rogers, 75.

37 https://sabr.org/bioproj/person/Tommy-Tatum/.

38 Robin Roberts and C. Paul Rogers III, *The Whiz Kids and the 1950 Pennant* (Philadelphia: Temple University Press, 1996), 48-52.

39 Red Barber, *1947 – When All Hell Broke Loose in Baseball* (New York: Doubleday & Co., 1982).

40 Chris Lamb, *Blackout: The Untold Story of Jackie Robinson's First Spring Training* (Lincoln: University of Nebraska Press, 2004),

41 Lamb, 83-90; William Brown, *Baseball's Fabulous Montreal Royals* (Montreal: Robert Davies Publishing, 1996), 97.

42 Jackie Robinson as told to Wendell Smith, *Jackie Robinson – My Own Story* (New York: Greenberg Publishers, 1948), 79; Lamb, 135-136.

43 Kostya Kennedy, *True—The Four Seasons of Jackie Robinson* (New York: St. Martin's Press, 2022), 22.; Lamb, 140-141.

44 Robinson had played relatively few games at Pasadena Junior College and UCLA, where baseball was perhaps his fourth best sport while in college, had played 34 games with the Kansas City Monarchs of the Negro American League in 1945 and barnstormed in Venezuela briefly after that season. James W. Johnson, *The Black Bruins: The Remarkable Lives of UCLA's Jackie Robinson, Woody Strode, Tom Bradley, Kenny Washington, and Ray Bartlett* (Lincoln: University of Nebraska Press, 2017), 56, 60, 103.

45 Lamb, 94-95.

46 Teammate Lou Rochelli, whose was also in line for the second base job, helped Robinson transition to second and taught him how to turn the double play, a gesture Robinson never forgot. Jackie Robinson, *I Never Had It Made: An Autobiography* (New York: Putnam, 1972), 44.

47 Kennedy, 17; Brown, 99.

48 This was especially true because the Dodgers were short on pitching but had Pee Wee Reese at shortstop and Eddie Stanky at second base, both front-line major leaguers. Kennedy, 29-30.

49 In two significant actions of acceptance, manager Clay Hopper, who was from Mississippi and was coaching third, slapped Robinson on the back as he crossed third base and the next batter, George Shuba, shook Robinson's hand as he crossed the plate. Brown, 101-102; Kennedy, 32. George "Shotgun" Shuba, as told to Greg Gulas, *My Memories as a Brooklyn Dodger* (Youngstown, Ohio: City Printing Company, 2007), 32-34.

50 Kennedy, 32-33.

51 Robinson as told to Smith, *Jackie Robinson – My Own Story,* 105.

52 Robinson, *I Never Had It Made*, 46.

53 Robinson as told to Smith, *Jackie Robinson – My Own Story*, 106; Robinson, *I Never Had It Made*, 49.

54 Kennedy, 57.

55 Mark J. Steiner, "Jackie Robinson: History Made at the 1946 Junior World Series." https://sabr.org/journal/article/jackie-robinson-history-made-at-the-1946-junior-world-series/

56 Tygiel, 143.

57 Brown, 111-112; Anderson; Steiner.

58 Robinson, *I Never Had it Made*, 47.

59 Roberts and Rogers, 48. Of course, Roberts would later become the ace of the Philadelphia Phillies and face Jackie Robinson many times in the National League, including his defeat of the Dodgers on the last day of the season in 1950 to clinch the pennant for the Whiz Kids.

60 Robinson received 12 of 24 first-place votes while Musial received 5.

61 The results of the sportswriters' poll was announced at the sixth game of the Little World Series between Montreal and Louisville, after the International League playoffs had concluded. "Oriole' First Sacker Voted Most Valuable," *Sault Star* (Sault Ste. Marie, Ontario, Canada), October 5, 1946: 13.

62 Brown hit five home runs while Robinson hit only three, including the three-run shot on Opening Day. But both were among the league leaders in doubles with 27 and 25 respectively.

63 Eddie Robinson was also very difficult to strike out, especially considering he was a power hitter. In 1946 he struck out only 47 times in 607 plate appearances.

64 Robinson, *I Never Had It Made*; Robinson as told to Smith, *Jackie Robinson – My Own Story.*

65 Rachel Robinson also did not allude to the 1946 MVP voting in her memoir about her life with Jackie. Rachel Robinson with Lee Daniels, *Jackie Robinson – An Intimate Portrait* (New York: Harry N. Abrams, Inc., 1996).

66 The first-place vote for Wallaesa was indeed puzzling as he split the season between Toronto and the Philadelphia Athletics, batting .253 in 63 games for the sixth-place Maple Leafs.

DEADLY BUS TRIPS HARD TO FORGET

By Jim Price

Blessedly, professional baseball has had very few terrible moments, incidents that end with loss of life, calamity, or great destruction, leaving behind indelible memories.

Serious fans almost everywhere know about these, as readily as they recall the feats of Babe Ruth and Walter Johnson, the durability of Lou Gehrig and Cal Ripken, the shame of the Black Sox, or the recurring dominance of the New York Yankees.

As I discovered at my first SABR convention, fans also respond to mention of my home, Spokane, Washington, with questions about the bus accident that killed nine of that city's players. Almost eight decades later, that 1946 catastrophe remained the worst of its kind in American professional sports. The second worst involved another minor-league team, the Duluth Dukes, and its bus in another league just two years later.

Those and a few less frightful events underline the perils of minor-league travel and team travel in general. Most known examples were a consequence of late-night bus rides. All baseball-related fatal accidents involved lower minor-league or college teams. In almost a century and a half, no major-league American sport has had a team-travel fatality.

Both deadly accidents took place in the aftermath of World War II. Nationwide, worn-out vehicles and parts shortages often left passenger equipment in precarious condition. Even in our own lives, deferred maintenance can take its toll.

Since then, with Major League Baseball wielding almost complete oversight of the professional game, standards are higher and the buses better. Nonetheless, in the lower minor leagues, where smaller cities may be separated by hundreds of miles, late-night bus rides remain the most affordable option. Not all notable bus

Jack Gillis, Minneapolis Star, July 24, 1948. Courtesy Minneapolis Star.

The bus, carrying members of the Duluth, Northern League team, is shown on July 24, 1948, after it collided with a truck that that had crossed the center line. Five Duluth players perished in the accident.

accidents occurred long ago. Not all involved professionals. Only a few ended in death. Considering the number of trips over many decades, the national pastime should give thanks that the consequences haven't been worse.

The basic facts of Spokane's disaster, while the city's team was a member of the Class-B Western International League, are well known. But details, collected over seven-plus decades, describe personal tragedy, horror, pain or heartbreak. A few were life-changing, not always in a good way.

The second terrible accident involved a 1948 Northern League team, the Dukes from Duluth, Minnesota. This is not as well-remembered. Horrible things happened there, too. In two years, the profile of minor-league baseball had changed quite a bit. Most minor leagues had not operated since 1942. By war's end, many experienced minor leaguers had played in fast company, some of it in the service. As a result, in 1946, pro ball was awash with talent. With the economy on the rise, and television not yet ubiquitous, fans flocked to ballparks in more than 300 markets. Three years later, the minors reached their peak with 59 leagues representing 438 cities.[1] They employed close to 7,000 players. Today, the constricted minor leagues include only 120 teams. Each major-league franchise has four affiliates.

The Spokane and Duluth teams were typical of their year. Duluth's players in Class C were much younger, averaging 21.5 years. Put simply, they had far less history. Few had gone to war. Few were married. Only five had prewar experience. In 1946 the Indians players averaged 26.1 years old. All of them had played before or during the war. A clear majority were married. All but three had been servicemen. The WIL was the second-best league in the West.[2]

Spokane, with no apparent weakness, was a logical pennant contender. Veterans, not just the military kind, clogged the roster. They had Bob Kinnaman, the best pitcher, and top outfielder Levi McCormack from the city's 1940 and 1941 regular-season champions. Third baseman Jack Lohrke, on option from San Diego's Pacific Coast League team, and first baseman Vic Picetti were considered top prospects. Several teammates were in the midst of, or near the end of, long careers.

Lohrke, 22, had been in the Army, where he had survived combat at the Battle of the Bulge. Then, after his discharge, he was bumped off a military flight, which subsequently crashed, killing everyone aboard.[3] He would become known as "Lucky Lohrke," a nickname he disliked. Picetti was a protégé of Oakland manager Dolph Camilli, the former National League MVP. In 1945 Picetti had gone directly from high school to the PCL, where Camilli, who later told me, "He was the greatest prospect I ever saw come straight out of high school," benched himself so Picetti could replace him in the lineup.[4]

Five veteran right-handers led Spokane's pitching staff. All of them had played before the war. Former Washington State College star Kinnaman, a 22-game winner for the 1941 Indians, belonged in the Coast League. But, like Picetti and outfielder Bob Paterson, he'd been crowded off Oakland's roster by prewar regulars.

Milt Cadinha and Joe Faria were boyhood friends from Northern California's East Bay area. Cadinha, already known to WIL fans, had twice won 13 games for Tacoma (in 1940 and 1941), and he was off to an 8-1 start.[5] Darwin "Gus" Hallbourg and Dick Powers also came on option from San Diego. Hallbourg had 45 wins over three pro seasons. Powers, a seasoned East Bay semipro, had spent the last two years with Sacramento in the PCL.

Like Paterson, the other regular outfielders, Bob James and McCormack, could hit. McCormack, 33, a handsome Native American from the Nez Perce reservation, had starred for both Spokane title teams. George Risk, a former football and baseball standout at Oregon's Pacific University, was the shortstop. He and infielder Fred Martinez, a Dodgers farmhand before the war, were batting well above .300. League veteran Mel Cole was set to be the catcher, but instead, plagued by injuries, he became the manager. Just before Opening Day, team owner Sam Collins fired Glenn Wright because the former National League infielder had disappeared on a drunk. When Wright managed Wenatchee's first-place team in 1939, Cole had been his catcher.[6]

Recently, Collins had signed a pair of seasoned pros, each with a bit of big-league experience. Ben Geraghty succeeded Martinez at second base. Chris Hartje, a former Brooklyn Dodger who had been working out with Oakland, was going to step in for Cole.[7]

On Monday morning, June 24, 1946, Spokane players gathered outside Ferris Field, waiting to board the bus that would carry them almost 325 miles over land and sea. Ahead, with the season nearly half over, lay a weeklong series with Bremerton. Summer had begun, but it was wet and dreary. This would be a long, slow trip, maybe 12 hours, twice as long as it takes today.

The wooden ballpark, built as a 1936 WPA project, shared the former Spokane Interstate Fairground with a thoroughbred racetrack, three miles east of downtown, just north of Sprague Avenue, which intersects the city. In those days, Sprague doubled as a segment of US 10, stretching east toward the Idaho state line and west toward Seattle.

On Sunday, Spokane had divided a split doubleheader with Salem, winning the night game, 11-10, with the help of Lohrke's four hits.[8] The team picture, which became a collectible, was taken between games. Salem, after opening the season with a 13-game win streak, now clung to the lead, barely ahead of Wenatchee, with three teams crowded behind them. All five had winning records. Though the Indians were fifth, with a record of 32-26, 5½ games behind.[9]

Cole and 15 teammates boarded their Washington Motor Coach charter, a 20-passenger version of a school bus, a bit before 11:00 A.M. Glen Berg, young but experienced, had the wheel. Cadinha, Faria, and their wives had gone ahead in Faria's prewar Buick.

With two-lane highways the norm, they would mostly follow the route that has since become Interstate 90, heading south to Ritzville, west through the Columbia Plateau – among the world's largest deserts – and across the Columbia River, farther west to Ellensburg, then over Snoqualmie Pass to Seattle, where they would catch a ferry.

A couple of hours after the team left, business manager Dwight Aden, who had been the team's prewar center fielder, received a call from San Diego. The Padres had recalled Lohrke, who was hitting .345 and had 28 extra-base hits. Long-distance phone lines were out of service in the middle of the state, so Aden asked the state patrol to get an Ellensburg officer to deliver the message when the Indians stopped to eat at Webster's Café.[10]

The team arrived about 5 o'clock. While the players ate, Berg drove to the company's local garage, hoping to replace the bus. Told he had a better vehicle than anything on the lot, he settled for minor repairs. When Berg rejoined the team, Lohrke grabbed his gear, said goodbye, hitchhiked back to Spokane and, after hearing the dreadful news, caught a train to San Diego.

The team continued west. As a holdover from the war, there was no daylight saving time, so the overcast was fading to dusk, and the drizzle had turned into mist, as the bus labored up and over Snoqualmie Summit. At about 8:00 P.M., it rounded Airplane Curve and started down the long straightaway. In those days, US 10, one lane in each direction, hugged the southern edge of the deep, narrow canyon. Stout wood posts, strung with cable, separated westbound traffic from the ravine.

Hallbourg told the *Seattle Daily Times* that he had seen the Snoqualmie River glistening far below. The view prompted him to twist in his front-row seat and tell Kinnaman, two rows back, "'This would be a hell of a place to go over, wouldn't it?' I turned back, and we were going through the fence."[11]

The Indians were almost three miles past the summit when, as Berg, McCormack, and Geraghty told investigators, a black, eastbound sedan came into view, crowding the center line. It may have clipped the bus. Berg swerved rather than applying the brakes, fearing he might lose traction on the slick road. But the right-side wheels slipped onto the shoulder. Though he nursed the front back onto the pavement, the rear duals ricocheted off the lip and slid the bus sideways into the cable, where it began clipping off posts. After 100 feet or so, it broke through. Tumbling down the rocky hillside, the bus struck a boulder, caught fire, bounced onto its left side, struck another big rock, then rolled again before stopping right side up, astride a log. It had fallen an estimated 350 feet, scattering men and equipment across the hillside. After moments of stunned silence, the gas tank exploded.

Six died at the scene. Cole, Risk, and Paterson, seated on the left side, burned to death. Fire or blunt force trauma killed Kinnaman, Martinez, and James, who sat right across the aisle. Picetti, spread-eagled on a boulder with terrible injuries, died on the way to Seattle's Harborview Hospital. Reserve pitcher George Lyden died around noon the next day. Hartje, burned over most of his body, passed away on Wednesday. He and Lyden had been with the Indians less than a week.

Survivors ejected through one of the aluminum-framed windows were seriously injured. Geraghty, launched almost at once, struck a boulder that left him with a gaping scalp wound and a broken knee. Powers had a skull fracture, a broken neck, and a broken collarbone. Although McCormack, lame in one hip, walked away, his nose was smashed.

Those still on board escaped through window openings. Hallbourg struggled to free his hips and ended up with burns on his pitching arm. Pete Barisoff, the staff's only left-hander, also crawled out. When he heard Irv Konopka crying for help, he dragged the backup catcher through the empty frame. Konopka, a former University of Idaho football player drafted by the Detroit Lions, had a broken shoulder, while Barisoff suffered a foot injury.

Berg, engulfed in flames, escaped through the battered doorway. He remained in Seattle's Virginia Mason Hospital for almost four months, burned badly on his arms, legs, and head.[12] Later, he became a truck driver, admired for his safety record.[13]

By the time rescue teams arrived, they worked in steady rain. The fire burned until dawn.

Professional baseball responded without precedent. The major leagues contributed $25,000 from All-Star Game receipts. PCL rivals Seattle and Oakland (managed by Casey Stengel) played a Ferris Field exhibition. Wenatchee hosted Sacramento, its parent club. Including donations from leagues, teams, and fans, the Spokane Baseball Benefit Fund raised $118,567.41, the equivalent of about $1.9 million in 2024 dollars.[14] Supplemented by bus company insurance, distributions were prorated. Cole, Martinez, and Hartje left pregnant wives, and widows with children received larger shares.[15]

Collins had secretly planned to send Picetti, homesick for his widowed mother and fiancée, home for a few days, after the Bremerton series. Instead, the women escorted his body back to San Francisco and buried him with his wedding ring.[16]

With a lineup cobbled together from Western International League rivals, former professionals and a semipro or two, Spokane resumed its schedule on the Fourth of July. Although Cadinha, Faria, and Hallbourg anchored the pitching staff, the Indians were nearly inept at the plate and in the field. They finished with a 54-78 record. Glenn Wright stepped in as manager until Geraghty was able to take over.

Geraghty stayed on in 1947. Stocked with prospects from the Brooklyn Dodgers, his old organization, he guided the Indians to within one percentage point of the WIL title. He went on to become a legendary, pennant-winning minor-league manager, haunted by the accident, and a protector of developing players, particularly Henry Aaron. However, a heart attack killed him in June of 1963. He was only 50 years old.[17]

Powers recovered, but it took almost two years. He worked as a meat broker and a real estate agent. McCormack rejoined the Indians in 1947 and played well until his aching hip forced him into retirement. He became a mail carrier. The three active pitchers and Barisoff played in 1947, then moved on with their lives. Cadinha became an insurance agent. Faria ran an East Bay celebrity hangout. Hallbourg settled east of them, near Modesto, where he spent 37 years with Pacific Telephone.[18]

Barisoff and Konopka weren't so fortunate. Barisoff died on November 12, 1949, trapped inside when fire swept through his Los Angeles County home. Konopka, who saw action with Boise's Pioneer League team in 1949, died of cancer in 1970.[19]

Lohrke played with the San Diego Padres for the rest of the season and batted .303 with 8 home runs and 48 runs batted in. He went on to seven seasons in the National League (with the New York Giants and Philadelphia Phillies) and he ended his 15-year professional baseball career as player-manager with the Tri-City Braves of the Northwest League. Afterward, he worked as a security guard in San Diego.[20]

Today, as part of Interstate 90, the former US 10, cut further into the hillside, carries only eastbound Snoqualmie Pass traffic. Westbound vehicles follow a relatively new path on the north side of the canyon.

A SECOND DISASTER

Exactly 25 months after Spokane's accident, right around noon on a sunny Saturday, July 24, 1948, Duluth Dukes manager George Treadwell and four of his players died north of St. Paul, when a truck loaded with dry ice veered across the center line and slammed into their team bus.[21] The Minnesota-based Dukes, losers of two one-run games the night before in Eau Claire, Wisconsin, were headed north on Highway 36 just before its intersection with Dale Road. They were bound for St. Cloud, contenders with a 40-34 record.[22]

By contrast, most of the ongoing news coverage of this accident came from league cities and their neighbors. Probably, it was underreported. Except for immediate notice, it attracted little attention from the national media. There was no unusual setting. There were few complex backstories. There was surprisingly little drama. Most of it unfolded in less than two hours. But it was awful.

Minnesota Highway Department investigators determined that the washboard section of road thought to be the cause was more than 30 yards from the point of impact. Instead, they speculated that the truck's worn steering mechanism may have failed, causing the driver, James Grealish, to lose control. Grealish, a Marine veteran with a wife and three daughters, and Treadwell, well known in the lower minor leagues, died instantly.

The truck had hit the 18-passenger former school bus on the left front corner, knocking it onto its right side. Their gas tanks ruptured and both vehicles burst into flames. A farmer named Frank Kurkowski, working nearby, heard the crash, ran to the scene, broke out the rear bus window and dragged five men to safety. Passing motorists rescued the rest.

Outfielder Gerald "Peanuts" Peterson, pitcher Don Schuchman, and outfielder Gil Krirdla, who played under the name Gil Trible, among the few Dukes with previous pro experience, also died on impact or burned to death. Second baseman Steve Lazar, his head split open, died two days later. Every survivor was injured to some degree. Many had burns. Some had inhaled toxic fumes. Several had fractures. Seven remained in critical condition for days.[23]

Pitcher Don Gilmore and all-star catcher Bernie Gerl were hurt the worst. In addition to burns, Gilmore was left with a broken left thigh and a mangled right ankle.[24] Gerl, the last man rescued, had extensive burns and internal damage caused by the fire and its fumes. "My face looked like a breaded pork chop," he recalled in 2013. "It made hamburger out of a lot of the guys. To describe some of the injuries, you couldn't write it."[25]

Duluth outfielder Chris "Bud" Dubia had a broken jaw, broken ankle, and broken ribs. Rookies Don Ritonya (broken arm, broken jaw, and broken leg) and John Vanderwier (fractured pelvis, deep wounds, and internal injuries), made the critical list though neither had pitched in a game. Shortstop Joe Becker, whose dad (also named Joe Becker) managed in the Western League, had lost skin on his left hand. He and pitcher Sam Paitich, his face badly burned, were hospitalized until the end of the year.[26]

The funeral service for Peterson, once a multisport star at Proctor High School, on Duluth's rural outskirts, and the most popular player for the 1947 Dukes, attracted almost 2,000 people. Treadwell's service, right across the state line in Superior, Wisconsin, drew an estimated 1,000.[27]

First baseman Mel McGaha and infielder Elmer Schoendienst, whose older brother Red was the second baseman and future manager of the parent Cardinals, were less injured. Both resumed their careers in 1949. McGaha, after years as a minor-league player-manager, managed the American League teams in Cleveland and Kansas City. Elmer Schoendienst spent a year in the Central League then gave it up and played semipro ball with another brother, Frank.[28]

Most of the others played only a year. Lou Branca, after pitching for the Dukes in 1949, coached the high-school team in Rochester, Minnesota, home of the Mayo Clinic, and ended up in the state coaches hall of fame. Recently married Eull Clark played in 1949. Dubia didn't return to action until 1950, when he split 29 games between Duluth and Aberdeen. Then he rejoined the Army and retired, highly decorated, as a colonel. Vanderwier made a belated debut in 1950,

Courtesy of David Eskenazi.

A memorial program was conducted in Spokane in July to commemorate the eight Spokane players and the bus driver, who died on June 24, 1946, when their team bus careened off a narrow road in the Cascade Mountains.

posting an 8-6 record for Hamilton of the PONY League. Paitich, who was on the team but never got into a game, became a local tavern owner.[29]

Aces Joe Svetlick (10-4, 2.39) and Bob Vogeltanz (10-3, 2.54) also played only one more year. Svetlick, after completing the 1948 season, pitched well again in 1949, then joined the Air Force. Vogeltanz, promoted to Columbus of the Sally League, won twice in relief. But his thigh injury flared up, and the short, stocky ex-Marine was finished by June.

Gilmore, also a pitcher, became a law officer and owned a security company. Beginning in 1969, he served six terms as a Republican state legislator in Ohio.[30]

"There are people who have been through things as horrible and terrifying as that was," he told the *Duluth Tribune/News* at a 40th anniversary gathering in 1988. "But it's been 50 years and I still dream about it twice a week."[31] Gilmore died on October 15, 2003, at the age of 75.

Only one other persisted. Gerl, who had lost 70 pounds during 40 days of hospitalization, underwent more than a year of intense recovery. After sitting out 1949, he batted .302 in 1950 for a St. Louis affiliate, Montgomery in the Southeastern League. After another year off, he rejoined Duluth, which needed a catcher, in 1952 and 1953. He liked to brag that, in his final season, he drove in more runs than Fargo-Moorhead's hometown rookie hotshot, outfielder Roger Maris. Afterward, Gerl, a lifelong resident of Joliet, Illinois, went to work in his local Coca-Cola warehouse. He took charge five years later, and then became a regional Coke executive.[32]

Professional baseball and the public again responded generously. The league's other seven teams loaned a dozen players. The Cardinals organization sent nine. The American Association's Triple-A franchise in Minneapolis loaned another. Led by a fundraising effort highlighted by home-and-home Northern League benefit games and broadcast over radio stations in four states, more than $75,000 was raised and distributed to families of the victims.

Like Spokane, Duluth had a player who avoided possible death. St. Louis had promoted an 18-year-old right-hander named Sam Hunter, who missed the train that would have taken him from Chicago to Eau Claire, Wisconsin. Instead, he caught a bus and, by the time he arrived, the team had gone.[33]

Duluth returned to action seven days after the accident, meeting Superior, its Northern League neighbor from across the Wisconsin state line. Ted Madjeski, in his third year as a player-manager at age 26, succeeded Treadwell as manager. The Dukes finished the season with 53 wins and 61 losses.

Surviving players held 30th and 40th reunions at the city's Wade Stadium. Five teammates joined Gilmore and Gerl, who gathered on the 30th anniversary for a July 21, 1978, *Duluth Herald* photo. By the 50th anniversary. Gerl was the only one left. Nonetheless, he made the eight-hour drive for 15 straight years, a streak that didn't end until 2010.[34]

Viewed from the distance of time, Gus Hallbourg and Bernie Gerl, each a last survivor, modeled gratitude and fulfillment while living many more productive decades.

"I am one of the great lucky guys alive," Hallbourg said before the 50th anniversary of Spokane's accident.[35] He'd completed a fine career. He golfed. He gardened. He was popular in his community. He had a loving family. When he died on October 13, 2007, he was 87 years old.

Gerl also made the most of his remaining years. He, too, dreamed about his terrible day. But there he was, two years later, successfully back in uniform, married after a six-month postponement, using the insurance settlement to buy and furnish a home, and traveling the world for his employer. He had nine grandchildren and a fleet of great-grandchildren. In later years, he relished his time in the spotlight as the man who refused to let us forget his unfortunate teammates.[36]

Gerl, the last of the last survivors, died on November 7, 2020. He was 94 years old.

No other American professional teams in any sport have experienced fatalities.

Only one serious accident has affected a major-league team. That involved the California Angels. On May 21, 1992, the first of two team buses, headed to Baltimore from New York City, swerved off the New Jersey Turnpike at 1:50 A.M. and plunged into a grove of trees. The bus rolled onto its right side and left a dozen team members injured.[37]

Manager Bob "Buck" Rodgers, briefly trapped in the wreckage, was hurt the worst. The former Angels catcher suffered a crushed right elbow, a damaged left knee and a broken rib. He didn't rejoin the team until August 28. The driver, who had had five speeding violations, was cited for careless driving.[38]

When it came to bus accidents, baseball's other known multiple player deaths involved amateurs. Other minor-league incidents did not end in athlete death. The numbers are small. That may be a miracle.

SOURCES

In addition to the sources mentioned in the Notes, the author consulted Baseball-Reference.com.

Descriptions and details of the Spokane accident represent accumulations of information from the June 25-29, 1946, editions of the *Spokesman-Review* and *Spokane Daily Chronicle*, the *Seattle Daily Times*, *Seattle Post-Intelligencer*, and the *Seattle Star*, along with dispatches from the Associated Press and United Press, and the author's telephone conversations with survivors and their families. Many of these details have been printed in his *Spokesman-Review* anniversary stories on June 22, 1986, June 24, 1996, June 18, 2006, and June 19, 2016.

NOTES

1 Lloyd Johnson and Miles Wolff, eds., *The Encyclopedia of Minor League Baseball*, 2nd Edition (Durham, North Carolina: Baseball America, Inc., 1997).

2 Baseball-reference.com provided rosters and player records for the 1946 Spokane and 1948 Duluth teams, supplemented by the author's interviews.

3 Ron Fimrite, "O Lucky Man," *Sports Illustrated*, November 14, 1994.

4 Author's telephone interview with Camilli in June 1986, reported in the author's article in the *Spokesman-Review*, June 24, 1986.

5 Cadinha went on to win 16 games (against seven losses) in 1946 for Spokane.

6 Conversations with Dwight Aden and various surviving players.

7 Various articles printed in the *Spokane Spokesman-Review*, June 17-20, 1946.

8 "Spokane Wins Salem Series, 4-3," *Spokane Spokesman-Review*, June 24, 1946: 7.

9 "Spokane Wins Salem Series, 4-3."

10 Author's 1986 conversations with Aden and his phone conversation with Lohrke.

11 Hallbourg repeated this quote, frequently printed in the accident's aftermath, to the author in their June 1986 telephone conversation.

12 This and other Glen Berg details came from the author's several conversations with his daughter Debbie and were summarized in the author's Berg obituary for the *Spokane Spokesman-Review*, November 2, 2003.

13 Berg had driven more than a million consecutive accident-free miles, according to a telephone conversation with Teamsters Local 690, Spokane, on October 31, 2003.

14 CPI Inflation Calculator, accessed October 1, 2023, and updated April 16, 2024.

15 "Bus Crash Fund Totals $114,805," *Spokane Spokesman-Review*, December 21, 1946: 10. Details updated in author's telephone interview with Pat Lyden, June 2016.

16 Conversations with Dwight Aden in June 1986 supplemented in June 2006 during telephone interviews with Vic Picetti's sister, Bev Schumann, and his former fiancée, Bety Evans King.

17 "Survivor of Smash Ben Geraghty Dies," *Spokane Chronicle*, June 18, 1963: 13. Aaron's admiration detailed in Kenny Kerr, "Kenny Kerr's Korner," *Bristol* (Tennessee) *Herald Courier*, October 10, 1974: 21.

18 From the author's telephone conversations with Powers, Cadinha, Faria, and Hallbourg in June 1986.

19 "Survivor of 1946 Wreck Dies in Fire," *Spokane Spokesman-Review*, November 15, 1949: 15. Konopka's death was detailed in Mike Lynch and Alden Cross, "Baseball's Darkest Night," *Spokane Spokesman-Review*, June 20, 1971: 109-112.

20 See https://www.baseball-reference.com/register/player.fcgi?id=lohrke001jac.

21 "Four Deaths, Injuries Riddle Dukes' Roster," *Eau Claire* (Wisconsin) *Leader-Telegram*, July 25, 1948: 10.

22 "5 Die, 14 Hurt in Bus-Truck Crash," Minneapolis *Star Tribune*, July 25, 1948: 1; Halsey Hall, "Northern League Continues; Help Promised Duluth," *Minneapolis Star Tribune*, July 25, 1948: 31.

23 "5 Die, 14 Hurt in Bus-Truck Crash."

24 "Eight Duluth Players Still Stick by Game," *Rapid City* (South Dakota) *Journal*, August 6, 1948: 11.

25 Jon Nowacki, *Duluth News-Tribune*, July 18, 2013 (page unknown).

26 "'Duluth Fund' Contributions Total $115," *Johnson City* (Tennessee) *Press*, August 12, 1948: 32.

27 "Send 26 Players to Bolster Dukes," *Minneapolis Star-Tribune*, July 28, 1948: 17.

28 See https://www.baseball-reference.com/register/player.fcgi?id=schoen001elm.

29 "Col. C.F. Dubia dies at 66," *Columbus* (Georgia) *Ledger-Enquirer*, July 31, 1990: 27.

30 H.R. 142, In Memory of Don Gilmore, Ohio House Journal, January 27, 2004.

31 Jon Nowacki, *Duluth News-Tribune*, July 12, 2008 (page unknown).

32 Author's telephone conversation with Gerl in June 2016.

33 Joel Rippel, "The 1948 Duluth Dukes Bus Crash," *The National Pastime* (Society for American Baseball Research), 2022.

34 Dave DeLand, "A Vivid Memory," *St. Cloud* (Minnesota) *Times*, July 24, 2015: A1, A2, A4.

35 Personal conversation with author, 1998.

36 Author's telephone conversations with Gerl, June 2016.

37 "12 are injured as Angels' team bus crashes," *Atlanta Journal*, May 21, 1992: 85.

38 Helene Elliott, "13 Injured in Angel Bus Crash," *Los Angeles Times*, May 22, 1992: C1.

PETE HUGHES: GREAT PLAYER, BAD TIMING

By Will Christensen

A great quote sums up why most people – even dedicated baseball fans – have likely never heard of Pete Hughes.[1] The sports editor of the *Winnipeg News* wrote about the right fielder for the local club in the legendary ManDak League in 1953:

"For our money, Hughes gives away more runs than he manufactures. He's too slow afoot and almost has to hit a triple to get to first base. Then, in the field, he's not a very sure catch when he does manage to get under a ball. If we were manager Ken Meyers, we wouldn't get rid of Hughes, but we'd use him in a pinch hitting role, where he'd no doubt prove valuable to the club."[2]

This was written after a game in which Hughes, at the advanced age of 38, dropped two fly balls (his first two errors of the season).[3] But what Maurice Smith did was suggest turning the league's most potent offensive force into a bench warmer.

For all Hughes did that season was set a league record for home runs (13) while leading the league in RBIs – finishing fifth in batting at .324 – and leading the league in walks.[4] Preliminary research indicates Hughes probably walked around 100 times in the 74 games he played,[5] so his OBP probably was in the neighborhood of his career .530 average.

That's right: A .530 OBP for an entire career – of 1,333 games. As you might suspect, that's a record for anyone who played more than a handful of games in Organized Baseball.

In fact, Hughes ranks first or second – usually first – in the most important averages as far as assessing offensive value among minor-league players who played at least 1,000 games:

On-Base Percentage:

Hughes	.530
Joe Bauman	.487
Howard Weeks	.481

Slugging Average:

Bauman	.702
Gordon Nell	.639
Hughes	.637

OPS:

Bauman	1.189
Hughes	1.167
Pud Miller	1.062

Secondary Average:

Hughes	.674
Bauman	.652
Joe Pactwa	.542

Run Average:[6]

Hughes	.592
Bauman	.589
Ray Perry	.485

Runs Created / Game[7]

Hughes	13.88
Bauman	12.78
Buzz Clarkson	10.83

Runs Created / Year[8]

Hughes	171
Bauman	163
Rasty Wright	144

Until steroids came along, Joe Bauman was the all-time record-holder for home runs in a season, at 72.[9] No less of a media celebrity than Keith Olbermann wrote about him.[10] As for Hughes, he got a brief back-of-the-book article by Tony Salin in *Baseball's*

Forgotten Heroes (Bauman got a full profile in the same book), and that's pretty much it.[11]

Who was Pete Hughes? Good question. Little is known about his life before he broke into pro ball at the relatively advanced age of 22, and less is known about him after he left following that 1953 season. Hughes apparently got into baseball during high school in Los Angeles, and later on, he was a swimming pool technician.[12] Along the way, he got married and had a son and daughter,[13] but if a post-career profile, aside from Salin's, was written about him, it remains to be discovered.

In the years from 1937 to 1953, however, and particularly after World War II, Hughes drew a fair amount of ink while dominating every league he played in. He never played more than 134 games in a season, so, aside from the walks, his season totals don't look overly impressive. Here's what Hughes did from 1946 to 1952:

Year	G	AB	R	H	2B	3B	HR	RBI	BB	BA	OBP	SLG	RC
1946	119	364	109	124	25	1	30	121	132	.341	.518	.662	127
1947	133	442	180	164	36	8	38	167	193	.371	.569	.747	186
1948	132	415	142	144	38	5	21	118	207	.347	.566	.614	159
1949	123	408	156	143	31	9	24	126	210	.350	.574	.647	164
1950	107	369	104	145	25	4	19	108	131	.393	.557	,637	134
1951	116	363	64	114	29	1	19	95	144	.314	.513	.556	115
1952	123	377	123	138	22	6	28	131	180	.366	.577	.679	155

Now here's what Hughes' average OB season after World War II was in a 162-game context:

Yrs.	AB	R	H	2B	3B	HR	RBI	BB	BA	OBP	SLG	RC
5.27	520	167	185	39	6	34	164	227	.355	.555	.651	197

That's an average of 412 times on base per 162 games, without counting his HBPs. For context, the major-league record for one season is 379 in 153 games.

At this point, one might ask: Why didn't this guy get even a sniff at the majors?

He didn't fit the profile of what a good ballplayer was supposed to be. Because of two broken legs early in his career,[14] Hughes didn't have much speed, so he couldn't cover a lot of ground in the field.

Also, his timing stunk. In 1941 Hughes hit .318 in the Class-B Western International League, with a league-leading 34 homers, 125 RBIs, a league-leading 139 runs, and, of course, a league-leading 156 walks. He appeared poised for a promotion, even to the Double-A Pacific Coast League.[15]

But Uncle Sam came calling, and Hughes instead served in the US Army Air Corps for the next four years.[16] When he'd done his duty, Hughes was 31, and major-league ballclubs weren't interested in a 31-year-old slow-footed rookie who hadn't played higher than Class-B ball – no matter how many runs he put on the scoreboard.

Hughes put a ton of runs on the scoreboard. His teams, fans and sportswriters noticed. Hughes played on five championship teams and was an all-star eight times in 12 years.[17]

Times change, and there's no doubt that had Hughes come along more recently, he not only might make the majors, but might have a career. It might not be an all-star career, but it would be enough for him to accumulate a few back-of-the-baseball-card highlights along the way.

This article was edited by Thomas Rathkamp and fact-checked by Tony Escobedo.

NOTES

1 Hughes has often been referred to as Gabriel "Pete" Hughes, but the best evidence suggests that Gabriel was his middle, not first, name, based on his World War II registration card, the Social Security Index and Hughes's obituary. Also, according to multiple census forms, he was listed as a Junior.

2 Maurice Smith, "Time Out with Maurice Smith," *Winnipeg Free Press*, May 28, 1953: 26.

3 "Brandon Routs Royals by 11-2 at Winnipeg," *Minot* (North Dakota) *Daily News*, May 28, 1953: 10.

4 "Scarborough Tops Hitters," *Winnipeg Free Press*, September 4, 1953: 24. The ManDak League didn't release complete official statistics, but in this report, Hughes was called "the most walked man in the league."

5 An examination of the box scores of 23 random games Hughes played in 1953 shows 31 walks compared with 76 at-bats. Extrapolating that ratio out to the 241 at-bats noted in the *Winnipeg Free Press* would result in 98 walks.

6 Run Average was unveiled in *The New Bill James Historical Baseball Abstract* (New York: The Free Press, 2001). It is an attempt to put run production into the context of a batting average and is figured thus: (Runs + RBI) / At-bats.

7 The method of figuring runs created was taken from formulas presented in the *All-Time Major League Handbook*, (Skokie, Illinois: Stats Inc. Publishing, 1998).

8 Runs Created per Year is runs created per 144 games.

9 See Bauman's SABR biography by Bob Rivers at https://sabr.org/bioproj/person/joe-bauman/.

10 Keith Olbermann, "One for the X-Files in a Season of Inalienable Glory, Roswell's Joe Bauman Hit 72 Homers," *Sports Illustrated*, August 31, 1998. https://vault.si.com/vault/1998/08/31/one-for-the-x-files-in-a-season-of-inalienable-glory-roswells-joe-bauman-hit-72-homers, accessed January 26, 2023.

11 Tony Salin, *Baseball's Forgotten Heroes* (Lincolnwood, Illinois: Masters Press, 1999). Hughes's profile filled two pages; Bauman's 16.

12 "Pioneer League Moundsmen No Mystery to Pete Hughes," *Salt Lake* (Utah) *Telegram*, August 10, 1939: 13; "Obituaries," *Riverside* (California) *Press-Enterprise*, August 1, 2001.

13 Clyde Giraldo, "Stengel Says Other Clubs Ought to Hunt for Hawkins," *San Francisco Chronicle*, February 26, 1946: 18; "Obituaries," *Riverside Press-*

Enterprise. It isn't clear whether Edith Hughes was the mother of Hughes's two children.

14 Ty Cobb, "Inside Stuff," *Nevada State Journal* (Reno), April 17, 1949: 11. A broken leg in 1938 limited Hughes to just eight games that year.

15 "Dan Escobar May Be Lost Thru Draft," *Oregon Journal* (Portland), March 11, 1942: 15. Hughes had been acquired by the Portland Beavers of the Pacific Coast League and was expected to at least get a tryout with the team that spring.

16 "Stengel Says Other Clubs Ought to Hunt for Hawkins." Another story says Hughes served in the Philippines. Hughes said he was overseas for a year but gave no location.

17 Lloyd Johnson and Miles Wolff, eds., *Encyclopedia of Minor League Baseball*, Third Edition (Durham, North Carolina: Baseball America, 2007). The championship teams were Ogden 1940, Spokane 1941, Las Vegas 1949, El Centro 1950, and Tijuana 1952. Hughes also was an all-star in 1937 (DeLand), 1939 (Ogden), and 1947 (Phoenix).

THE LONG AND SHORT OF IT: W.C. "BILL" THOMAS AND ANTONIO "LITTLE TONY" FREITAS

By Len Pasculli

This is the story of two of the greatest pitchers in the history of the minor leagues. One was a lean right-hander, 6 feet tall, 175 pounds, who pitched from 1926 to 1952 for 24 different teams in 24 seasons, but he never pitched in the major leagues. He did not pitch professionally in 3½ seasons during that stretch. (More on that later.) Let's call this player "W.C."

The other was a short fella, a lefty who stood, by his own account, a fraction below 5-feet-8 and weighed about 160 pounds. He pitched from 1928 through 1953 but only for 23 seasons within that span because he lost three seasons to military service. Let's call him "Little Tony." Little Tony *did* pitch in the major leagues in five of those 23 seasons (1932-1936). However, when he was invited to return to the big leagues two years after he left, he respectfully declined.

"W.C." is William Clinton "Bill" Thomas. Thomas was born in East Prairie, Missouri, on January 9, 1905 (or 1907 or 1908); little else is known about Thomas's life before or after Organized Baseball.[1] What *is* known is that W.C. set minor-league records for games pitched (1,016), innings (5,995), wins (383), losses (347), hits (6,721), and runs (3,098).

To put some of these numbers in perspective, as of this writing, only 13 pitchers appeared in more than 1,016 *major*-league games. Five of them – Mariano Rivera, Dennis Eckersley, Hoyt Wilhelm, Trevor Hoffman, and Lee Smith – are in the National Baseball Hall of Fame. The only major-league pitchers who pitched more than 5,995 innings are Cy Young and Pud Galvin; and Cy Young and Walter Johnson are the only pitchers who had more than 383 big-league wins. Those pitchers are also in Cooperstown.

"Little Tony" is Antonio "Tony" Freitas Jr. (pronounced FRAY-tis), born on May 5, 1908 (some records say 1910), in Mill Valley, California. His parents Antonio and Maria, immigrants from Portugal, met and married in Mill Valley in 1903. Freitas was an unassuming man and a fan favorite. He liked fishing and hunting, playing locker-room pranks and the accordion, and fast cars.

Although Freitas's minor-league statistics are not quite as rarefied as Thomas's, he ranks fourth on the list of all-time winningest minor-league pitchers, after three right-handers: Oyster Joe Martina (1910-1931) is second behind Thomas with 349 wins and George Washington Payne (1913-1940) is third with 348, followed by Freitas with 342.[2] Martina had seven 20-win seasons; Freitas had nine (as did Charles "Spider" Baum), the best mark of all minor-league pitchers.[3]

From Minor-League Stars *(SABR, 1978)*

Bill Thomas.

For his achievements, Freitas was voted by SABR members in 1984 as the best minor-league pitcher of all time.[4]

Thomas got his break at the age of 21 in 1926, when he played for the Hanover (Pennsylvania) Raiders in the Blue Ridge League (Class D). He finished with 15 wins – tops on his team – and he led the league with 35 games and 246 innings pitched. In 1927 he pitched 244 innings and picked up 16 wins for the Charleroi (Pennsylvania) Babes in the Middle Atlantic League (Class C); he appeared in a league-best 41 games. Thomas averaged 42 games, 250 innings, and 16 wins in the 24 seasons he played.

Freitas got his start when he signed with the Sacramento Senators of the Pacific Coast League in 1928 at age 20. It was classified as a AA league (commonly called Double A), which in Freitas's day was the highest minor-league classification. Many have called the PCL "a third major league." After some seasoning in the Arizona State League, Freitas became a regular in the Senators' rotation and led the team in wins in both 1930 and 1931 (19 wins each time).

Driving fast was Freitas's only vice. He received a number of speeding tickets through the years and one landed him in Marin County (California) jail for five days. It happened in the summer of 1931. When Freitas was sentenced, he and Buddy Ryan, his manager, pleaded with and persuaded the judge to allow Freitas – with a deputy escort – to go to San Francisco to pitch his scheduled start against the Missions. Ryan knew scouts would be there to see Freitas. After winning the game, Freitas was returned to his cozy confines behind bars.

Freitas's automobile-related risk-taking may have been a reason to dissuade major-league teams from purchasing his contract in those early years. Or perhaps it was his short stature. Or maybe the lack of a good fastball was the reason. Freitas was a control pitcher and relied almost entirely on his curveball and changeup. But he just had to get a major-league team to take a chance on him. And he did.

On May 5, 1932, Freitas, the "Portuguese Portsider,"[5] took the mound for Sacramento on his 24th birthday and pitched a no-hit, no-run game against the Oakland Oaks. The performance did not go unnoticed. Connie Mack, owner and manager of the Philadelphia Athletics, needed rotation depth for his three-time reigning American League champions and traded Jimmie DeShong and cash to get Freitas.

Freitas debuted for the A's on May 31, 1932, at Shibe Park against the Washington Senators and turned in a splendid performance. He pitched 10 innings and allowed three runs on seven hits when Mack handed the ball to veteran George Earnshaw in the top of the 11th inning. The A's lost the game, 5-4, in the 12th.

Freitas played two seasons with the Athletics. He had a 12-5 record in 1932 but fell to 2-4 with one save[6] in 1933 before he was optioned to Double-A Portland. In 1934 Freitas turned himself around with the St. Paul Saints in the Double-A American Association and he was traded to Cincinnati for Jim Lindsey, Ivey Shiver, and cash.[7] He played three seasons for the Reds, starting with a 6-12 record and one save in 1934 and a 5-10 record with two saves in 1935.[8]

In the 1936 season, Freitas got off to a slow 0-2 start and the Reds sold him to the Columbus Red Birds, a Double-A St. Louis Cardinals affiliate. For a second time (counting the California judge as the first time), Freitas applied his charm. He persuaded the Cardinals' general manager, Branch Rickey, to transfer him from Columbus to the Sacramento Solons[9] in the PCL, also a St. Louis affiliate, so that he could be closer to home. Rickey arranged it to happen in 1937.

More than halfway across the country from Sacramento, Thomas made the rounds. He advanced quickly early in his career but then got stalled in the higher minors over the next nine years. From 1928 through 1936, Thomas was sold, traded, or otherwise transferred from West Virginia to Oklahoma to Indiana to Tennessee, back to Pennsylvania where he started, then Louisiana, with a couple of short stops in Texas and Wisconsin mixed in. It seemed that the road was *his* home.

With a record of 159-145 in 419 appearances from 1926 through 1936, the scouts undoubtedly were bird-dogging Thomas. Yet he never got the call. Major-league teams could not have had the same doubts about Thomas's body type that they had with Freitas. Also, Thomas was a good fielder (so was Freitas) and a good hitter (Freitas was not).

Perhaps, instead, Thomas's lack of a good fastball was the reason the scouts shied away from him. Like Freitas, Thomas was a curveball pitcher, with good control. His 3.71 career ERA was serviceable, not stellar.

As fate would have it, these two pitching giants – figuratively speaking, in Freitas's case –

turned up in the Pacific Coast League on the same day – Opening Day, April 3, 1937. In December 1936 the Seattle Indians traded an aging Ed Wells to get Thomas. Sacramento hosted Seattle on Opening Day. Freitas pitched and lost to the Indians, 6-4. The next day, Thomas pitched Seattle to a 7-3 win over Sacramento. The six years from 1937 through 1942 give statisticians a perfect lens through which to view and compare these two stars.

Thomas played for four PCL teams in 1937-1942: Seattle, Portland, San Diego, and Hollywood.[10] In those seasons, he pitched 1,566 innings in 269 games with a won-lost record of 89-103.[11] He turned 38 before the 1943 campaign began. Thomas was probably too old to jump to the big leagues at the time, even with the hundreds of vacancies created by the major leaguers who went off to war.

Meanwhile, happy to be home in Sacramento, Freitas ran off two consecutive 20-win seasons in 1937 and '38. Branch Rickey told Freitas that he would like to buy his contract to come back and play in the majors again. To Rickey's astonishment, Freitas explained that he would prefer to remain in Sacramento. He had his reasons: Freitas liked the regularity of the PCL schedule; he disliked the weather away from California; and the opposing lineups were tougher in the big leagues. Besides, he had already experienced the triumph of being there. So, he stayed in Sacramento. From 1937 to 1942, Freitas pitched 1,839 innings in 244 games and won at least 20 games each season. His won-lost record was 133-88.

In 1943, at the height of his playing career and coming off a remarkable 1942 season when he helped the Solons win their first league championship with a save and a win in a doubleheader on the final day of the season, Freitas enlisted in the US Army Air Forces (renamed from the U.S. Army Air Corps in 1941.)

After the 1943 season, Thomas once again bounced around the country. The Hollywood Stars sold his contract to the Knoxville Smokies, a lower classified team (Class A1) in the Southern Association (which midway through the season moved and became the Mobile Bears). Three years later, Thomas landed in Houma, Louisiana, in the Class-D Evangeline League. At the age of 41, Thomas's performance in 1946 was outstanding. He pitched 353 innings, won 35 games, and lost only seven.

The legendary Bill James says this about Thomas's season: "Now granted, that wasn't much of a league, but 35 wins are a bunch. No other pitcher, anywhere in organized baseball, at any age, has won 35 games in any other season since 1922."[12]

The little information published about Thomas's personal life and personality creates an impression that he was mysterious, or sullen, or ornery – or all three. One sportswriter called him "somewhat screwy."[13] Once when Thomas was in Portland playing for the Beavers, he and his batterymate, George Dickey (younger brother of New York Yankee Bill Dickey), exchanged punches in the dugout, accusing each other of costing the game they just lost.[14] Another time, when Thomas played for the Houma Indians, he was suspended and fined $25 for "using profanity on the field."[15] In baseball, all players are competitive. Some are quietly competitive, like Tony Freitas. Some are less quiet, like Bill Thomas.

Much has been written about rampant gambling in the minor leagues during the post-World War II years. In 1947 the Houma team, which had won the 1946 league championship by a wide margin, was investigated on allegations that several players, including Thomas, were involved in throwing games during the prior year's playoffs. One of the accusations against Thomas is explained in this way: After World War II, "the Brooklyn Dodgers engaged in a thorough housekeeping of the Mobile farm club" by assigning older players to Houma to make room for younger players in

Courtesy TCDB

Tony Freitas.

Mobile, and those assigned players "who were good enough for higher levels of ball, were willing to play in Class D for the benefits of dealing with the gamblers in Louisiana."[16]

In January 1947, Houma's manager and four players – Thomas and two others from Houma and one from Abbeville, Houma's playoff opponent – were banned from baseball for life by the National Association, then the minor leagues' governing body. Thomas and one other player successfully appealed and were reinstated 2½ years later.[17]

Thomas finished the 1949 season with Houma and then played the next years for whichever team would take him – all in the low minors. He pitched 728 innings after his 42nd birthday and accumulated 52 more wins. Thomas retired after the 1952 season at age 47.

When Freitas came out of the service in 1946, he was a little rusty but was still able to compete at the minor leagues' highest level (AAA, or "Triple A," under baseball's new scheme) for four more seasons with Sacramento. He lost his string of 20-win seasons, but he collected 45 wins against 53 losses.

In the next four seasons, first with Modesto then with Stockton, in the Class-C California League, Freitas pitched 1,048 innings after *his* 42nd birthday. Like Thomas, Freitas too was able to put up good numbers against the younger minor leaguers – 20, 25, 18, and 22 wins in 1950-1953 (in the second and fourth of those seasons, he led the league).

Before he retired as a player, he was the player-manager of Modesto and Stockton for one season each. After that he coached and then managed the Sacramento Solons in 1954 and 1955 before fully retiring from the game. Freitas said in various interviews that he might not have been cut out to be a manager, but that he had no regrets about his playing career.

It was a remarkable quarter-century in an interesting time in minor-league history for W.C. and Little Tony – men who were not so different in so many ways, but worlds apart in others.

That's the long and short of it.

ACKNOWLEDGMENTS

Special thanks to SABR members Zak Ford and David Jerome for sharing their interest in and information on these two subjects deriving from their unpublished research, Ford on Freitas and Jerome on Thomas; to Tom Emerson and Frank Longo, SABR members and longtime friends, for their editorial assistance; and to Cassidy Lent, manager of reference services at the National Baseball Hall of Fame and Museum, for supplying copies of news clippings from the files in Cooperstown.

This article was edited by Thomas Rathkamp and fact-checked by Mike Huber.

NOTES

1 Very little personal information on Thomas has been found in the public domain at this time. The birth information cited here is from Thomas's World War II draft card application available through Ancestry.com. The other birth dates appear elsewhere. The SABR site contains a collection of *The Sporting News* Player Contract Cards including one on Thomas. The National Baseball Hall of Fame and Museum library has no file on Thomas. Two SABR researchers corroborated the absence of personal information about Thomas: George W. Hilton in the final paragraph of "The Evangeline League Scandal of 1946" (published in SABR's *Baseball Research Journal* in 1982) and David Jerome in an email to the author on January 12, 2024.

2 For purposes of this article, the statistics used for Thomas, Martina, Payne, and Freitas were those published in the SABR book *Minor League Baseball Stars*, vol. I (1978) [all three volumes are available online at https://profile.sabr.org/page/research-resources], which were later compiled in Lloyd Johnson, ed., *The Minor League Register* (First Edition) (Durham, North Carolina: Baseball America, Inc., 1994). The author compared the two sources and found that they were identical except where Johnson made one improvement: He included in Thomas's statistics the one game he pitched (and lost) for the Wenatchee Chiefs on July 31, 1937, before William G. Bramham, the president of the National Association of Professional Baseball Leagues, disallowed the trade between the Seattle Indians and the Chiefs that included Thomas. The statistics published by baseball-reference.com for the four pitchers are different from those appearing in the SABR book and in the *Register*. The author contacted baseball-reference.com with some suggested improvements on the Freitas statistics and was advised that "[B-R's] process for reviewing historical minor league data is to work through each league-season systemically. They have written up a summary of their working methods here, which may be of interest: https://www.chadwick-bureau.com/doc/historical/. This is a very active area of research, so coverage of this era should be much more complete over the coming few years." (Aidan Jackson-Evans, Sports Reference, LLC, personal communications [via email], January 3, 2024.)

3 More about Martina and Payne, whose careers were done before World War II: Martina played only eight games in Class AA (the then highest level of minor leagues), but he did pitch in 24 games for the Washington Nationals in the American League in 1924 – a 34-year-old rookie. (He managed a 6-and-8 record.) Payne pitched in more high-minors games than Martina did, but he appeared in only 12 major-league games. At age 31, he played for the 1920 Chicago White Sox with teammates who had not yet been banned from baseball, and he picked up one win and one loss. Payne's final win came in 1940 with the Worthington (Minnesota) Cardinals, a Class-D affiliate of the St. Louis Cardinals in the Western League, when he was 51 years old. It must be at least mentioned when looking at the closeness of the number of wins among Martina (349), Payne (348), and Freitas (342) that the bulk of Martina's and Payne's wins came in minor leagues classified below Double A, while Freitas's wins were mostly in Double A/Triple A, and that neither pitcher lost time during his careers as Freitas did, although Martina did retire at 41, which was much younger than the age at which the other two retired.

4 Society for American Baseball Research, *Minor League Baseball Stars*, vol. II (1985), 9-14.

5 First use of this nickname for Tony Freitas first appeared in Pacific Coast News Service, "Tony Freitas of Oakland Sacs' Hero," *The Oakland Post-Enquirer*, April 19, 1930: 23. It appeared in newspapers across the country after that.

6 Saves were not an official major-league statistic until 1969. Saves noted of pitchers before that were awarded retroactively by researchers.

7 This trade was so typical of the deal structure in which minor-league teams frequently engaged during this time period. Lindsey and Shiver were on the downside of their career; Freitas was a young prospect. And the often-struggling minor-league team always welcomed a cash component from the major-league team.

8 Freitas was good enough to be the starting pitcher on Opening Day on two occasions in the majors. He did it once in each league, a rarity: On April 12, 1933, he opened the season for the Athletics in the AL and on April 16, 1935, for the Reds in the NL. He lost both games.

9 The Sacramento Senators changed their name to the Solons after the Cardinals purchased the team in 1935. Sacramento is California's state capital and Solon was an ancient Greek legislator; "solon" is also slang for a member of a legislative body.

10 Thomas played one game for the new Wenatchee (Washington) Chiefs in the Class-B Western International League on July 31, 1937. See Note 2 above.

11 In 1943, his final year in the PCL, Thomas played for Hollywood while Freitas was in the military, so his stats for that year are not included in the comparison between the two pitchers: Thomas pitched 249 innings in 52 games, but his record slipped to 11-21 before he was sold to Knoxville.

12 Bill James, *The Bill James Historical Baseball Abstract* (New York: Villard Books, 1986), 198.

13 Tom Anderson, "From Up Close," *Knoxville Journal*, April 30, 1944: 11.

14 Associated Press, "Pitcher, Catcher Fight in Dugout," *Nevada State Journal* (Reno), August 23, 1938: 8.

15 "Thomas Fined $25, Suspended," *The Sporting News*, June 5, 1946: 32.

16 George W. Hilton, "The Evangeline League Scandal of 1946," *Baseball Research Journal* (SABR), 1982.

17 Thomas did not play professional baseball in 1930, for a reason that has not yet been determined. Taken together with the Evangeline incident, he lost a total of 3½ years of pro ball.

LEGENDARY COMEDY DUO SWINGS OPEN CRACKERS SEASON

By Brian Williams

Bud Abbott: Well Costello, I'm going to New York with you. You know Bucky Harris, the Yankees' manager, gave me a job as coach for as long as you're on the team.
Lou Costello: Look, Abbott, if you're the coach, you must know all the players.
Abbott: I certainly do.
Costello: Well you know I've never met the guys. So you'll have to tell me their names, and then I'll know who's playing on the team.
Abbott: Oh, I'll tell you their names, but you know it seems to me they give these ballplayers nowadays very peculiar names.
Costello: You mean funny names?
Abbott: Strange names, pet names ... like Dizzy Dean...
Costello: His brother Daffy.
Abbott: Daffy Dean ...
Costello: And their French cousin.
Abbott: French?
Costello: Goofe.
Abbott: Goofe Dean. Well, let's see, we have on the bags, Who's on first, What's on second, I Don't Know is on third. ...[1]

While Bud and Lou touched their audience's funnybones through a variety of vaudeville, radio, film, and, later, television acts, this baseball-themed gem seemed to gravitate to the top of the pair's repertoire. Most baseball fans and comedy sketch aficionados can still recite much of Abbott and Costello's classic skit. Fewer may know about the skit's appearances on the baseball field and in American popular culture.

On Friday, April 16, 1948, Bud and Lou's live performance of "Who's on First?" graced a professional baseball team's Opening Day at the ballfield at the corner of Atlanta's Ponce de Leon Avenue and Lakeview, known at the time as Ponce de Leon Park.

This was one of several appearances by the comedy duo in the Atlanta area that weekend. Bud and Lou visited a federal penitentiary and two hospitals the day before the game. One hospital patient, Patrolman R.C. West, was a specific target of their humor. They wanted to lift the spirits of the police officer, whose leg had been amputated after a recent gun battle. Abbott and Costello joked with the heroic officer and the nursing staff. That evening, they entertained overflow audiences with two live shows at the Paramount Theater, coinciding with the opening of their new comedy film, *The Noose Hangs High.*

The next day the comedy team stepped onto the same field as two teams in the Southern Association. With twilight spring temperatures hovering in the mid-60s, the Birmingham Barons and Atlanta Crackers prepared to begin a new season before 21,812 eager fans.[2] Suddenly, Bud Abbott and Lou Costello stepped to the microphone stand at home plate.

Atlanta's Ponce de Leon Park erupted with laughter throughout the skit featuring its original comedy team. The huge crowd hung on every line.

Bud Abbott: You throw the ball to Who?
Lou Costello: Naturally.
Bud Abbott: That's it.
Lou Costello: Same as you! Same as YOU! I throw the ball to Who. Whoever it is drops the ball and the guy runs to second. Who picks up the ball and throws it to What. What throws it to I Don't Know. I Don't Know throws it back to Tomorrow, triple play. Another guy gets up and hits a long fly ball to Because. Why? I don't know! He's on third and I don't give a darn!
Bud Abbott: What?
Lou Costello: I said I don't give a darn!
Bud Abbott: Oh, that's our shortstop.[1]

Abbott and Costello regaled the standing-room Opening Day crowd for a full 15 minutes before taking their bows and yielding to the Crackers' starting defenders. The fans roared their approval and eagerness to begin a new season. After all, the Crackers played before an average crowd of 5,309 in 1947[3] while this Opening Day attendance eclipsed 21,800. The previous record crowd (21,500) at the park watched a 1946 spring game that the Crackers hosted against the Yankees.

One of those in attendance was Pearl Sandow, who missed only one Crackers home game between 1934 and 1966. She switched allegiance when the Braves brought their National League team to Atlanta. Pearl attended more than 1,850 Crackers games at Ponce de Leon Park before she advanced to the majors and, ultimately, the fans section of the Baseball Hall of Fame. On this day Pearl followed her usual routine of leaving her federal Housing Department career and heading directly to the ballpark.[4]

Once baseball took center stage, the two Southern Association teams sought to entertain the masses following so-so performances the previous season. In 1947 the Crackers rode an average of just under five runs per game to a 73-78 record, 20 games off the pace set by the Mobile Bears. The Barons (73-80) stayed on the heels of Atlanta in the standings, as well as in team batting and pitching. Only Memphis and Little Rock fared worse. The top two teams, Mobile and the New Orleans Pelicans, won more than 90 games.

Kiki Cuyler's Crackers opened this season's scoring on a first-inning infield single by Neb Wilson. Atlanta threatened to score more; however, Birmingham starting left-hander Irv Medlinger wriggled out of the inning with a pop fly and a strikeout.

The Barons took the lead in the third as former Cracker Tommy O'Brien smoked a two-run double down the left-field line. In the sixth, O'Brien, a wartime major leaguer with Pittsburgh, recorded his second hit of the game and scored on a fly ball by player/manager Fred Walters.

The Crackers came storming back in the bottom half keyed by catcher Red Mathis, who doubled in a pair. The go-ahead run scored on a passed ball to give Atlanta a 4-3 lead.

The Barons reknotted the score at 4-4 in the top of the seventh. Then Carl Lindquist relieved for the Crackers and stifled the Birmingham rally. Lindquist had pitched 21⅔ innings for the Boston Braves during World War II.

The Crackers broke the tie by tallying three two-out runs in their seventh-inning turn. Two walks, two singles, and Mathis's second double of the day did the damage. Atlanta added three more runs in the eighth off reliever Mike Gast. The Barons scratched out a run in the final frame without a hit, thanks to catcher's interference, a throwing error, and a fly out.

Southpaw Bill Kennedy earned the win. He finished the season at 15-15, and recorded one win in three years of major-league roster time. Birmingham's George Washington Wilson led all hitters with three safeties in this season opener. He wrapped up his 1948 season hitting .335 with 27 home runs. In 1952 Wilson debuted in the majors with the New York Giants and eventually logged time with the Yankees as well. In addition to Wilson's three, the Barons logged 11 more hits in the game, yet could only dent the plate five times. The 11-5 defeat to the Crackers did not deter the Birmingham squad, which went on to win the 1948 Southern Association championship with a record of 84-69. In the playoffs, the Barons disposed of Memphis and Nashville in two 4-2 series wins, even though both teams had finished with better regular-season records.

The Crackers, meanwhile, fell to sixth place and completed another mediocre season (69-85). The most memorable point of that season for the Crackers' faithful may have been that first victory and the legendary Abbott and Costello's pregame performance of "Who's on First?"

"Who's on First?" has had a remarkably long run. The skit originated almost a decade before Abbott and Costello's live performance at the Crackers' opener. It debuted in 1937 on a vaudeville revue tour. Then, a year later, in March 1938, after joining the cast of *The Kate Smith Hour* radio program, Abbott and Costello treated radio listeners to "Who's on First?" Their first film, *One Night in the Tropics*, included the skit, which was becoming so popular that the comedy duo copyrighted the routine in 1944. They also included it in their 1945 film *The Naughty Nineties*, which some consider their finest recorded performance.

"Who's on First?" reached Cooperstown in 1953, eight years after Abbott and Costello's Atlanta performance, when a golden record of the skit was added to the permanent display on the second floor of the National Baseball Hall of Fame and Museum. At the time of the announcement, Costello said, "This is many times better than getting an Oscar." A video of the stellar *The Naughty Nineties* version still plays on screens inside the Hall.

During the 1956 World Series *The Steve Allen Show*, a variety hour on NBC-TV, featured a salute to baseball. Guests on the show included Mickey Mantle and Claire Ruth, Babe Ruth's widow. Steve Allen then introduced "two men who have made a very unique contribution to the game in a lighter vein." The 58-year-old Abbott and 50-year-old Costello came on stage in their baseball uniforms along with two executives from the Hall of Fame to talk about the new display in Cooperstown. After the applause died down, Allen introduced what some claim to be the final performance of "Who's on First?" Fittingly, the very next day, Don Larsen pitched his World Series perfect game. Within a year the Abbott and Costello comedy team broke up.

Despite the duo's split, the reach of the skit continued to grow. A "Who's on First?" board game was marketed in the 1970s. *Time* magazine named the routine "Best Comedy Sketch of the 20th Century" in a 1999 issue. The Library of Congress placed an early radio recording of the piece in its National Recording Registry in 2003. Two years later – 66 years after its initial performance – the line "Who's on First?" was included on the American Film Institute's list of 100 memorable movie quotes.

"Who's on First?" succeeded in breaking generational barriers and lives on to entertain millions of baseball and comedy fans. On an MLB Network "Who's on First?" special in 2012, Jerry Seinfeld helped explain why: "Any great comedy is how far can you take this silly idea. I mean the initial idea is just a first baseman named 'Who.' And then you get the 'What,' then the 'I Don't Know,' and it keeps going. You think it's out of gas, and it's not. That's what makes this great."[5]

From Max Patkin, the Clown Prince of Baseball, to today's team mascots; from dogs serving as batboys to a famous comedy team performing its most famous skit to promote a new movie and entertain a pregame crowd on Opening Day in Atlanta in 1948, baseball and fun have always been on the same team.

THE "WHO'S ON FIRST?" TEAM LINEUP

First Base: Who
Second Base: What
Third Base: I Don't Know
Left field: Why
Center field: Because
Pitcher: Tomorrow
Catcher: Today
Shortstop: I Don't Give a Darn
The right fielder is never named.

This article was edited by Cathy Kreyche and fact-checked by Kevin Larkin.

SOURCES

Williams, F. M. "Crackers Lick Barons in Debut Before 21,812," *Atlanta Constitution*, April 17, 1948.

Bennett, Byron. "Atlanta's Other Lost Ballpark – Ponce De Leon Park." *Deadball Baseball,* August 5, 2013. https://deadballbaseball.com/2013/08/atlantas-other-lost-ballpark-ponce-de-leon-park/.

Walker, Buss. "Mawnin'!," *Chattanooga Daily Times*, April 19, 1948.

Fenster, Kenneth R., Georgia State University Perimeter College. "Pearl Sandow, 1902-2006." https://www.georgiaencyclopedia.org/articles/sports-outdoor-recreation/pearl-sandow-1902-2006/.

Francis, Bill. "Who's on First Joined the Hall 60 Years Ago." National Baseball Hall of Fame. February 6, 2016. https://baseballhall.org/discover/short-stops/whos-on-first.

"1947 Southern Association." Baseball Reference. BR Bullpen. https://www.baseball-reference.com/register/league.cgi?id=92db4b25 (statistics on the 1947 season).

"Ponce de Leon Park." *New Georgia Encyclopedia* (n.p.: Georgia Humanities, University of Georgia Press, n.d.). https://www.georgiaencyclopedia.org/articles/sports-outdoor-recreation/ponce-de-leon-ballpark/.

"Who's on First?" Baseball Reference. BR Bullpen. https://www.baseball-reference.com/bullpen/Who%27s_on_First%3F ("Who's on First?" history).

NOTES

1 "Who's on First?" script. https://abbott-and-costello-whos-on-first.info/whos-on-first-script/.

2 Atlanta Crackers 1948 Attendance figures and roster. https://www.statscrew.com/minorbaseball/roster/t-ac10221/y-1948.

3 Atlanta Crackers 1947 Attendance figures. https://www.statscrew.com/minorbaseball/roster/t-ac10221/y-1947.

4 Kenneth R. Fenster, Georgia State University Perimeter College, "Pearl Sandow, 1902-2006." https://www.georgiaencyclopedia.org/articles/sports-outdoor-recreation/pearl-sandow-1902-2006/.

5 Bill Francis, "Who's on First Joined the Hall 60 Years Ago," National Baseball Hall of Fame. February 6, 2016. https://baseballhall.org/discover/short-stops/whos-on-first.

THE ARRIVAL OF THE SPRINGFIELD CUBS SIGNALED THE DEMISE OF NEWARK'S LEGENDARY BEARS

By Robert Cvornyek and Douglas Stark

On Monday evening, February 6, 1950, a cold winter night laced with thoughts of Opening Day two months away, Municipal Auditorium in downtown Springfield, Massachusetts, was filled with fans whooping and hollering as the newest baseball team, the Springfield Cubs, was introduced. Sponsored by the Springfield Chamber of Commerce, the "Meet-the-Manager" Night, as it was billed, witnessed a capacity crowd as they greeted manager Stan Hack of the Springfield Cubs, manager Frankie Frisch of the Chicago Cubs, International League President Frank J. Shaughnessy, and Jack Sheehan, chief of the Chicago Cubs farm system.[1] Signs welcoming Hack and the International League adorned the auditorium. As sports reporter Walter Graham captured the following day in the *Springfield Daily News*, "The whole affair was a bang-up success and the Chicago Cubs folks had reason to feel ever so happy about it all."[2]

The event was designed to formally introduce the Springfield Cubs, the Triple-A International League affiliate of the Chicago Cubs, as the newest baseball team in Springfield. The evening also featured a well-deserved thank-you to Jack Sheehan, "the man who spearheaded the movement that resulted in this city getting the Newark franchise." As Sheehan reflected the day after the event, "It has always been my contention that Springfield and Western Massachusetts is a great sports area, and the wonderful turnout of fans last night makes my conviction stronger than ever. I express the sincere thanks of the entire Chicago Cub organization for all who took part in the affair. With fans like this, I don't see how International League baseball in Springfield can miss."[3]

Indeed, optimism was high as Springfield welcomed not only a new team but a new decade, the 1950s. Neither baseball nor the Cubs were a new venture for Springfield, though. The Springfield Cubs had been a member of the eight-team Class-B New England League in 1948 and 1949. In 1948 the Cubs finished in sixth place, failing to qualify for the playoffs, but the following season, the team improved to fourth place and a playoff berth. After defeating the Pawtucket Slaters in a best-of-three series, they then lost to the Portland Pilots in a best-of-seven championship series. At the conclusion of the 1949 season, however, the league folded, temporarily leaving Springfield without a professional baseball team.

The Chicago franchise strongly believed that Springfield still possessed a strong market, as evidenced by the team's attendance figures. For the 1948 season, the Cubs finished second in the league with attendance of 95,406, and in 1949 they led the league with 102,387 fans passing through the turnstiles.[4] For

SABR: The Rucker Archive.

Jacob Ruppert.

SABR: The Rucker Archive.

George Weiss.

Cubs executives, Springfield was viewed favorably as a good baseball town, in the parlance of the day, that would continue to support professional baseball.

Sheehan and the Cubs wasted little time in trying to secure another franchise for Springfield, but time was of the essence, so Sheehan quickly went to work and soon found that the Newark Bears team, the Triple-A affiliate of the New York Yankees, were for sale. The Bears were considered the gold standard in terms of minor-league baseball.

In the 1930s and 1940s, Newark Bears fans enjoyed watching one of the most successful minor-league teams in baseball history. In 1931 Jacob Ruppert, principal owner of the New York Yankees, purchased the team from financially strapped newspaper editor Paul Block for an estimated $350,000. The acquisition included Davids Stadium, a relatively new ballpark built in 1926 and located on Wilson Avenue in the city's East Ward, colloquially known as the Ironbound neighborhood. The facility was renamed Ruppert Stadium soon after the takeover. According to historian Neil Sullivan, Ruppert, who amassed a fortune in his father's beer business and later real estate, wisely surrounded himself with men who knew the game. In particular, he persuaded George Weiss, vice president, and general manager of the Baltimore Orioles, to accept an offer to run the Newark club in the International League and build an overall stronger farm system for the Yankees.[5]

Weiss remained with the Yankee organization for 28 seasons, from 1932 to 1960, first as the architect of the farm system before becoming New York's general manager in 1948 (and being elected to the National Baseball Hall of Fame in 1971). By 1940, the Yankees controlled nine minor-league teams and operated at all levels of competition, with Newark being considered as the "crown jewel" of its minor-league system. True to its name, the Newark franchise consistently developed talent for its parent organization, and the Yankees claimed seven American League pennants between 1936 and 1943. The Bears also enjoyed success as contenders for the International League crown. During the Bears' 18-year existence in Newark, the team finished first in the International League in 1932, 1933, 1934, 1937, 1938, 1941, and 1942. The Bears advanced to the league playoffs an additional nine times, missing only the 1947 and 1949 seasons. The team defeated its playoff rivals in 1937, 1938, 1940, and 1945.[6]

Understandably, it was the 1937 ballclub that received the most praise and attention. Once named the Minor League Team of the Century by the readers of the publication *Baseball America*, the 1937 Bears captured one of the team's three Little World Series championships. According to New Jersey baseball historians Ronald Meyer, James DiClerico, and Barry Pavelec, the greatness of this team rested on three achievements. First, the team finished an astonishing 25½ games in front of the second-place Montreal Royals. Second, the Bears captured the Little World Series by defeating the Columbus Red Birds of the American Association in dramatic style. After losing the first three games, Newark stormed back to win the last four games. Finally, the team managed to send every starter to the major leagues. Among the players who graduated to the big leagues were Joe Gordon, Babe Dahlgren, George McQuinn, Jim Gleeson, Bob Seeds, Nolen Richardson, Buddy Rosar, Atley Donald, Joe Beggs, Vito Tamulis, and Steve Sundra. The most beloved member of the squad, Charlie "King Kong" Keller, played 13 seasons, mostly with the Yankees, where he joined Joe DiMaggio and Tommy Henrich as the organization's premier outfield combination. In later years, other stars including Yogi Berra, Bobby Brown, Johnny Lindell, George Stirnweiss, and Hank Majeski advanced to the majors after spending time in Newark.[7]

In late December 1949, Newark fans experienced the unthinkable when the Yankees entertained offers to purchase the Bears franchise. The Cubs entered a bid for the team after the New England League disbanded, leaving the Chicago affiliate without a home. The Cubs took an option on the Newark Holdings until January 15. 1950. After hearing the news, Newark City Commissioner Meyer C. Ellenstein contacted Parke Carroll, the Bears' general manager, to discuss keeping the team in Newark. Bears fans had complained about inadequate transportation to Ruppert Stadium and the offensive smell that engulfed the park. "Transportation can be corrected," Ellenstein stated, "and the smoke and smells I've been hearing about can be eased too." Carroll considered the city's response but deferred any decisions regarding the team to Dan Topping, president and co-owner of the Yankees.[8]

Topping understood that the decision to sell the Bears had little to do with transportation and pollution. Both he and Weiss knew that multiple factors contributed to the sale. The competition from live television and nearby major-league ballparks – the Yankees, Giants, and Brooklyn Dodgers were just across the Hudson River – had cut attendance to 90,000 in 1949, a far distance from the record high attendance of 345,000 in 1932. Moreover, the Yankees chose to reorganize their entire farm system with a goal toward greater specialization in player development. The Bears were one of five farm teams the Yankees eliminated. With the removal of Newark, the Yankees retained only one Triple-A team, the Kansas City Blues of the American Association. Weiss, the man who built the Yankees dynasty with Newark's muscle, officially cited attendance and reorganization as major reasons to sell the team.[9]

In December 1949, discussions heated up. Springfield was not the only city being considered for the Bears. At the National Convention of Professional Baseball held in Baltimore, Weiss indicated that Springfield; New Haven, Connecticut; and Québec City all represented viable options for the sale and relocation of the Newark franchise. Part of the negotiations for bringing a Triple-A team to Springfield centered on the ballpark. Pynchon Park had been part of the discussions in 1947 when the National League Chicago Cubs agreed to relocate the minor-league Cubs to the New England League. At that time, the Cubs leased the park from the City of Springfield and quickly set about making the necessary upgrades. They desired "to revive baseball in this area and to transform Pynchon Park into a place where people could spend their evenings and Sunday afternoons enjoying their favorite American sport."[10] At that time, it included a new corrugated steel fence, new grandstand and concession stand, improved fire safety measures, doubling the number of entrances, paving the parking lot, and resodding the infield, all for a reported cost of $5,000.

On January 6, 1950, the *New York Times* reported that top officials in the Cubs organization, including John T. Sheehan and Earl Nelson, asked civic and business leaders in Springfield to raise $250,000 to totally renovate Pynchon Park and upgrade facilities consistent with the quality of an International League baseball club. After all parties reached a satisfactory agreement, the Cubs officially announced the purchase of the Newark Bears on January 12.[11]

With the purchase and relocation, Springfield now hosted an International League team, the second of two Triple-A franchises for Chicago. (The Los Angeles Angels still operated in the Pacific Coast League.) It also meant that there would be a marked improvement in the quality of players who spent time in Springfield. For comparison, only four players from the team's two New England League years ever played in the majors, while the 1950 team alone saw 22 players get the call to the big leagues at some point.

Optimism greeted the Springfield Cubs for the 1950 season, generated by legendary Cubs third baseman Stan Hack, who had been a five-time All-Star and a

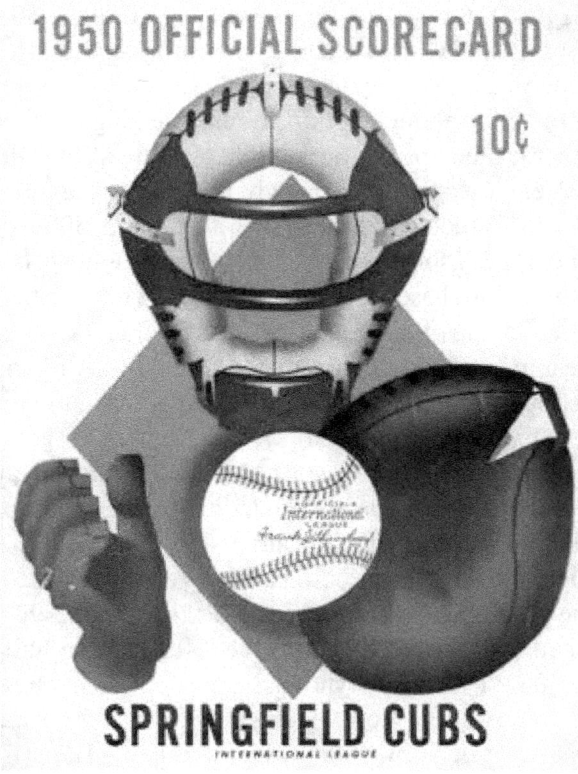

Courtesy Wood Museum of Springfield History.

Springfield Cubs official scorecard, 1950.

SABR: The Rucker Archive.

Springfield Cubs manager Stan Hack.

key player for three Chicago pennant winners (1935, 1938, 1945). On a cold and blustery April 22, 1950, the Springfield Cubs welcomed the Buffalo Bisons to Pynchon Park. Five thousand fans saw the Cubs lose their opener, although optimism remained high as the weather heated up. The Springfield team finished fifth out of eight teams and narrowly missed the playoffs with a 74-78 record. Despite hovering around .500 for most of the season, the team did have its bright spots, including third baseman Randy Jackson, who won the league's rookie of the year award and would go on to a 10-year major-league career that included two All-Star selections. Fans continued to support the team in 1950 as they had in 1949, with 201,217 fans coming through the gates. During that season, 22 Cubs players eventually played in the majors, including pitcher Warren Hacker and catcher Smoky Burgess.

Over the next three seasons, however, the fortunes of the team gradually sank. In 1951 the team (63-90) finished in last place. Attendance fell nearly in half to 105,052. Bill Kelly, who had managed the declining fortunes of the Los Angeles Angels in 1950, was the manager of Springfield in 1951 and 1952. The primary bright spot occurred on April 12, 1951, when a preseason exhibition game with the Boston Red Sox (the Red Sox won, 5-2) attracted a crowd of 10,736, at that time the largest ever for a baseball game in Western Massachusetts. Fourteen Springfield players would go to or had played in the majors, including catchers Nelson Burbrink and Harry Chiti and pitchers Monk Dubiel and Vern Fear. Fans also enjoyed seeing some players who were nearing the end of their careers, including infielder Emil Verban, and outfielder Stan Spence.

The team did not fare much better in 1952, with a mark of 65-88 and another last-place finish, 31 games behind the first-place Montreal Royals. Attendance improved slightly to 107,675. After the season, manager Kelly's services were not retained. Again, a highlight was another early-season game against the Red Sox at Pynchon Park; this time 9,160 fans watched the Cubs lose, 6-1. Much like previous seasons, though, the fans did have an opportunity to watch major-league talent: 20 members of the Springfield Cubs had played or would play in the major leagues.

With Kelly out as manager, the Cubs introduced their third manager in four seasons – Bruce Edwards. But the wheels came off the team in 1953 as it again landed in last place with a 51-102 record, costing Edwards his job toward the end of the season. Jack Sheehan finished up as manager. Attendance mirrored the fortunes of the team on the field and plummeted to 85,281. This represented a nearly 60 percent decline over the four seasons. The fans did have something to cheer about as they watched future big-league pitchers Don Elston, Dave Hillman, and Jim Brosnan hone their craft.

What began with an optimistic start with the team's official announcement in the winter of 1950, ended with a giant thud by the fall of 1953. Many reasons were cited for the team's demise. Although the Cubs had won the 1945 National League pennant, by the 1950s the team was mired in the second division. During the four seasons that the Cubs oversaw their Springfield affiliate, Chicago finished in seventh place twice, fifth once, and eighth once in the eight-team National League. Without the necessary talent to stock a faltering major-league team, it became even more difficult to stock a Triple-A franchise, let alone two of them. Neither Triple-A team fared well, and the Springfield team did not always get the Cubs' best prospects.

During the Cubs' four years in Springfield, the team – as well as the International League as a whole – was dominated by Montreal, the top farm club of the Brooklyn Dodgers. Future Dodgers stars Junior Gilliam and Sandy Amoros made game appearances in Springfield during the 1952 and 1953 seasons. The Royals team also featured a lefty pitcher by the name of Tommy Lasorda, who loved to pitch at Pynchon Park. While later managing the Los Angeles Dodgers, Lasorda once remarked, "I loved that Springfield ballpark with its deep fences. If I could have pitched there all the time, I'd be in the Hall of Fame."[12]

In September 1953, Chicago placed the Springfield team up for sale. Roberto "Bobby" Maduro was the majority owner of the Havana Cubans and desired to have a major-league club in Cuba. He purchased the rights to the Springfield franchise and received permission to relocate the team to Cuba, with the new name of the Havana Sugar Kings. In 1954 the Red Sox were New England's lone professional baseball franchise. Baseball would be dormant in Springfield until 1957, when the Springfield Giants of the Eastern League became the final professional team to call Pynchon Park home. They lasted until 1965, when low attendance, once again a recurring theme, forced them to relocate to Waterbury, Connecticut. A year later, in 1966, Pynchon Park burned to the ground. Professional baseball has yet to return to Springfield.[13]

Edited by Marshall Adesman and fact-checked by Mark Richard.

NOTES

1 Walter Graham, "'Meet-the-Manager' Night at the Auditorium Here Results in Capacity Crowd to Welcome Stan Hack and Other Baseball Notables," *Springfield Daily News*, February 7, 1950: 22.

2 Graham.

3 Graham.

4 Lloyd Johnson and Miles Wolff, eds., *The Encyclopedia of Minor League Baseball* third ed. (Durham, North Carolina: Baseball America, Inc.), 2007.

5 Neil J. Sullivan, *The Minors: The Struggles and Triumph of Baseball's Poor Relation from 1876 to the Present* (New York: St. Martin's Press, 1990), 132-148; Ronald A. Mayer, *The 1937 Newark Bears: A Baseball Legend* (New Brunswick, New Jersey: Rutgers University Press, 1994), 10-18. See also, "Ruppert Acquires the Newark Club/Owner of Yankees Buys Block's Holdings Outright – Price Reported at $350,000," *New York Times*, November 13, 1931: 33. Information on the Newark Bears adapted from Robert Cvornyek, *Baseball in Newark* (Charleston, South Carolina: Arcadia Publishing, 2003), 31-32.

6 Sullivan, *The Minors*, 142-144; Mayer, *The 1937 Newark Bears*, 19-26.

7 James M. DiClerico and Barry J. Pavelec, *The Jersey Game: The History of Minor League Baseball From Its Birth to the Big Leagues in the Garden State* (New Brunswick, New Jersey: Rutgers University Press, 1991), 85-90. See also "Newark's Baseball History Has Been a Colorful One," *Newark Evening News*, January 13, 1950, located in the subject files of the New Jersey Reference Room in the Newark Public Library.

8 "Ellenstein, Newark, Offers Aid to Bears," *New York Times*, January 17, 1949: 25; "Newark Officials Plan Aid to Bears, *New York Times*, January 20, 1949: 40.

9 "Report Topping Set to Sell Newark Club," *New York Times*, November 11, 1948: 40; John Drebinger, "Yanks Drop 5 Minor League Teams as Club Reorganizes Farm Policy/Bombers to Aim for Greater Specialization in Developing Players – Will Operate School in Phoenix Under New Plan," *New York Times*, December 31, 1949: 11.

10 See also Roscoe McGowen, "Hartung, Lohrke in Giants Fold; Yankees Sell Newark Franchise/Cubs Will Place Team in Springfield, but Take No Bear Players ...," *New York Times*, January 13, 1950: 34.

11 The 1950 Official Scorecard, Springfield Cubs, Wood Museum of Springfield History, Springfield Museums, Springfield, Massachusetts.

12 "Stadium Fund Proposed: Cubs Ask Springfield to Spend $250,000 for Baseball Club," *New York Times*, January 6, 1950: 30.

13 Garry Brown, "When Pynchon Park Went Triple A: The 1950-1953 Springfield Cubs," masslive.com, April 15, 2018, https://www.masslive.com/sports/2018/04/when_pynchon_park_went_triple.html#:~:text=Local%20baseball%20fans%20greeted%20the,6%2C%20to%20the%20Buffalo%20Bisons.

NO MINOR MATTER: MID-CENTURY GREATNESS IN THE TAR HEEL STATE

By Bill Pruden

In the immediate aftermath of World War II, minor-league baseball enjoyed unprecedented popularity. The year 1949 marked its peak with the minors boasting 59 leagues and 448 teams.[1] Nowhere was this renaissance more evident than in North Carolina. Baseball has long been popular in North Carolina – only Texas has had more cities and towns that have hosted teams at one time or another. The period from 1946 to 1951 saw the popularity of minor-league baseball in the Tar Heel State reach an all-time high.[2] If a town did not boast a team, it wanted one and the number only grew. The 1946 season saw the state sporting 33 teams in six leagues. That number increased to 36 in 1947 and 44 in 1948, fueled by the creation of the Western Carolina League. There were 43 teams in 1949.[3] No less reflective of the game's health was the fact that attendance from 1947 to 1949 achieved levels that were not seen again until the 1980s, an especially impressive fact considering that from 1950 to 1980 the state's population grew by just under 45 percent, shooting up from 4,061,929 to 5,881,766.[4]

SABR: The Rucker Archive

Wilmer "Vinegar Bend" Mizell.

The state also boasted a healthy contingent of Black players who played in a strong semipro circuit, and although there were no formal Negro League teams in North Carolina, these semipro teams served as something of a minor-league system of their own for the Northern Negro League franchises.[5] Indeed, the popularity of baseball among the Black population was high and many towns of the times had both White and Black teams which, while strictly maintaining the segregation policies – both the legal and the customary – of the time, often shared the town's ballparks for their games.[6]

As impressive as these numbers are, minor-league baseball in North Carolina was not just about the interest or the level of activity. Minor-league baseball in North Carolina was about more than, as the saying goes, just showing up. It was also about showing off, if you will, and the resultant quality of North Carolina's minor-league baseball during this period was no less worthy of note. In fact, during this minor-league heyday, North Carolina was home to two teams, the 1950 Winston-Salem Cardinals and the 1951 Charlotte Hornets, whose performances earned them inclusion as numbers 61 and 36 respectively on the list of the "Top 100 Minor League teams of All-Time" that Minor League Baseball compiled and released in 2001 as part of the sport's centennial celebration.[7] For North Carolinians, the designations were a well-deserved pair of honors that recalled and recognized an important period in North Carolina sports history. It was an exciting time and while it didn't last, the memories of those teams and their accomplishments, occurring against the backdrop of major changes in both the game and American society, make them worthy of study and celebration. This is especially true at a time when the place of both baseball and the minor leagues within the American sports landscape were being scrutinized as never before.

The 1950 Winston-Salem Cardinals were a phenomenon that captured the hearts and imagination of the Piedmont community. In a region that had no major-league teams, the minors not only represented the connection to the big leagues, but they were also a central part of the community, a form of entertainment, but more than that, a shared experience. Indeed, it was no accident that in 1949 Winston Salem mayoral candidate Marshall Kurfrees included a winning team for the city among his campaign promises, for he understood the role the team played in the community. It resonated with the city's residents – and voters. Indeed, one commentator later said that the Cardinals' championship run in 1950 all but guaranteed the success of Kurfree's 1951 reelection effort.[8]

The group that did this was a distinctive, but at the same time representative, collection of baseball talent that came together as a team to produce one of the finest seasons in North Carolina baseball history. Termed "one of the more talented teams to ever play in the state" by author Chris Holaday, one of the most respected observers of the state's minor-league landscape, the 1950 Cardinals totally dominated the Carolina League, ultimately finishing 19 games ahead of second-place Danville while compiling a record of 106-47, amassing a win total that remains the Carolina League record.[9]

With player-manager George Kissell pledging at the outset that the Cardinals would be "the hustlingest and runningest ball club" in the league, they won eight of their first 10 games and were never headed.[10] And they won exactly as Kissell said they would, stealing four bases in their opener against Fayetteville, and pilfering a total of 16 in the first 10 games and 40 in their first 18.[11] No less telling was the fact that twice in the season's opening weeks hustling Cardinals baserunners scored from second base on infield outs.[12] A young energetic team, one whose average age was only 20, they continued that fervid pace, ending the month of May with a mark of 30-11.[13] But that was only the beginning as they would go on to achieve a record winning streak.

In the midst of the streak, in a colorful example of the relationship between the team and the city, as well as the spirit that infused the whole season, on June 14 almost 5,000 fans crowded into Southside Park to witness a pregame milking contest that included both players and managers from the Cardinals and the Raleigh Capitals. Cardinals pitching ace Wilmer "Vinegar Bend" Mizell won the contest and then went out to take a shutout and a 5-0 lead into the eighth inning. However, his milking effort apparently caught up to him and a tired Mizell gave up six runs – and the lead – in the inning. But in a way that marked the team's effort all season, Jim Neufeldt hit a two-run home run to save the day and keep the streak alive. That win, the Cardinals' 13th in a row, tied the 1948 record set by Burlington. The Cardinals won three more to extend the streak to 16 – still the league record – before they came up short on June 16, losing to the Durham Bulls.[14]

The Cardinals were so dominant that they engendered significant jealousy around the league. On a number of occasions, the team found itself on the receiving end of fan abuse. The most noteworthy incident came after a pitch by Burlington pitcher Al Cleary broke J.C. Dunn's arm: The Burlington crowd showered the defenseless Dunn with debris as he exited the field.[15] Meanwhile, there were reports that the Burlington team officials refused to either call a taxi or provide a car to take Dunn to a hospital, leaving the Cardinals to do so in the team bus.[16]

All of this was a product of some impressive baseball talent. Reflective of the Cardinals' depth of talent, only Lee Peterson's 21 wins topped any of the major statistical categories. Peterson's effort was only one of the many impressive pitching performances the Cardinals staff claimed. Beyond Peterson, the staff was anchored by future major leaguers – 19-year-old Mizell, who posted a record of 17-7 with 227 strikeouts and a 2.48 earned-run average, and relief ace Bobby Tiefenauer, who almost matched Mizell, with 16 wins against 8 losses.[17]

On the offensive side, the team, which led the league with 782 runs as well as 88 home runs, was led by player-manager and third baseman George Kissell, who hit .312. Supporting Kissell were outfielder Dunn, who joined the team in early May from Omaha in the Western League and hit .307; outfielder Russ Rac, whose .287 average was the leader among those with enough plate appearances to qualify for the batting title; and shortstop Jon Huesman, who stole 43 bases on his way to scoring 116 runs.[18] In addition, the team boasted a solid infielder, Earl Weaver, at second base. Only 19, Weaver hit .276 with 60 runs batted in and 57 runs scored in 127 games. That total was limited by a five-stitch spike wound, a midseason case of the flu, and, most debilitating, a broken thumb in August that sidelined him late in the season, although the feisty infielder returned in time for the postseason.[19] Such resilience was typical for a player who even in his teens was recognized for his leadership abilities and a knack for winning, a talent that was evident in a minor-league career that saw him on league champion teams for each of the 1948-1951 seasons.[20]

It was a singular collection of baseball talent, and, in the end nothing could stop the Cardinals from fulfilling their destiny. However, Carolina League regular-season champs often fell short when it came to the playoffs and for all of their regular-season dominance, the Cardinals were well aware of the fact that not since 1945 had the regular-season winner survived the gauntlet of the playoffs to emerge as Carolina League champions.[21] As the playoffs began, facing fourth-seeded Reidsville, the Cardinals seemed intent on burying the ghosts of the past and when they won the first two games, the mission seemed all but accomplished. However, they stumbled in Games Three and Four, but with Mizell on the mound for game five, they thrashed Reidsville 11-2 to take the series.[22]

They did not need such dramatics in the final series, dispatching Burlington – which had upset Danville in the other first-round match – in five games in the best-of-seven series. The first game was a nailbiter but the pitching that had been the team's hallmark all year was again exceptional, holding Burlington scoreless until first baseman Neal Hertweck hit the first pitch he saw over the right-field fence in the 13th inning to secure the win.[23] While they dropped Game Two, 6-2, the team quickly regrouped.[24] Then, showing their mettle, they won Game Three despite getting only four hits. One of them was Gene Barth's seventh-inning three-run home run that secured the 8-5 victory.[25]

On September 26 the Cardinals' season-long mission was completed as Mizell scattered eight hits while Weaver's bases-loaded single in the sixth inning provided the runs needed to bring the championship home to Winston-Salem. It also allowed the newly crowned Carolina League title holders to stake their claim to being the finest team ever to grace a North Carolina minor-league diamond.[26]

One of the competitors for that designation was the 1951 edition of the Charlotte Hornets. Coming just a year after the Cardinals' heroics, the performance of the Hornets as they cruised through the 1951 Tri-State League schedule was no less dominant than what the Cardinals had achieved in 1950. The Hornets won the regular-season crown in spectacular fashion, completing the year with a record of 100-40 while finishing 15 games ahead of second-place Asheville.[27] However, unlike the Cardinals, the Hornets were unable to continue the magic in the postseason, falling in stunningly unexpected fashion to fourth-place Spartanburg in the first round of the playoffs. It was a devasting finish to a season that had seemed charmed – one which, as it unfolded, had the makings of the kind of team that people would talk about for years to come.

Indications that it might prove to be a special season were there from the beginning. The team raced to a 16-4 start after 20 games, and while Asheville actually did them one better, opening with a 17-3 mark, the Hornets kept up their torrid pace. They reached first place on May 15 and never looked back, remaining in the top spot the rest of the season.[28]

Like the Cardinals, the Hornets were led by a player-manager – in this case, Cal Ermer. Ermer, who also manned second base, led by example (he batted .297) and through strength of character. He helped the club navigate the ups and downs of the long grind of the baseball season. Under Ermer's leadership, they continued to put distance between themselves and second-place Asheville, which finished 15 games behind the Hornets.[29] Indeed, given that record, as teams headed into the playoffs, the Hornets were riding high. As the top seed, they had earned the right to start at home, against Spartanburg, which had finished 27 games back of the regular-season champ.

But the Hornets quickly ran into trouble. In the opener, they lost a pitchers' duel, 2-1. While Spartanburg garnered only four hits, it picked up one run in the first when a triple by Al Neil drove in Al Smith, who had singled. Then in the fourth, they sealed things on Tex Dargie's home run.[30] The Hornets regrouped in Game Two, securing a 4-3 win in another close contest.[31] However, playing at Spartanburg, the Hornets lost a pair of one-run games. Game Three, a 9-8 heartbreaker for the Hornets, saw Spartanburg pitcher Don Van Nest take things into his own hands, hitting a game-winning eighth-inning home run.[32] Then in Game Four, with their backs to the wall, behind 4-0 entering the top of the ninth, the Hornets fought back valiantly, only to lose 5-4, a loss that brought their magical season to a crashing halt.[33]

Reflective of the feeling the team had inspired in the Charlotte community, in the immediate aftermath of the gut-wrenching series of one-run losses, fans organized an impromptu farewell dinner on the night after the final loss, stressing the team's accomplishments and not the deeply disappointing end. Manager Ermer spoke of each player. He highlighted his contribution, and each commentary summarized the ups and downs that characterized the season and minor-league baseball in general. It is a distinctive odyssey where every year young men, in pursuit of a dream, play their hearts out in the hope that one day they will make it to the big leagues.[34] As Ermer talked about the pitcher Suvern Wright "who wanted to win [the team's 100th] as much as any he ever pitched," or Dick Guyton ("the best center fielder in the league and I don't give a damn what they say about any all-star team"), or Buck Fleshman ("just 20 years old but he really did a job"), he was talking about the realities of minor-league baseball with its unique bonds.[35]

The fans' gesture and Ermer's remarks served as poignant reminders of the way minor-league baseball of that era was about more than just winning and losing, however important that was. It was also about a community connection; and this event represented a reaffirmation of the fans' appreciation. It also reflected their determination that an unfortunate upset in the season's final series would not be allowed to wipe away the rest of the season.

Further evidence of the bond that had been established between the team and its home city was the September 26 full-page advertisement appearing in the *Charlotte Observer*. Headlined "1951 Tri-State League Champions," the ad featured an aerial view of the ballpark and the playing field and below it were the words: "The Management, Officials, and Directors of the Charlotte Hornets Baseball Club Wish to Express Their Appreciation to the Club's Fans for Their Loyal Support During the 1951 Baseball Season."[36] In addition, soon after the season ended, Ermer was presented with a car from appreciative fans, further evidence of the chord the team had hit with the Charlotte community.[37]

In fact, the fans had it right. As disappointed as the team was, the early elimination could not wipe away an exceptional regular-season performance. Indeed, their domination of the Tri-State League was evident in virtually every major statistic. They led the league with a team batting average of .287; 940 runs (6.7 per game); 1,384 hits; 79 triples; 828 walks; and 819 RBIs. Reflective of the same keen eye that had garnered the league-high walk total, they also had the fewest strikeouts, 546. The Hornets' only real offensive deficiency was a lack of power as the team finished seventh in home runs with only 40.[38]

As much depth as these team offensive figures reflect, the Hornets also boasted the league's top individual offensive performer in Cuban outfielder Frank Campos. Campos crafted a .368 batting average – highlighted by a 27-game hitting streak that fell one short of the league mark. He had only 20 strikeouts in over 550 plate appearances. His average earned him the league's batting title and, combined with his 103 runs batted in, helped him earn the league's Most Valuable Player Award. He was the team's only player selected for the Tri-State League's all-star team. Indeed, that fact, to which Ermer alluded in his comment about center fielder Dick Guyton, had led team official Frank Howser to call the Tri-State League a "bush league," asserting that given the team's dominance, it was "an outright insult" that only one Hornet (as well as manager Ermer) had been chosen for the all-star team.[39]

All of this offense was complemented by a first-rate pitching staff, led by 20-game winner Levi "Buck" Fleshman, who posted a 20-9 record. He was ably backed up by Jerry Lane at 17-7, Bob Danielson with an 11-3 record, Mark Harley Grossman who posted a 10-2 mark, and Suvern Wright, who anchored the staff with an unblemished 7-0 record. And backing up the pitching staff was a defense that led the league in

SABR: The Rucker Archive

Bobby Tiefenauer.

SABR: The Rucker Archive

George Kissell.

fielding percentage.[40] While the season had not ended the way anyone associated with the Hornets wanted, the 1951 campaign nevertheless represented a historic achievement.

For most individual players, and even managers and coaches, the association with a minor-league team is usually short, often fleeting. The significance of a minor-league season is as often reflected in the subsequent careers for which they are part of the foundation as in their actual accomplishments. In many ways, their 1950 accomplishments notwithstanding, that was particularly true for the 1950 Winston Salem Cardinals, whose roster included a number of players who rose to greater prominence both in and out of baseball. Most prominent among the Cardinals alumni was Earl Weaver, whose time with the team, indeed, his whole minor-league career, was a precursor for his future Hall of Fame managing career. He never made it to the major leagues as a player, but his first managing assignment came in 1956 with the Knoxville Smokies. In 11 seasons as a minor-league manager, Weaver won three championships before he rose to the major leagues, moving from first-base coach to manager of the Baltimore Orioles in 1968. In 17 seasons, he led the team to six division titles, pennants in 1969, 1970, 1971, and 1979, and a World Series championship in 1970. He was inducted into the Baseball Hall of Fame in 1996.[41]

Meanwhile, for Weaver's teammate, manager, and mentor George Kissell, whose calm hand was so important in guiding the young Cardinals team to the championship, the 1950 season represented an early stage of what became a legendary career in the St. Louis Cardinals organization as a minor-league manager and coach.[42]

Also noteworthy were the future careers of Mizell and Tiefenauer. Both went on to substantive major-league careers, with Mizell pitching for nine seasons from 1952 to 1962 – he lost two seasons to military service. He compiled a career record of 90 wins and 88 losses with an ERA of 3.85. His best year was 1960, when a midseason trade landed him in Pittsburgh, where he was 13-5 for the pennant-winning Pirates. He made two appearances in the Pirates' World Series win, making the start in Game Three.[43] In addition, following his baseball career Mizell, who had settled in Midway, North Carolina, during the 1950 season, got involved in politics. He eventually won election to Congress in 1968. A Republican, he twice won reelection before being upset in 1974, a victim of the Watergate-fueled Democratic landslide.[44]

Meanwhile, Bobby Tiefenauer went on to spend at least parts of 10 seasons in the big leagues as a reliever. He played for six different teams during that span with his most successful year being 1964, when he recorded 13 saves for the Milwaukee Braves.[45]

While they did not boast the same level of later baseball accomplishments that the Cardinals did, some of the 1951 Charlotte Hornets took their careers to the next level. Star outfielder Frank Campos was not given much time to grieve the Hornets' playoff fate, as he was called up by the Washington Senators soon afterward. Hitting .423 in eight games, he would play for the team in 1952 and part of 1953, in a major-league career that consisted of 71 games.[46] Hornets catcher Bob Oldis had the longest major-league career of any team member, joining the Senators in 1953 and playing his final game with the Phillies in 1963, having spent time with the Pirates as well as back in the minors. Outfielder Bruce Barmes had a five-game major-league career as part of the 1953 Senators. Meanwhile, pitcher Jerald Lane's 31 total games with the 1953 Senators and 1954-1955 Cincinnati Reds led the pitching corps, while Harley Grossman and Diz Sutherland both had the proverbial "cup of coffee," each appearing in one major-league game.[47]

The two seasons enjoyed by the Winston-Salem Cardinals in 1950 and the Charlotte Hornets in 1951 not only represented the high-water mark of success and excellence in North Carolina minor-league baseball, but they came at the peak of the game's popularity in the Tar Heel State and in that way their place in the state's sports pantheon is even more secure. At the same time, those seasons in many ways represented the end of an era, for both of those seasons were played out against a rapidly changing racial backdrop in the United States. With Jackie Robinson having integrated the major leagues in 1947, joined in the ensuing years by the likes of Larry Doby, Roy Campanella, and others, the minor leagues would surely follow suit, and yet given the predominance of Southern teams in the minor leagues, it would not be easy. But it would come, changing the face of the game and the society it represented.[48] In the meantime, the fans of the Winston-Salem Cardinals and the Charlotte Hornets could revel in the memories of having witnessed some of the best baseball the North Carolina minor leagues had to offer.

This article was edited by Thomas Rathkamp and fact-checked by Ray Danner.

NOTES

1 David P. Kronheim, "Minor League Baseball, 2012, Attendance Analysis," Number Tamer, https://ballparkbiz.files.wordpress.com/2013/01/2012-minor-league-attendance-analysis.pdf.

2 Jim L. Sumner, "Baseball," in William S. Powell, ed., *Encyclopedia of North Carolina* (Chapel Hill: University of North Carolina Press, 2006), 94.

3 J. Chris Holaday, *Professional Baseball in North Carolina: An Illustrated City-by-City History, 1901-1996* (Jefferson, North Carolina: McFarland & Company, Inc., Publishers, 2006), 5.

4 Holaday, 5; Historical Population Change Data (1910–2020). Census.gov. United States Census Bureau; https://www.census.gov/data/tables/time-series/dec/popchange-data-text.html.

5 Gwendolyn Glenn, "Negro League Roots Found Deep in North Carolina History," WFAE, September 4, 2020; https://www.wfae.org/sports/2020-09-04/negro-league-roots-found-deep-in-north-carolina-history.

6 Holaday, 199.

7 Bill Weiss and Marshall Wright, *The 100 Greatest Minor League Baseball Teams of the 20th Century* (Denver: Outskirts Press, 2006).

8 "Campaign promises ..." North Carolina Collection, Forsyth County Public Library; https://northcarolinaroom.wordpress.com/2012/11/23/campaign-promises/. 1951 was the first of Murfree's five reelection victories as he served as Winston-Salem mayor from 1949 to 1961.

9 Holaday, 189; Weiss and Wright, 129.

10 Jim L. Sumner, *Separating the Men from the Boys: The First Half-Century of the Carolina League* (Winston-Salem, North Carolina: John F. Blair, Publisher, 1994), 36.

11 Sumner, *Separating the Men from the Boys*, 36; "Carolina League Sidelights," *Danville* (Virginia) *Bee*, May 18, 1950.

12 Sumner, *Separating the Men from the Boys*, 36.

13 Elton Casey, "Youthful Twins Run Durham Bulls Dizzy," *Durham* (North Carolina) *Sun*, May 10, 1950.

14 Sumner, *Separating the Men from the Boys*, 36.

15 Sumner, *Separating the Men from the Boys*, 37.

16 Sumner, *Separating the Men from the Boys*, 37.

17 Weiss and Wright, 129-130.

18 Weiss and Wright, 129-130.

19 Bill Kerch, "Stars in the Making," *St. Louis Globe-Democrat*, August 11, 1950.

20 "Cardinals Spring Lineup Had Stan Musial, Earl Weaver," RetroSimba: Cardinals History Beyond the Box Score, January 30, 2013, https://retrosimba.com/2013/01/30/cardinals-spring-lineup-had-stan-musial-earl-weaver/.

21 Sumner, *Separating the Men from the Boys*, 37.

22 Sumner, *Separating the Men from the Boys*, 38.

23 "Winston Cops Win in 13th," *Durham Morning Herald*, September 22, 1950.

24 "Burlington Bees Beat Winston-Salem, 6-2," *Raleigh* (North Carolina) *News and Observer*, September 23, 1950.

25 "Twin-City Takes Lead in Play-Off," *Durham Sun*, September 25, 1950.

26 "Winston Cops Play-Off Title," *Durham Sun*, September 27, 1950.

27 Weiss and Wright, 240.

28 Weiss and Wright, 238.

29 Weiss and Wright, 238.

30 "Champion Hornets Lose First Playoff Game," *Sumter* (South Carolina) *Daily Item*, September 6, 1951.

31 "Charlotte Even in Play-offs," *Rocky Mount* (North Carolina) *Telegram*, September 7, 1951.

32 "Peaches Beat Charlotte, 9-8," *Knoxville Journal*, September 8, 1951.

33 "Peaches Eke Hornets, 5-4," *Greenville* (South Carolina) *News*, September 9, 1951.

34 Eddie Allen, "Hornets Hit Peak With 100 Victories," *Charlotte* (North Carolina) *Observer*, September 26, 1951.

35 Allen, "Hornets Hit Peak With 100 Victories."

36 "1951 Tri-State League Champions," *Charlotte Observer*, September 26, 1951.

37 "Hornet Manager and Remembrance of 1951 Flag," *Charlotte Observer*, September 17, 1951.

38 Weiss and Wright, 238.

39 "Club Official Says Loop Is 'Bush League,'" *Macon* (Georgia) *News*, September 6, 1951; "Champion Hornets Lose First Playoff Game," *Sumter* (South Carolina) *Daily Item*, September 6, 1951.

40 Weiss and Wright, 238.

41 Warren Corbett, "Earl Weaver," SABR BioProject, https://sabr.org/bioproj/person/earl-weaver/.

42 Warren Corbett, "George Kissell," SABR BioProject, https://sabr.org/bioproj/person/george-kissell/.

43 "Vinegar Bend Mizell," Baseball Reference, https://www.baseball-reference.com/players/m/mizelvi01.shtml; "1960 World Series," Baseball Reference, https://www.baseball-reference.com/postseason/1960_WS.shtml.

44 Bart Barnes, "Wilmer D. 'Vinegar Bend' Mizell Dies at 68," *Washington Post*, February 24, 1999.

45 "Bobby Tiefenauer," Baseball Reference, https://www.baseball-reference.com/players/t/tiefebo01.shtml.

46 "Frank Campos," Baseball Reference, https://www.baseball-reference.com/players/c/campofr01.shtml.

47 Weiss and Wright, 239-240.

48 Bruce Adelson, *Brushing Back Jim Crow: The Integration of Minor-League Baseball in the American South* (Charlottesville: University Press of Virginia, 1999).

THE 1950 QUÉBEC BRAVES

By Martin Lacoste

On September 20, 2002, the Los Angeles Dodgers played a doubleheader against the Arizona Diamondbacks and scored five runs in the eighth inning to come back and take game one 6-5. This gave the Dodgers a season record of 103-44, a .700 winning percentage (briefly, as they lost game two), a feat rarely accomplished in Organized Baseball. Over a full season (minimum 120 games), a .700 winning percentage had been achieved only three times in the major leagues since 1950. From the list of the *100 Best Minor League Baseball Teams* as selected by historians Bill Weiss and Marshall Wright in 2001, only 12 teams since 1950 achieved this feat. The ninth-best record takes us north of the US border to a perennially last-place team that in very short order built a dominant championship squad. Here is the story of the 1950 Québec Braves.

PROLOGUE

The Canadian-American League (also referred to as the Can-Am League) was a Class-C league that ran from 1936 to 1951, minus a hiatus in 1943-45 because of World War II. The Québec Athletics ("Les Athlétiques") joined the Can-Am League in 1941 from the Provincial League, and in their first two seasons never rose above sixth place (of eight teams). After the war, the team, renamed the Alouettes, languished at the bottom of the standings for three years. In 1947, the Alouettes won less than a third of their games and finished a dismal 40½ games behind the league leaders. In 1948, though slightly improved, they finished with a lowly .406 winning percentage. Despite this, they remained a popular team throughout, ranking in the top three in the league in attendance each year. Fans were about to be rewarded for their unfailing support.

The 1949 season proved to be a dramatic turnaround for the team. Rebranded the Braves (much like Alouettes, another conveniently bilingual nickname), they began to operate independently, as their former agreement with the New York Giants was seen as less than beneficial: "There is no doubt that the Giants' management had been less than generous in directing talent toward their Québec affiliate," wrote a SABR researcher.[1] As an independent team, the Braves were free to sign veteran players, many of whom brought experience of playing at higher levels (or the majors). These signings raised the average age of the players substantially (at 27.3, four years above the league average), but this experience, along with a new manager in former major-league All-Star Frank McCormick, helped Québec to finish first after regular-season play with a stellar record of 90-48, 14½ games ahead of the second-place Oneonta (New York) Red Sox. Fan support was also at an all-time high: Fan support was also at an all-time high: The team led the league in attendance and almost tripled the attendance of Oneonta, whom they swept in the playoff finals.

THE PLAYERS

An eventful offseason leading up to 1950 appeared to thwart a possible a championship repeat, starting with the announcement that the team was being sold to a new owner/president, Dr. Joseph A. Bellemarre.[2] At virtually the same time, it became evident that the manager who led them to their first Can-Am championship, Frank McCormick, would likely not be returning. On January 20 it was confirmed that another former major-league All-Star, most recently with the Yankees, George McQuinn, would helm the Québec Braves for the 1950 season.

Despite the managerial change, it is likely that the similarities between McCormick and McQuinn effected a smooth transition. Neither had had managerial experience before their tenure with Québec but were both All-Star first basemen with strikingly similar major-league experience. (McCormick played in 1,534 major-league games, hit 128 home runs, and was named an All-Star nine times; McQuinn played in 1,550 games, hit 135 home runs, and was an All-Star seven times.) Each also won a World Series ring, McCormick with Cincinnati in 1940 and McQuinn with the Yankees in 1947, and both were player-managers. Though McQuinn was 39 when he started with Québec (McCormick was 37), he had more impact at the plate. (McCormick batted .143 in only 21 at-bats while McQuinn hit .318 over 242 at-bats.) McQuinn would stay on to manage Québec until 1954, then managed teams in Atlanta, Boise, and finally Topeka in 1958. He then returned "closer to his [Arlington, Virginia] home and became a scout for the Washington Senators"[3] and "later scouted for the Montreal Expos before retiring from baseball in 1971 after 42 years in the game."[4]

The 1950 season was heavily shaped by the previous season, and by the fact that a good number of the players from 1949 (14 of 24, including many of their regulars) returned to the Braves. The 1950 club was still independent and again was the oldest team in the league (average age 26.5, well above the league average of 22.8).

The 1949 Québec Braves pitching staff allowed the fewest runs in the league, and their top four starters, who had combined for a record of 65 wins and 36 losses, all returned to Québec for 1950. No starting pitcher on the Braves had an ERA above 4.00, which contributed in no small part to their outstanding season. The pitching staff for 1950 consisted of:

Albert Fred Belinsky	From Norwalk, Connecticut, Belinsky had been with Québec in 1948, but with minimal run support, registered only six wins. In 1949 he almost doubled his win total, finishing 11-9, but he reached his peak in 1950, doubling his win total yet again, leading the team (and league) with 22 wins. He joined his teammate Hal Erickson as two of only four Can-Am pitchers who finished with an ERA under 3.00, sneaking in with 2.99. He would play briefly with Hartford of the Eastern League in 1951 before joining the US Army.
Alexander Danelishen	Cleveland-born, he played Class-A and Double-A ball before joining Québec in 1949, when he pitched to an 18-12 record. He virtually equaled this in 1950 at 18-11 and remained with the team the following year and played a few more seasons in the Provincial League.
Harold James Erickson	The senior member of the Québec pitching rotation, Hal Erickson had pitched for several minor-league teams, notably the Triple-A International League Syracuse Chiefs, before signing with Québec in 1949. Much like Danelishen, his 1949 and 1950 campaigns were virtually identical, though he was the only pitcher to win 20 games for the Braves in both seasons (21-6 and 20-7). He led the league in ERA (by a substantial margin – 2.40 compared with 2.81 by Oneonta's John Gilbert, who had the second best mark) and strikeouts (205). He was traded before 1951 to the Cleveland Indians organization and enjoyed another 20-game season with Cleveland's Double-A Dallas Eagles in 1952. This caught the attention of the Detroit Tigers, who traded for him in the offseason and promoted him to the major-league team in 1953 as a 33-year-old rookie. He pitched in only 18 games before being sent down to Triple A.
John Nansteel	The only left-handed pitcher on the team, Pennsylvania-born Nansteel played with Peekskill of the North Atlantic League before joining Québec in 1949 and went 15-9. He too enjoyed a similar campaign in 1950, finishing with a 13-8 record. He played the following season with Trois-Rivières of the Provincial League.
Younger/ Ambrose/ Meau	The 1950 Braves pitching staff was rounded out by these three. Two of them, Bud Younger and John Ambrose, functioned as fifth starters when needed, while Alfred Meau was their primary relief pitcher. Younger had pitched with Québec in 1948 and had "proven his value with the Alouettes"[5] by leading the team in ERA that year. "It was no secret to anyone that, since his departure from Québec, Younger had only one wish, to return to the old capital,"[6] and so he and the Braves were equally content with the reunion, though he did ask, for personal reasons, to report to the team at the end of May. The addition of Younger might have prompted the reliever Meau to believe his playing time would become more sporadic and led to his decision to leave the club on June 12 to spend more time with his family. Younger meanwhile finished with a 10-5 record, while John Ambrose finished 9-2.

In terms of position players, here too we see a preponderance of players returning from the 1949 squad.

First Base	George McQuinn & Vernon Shetler	For the first few months of 1950, first base was shared between player-manager McQuinn and Vernon "Moose" Shetler. Despite being named league MVP in 1949 after leading the league with 133 RBIs and amassing 64 RBIs in 55 games to start the 1950 season, the veteran Shetler was released by the Braves on July 12, only to be picked up within a few days by Auburn of the Border League. Upon Shetler's release, McQuinn became the regular first baseman, and finished the season with a .318 batting average, second highest on the team.
Second Base	Wally Williams & Mike Fandozzi	Second base was also shared between primarily two players whose skills complemented each other nicely. While Chicago-born Wally Williams, one of two Black players on the team, was an exceptional hitter who batted .314 with 54 RBIs, Mike Fandozzi was the superior fielder, with a .971 fielding average (compared to Williams's .929 average). Williams was signed as a 19-year-old by the Boston Braves while on tour as a saxophonist with a professional jazz band and stayed on with Québec in 1951. Fandozzi meanwhile became a local fan favorite who manned second base with Québec through 1955. He continued to play in the minor leagues at various levels up to Triple A until 1966.
Shortstop	Edward Hamel	Williams and Fandozzi also took turns playing shortstop when the regular shortstop, Edward Hamel, was not available. Hamel, too, had been on the 1949 Québec squad and batted a respectable .286 with Québec in 1950.
Third Base	William Sinram	The infield was anchored by the sure-handed third baseman William Sinram, from Long Island, New York, who also had been with Québec in 1949. Among regular third basemen, he led the league in fielding percentage, though his season was cut short by season-ending surgery in early September.
Left Field	Garland Lawing	In left field, Garland "Butch" Lawing had cups of coffee with Cincinnati and the New York Giants in 1946, amounting to a total of only 15 at-bats in 10 games, but had great success in the minor leagues. After batting .379 with Ogdensburg of the Border League in 1948, he led the Can-Am League in 1949 in runs scored, doubles, walks, and slugging percentage, and came in second in batting average (.342) to his teammate Pete Elko. In 1950 Lawing again led the league in doubles and walks, but most notably won the Triple Crown (.346, 19 home runs, 141 RBIs). This earned him the league MVP, the second consecutive year the honor went to a Québec player (Shetler in 1949). Lawing moved on to West Palm Beach in the Florida International League for a few seasons, but never again reached the level he attained while with Québec.

Center Field	Louis Palmisiano	Playing in all but four games for Québec, the most reliable position player was the diminutive but scrappy center fielder Louis Palmisiano. At 5-feet-7, he was among the shortest players in the league, but his productivity and versatility enabled him to be a regular fixture in the Braves lineup. He spent several seasons in the Cleveland organization as a pitcher and pitched in a few games while with Québec in 1949, but by 1950 had fully converted to playing center field. He finished the season with a solid .304 batting average and led the league in runs scored with 130.
Right Field	Pete Elko & John Werner	Rounding out the outfield for the first half of the season was the hard-hitting Pete Elko, already mentioned as the league's leader in batting average the year before at .348. The veteran Elko had had brief stints with the Chicago Cubs in 1943 and 1944, but much like Lawing, his greatest success was achieved in the minor leagues. He continued to hit well in 1950 (.305 with Québec) and was the Braves' regular right fielder until he was sold to one of their rivals, the Rome (New York) Colonels, in the middle of a doubleheader on June 11. Elko's departure allowed part-time catcher and first baseman John Werner to take his place in right field, and he proved a capable replacement, finishing second on the team with 15 home runs and hitting a very respectable .286. The Philadelphia native spent three more seasons with Québec.
Catcher	Charles Alltop & William Kivett	Indianapolis-born Charles Alltop had been the Braves' most dependable catcher in 1949, and he continued to be among the best-fielding catchers in the league in 1950, while hitting a decent .254 and driving in 57 runs. He left in late August to join the Army, at which point the Braves picked up the light-hitting William Everett "Bernie" Kivett, recently released by Ottawa of the Border League, who remained behind the plate from August 18 until the end of the season. Though he did not fare too well at the plate, batting only .185, Kivett was as solid defensively as Alltop, both with .981 fielding percentages. John Werner also spent 28 games behind the plate for the Braves.

Four other players appeared briefly on the 1950 Québec roster, but their distinct and intriguing stories are each worth noting.

Robert Adamson	Robert Adamson, only four years after Jackie Robinson's debut in 1946 down the road in Montreal, was the second Black player to play for the Braves, playing sporadically in the outfield in 1950.
Thomas Ambrose	Thomas Ambrose was brought in as a (very) late-season substitute (and potential emergency reserve for the playoffs if needed) at second base for the Braves. The older brother of pitcher John Ambrose, he appeared in the final four games of the regular season before giving way to regular Wally Williams for the playoffs, which avoided a minor controversy as the Oneonta Red Sox vehemently opposed his potential appearance in the playoffs.[7]
Joseph Galioto	Only two players were present in Québec's rise from worst to first from 1948 to 1950 – one was Albert Belinsky; the other was Joseph Galioto. Used sparingly as a pitcher in 1948 and 1949, he was used even less in 1950, as he was brought in as a pinch-runner in the ninth inning on Opening Day for the pinch-hitter Shetler. Not only did he not score, but he never again appeared in a game with the Braves, which ignominiously left his final season statistics as simply one game played. The papers mentioned in the middle of May that he simply "disappeared."
Jean-Louis Leclair	Lastly, perhaps a yet more intriguing addition to the club arrived on August 4 during a doubleheader against the Schenectady Blue Jays, when the Braves invited local sports star Jean-Louis "Jackie" Leclair to try out with the team as a catcher. His debut was to be the day before, but the game was rained out after only half an inning. But with almost 2,500 fans in attendance despite the weather, and Leclair impressing McQuinn enough in the short outing, he was slated to catch the first game of the doubleheader. The "catch" is that Leclair was better-known to fans as a hockey star, born in Québec City, and who played in several minor Québec hockey leagues, most recently with Québec in 1948, and with Ottawa in 1949-1950, while also playing amateur baseball for Levis. The Braves' interest in him may have been in part publicity stunt, part out of necessity, with the team down a catcher with Alltop needing to rest because of a strained shoulder muscle. Though it was intended Leclair would play only the first game, between getting a hit in his first at-bat and adding a sacrifice later in the game, and committing no errors behind the plate, he was put in to catch in place of Werner for game two. This was also helped by the fact that he is said to have been "the focus of one of the best attendance numbers"[9] of the season (in fact, the highest attendance figure for the entire second half of the season, including the playoffs). Leclair's appearance almost seemed to eclipse the fact that his batterymate, Bud Younger, pitched a no-hitter in game one (and Erickson allowed only three hits in the nightcap). He was slated to catch two days later against Amsterdam, but Werner ended up behind the plate, with no mention of why Leclair was not present, or why Leclair never returned behind the plate for Québec. But by playing the doubleheader, he became the only local player, let alone Canadian, to play on the Braves in 1950. His hockey career continued to blossom, and he reached the NHL for three seasons (1954-55 to 1956-57) with the Montreal Canadiens, and his name can be found on the Stanley Cup as part of the winning 1955-56 Canadiens team.

THE 1950 SEASON

With an even more impressive roster than the year before, there was a good degree of confidence in the team repeating its success from 1949. April 26 was opening day for the 1950 Can-Am League, and Québec started off the season with a 5-3 road loss to the Rome Colonels. But they wasted no time racking up wins as they took the next four games, starting with a 20-4 drubbing of Pittsfield (Massachusetts). The Braves finished the month of May in a tie for first place with Schenectady with a record of 24-9.

June witnessed several stellar pitching performances by their elite pitching staff, including a one-hitter by Belinsky on June 5 against Schenectady, a two-hitter by Younger on June 7 vs. Amsterdam (aided by six RBIs by Shetler), and a two-hit shutout against Schenectady, again by Belinsky, on June 20. The worst pitching performance to this point in the season occurred on June 8, when three pitchers allowed 12 runs to Amsterdam. But even this did not result in a loss, as the offense came through with a season-high 24 runs, led by Butch Lawing who went 5-for-5 with seven RBIs (he drove in this same amount on July 23 against Gloversville-Johnstown (New York)). The otherwise dominant pitching contributed to a 28-6 June record, and by the Canada Day holiday on July 1, Québec had pulled 4½ games ahead of Schenectady with an impressive 52-15 record.

July featured two more stellar pitching performances by Belinsky – a 2-1 one-hit win on July 16 vs. Rome and, in his next start four days later, a no-hitter against Pittsfield. The Braves continued to pull further ahead of the rest of the league in July, ending the month with a record of 72-23, 10½ games ahead of the Schenectady Blue Jays.

The Braves started the month of August going 5-1, highlighted by the no-hitter by Younger on August 4, and grand slams on consecutive days by Lawing and Werner on August 5 and 6. But the rest of the month was less than spectacular, as personnel changes destabilized the lineup and the team was likely stretched due to nine doubleheaders, including four in a row, many of which were the result of games being rained out. A season-high five-game losing streak contributed to a mediocre August record and allowed Schenectady to pull to within four games as of September 1. But a six-game winning streak (all against the Trois-Rivières Royals) and a strong 9-1 finish to end the season resulted in a final regular-season record of 97-40, fully 7½ games ahead of second-place Schenectady.

At the close of the regular season, in addition to the individual accomplishments of players like Lawing, Erickson, and Belinsky, the Braves as a team led the league in batting average (.280), runs scored (899), and walks (1,009, not far from their hit total of 1,242), averaging over seven walks per game. The pitching staff also allowed the fewest runs per nine innings (4.23), which, combined with their offensive strength, positioned the Braves as the favorites heading into the playoffs.

THE PLAYOFFS

The Braves began the Can-Am Championship playoffs with a best-of-seven semifinal against the third-place Oneonta Red Sox. After a commanding 9-2 victory in the opening game on September 12, a double by right fielder John Werner in the bottom of the ninth to score Lawing gave the Braves a walk-off victory, and a 2-0 series lead. In game three on September 16 (after the game was rained out the previous day), the Braves and Red Sox were tied 2-2 after six innings, but the Braves' eight-run seventh inning broke the game open and resulted in a 10-4 win. Facing elimination, the Red Sox scored a run in the bottom of the eighth inning of game five to break a 4-4 tie and avoid being swept.

The Braves hoped to clinch the series on September 18 and came out strong in the first inning with five runs. But Oneonta fought back and took a sizable 11-6 lead after five innings. Alex Danelishen was the third pitcher for the Braves, and he shut down the Red Sox for the next three innings. He also went 3-for-3 at the plate to help the Braves claw back and tie the game, 11-11, after eight innings. In the ninth inning, Danelishen's fourth hit of the day brought in the second run of the frame, and he kept the Red Sox scoreless in the bottom of the ninth to secure the victory and the series.

Meanwhile, in the other semifinal series, the fourth-place Amsterdam Rugmakers upset the Schenectady Blue Jays by defeating them 11-7 for a 4-2 series win. The Braves then faced the Rugmakers for the Can-Am Championship.

In the series opener, Albert Belinsky scattered seven hits, while the Braves scored seven runs in the first inning and were led by the light-hitting catcher Kivett and shortstop Hamel who each had three hits and three RBIs. Butch Lawing also hit the only home run of the finals to seal the 15-7 home victory.

The second game started off much like the first, with the Braves taking advantage of five walks by Rugmakers pitcher Wally Burnette and an error to score three runs. Lawing drove in Williams in the second inning with a single to increase the lead to 4-0. Meanwhile, Braves starter Hal Erickson had a no-hitter after six innings, but Amsterdam rallied to score one in the seventh and two in the eighth to make the score 4-3. Still in the eighth, the game now on the line, Rugmakers' standout catcher (and future major-league All-Star) Gus Triandos came up with the bases loaded with two outs. But Erickson induced Triandos to hit a roller to Fandozzi to end the rally, and the Braves held on, despite getting only four base hits, with a 4-3 victory to take a 2-0 series lead.

The series moved to Amsterdam, and game three turned out to be a lopsided victory for the Braves, as they pounded out 15 hits and Danelishen scattered five hits to defeat the Rugmakers 9-2.

In game four, in front of a dejected Amsterdam crowd of 304, Québec took an early 5-0 lead after three innings. After a good start, Braves pitcher Nansteel was chased to the showers after allowing two runs in the fourth inning, but Bud Younger came in and threw 5⅓ shutout innings to secure the win and complete the sweep with a decisive 6-2 win. The hitting standout of the series proved to be, surprisingly, catcher Bill Kivett, who added three more hits to finish the playoffs with a .571 batting average and five RBIs and was instrumental in helping the Braves secure their second consecutive Arthur E. Ford Trophy for winning the Can-Am Championship for 1950.

EPILOGUE

Québec remained a highly successful draw in 1950, with a total attendance of 123,352, almost triple the average of the other Can-Am teams (47,111). But despite their success on the field and at the gate, the return of the Provincial League to the National Association after "yet another fling as an 'outlaw' loop"[10] proved too tempting. Québec and Trois-Rivières decided to "rejoin their countrymen"[11] and transferred out of the Canadian-American League. This had the added benefit of dramatically decreasing travel time for the teams that remained. Despite this, the Can-Am League sputtered along in 1951 as a six-team league, but without its largest draw, and with growing competition from radio and television broadcasts, league attendance dropped by 60 percent. Every team lost money, and the Can-Am League ceased operations after the 1951 season.

The Braves meanwhile finished fourth in the 1951 Provincial League, with a more moderate record of 65-58, but returned to their winning ways and won the league championship the next four years, until the Provincial League like many minor leagues in the 1950s, succumbed, folding after the 1955 season.

This article was edited by David Siegel and fact-checked by Kevin Larkin.

SOURCES

In addition to the sources cited in the Notes, the author consulted Baseball-Reference.com.

Weiss, Bill and Marshall Wright. "100 Best Minor League Baseball Teams," the Official Site of Minor League Baseball, https://secure.milb.com/milb/history/top100.jsp.

Québec newspapers are available online at Bibliothèque et Archives Nationales du Québec (https://numerique.banq.qc.ca/).

NOTES

1 Daniel Papillon, "The Québec Braves: A Baseball Dynasty," *Dominionball* (Cleveland: Society for American Baseball Research, 2005), 114.

2 "La Franchise des Braves de Québec au Dr J.-A. Bellemarre," *Le Soleil* (Québec), December 30, 1949: 18.

3 C. Paul Rogers III, "George McQuinn," SABR Baseball Biography Project, https://sabr.org/bioproj/person/George-McQuinn/, accessed September 6, 2022.

4 Rogers.

5 "Younger a signé pour les Braves," *Le Soleil*, March 18, 1950: 21.

6 "Younger a signé pour les Braves."

7 "Oneonta s'oppose à la présence du joueur d'intérieur: Thomas Ambrose," *Le Nouvelliste*, September 8, 1950: 10. Because he played in only four games, he is often not shown in official records.

8 "Pichenettes," *Le Soleil*, May 19, 1950: 32.

9 "Partie sans point ni coup sûr," *L'Action Catholique*, August 5, 1950: 12.

10 Daniel Pietrusza, *Baseball's Canadian-American League* (Jefferson, North Carolina: McFarland & Co, Inc., 1990), 185.

11 Pietrusza, 85.

LIFE IN THE BUSH LEAGUES OF BASEBALL'S PAST

By Norman L. Macht

Cal Ripken Jr. has said, "I had the most fun in baseball in my first year in the minor leagues than at any other time in baseball. Once you get to the major leagues, it's more of a business." In my more than 50 years interviewing ballplayers, I often started by asking about those early years. I never met Goldie Holt, but I heard his story from several players.

GOLDIE HOLT

Goldie Holt, who racked up more bus miles as a minor-league player and manager between 1925 and 1958 than an astronaut's mileage log on a trip to the moon, was managing in Ponca City, Oklahoma, in the Western Association in 1938. The team traveled in an antiquated bus with straw seats, and the players often had to get out and push it. One night it died – again – and they pushed it to the side of the road.

Holt had had enough. "We'll fix this once and for all," he said. "Get all the stuff out of the bus."

The players emptied the bus, then drained gasoline from the fuel tank and poured it all over the bus. Holt lit a match.

Just then a Greyhound bus came along. The driver saw the fire and slammed on his brakes. He leaped out with a fire extinguisher, put out the fire and saved the bus.

As soon as he got back in his Greyhound and drove away, the determined Holt lit it again.

They got a new bus.

JIMMY WILLIAMS

Only a true baseball lifer could enjoy a 40-year career – all but the last seven of them in the minor leagues -- and finish with a smile, a million stories, and not a bit of regret over what might have been. Jimmy Williams played in over 2,000 games at every level from Class D to Triple A before finishing his career as a coach for the Baltimore Orioles from 1981-1987, earning a prize that eluded a lot of big-league Hall of Famers: a World Series ring. He shared his stories with us during several visits at his home in Baltimore.

To comprehend what follows, one needs to understand the chain-gang system that once prevailed in baseball. It was created by Branch Rickey when he presided over the St. Louis Cardinals in the mid-1920s and installed in Brooklyn when he moved there in 1943. Jimmy Williams batted .288 in 18 years in the Dodgers' system, and never swung a bat in the major leagues. His contract was sold from one Dodgers affiliate to another. There was no escape.

But the affable Williams never complained as he traversed the Dodgers' gulags from Kingston in the North Atlantic League to Montreal (International

SABR: The Rucker Archive.

Monte Weaver.

League), making 15 stops in all. Most of those years he played at Double-A Mobile and Atlanta and Triple-A Montreal, where life was good and the salaries were better than some big-leaguers earned. Remember, this was a time when only the stars – Joe DiMaggio, Ted Williams, Mickey Mantle, Stan Musial – strode in the thin air of the $100,000 stratosphere. Like most minor-league nomads, Jimmy Williams held other jobs during the winters; for 37 years he never lived and worked a full year in the same town.

Jimmy spent most of his rookie season at Sheboygan in the Wisconsin State League. When the train pulled into the station, he was a third baseman. But when he walked out of the depot, he became an outfielder.

"It was 5:30 in the morning when I got there, too early to call the general manager, so I sat down to wait and got to talking to a guy sweeping out the station. He saw my bag and asked if I was coming to join the Indians and I said yeah.

"He said, 'What position do you play?'

"I told him third base. 'Oh,' he says, 'we got the best third baseman in the league.'

"I said, 'What about short?'

"He says, 'Our shortstop looks like he's going to be rookie of the year. He can really pick it.'

"I said, 'What about second?'

"'Oh, that's Tommy Bartose. He's been with us for years and, besides, he drives the bus.'

"So I'm sitting there thinking all this over and then it's time to call the GM and he comes and gets me and takes me around town and we go to meet the manager, Joe Hauser, who says to me, 'What position do you play?'

"I said, 'What do you need?'

"'A left fielder,' he says.

"'I play left field,' I said.

"And that's how I became an outfielder."

Like many players, Williams remembers his rookie year at Sheboygan with special fondness. He batted .385 with 105 RBIs in 86 games. And he was named Rookie of the Year, not the shortstop.

"We ran away with the pennant. But what stands out most is the bus rides, talking baseball for hours. At night after a road game, we'd pass through these small towns in Wisconsin, and the manager Hauser, would say, 'Let's let them know we're going through their town.' So no matter how late it was, we all sang 'Take Me Out to the Ball Game' every time we rode through a town."

Hauser, the home-run king of the minors, who hit 63 for Baltimore in 1930 and 69 in 1933 for Minneapolis, taught Williams a batting lesson he never forgot. "Joe was 48 then, a left-handed batter. He'd grab a new bat and tell us, 'This is what hitting is all about. I'm going to hit the ball to left field.' Ping. He'd hit it to left. Didn't matter where the pitcher threw it. Then he'd say, 'I'm going to hit it to center,' and he did. Then he'd point to right and hit one there. 'You hit for power this way,' he demonstrated, and hit one over the fence.

"Then he'd show us the bat. There was one mark on it the size of the ball. He had hit every one on the sweet spot of the bat. 'That's the secret of hitting,' he said. That, and hitting the ball out in front of the plate, is all the secret to hitting I ever found."

After his playing days, Williams managed in the minors for 17 years, beginning at Santa Barbara (Class A, California League) in 1963. He worked at every level except rookie leagues in the Dodgers, Kansas City A's, Houston, and Baltimore organizations, winning four pennants. He was a strict disciplinarian, making rules and sticking to them. "If I said the bus leaves at 2, we left at 2, and if some guy came running up two minutes later, he was out of luck."

But he also knew the value of a few cases of beer in the clubhouse after a game to keep the players together talking baseball instead of dressing quickly and scattering. He taught as much from the manager's traditional seat by the door on the all-night bus rides as he did on the field. But he never hankered to be a big-league manager.

"Sparky Anderson is younger than I am, but he sure doesn't look it," he said in explanation.

MEL PARNELL

Mel Parnell was the winningest southpaw in Boston Red Sox history, 123-75 over 11 years beginning in 1947.

"I broke in at Centreville, Maryland, in the Class D Eastern Shore League. It was a friendly town. Everybody knew everybody. We stayed at a boarding house. A local hardware man ran the club. We had a horse to cut the grass. No road trips. We rode the bus home at night after every away game, had a ball holding amateur contests where everybody got up and took a turn doing something, maybe stop and raid a watermelon patch on the way. We were all young. No family responsibilities. Those minor-league days were the most fun I ever had in baseball. Once you get up to the major leagues, it becomes more businesslike."

ARTHUR RHODES

Left-handed pitcher Arthur Rhodes pitched for nine teams over his 20-year career, the last 15 primarily as a middle reliever against left-handed batters. Rhodes threw his first professional pitch at 3 o'clock in the morning for the Class D Bluefield Orioles (Appalachian League) in 1988.

"I was just out of high school in Waco, Texas, signed a contract and headed for Class D Bluefield in West Virginia. I just had time to find a place to live and the next day we got on a bus to go to Burlington, North Carolina, for two games. I hadn't even thrown on the side. I was on a pitch limit because I had thrown so much in high school. I was in the dugout until the seventh inning, then went out to the bullpen."

The game was tied 2-2 after nine innings, and it went on and on.

"I had nothing to eat during the game, just tried to drink a lot of water, eat sunflower seeds, chew bubble gum. It got midnight.

"Then it was 3:00 A.M., and I was the last pitcher in the bullpen. I had to get up and start throwing and then I was wide awake, raring to go. I wanted to throw so bad I didn't mind going out there at 3:00 A.M. I pitched the 26th. We scored a run in the 27th and I got three outs to end the game. It was my first pro game and first pro win.

The game time was 8 hours and 15 minutes, the longest continuous game in history. Bluefield coach Frank Klebe recalled, "We had to get on the bus to go home, a 3½-hour ride. There was nothing open anywhere to get something to eat. We stopped at an all-night gas station on the way and cleaned out whatever snacks and crackers they had."

MONTE WEAVER

Monte Weaver was a right-handed pitcher for Washington 1931-1938 and the Red Sox in 1939. He was the losing pitcher in an 11-inning 2-1 loss to Carl Hubbell and the New York Giants in Game Four of the 1933 World Series.

"I was working on a master's degree in mathematics at the University of Virginia and teaching when Dr. Booker, a surgeon who owned the Durham club in the Class C Piedmont League, offered me a $500 bonus, $275 a month, and 25 percent of any sale price in 1928.

"Our manager was George "Possum" Whitted, who had been on the 1914 Miracle Braves. He was also the first baseman, bill payer, and groundskeeper. We had a skin infield and every morning he attached a scraper to the back of his Ford roadster and scraped the infield. The ballpark was next to a tobacco warehouse. The smell was so strong it almost made me sick. I tried chewing once, but that was enough.

"One day I was pitching and the batter hit a line drive that split my chin wide open. I went down and Whitted came running over. My chin was bleeding profusely and all he said to me was, 'Don't get blood on your uniform.' The laundry bill was the first thing on his mind. There was a doctor in the stands and he dragged me out to his car and put some metal clips on the cut until I could get to a hospital. I was back pitching three days later, stitches and all.

DON ZIMMER

Infielder Don Zimmer was a baseball lifer; 12 years as a player (1954-1965), four of them with Brooklyn and two with the Los Angeles Dodgers; 12 years as a manager for the San Diego Padres, Boston Red Sox, Texas Rangers, and Chicago Cubs; and 25 years as a coach, the last 11 for the New York Yankees (1996-2006).

"I signed with the Dodgers right after graduation from high school in Cincinnati in June 1949. I got on a train and went to Cambridge, Maryland, in the Eastern Shore League. Class D. They had told me to go to the hotel in town, an old white building. The first thing I always did, from that day on, whenever I went into a town, I went to the local newspaper office and had the paper sent to my father.

"I called the ballpark. The general manager said, 'Where are you?'

"'I'm at the hotel.'

"'Be out in front and I'll pick you up in 20 minutes.'

SABR: The Rucker Archive.

Don Zimmer in Cuba, 1952.

"It's about 4 o'clock in the afternoon and it was hot. He came in a pickup truck. I got in and we go to the ballpark. He introduced me to the players. In Class D baseball you were allowed so many veterans and so many limited-service players. The rest were rookies, like me. The manager said to me, 'You ready to play tonight?'

"'Yes, sir.'

"They had a veteran third baseman, Hank Parker, and a veteran pitcher, Zeke Zeiss. He was 28 years old, the best pitcher on the team. About my fourth game, I was playing shortstop. Zeiss is pitching. Here came a groundball, took a bad hop and hit me in the neck. You figure it's called a hit. The next ball I went to field took a bad bounce and hit me on the right shoulder.

"There was a wooden outhouse over beyond first base. The third ball hit to me, I finally caught one. I threw it over the first baseman's head and hit the outhouse. I figured that was my first real error. Two innings later another ball's hit over my head between me and the left fielder. I go back figuring the left fielder's going to run me off the ball. I don't hear him. I reach out. The ball hit my glove and fell on the ground.

"Later I make another error and we lose. I had botched up the game. As we're walking off the field, I happen to be walking behind Parker and Zeke Zeiss. The pitcher said to Parker, 'What are we doing with this guy? He can't play a lick.'

"Parker said, 'Let me tell you something. You're 28 years old. This kid played in high school a week ago. Give him a chance.'

"I never forgot that. I always respected Hank Parker for kinda sticking up for me.

"A few days later I got a call from my dad. He said, 'Well, it didn't take you long to set an Eastern Shore League record.'

"I said, 'What's that, dad?'

"'You made six errors in one game.'

"'Well, I remember making three legitimately.'

"I had a room in a boarding house. We rode in yellow school buses, straight backs, for road trips. It was quite an experience. Eighteen years old, scared to death, going away for the first time, guy picks you up in a truck to take you to the ballpark."

This article was edited by Marshall Adesman and fact-checked by Mike Huber.

BASEBALL IMMORTALS INVADE THE COTTON BOWL FOR THE 1950 TEXAS LEAGUE OPENER

By C. Paul Rogers III

The Cotton Bowl Stadium in Dallas dates to 1930, when it was known as Fair Park Stadium, since it was built on the State Fairgrounds. Its fame was originally from its hosting of the annual Cotton Bowl football game, which was played there from 1937 until 2009. In the late 1940s the Cotton Bowl was also commonly referred to as "The House that Doak Built" because the demand to watch SMU's triple-threat running back Doak Walker necessitated adding a second deck on both sides to increase capacity to over 75,000.

For one night in 1950, however, the Cotton Bowl was also the improbable site of a Texas League baseball game between the Dallas Eagles and the Tulsa Oilers. The game was the brainchild of Eagles flamboyant owner Dick Burnett, who wanted to start the 1950 Texas League baseball season by breaking the minor-league attendance record. By doing so, he hoped to put Dallas on the map for a major-league franchise, since rumors were rampant that several teams, including the St. Louis Browns, were considering relocation. He also hoped that a blockbuster start to the Texas League season would increase local interest in the Eagles and improve attendance for the rest of the season.[1]

Burnett was an oilman from Gladewater in deep East Texas and had purchased the franchise in 1948 for $550,000 from a group headed by George Schepps. He promptly changed the name of the team from the Rebels to the Eagles and immodestly renamed the team's ballpark Burnett Field. It held 10,500 people and was located in the Oak Cliff section of Dallas, by the Trinity River just south of downtown.[2]

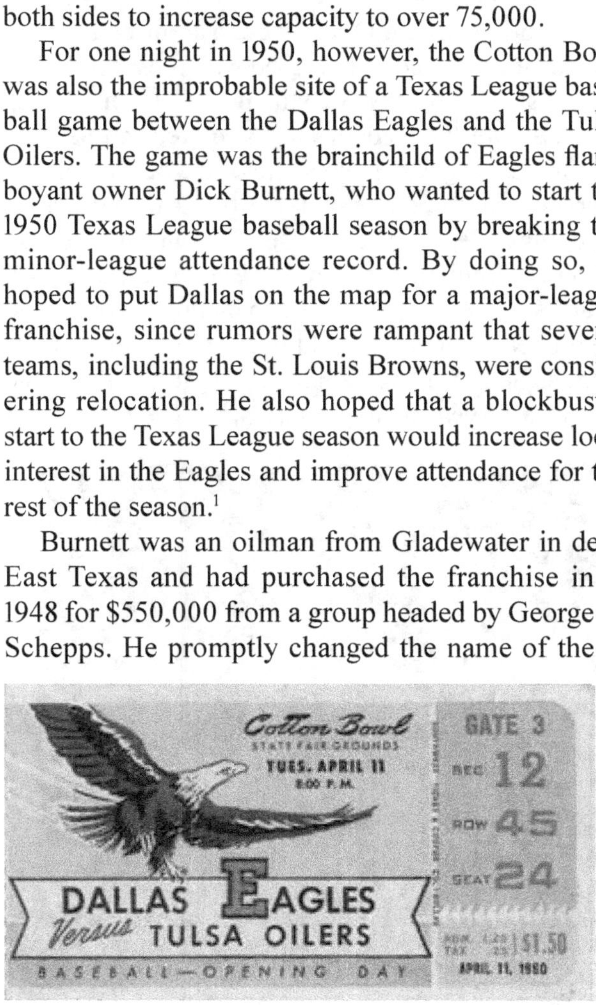

Courtesy C. Paul Rogers.

Cotton Bowl ticket.

The minor-league paid admissions record was supposedly 56,391, set by the Jersey City Giants in their 1941 Opening Day against the Rochester Red Wings.[3] That figure was subject to interpretation, however, since the Jersey City ballpark held only 25,000 and there was not a turnstile count of how many actually attended the game.[4] Also, Burnett probably was aware that a 1944 Little World Series game in Louisville between the Louisville Colonels and the Baltimore Orioles had drawn 52,833 by actual turnstile count.[5]

Burnett had already made waves prior to the 1950 season by signing former Chicago Cubs manager Charlie "Jolly Cholly" Grimm at the unheard-of salary of $30,000 to manage the Eagles.[6] Although there were many skeptics, Burnett set about trying to break the attendance record by securing nine baseball immortals to take the field to start the game for the Eagles. Burnett started at the top by contacting Ty Cobb, and when Cobb agreed, others quickly committed as well.[7] In all he secured Tris Speaker, Dizzy Dean, Mickey Cochrane, Charlie Gehringer, Frank "Home Run" Baker, Duffy Lewis, Travis Jackson, and Grimm, a top-notch first baseman in his playing days, who of course had to be there anyway.[8]

Burnett pulled out all the stops in promoting the game, enlisting the help of the local print and radio media. He got a big boost early on when the First National Bank purchased 15,000 tickets and distributed them to high-school students in Dallas and Highland Park.[9]

Opening Day was on April 12, and the day began with a luncheon at the Town & Country Restaurant near downtown, attended by 200 invited guests, including Texas Governor Alan Shivers and the assembled baseball legends.[10] Gordon McClendon, president of the Liberty Broadcasting System, served as emcee and interviewed the former players to a national radio audience, asking each what their most memorable moment in baseball was. When it was Ty Cobb's turn, Cobb told a story and punctuated it with a couple of well-chosen swear words, prompting McClendon to grab the mike and say, "Oh well, the Liberty Broadcasting System has been on the air now for two years and I guess that's long enough anyway."[11]

After the luncheon, the dignitaries were escorted down a parade route through downtown and out to Fair Park. Game time was 8:00 P.M. but most of the crowd of 53,578 fans were there by 6:30 to watch the old-timers take batting practice. They were treated to an assortment of line drives by the 62-year-old Tris Speaker and then a bunting exhibition by Ty Cobb, who was 63. Then Cobb called out to batting practice pitcher Rube Fischer, "Over second base," and delivered the next pitch on a line directly to center field.[12] Cobb and Home Run Baker, who was 64, wowed the crowd with the longest drives into the stands.[13]

Pregame festivities began at 7:15 and were elaborate, with bathing beauties from Greenville, Texas, parading around the field in swimsuits buttressed by holsters and six-shooters, and a performance by the Kilgore College Rangerettes, hoisting miniature bats rather than batons. The collegians' precision and jitterbug dancing reportedly "delighted the crowd."[14]

The public-address announcer introduced the old-timers to warm applause as they took the field one by one. Cobb had been first listed as the center fielder, but announced in the clubhouse before the game that he would play right field. "There's only one center fielder," he said. "Speaker plays center."[15] Duffy Lewis (age 61) rounded out the outfield in left while the infield consisted of Grimm (age 51) at first, Charlie Gehringer (46) at second, Travis Jackson (46) at shortstop, and Baker at third. Dizzy Dean, a relative youngster at 40, was on the hill pitching to Mickey Cochrane, who was 47.

The layout for baseball was unusual, to say the least. To cram a baseball diamond into the legendary football facility meant that the foul lines to right and left field were only about 200 feet from home plate. Dead center field was probably 500 feet or more away. Special ground rules were put in place so that any ball flying into the stands was a ground-rule double. Also, the only dirt portions of the field were the pitcher's mound and the batter's box, but the grass in the basepaths was cut shorter than in the outfield.[16]

Governor Shivers threw out two first pitches from the mound to batterymate Burnett which "umpire" Dizzy Dean, called strikes although neither was one. Then Tulsa's Harry Donabedian stepped to the plate to face Dizzy, who had earlier announced that "I'm gonna try to fog it in there and I hope nobody gets kilt."[17] Dean, who had a farm in nearby Lancaster, managed to get two strikes on Donabedian, but then walked him on a full count. Dean, of course, protested vigorously to the home-plate umpire and was tossed from the game. His teammates, in a show of supposed unity, followed Dean to the home dugout, to be replaced by the regular Dallas Eagles.[18]

Donabedian returned to home plate and batted again, promptly singling against the Eagles' Tom Finger to officially kick off the season in a game Tulsa won 10-3. The Oilers took advantage of the unusual layout, recording seven ground-rule doubles to three for the Eagles. The Oilers' young catcher Hobie Landrith was a casualty of the evening when he fractured his ankle sliding into home in the fourth inning.[19]

While the Eagles were not affiliated with a major-league team, the Oilers were a farm club of the Cincinnati Reds and were loaded with prospects.[20] The Oilers' shortstop, Roy McMillan of Bonham, Texas, debuted with the Reds in 1951 and went on to a 16-year major-league career as one of the best defensive shortstops in the game, making two All-Star teams. Slugging Oilers outfielder Bob Nieman jumped up to the St. Louis Browns in 1951 and played 12 big-league seasons with a career .295 batting average. And the broken ankle didn't hold back Hobie Landrith for long, as he had a late-season call-up to the Reds, the start of a 14-year major-league run.[21] The Oilers also

Courtesy C. Paul Rogers.

Pre-game Cotton Bowl baseball activities included the appearance of former major-league stars, from left: Tris Speaker, Ty Cobb, and Duffy Lewis.

had the veteran Eddie Knoblauch, who accumulated over 2,000 minor-league hits, mostly in the Texas League.[22]

Dotting the Dallas lineup were also future major leaguers like the 21-year-old Bob Buhl, who would go on to win 166 big-league games, mostly with the Braves and Cubs, and infielder Billy Klaus, who would have an 11-year major-league career as a utility infielder. The Eagles also featured a number of former big leaguers such as Johnny Beazley, Rugger Ardizoia, Heinz Becker, and Bob Malloy, who were playing out the string. Twenty-five-year-old hurler Wayne McLeland was the team's outstanding performer as he went 21-8 with a 2.49 earned-run average.[23]

Burnett's Cotton Bowl extravaganza was by any measure a great success. He did in fact break the minor-league attendance record measured by people in their seats[24] and blew by the Texas League attendance record of 16,018, set in 1930 by the Fort Worth Cats.[25] Not surprisingly, Burnett also won the Metroplex attendance battle for the evening as the Cats drew 3,852 to their opener that night in Fort Worth.

Afterward an ecstatic Burnett declared that the turnout proved that Dallas was ready to support a major-league franchise, if only he could get one to relocate.[26] That point was perhaps debatable because 24 hours later, the Eagles drew only 1,048 fans back in Burnett Field for their second game of the season, again against Tulsa. Afternoon rains and a chilly wind doubtless had something to do with the poor showing.[27]

The Eagles, buttressed by their opening throng, drew 317,592 fans for the season, tops in the league. They led the Houston Buffs by about 60,000 fans, which means that if one takes out the Cotton Bowl game, the two major Texas cities were about dead even. But perhaps more telling is that the Eagles outdrew two major-league franchises in 1950. The Philadelphia Athletics drew 309,805 patrons to Shibe Park while the St. Louis Browns attracted only 247,131 to Sportsman's Park.[28] Of course, within four years both franchises, located in two-team cities, moved to Kansas City and Baltimore, respectively, not Dallas or Houston.

Although also known for his volatile temper, Dick Burnett continued to be a progressive innovator, sort of a minor-league version of Bill Veeck. In 1952 he integrated the Texas League when he signed Negro League veteran pitcher Dave Hoskins to a contract. It turned out to be a great move competitively as well as socially as the 34-year-old went 22-10 and, as a sometime two-way player, batted .328 in 62 games to lead the Eagles to Dallas's first pennant since 1936.[29]

Burnett was named Minor League Executive of the Year in 1953 by *The Sporting News* but sadly died of a heart attack in 1955 at the age of 57 while watching his Eagles play in Shreveport. Although he did not live long enough to see major-league baseball come to the Metroplex, he certainly helped set the foundation for what was to come.

The Cotton Bowl, meanwhile, left baseball behind and reverted to its place as one of the preeminent football venues in the country. Not only did it host the annual Cotton Bowl game for 72 years[30] but the Red River Rivalry, the annual grudge match between the Universities of Texas and Oklahoma, has been played there every year since 1932. The State Fair Classic, typically between Prairie View A&M and Grambling, is a staple of the State Fair. The Cotton Bowl was for many years the home stadium for the SMU Mustangs and has served as home for three professional football teams, the NFL's Dallas Texans (1952)[31]; the AFL's Dallas Texans (1960-1962),[32] and the Dallas Cowboys (1960-1971).

In 1994 the Cotton Bowl playing surface was widened and the venerable old stadium played host to six World Cup soccer matches. Then on New Year's Day 2020, the annual Winter Classic National Hockey League game was held at the Cotton Bowl as 85,000 watched the Dallas Stars defeat the Nashville Predators. But no one since Dick Burnett has again suggested the revered old stadium for a baseball game.

This article was edited by David Siegel and fact-checked by Mike Huber.

NOTES

1 The fifth-place Eagles had drawn 404,851 spectators in 1949, tops in the league by well over 100,000 fans. That averaged to about 5,200 a game, but only half-filled Burnett Field. Lloyd Johnson & Miles Wolff, eds., *The Encyclopedia of Minor League Baseball, Second Edition* (Durham: Baseball America, Inc., 1997), 378.

2 Chuck Cox, "Recalling Our Field of Dreams," unidentified and undated article on file with the author.

3 "Minors' Paid-Admission Mark Held by Jersey City With 56,391," *The Sporting News*, April 18, 1950: 21.

4 James M. DiClerico and Barry J. Pavelec, *The Jersey Game: The History of Modern Baseball from Its Birth to the Big Leagues in the Garden State* (New Brunswick, New Jersey: Rutgers University Press, 1991), 101.

5 Frank Jackson, "Thinking Big in Big D in 1950," FanGraphs, January 12, 2012, https://tht.fangraphs.com/thinking-big-in-big-d-in-1950/.

6 Bill O'Neal, *The Texas League 1888-1987: A Century of Baseball* (Austin: Eakin Press, 1987), 104-105.

7 Larry Bowman, "Eagles in the Cotton Bowl," *Legacies – A History Journal for Dallas and North Central Texas*, Spring 1994: 25.

8 "Diamond Immortals Feature Eagle Opener," *Dallas Morning* News, April 11, 1950. All but Lewis and Grimm wound up in Baseball's Hall of Fame.

9 Bowman, 27.

10 Duffy Lewis was the last legend to arrive and missed the luncheon.

11 Bill Rives, "Cobb Quickly Retired as Talker After His Microphone Sizzler," *The Sporting News,* April 18, 1950: 22.

12 Bill Rives, "53,578 Cheer All-Time Stars at Dallas Opener," *The Sporting News*, April 11, 1950: 21.

13 "Diz Thought Barr's Head Should Rattle," *Tulsa World*, April 12, 1950.

14 Rives, "53,578 Cheer All-Time Stars at Dallas Opener," 22.

15 Kevin Sherrington, "Dallas' Ty Cobb, if Only for a Day," *Dallas Morning News*, April 8, 2012: 2C.

16 Rives, "53,578 Cheer All-Time Stars at Dallas Opener," 21.

17 Rives, "53,578 Cheer All-Time Stars at Dallas Opener," 22.

18 Frank Jackson, "Thinking Big in Big D in 1950."

19 John H. Turner, "54,141 See Cress Hurl Victory Over Eagles," *Tulsa Daily World*, April 12, 1950.

20 Tulsa finished in third place in the 1950 Texas League standings with an 83-69 record while Dallas ended up in fifth place in the eight-team league, with a 74-78 won-lost total.

21 In 1961 Landrith gained a certain notoriety when he was the first player selected by the New York Mets in the National League expansion draft.

22 Eddie Knoblauch was the uncle of 12-year major-league veteran second baseman Chuck Knoblauch.

23 McLeland had cups of coffee with the Detroit Tigers the next two years but finished his brief major-league career with an 0-1 record and an 8.56 ERA in 10 appearances.

24 The official tally showed 54,151 tickets sold with an actual attendance of 53,378. Jackson, 5.

25 Harry Gage, "Oilers Clip Eagles, 10-3, in Texas Loop Opener," *Dallas Morning News*, April 12, 1950.

26 "Opener Shows Dallas Ready for Big Time, Says Burnett," *The Sporting News*, April 18, 1950: 22.

27 Bill Rives, "Skid From 50,000 to 1,048 Fans in Dallas in 24 Hours," *The Sporting News*, April 18, 1950.

28 Johnson & Wolff, 389.

29 Kevin Sherrington, "Breaking Barriers," *Dallas Morning News*, May 21, 2000: 28B.

30 In recent years, the First Responder Bowl Game has sometimes been played at the Cotton Bowl around the first of the year.

31 The NFL Dallas Texans became the Baltimore Colts the following year and, after moving to Indianapolis following the 1983 season, became today's Indianapolis Colts.

32 The AFL Dallas Texans moved to Kansas City after the 1962 season to become the Kansas City Chiefs and, as of 2024, were winners of three of the last four Super Bowls.

MINOR LEAGUE BASEBALL AND AFFILIATIONS IN QUÉBEC: THE SOLUTIONS OR THE CAUSES OF ALL PROBLEMS?

By Christian Trudeau

On the afternoon of May 8, 1949, 4,000 fans crammed the stands in Drummondville, Québec, on Opening Day in the Provincial League, for a game against Sherbrooke. After the game, the Sherbrooke Athlétiques and the Drummondville Cubs drove to Sherbrooke for a rematch that night, playing in front of 4,200 spectators, with many undoubtedly having traveled the 50 miles to attend both games. If you could have told fans on that day about the future of the game, few would have believed that a mere six years later, professional baseball would be in its dying days locally, with most teams struggling to attract 500 spectators to a game.[1]

However, 1949 fans might have agreed that the situation could not last forever. The Provincial League operated outside of the umbrella of the National Association of Professional Baseball Leagues, which included all minor leagues recognized by the major leagues and which regulated transfers of players and salaries, among other things. Without NAPBL constraints, the salaries paid to many players in the Provincial League were too high for the league's level of play. On the field that day were Sal Maglie, Max Lanier, Adrián Zabala, Danny Gardella, Roy Zimmerman, Fred Martin, and Harry Feldman, all unable to find work elsewhere after being suspended by Commissioner Happy Chandler for signing with the Mexican League in 1945.[2] Also present were Silvio García, Claro Duany, and Quincy Trouppe, who lacked opportunities from the major leagues, which was still early in its integration process. Finally, teams also had strong local players in Roland Gladu, Stan Bréard, and NHL player Normand Dussault.[3]

It was reported years later that the weekly payroll of the Drummondville Cubs was around $2,500, a tremendous amount for a team in a city of 14,000.[4] League President Albert Molini, in an interview printed in *La Tribune de Sherbrooke*, explained how this was possible: "With such players, fans have the impression of seeing major league games. We can pay them high salaries with a system in which rich fans, merchants and firms guarantee salaries." The article went on to say, "Molini believes Drummondville is paying Max Lanier $12,000 in addition to certain bonuses, bringing his salary to $20,000. These bonuses include lodging, food, clothing and cash prizes from fans."[5]

The bubble partially burst in June when the Mexican League jumpers were reinstated. The league lost many of its stars like Lanier and Zabala, but was able to convince some, like Maglie, to stay. That 1949 season was successful on some level. League notoriety skyrocketed, the crowds were good, averaging between 1,500 and 2,000. The finances, however, were more problematic, and quickly Molini's efforts turned to joining the National Association, to rein in the out-of-control spending.

The move garnered almost unanimous approval. Paul Parizeau, of *Le Canada Newspaper* summarized the general opinion: "With the rivalries being settled with fistfuls of dollars, Provincial League teams were heading toward bankruptcy, and it is a guarantee that the league would not have survived long. … Did players like Max Lanier, for example, provide performances that warranted the salaries they were paid? Probably not. These players sat on their reputations, more anxious to get their paychecks than to perform to their full potential. … They simply waited for their recall by the major clubs and picked up whatever they could while waiting."[6]

The Provincial League joined the NAPBL for 1950, with all six teams from 1949 making the jump. Molini had argued for a Class-B designation, given the caliber it enjoyed and the large attendance it attracted, but to no avail. Given the population of its cities, it received a Class-C designation. Molini did, however, extract a few concessions. The usual Class-C salary cap of $3,400 monthly was increased by 5 percent, presumably for the added difficulties of operating in Canada. American players were to be paid in equal parts Canadian and American dollars. Teams were required to dress at least four rookies and no more than eight veterans for each game.[7]

Teams had to attract players to Québec, as they still operated independently, with no major-league affiliation. While more challenging given the lower salaries, newspaper columnists openly advocated for a system of bonuses to attract players, with the added benefit of keeping them "properly motivated."[8] The bonuses, however, nullified the biggest benefit of the NAPBL, its unofficial salary cap.

On the field, the transition was successful, so much so that Québec City and Trois-Rivières left the Class-C Canadian-American League for the Provincial League, in time for the 1951 season. The caliber remained high, in part because former Negro League players were targeted. For instance, the 1951 Sherbrooke Athlétiques won the pennant and the playoffs with a lineup that included Ray Brown, Claro Duany, Silvio García, and Terris McDuffie.

The Québec Braves came to the Provincial League in 1951 having a strong relationship with the Boston Braves. While not officially affiliated, the Québec Braves had enjoyed a partnership with the National League team in previous years. It had been quite fruitful, in fact, with the 1950 edition selected, in 2001, as one of the top 100 minor-league teams of all time, in celebration of the centennial of the National Association of Professional Baseball Leagues.[9] Moving to a formal affiliation in 1951, the Québec Braves were less dominant in their first Provincial League season, but had a stable roster, strong finances, and finished a solid fourth in the eight-team league.

There were only six teams for the 1952 season, but they all had affiliations in place.[10] League President Molini enlisted the help of George McDonald, former umpire supervisor for the minor leagues, to secure these partnerships as major-league teams were reducing the number of such affiliations. The affiliations were seen as a way to finally curtail the arms race. "In 1952, Provincial League teams will not need to spend fabulous amounts of money to sign players. They will be able to obtain players for reasonable salaries. Therefore, they will improve their financial situation while still providing excellent baseball to its fans. If next summer attendances for games in the Molini circuit are as large as last summer, teams can hope to turn a profit for the season."[11]

The news was well received across the league. For instance, the Montreal newspaper *Le Front Ouvrier* commented: "The caliber of the game will not be as strong this year, but spectators will no longer see these old-timers who have come to our city to pocket large salaries and then mock us. A fighting spirit will replace these overrated reputations, because these young players ... will only have one desire: to climb higher every day to reach the major leagues if possible."[12]

The league was even featured in a long article in the *Montreal Star*, after being mostly ignored by the English-language Montreal press. It mostly reflected on the evolution since the outlaw days but concluded that "[h]ockey may be our national game, but in these cities, they love baseball. Of the members, only Québec City operates a hockey team on a major scale. Yet they spend $100,000 to run a ballclub. It's a good league, Albert Molini says it's the best!"[13]

One group, however, was less happy with the changes: the veteran players, particularly the local ones, who were driven out of the league. Most found a new home close by, in two local leagues that filled the gap. The Laurentian League (mostly based north of Montreal) and the Québec Senior League (south of Québec City) had operated as loosely organized semipro leagues since the end of World War II but had grown as Provincial League teams shed veterans not of interest to their major-league bosses. In 1952 the level of these leagues was quite uneven, with some teams still operating almost exclusively with local players, but others had rosters that could compete in the Provincial League. In the Laurentian League, Lachute fielded many former Negro League players (Len Pearson, Jimmie Armstead, Pat Scantlebury, Walter Hardy, Len Hooker), while St. Jérôme opened its wallet so that Bob Wiesler, a well-regarded New York Yankees prospect, could fly in every weekend from his base in Syracuse, where he was serving in the Army. In the Québec Senior League, Roland Gladu brought former Sherbrooke teammates Ray Brown and Armando Roche to Thetford Mines, together with former opponent Ernest Burke. The main opposition came from Plessisville, led by local veterans Stan and Roger Bréard, Paul Martin, and NHL players Normand Dussault and Gilles Dubé, and helped by several veterans of the Provincial League.

Teams in smaller cities in both the Laurentian and Senior Leagues struggled to follow the leaders, and

Table 1: Attendance per season, Provincial League cities, 1947-1955[18]

	1947	1948	1949	1950	1951	1952	1953	1954	1955
Drummondville	79,100	81,720	100,000	110,350	87,615	40,192	35,200	36,302	
Farnham	21,000	37,500	70,700	62,151	33,519				
Granby	67,300	70,000	72,900	82,512	76,823	31,554	46,935		
Québec	*85,572*	*144,156*	*176,779*	*123,352*	103,712	111,800	115,943	105,269	101,695
Saint-Hyacinthe	34,000	83,600	73,200	89,521	57,476	60,147	30,501		
Saint-Jean	61,500	121,690	NA	86,268	48,500	61,899	49,000	35,222	45,000
Sherbrooke	37,000	88,400	84,766	95,053	100,933		58,288	44,541	38,509
Thetford Mines							75,298	47,334	35,556
Trois-Rivières	*59,961*	*80,747*	*76,672*	*46,339*	69,139	85,256	73,900	64,902	47,873

two teams disbanded before the end of the season. This gave the public a rare glimpse into the finances of one of the disbanded teams, Ste. Thérèse of the Laurentian League. For 2½ months of activities, expenses were $15,442, including $6,887 in salaries. Revenues were $9,963, for a deficit of $5,478.[14]

When local star Jean-Pierre Roy jumped his contract with Ottawa of the International league to join St. Eustache of the Laurentian League,[15] there was a threat that the league would be considered as outlaw, and its players ineligible for National Association play. Provincial League President Albert Molini offered his advice, cautioning that the path taken by the Provincial League, which had forced the hands of minor-league officials by becoming an inescapable outlaw league, was highly unusual, and that offering higher salaries than the minor leagues was a suicide. According to him, cities should have a team with a caliber corresponding to its means.[16]

The Provincial League fielded eight teams for 1953, as Sherbrooke returned with a new ballpark, its previous one having burned after the 1951 season. To accompany them, Thetford Mines was plucked from the Québec Senior League, killing the loop in the process. The prestige of joining the minor leagues made the move a no-brainer for Thetford Mines, once the financial issues were sufficiently resolved. As part of that discussion, it was learned that it cost about $50,000 to operate a team. With 63 home games, but many doubleheaders and possible rainouts, it required about $1,000 in revenues, or 1,200 paying customers, per home date.[17]

A few years before, attracting 1,200 fans per game was almost a given. In 1950 the league average was over 1,600 per game, and that was before accepting the bigger cities Trois-Rivières and Québec City, both with ballparks that could host up to 5,000 fans. But by 1953 that was a challenge, and only Trois-Rivières, Québec City, and Thetford Mines, where Provincial League baseball was a novelty, achieved it. Sherbrooke, a Cleveland Indians farm team, attracted only 58,288 fans, less than 1,000 per game, even with a pennant-winning team playing in a new ballpark. In their previous season in 1951, they had attracted 100,933 fans, about 1,750 per game. Saint-Hyacinthe, which attracted only 30,051 fans, gave up after the season. Granby, which had only 46,935 fans with a second-place team, also withdrew from the league, and the Provincial League shrank back to six teams for 1954. Attendance was also down for the International League's Montreal Royals. The factors that led to the slow but steady decline were like elsewhere in North America: more entertainment options, more families visiting their cottages, and of course television, although it arrived relatively late to Canada.[19] The Canadian Broadcasting Corporation started broadcasting in English and French in 1952. Some of the first broadcasts in French were Montreal Royals games,[20] although it was seen more as a factor in the attendance decline in the Provincial and Laurentian Leagues than for the Royals.[21] The Laurentian League president proposed another explanation: Canadian fans might differ from American ones, requiring a winning team to be interested.[22]

One potential factor mentioned in the decline, particularly in Sherbrooke where the Cleveland Indians directly managed their affiliate in 1953-54, was the lack of consideration given to local particularities. The general manager appointed by the Indians was said to have arrived from California with the mindset of having to show real baseball to an ignorant population. Operating the team in English only was also a major faux pas in a province where the majority of the population speaks French.[23] While foreign talent had been

Table 2: Major league players in the Provincial League, 1950-55[24]

	1950	1951	1952	1953	1954	1955
Future AL and NL players	5	12	8	6	7	6
Former AL and NL players	13	17	6	7	2	3
Former Negro League players	25	50	10	14	7	4

the main drivers of the Provincial League for many years, the teams were under control of local interests; with affiliation these local actors had little or nothing to say anymore, which inevitably led to such conflicts.

In the Provincial League, these forces were combined with the decline in the quality of play. While an imperfect measure, Table 2 lists the number of future and former American League and National League players, as well as the number of former Negro League players. The changes in the composition of the league are staggering. Farnham, which fielded an almost all-Black team, dropped out of the league after 1951, partly explaining the drastic decline in former Negro League players from 1951 to 1952, and demonstrated the aforementioned changes in focus. The few former Negro League players who remained after 1951 were mostly younger players considered to be prospects. Veterans were mostly gone. Many went to the Manitoba-Dakota League, but a decent number stayed in the Québec Senior League and the Laurentian League.

Already in 1949, there were warnings about the caliber of play: "Fans are seeing too high caliber baseball right now to accept Class C or Class D levels."[25] By 1953, fans were tired of the constant subscription drives to try to keep their teams afloat. While it might have made sense to give a few dollars to the local baseball team to acquire the former major leaguer who might help beat the rival town, it was a less interesting proposition to help the finances of a team with a roster partly controlled by the Philadelphia Phillies or Washington Senators.

The Provincial League's early advantage to break in young Black and Latino players quickly vanished. The difficult Canadian climate also proved to be a challenge, as the needs of the National Association stretched the schedule as much as the warm weather would permit, fitting 130 games into just over four months, from May to early September. Before 1950, the league was playing a 100-game schedule. And more than the quality of the players, it was the turnover that hurt the most, especially since many of the stars who were coming back every year were local players like Roland Gladu and Stan Bréard, now chased to the Laurentian League.[26]

If the level of play was a factor in the decline of the Provincial League, it was not the only one, as the Laurentian League, playing a style of baseball closer to the 1948-51 Provincial League, was also struggling mightily. To keep salaries under control, an affiliation with the NAPBL and major-league teams was considered. After the 1953 season, the league president, Dr. Alfred Cherrier, had a mandate from the team owners to apply for admission into the National Association. The plan was to join as a Class-C league, the same level as the Provincial League. While the two leagues would operate separately, Cherrier would encourage a playoff series between the two champions. While financial pressures were the main reasons for proposing affiliation, one factor mentioned was the ability to enforce contracts.[27] According to rumors, during the 1953 playoffs seven players threatened to quit unless given an extra $100 per week.[28] Similar stories had convinced the Provincial League to join the NAPBL in both 1939 and 1949.[29]

The plan received the support of George Trautman, president of the NAPBL, and admission was expected heading into their annual meeting in December 1953.[30] It never happened. It seems likely that the National Association, using its population guidelines, wanted to assign the Laurentian League to a Class-D level. For some of the owners, it was Class C or nothing, for fear of being seen as simply a feeder for the Provincial League.[31]

The Laurentian League continued outside of the NAPBL for 1954, but it was a struggle. Attendance numbers are tougher to find for the league, but we have a few examples.[32] In St. Jérôme, a town of 25,000, attendance fell from 44,000 in 1952 to 10,000 in 1954, in about 35 home games.[33] The situation was so dire that a fan climbed in a light tower and vowed to stay there until the team could attract a crowd of 1,000 spectators. He stayed there for seven days before being rescued by a crowd of 1,067 fans.[34] In Joliette, population 10,000, attendance fell from 36,000 to 20,000 over the same period, with deficits of about $10,000 per year. Owners claimed that 40,000 in attendance would have been enough to break even.[35]

The 1954 playoff finals featured two of the smaller markets, Lachute and Ste. Therese. One of the games drew only 300 spectators.[36] The next spring, owners pulled the plug, given the bulging deficits and lack of attendance.[37]

Meanwhile, the Provincial League was also in trouble. Drummondville, which five years earlier was the toast of the game, had suffered through three difficult years, drawing fewer than 650 fans per game. The team was replaced for 1955 by Burlington, Vermont, the first venture outside La Belle Province. It drew relatively well, 51,267 fans for the season. Sadly, while that would have been dead last in 1950, it was now the second highest draw, a distant second to Québec City, which drew 101,695 while winning its fourth consecutive playoff championship. Adding Burlington meant additional travel expenses, so on balance the addition was probably a net loss for the league.

As the season was fading, Albert Molini resigned as president of the league, a job he had held since 1948. Under his guidance the league rose from semipro to top outlaw league to the NAPBL to a full-fledged part of farm systems. Weakened by health issues, Molini had been less active in the last few years, perhaps exacerbating the issues the league was facing.[38] The league did not survive his departure.

Sherbrooke, dropped by the Cleveland Indians, quickly announced that it would not come back. Québec City, Thetford Mines, and Burlington were willing to continue, but Trois-Rivières and St. Jean were hesitant. George McDonald, who had occupied various roles in the Philadelphia/Kansas City Athletics organization, including as general manager in St. Hyacinthe, Burlington, and Ottawa (International League), and had helped Molini in 1952 secure affiliations, was named president.[39] He lobbied the National Association to allow a four- or five-team league for 1956, and President Trautman responded positively, claiming that while the Association was not interested in four-team leagues, "it would however make an exception for the Provincial League, because of its importance among Class C circuits. The Provincial League is an old league that deserves to survive." But when both Trois-Rivières and St. Jean failed to meet a mid-April deadline, it became evident that a three-league team was impossible, and the National Association pulled the plug.[40]

As a sign that the fortunes of minor-league baseball had rapidly changed, Trautman was now the one courting the Provincial League for a revival. In July 1956 he met with representatives of the league in Montreal.[41] When these representatives insisted on getting a Class-B league, the project did not go anywhere.[42] Trautman would try again in 1958, this time with Montrealer Frank Shaughnessy, president of the International League. The Provincial League would become a Rookie League, operating from early June to late August, limiting the weather problems.[43] Once again, the project did not materialize.

Meanwhile, baseball returned to its local roots. The new Provincial League contacted Trautman to return to the NAPBL in 1960.[44] It did not, but as American players were accepted in greater numbers, the level of play increased quickly. By the end of the 1960s, it was among the top leagues outside of the NAPBL, attracting players recently released by major-league organizations, as well as young Latino players.[45] As was the case two decades earlier, deficits soared, and the Rookie League project was considered once again.[46] Eventually, as the gap between Québec, Trois-Rivières, and the smaller cities increased, the two larger cities moved to the Double-A Eastern League for 1971. Sherbrooke followed in 1972, eventually replaced by Thetford Mines in 1974. By the end of the 1977 season, however, the Eastern League had left the province. While Québec and Trois-Rivières eventually returned to independent minor leagues, affiliated baseball has yet to return to the province.

This article was edited by Marshall Adesman and fact-checked by Mike Huber.

NOTES

1 Attendance figures are given in Table 1, below.

2 For more details on the so-called Mexican League jumpers and their link to Québec, see Bill Young, "From Mexico to Québec: Baseball's Forgotten Giants," *The National Pastime: Baseball in the Big Apple* (Phoenix: SABR, 2017).

3 Maglie, Lanier, Gardella, Zimmerman, Trouppe, and Bréard suited up for Drummondville, and Zabala, Martin, Feldman, García, Duany, Gladu, and Dussault for Sherbrooke.

4 The report totals $2,145 for 14 players but does not include Max Lanier. Sal Maglie is the highest paid, at $350 weekly. "Les potins du jeudi," *La Voix de l'Est*, February 19, 1976: 1-10. Throughout the article money figures are in Canadian dollars, roughly on par with the US dollar in the period considered. Population data is from the 1951 Canadian census, cited in "Les régions métropolitaines de recensement, Cahier 1," *Bureau de la Statistique du Québec*, 1998: 34-37.

5 Most of the quotes in this article are translated from French. "Lanier a plus à Drummondville que ne lui offrent les Cardinals," *La Tribune de Sherbrooke*, June 8, 1949: 16.

6 Paul Parizeau, "Du Soir au lendemain," *Le Canada*, January 19 1950: 8.

7 Claude Savary, "Vues et Revues sur les Sports," *Le Courrier de St-Hyacinthe*, March 24 1950: 12.

8 Parizeau.

9 See https://www.baseball-reference.com/bullpen/100_Best_Minor_League_Baseball_Teams, accessed September 5, 2022.

10 Sherbrooke took a year off as its ballpark burned to the ground in the night following the 1951 championship. Farnham, the smallest town in the circuit, dropped out of the league. In addition to Québec (Boston Braves), the other affiliations were St. Hyacinthe (Philadelphia A's), St. Jean (Pittsburgh), Drummondville (Washington), and Granby (Philadelphia Phillies). Trois-Rivières had a partnership with the New York Yankees that was short of a formal affiliation.

11 Bert Soulière, "Horizons Sportifs," *Le Canada*, January 9, 1952: 9.

12 Michel Beauregard, "Équipes jeunes, rapides, combattives," *Le Front Ouvrier*, May 10, 1952: 11.

13 Lloyd McGowan, "Minus Sal Maglie, Lanier, Molini Loop Boom," *Montreal Star*, May 31, 1952: 31.

14 Georges Bonin, "La Parade des Sports," *L'Éclaireur*, August 21, 1952: 8.

15 Roy claimed it was to be closer to his ill mother.

16 Paul Guertin, "La suspension de Jean-Pierre Roy aurait de sérieuses répercussions," *Le Front Ouvrier*, July 26, 1952: 10.

17 "Thetford Mines figurera-t-il dans la Provinciale l'an prochain," *Le Canadien*, October 2, 1952: 4.

18 Years Québec City and Trois-Rivières spent in the Canadian American League are in italics. Sources for seasons in the NABPL are the annual Sporting News Official Baseball Guides. The numbers for the 1947-49 Provincial Leagues are less reliable. Sources are "Ligue de baseball provinciale 1947," Le Clairon de St-Hyacinthe, October 10, 1947: 10, "Ligue de baseball provinciale 1948 - Statistiques officielles," Le Clairon de St-Hyacinthe, October *8, 1948: 10, R*oger Cyr, "Ça et là dans les sports," Le Clairon de St-Hyacin*the*, October 7, 1949: 10.

19 "Une baisse des assistances à Montréal," *Le Front Ouvrier*, August 8, 1953: 13. One distinction with the decline of minor-league baseball in the United States is the proliferation of air-conditioning, not as much a factor in Canada given the climate.

20 "Les premiers pas de la télévision de Radio-Canada," Radio-Canada, https://ici.radio-canada.ca/nouvelle/1046151/television-baseball-hockey-histoire-archives, accessed on August 17, 2022.

21 "Une baisse des assistances à Montréal," *Le Front Ouvrier*, August 8, 1953: 13.

22 "La ligue des Laurentides souhaite entrer dans le baseball organisé," *Le Front Ouvrier*, September 5, 1953: 13.

23 "Tribune Libre," *La Tribune*, September 24, 1953: 16.

24 Compiled from https://www.lesfantomesdustade.ca/mlb and with help from Gary Fink and his database of Black players in the first decade of integration.

25 Noël Sylvain, "Deux nouveaux lanceurs pour les Cubs de Drummondville," *Le Front Ouvrier*, July 23, 1949: 14.

26 Jean Chartier, "Randonnée Sportive," *La Tribune*, September 23, 1955: 10.

27 "La ligue des Laurentides souhaite entrer dans le baseball organisé."

28 Oscar Major, "Dans le monde sportif," *Le Samedi*, January 30, 1954: 11.

29 Christian Trudeau, "The 1938-40 Québec Provincial League: The Rise and Fall of an Outlaw League," *Baseball Research Journal* 50, No. 2 (Phoenix: SABR, 2021), 95-104.

30 "Sur le front du baseball: Une petit série mondiale?," *Le Clairon de St-Hyacinthe*, October 16,1953: 9.

31 Robert Desjardins, "En pleine lumière: La ligue des Laurentides n'est pas 'mûre' pour le baseball organisé," *Le Petit Journal*, December 20, 1953: 89.

32 Population numbers in this paragraph are from 1961. See "Les régions métropolitaines de recensement, Cahier 1," *Bureau de la Statistique du Québec*, 1998: 34-37.

33 "St-Jérôme n'aime plus le baseball," *Le Petit Journal*, October 24, 1954: 98.

34 "Jean Barrette met le pied à terre," *L'Avenir du Nord*, August 5, 1954: 9.

35 "Pas de baseball senior au stade de Joliette," *L'Action Catholique*, May 10, 1955: 16.

36 Gaston Laporte, "Les Sports en revue," *L'Avenir du Nord*, September 16, 1954: 7.

37 "Pas de baseball cet été dans la Ligue des Laurentides," *L'étoile du Nord*, April 13, 1955: 7.

38 Jean Chartier, "Le président Albert Molini donne sa démission," *La Tribune de Sherbrooke*, September 23, 1955: 10.

39 "George McDonald succède définitivement à Albert Molini," *La Patrie*, November 26, 1955: 68.

40 "Où en est le baseball? Trois clubs en mauvaise posture," *Le Nouvelliste*, April 17, 1956: 1.

41 "George Trautman désire faire revivre la Ligue Provinciale," *Montréal-Matin*, July 21, 1956: 21.

42 Albert Vidal, "Nouvelles et commentaires," *Le Courrier de St-Hyacinthe*, October 5, 1956: 12.

43 "Shaughnessy et Trautman réssusciteraient la ligue Provinciale – Assemblée à Montréal, le 3," *La Tribune de Sherbrooke*, August 27, 1958: 10.

44 "De Trautman, Paulin reçoit une réponse," *La Presse*, June 30, 1960: 12.

45 George Gmelch, *Playing with Tigers: A Minor League Chronicle of the Sixties* (Lincoln: University of Nebraska Press, 2016), 204.

46 André Gagnon, "Sports Atout," *La Tribune de Sherbrooke*, September 12, 1969: 2-2.

THE ENCHANTED 1950 SEASON FOR THE OLEAN OILERS

By Joe Marren

Olean, New York, sits in a plateau in the foothills of the Allegheny Mountains. It is surrounded by rolling hills whose forests burst into a rainbow of color in autumn, mimic crystal and silver spires in winter, explode with new life in the spring, and cover the land with cooling shade in summer. Residents and Chamber of Commerce types alike call it the heart of the Enchanted Mountains.

If enchanted means more than Disney movies – if it transcends celluloid life – then Olean can lay claim to some sports enchantment. But as the late Commissioner A. Bartlett Giamatti once said, baseball is also designed to break your heart. And Olean has had its share of that, too.

Yet Olean did rejoice from time to time.[1] In the early 1950s, the unaffiliated Olean Oilers of the Class-D PONY League won the 1950 Governor's Cup. It was the first club without any major-league ties to win the league title. Close behind in sports glory for the region, the St. Bonaventure University Brown Indians[2] men's basketball team finished with a 17-5 record in 1949-50 and guard Ken Murray was named a 1950 Associated Press Honorable Mention All-American. The basketball team was ranked as high as 17th in the AP poll during the 1950-51 season and finished 19-6, barely losing an NIT quarterfinal game to St. John's University, 60-58.[3]

BACKGROUND TO 1950

Prior to all that, the good times started rolling near the end of the nineteenth century and continued up to about the mid-twentieth, when impersonal math subtracted revenue loss from population loss to equal a franchise lost at the end of the 1962 season. Chronology tells the story:

Immediately west of the City of Olean are the Town and Village of Allegany, and within that neighborhood is St. Bonaventure University. At the back of campus, near the Allegheny River as it meanders its way to join the Monongahela in Pittsburgh to form the Ohio River that flows into the Mississippi, is the McGraw-Jennings Athletic Field. It's named for Baseball Hall of Famers John McGraw and Hugh Jennings, who played and coached at St. Bonaventure in the 1890s. Legend has it that they invented the bunt in what is today's Butler Gym on campus. That's not true, but any Bona grad will insist there is a grain of truth in it since McGraw and Jennings turned the bunt into the high-bounce Baltimore chop that bedevils infielders.

The 17-year-old McGraw left his home in Truxton, New York (about 26 miles south of Syracuse), for Olean in 1890 with a contract to play ball for Olean in the unaffiliated New York-Pennsylvania League. It didn't go well and he was released by the team after six games and numerous errors playing third base. To flesh that out for context, in 1890 the New York-Pennsylvania League was not affiliated with Organized Baseball. But times change and in 1891 the New York-Pennsylvania League was considered a legitimate minor league (its only year as such, according to *The Encyclopedia of Minor League Baseball*)[4] and Olean finished 42-55, 19½ games behind league champion Erie, Pennsylvania.

That was Olean's first brush with the minors, but not its last. In 1905 the Olean Refiners[5] of the Class-D Interstate League finished 8½ games behind the Coudersport Giants.[6] In 1906 the Refiners finished seventh in the eight-team league, 18 games behind the Erie Sailors. Olean disbanded on July 18, 1907, with a record of 12-35. A new team, the Olean Candidates, played to a 15-2 record and were in first place before the league itself disbanded on June 5, 1908.

A revised Interstate League emerged in 1914 and the new Olean Refiners finished that Class-D season with a 43-53 record, 14½ games behind the Jamestown Giants in the six-team league. If that wasn't disappointment enough, there was more set for 1915 when the Olean White Sox (52-30) finished two games behind the Wellsville Rainmakers (54-32).[7] However, Olean refused to participate in the postseason playoffs due to a dispute about the won-lost record of the Jamestown Rabbits, which had disbanded on August 14, 1915. Olean argued that Jamestown's record of 28-42 should not include any victories against Olean and, therefore, Olean should have won both halves of the season. But the league refused to change the records and Wellsville won the league title by default.[8] And that set the stage for a disastrous 1916 season, when Olean finished last in the then eight-team league and disbanded on July 12 with a record of 16-25. As was common then, few minor-league teams were affiliated with major-league franchises. But the next time Olean was represented in Organized Baseball, it was with the 1939 PONY League, with teams scattered across New York, Pennsylvania, and Ontario, and it was a Class-D farm team of the Brooklyn Dodgers.[9]

The Olean Oilers (a throwback name to the Refiners days) had the best record in the league's inaugural 1939 season, finishing 65-38 in the six-team circuit, five games ahead of the Hamilton Red Wings, a farm team of the St. Louis Cardinals. In the playoffs, Hamilton beat the Batavia Clippers, three games to two, and the Oilers beat Bradford (Boston Bees), three games to one. The Oilers took the title that year after beating Hamilton four games to two. The 1940 season proved to be almost a mirror image, with Olean finishing on top during the regular season with a 65-39 record, eight games ahead of the Clippers,[10] which Olean beat in the postseason series, four games to two.

After that, however, Olean was usually near the bottom of the standings, both in won-lost records and attendance. For example, Olean finished fifth in the six-team league in 1941 (48-61) and last in 1943 (43-66), when it was also last in attendance with 23,288 fans going to games at Bradner Stadium.[11] Following along, the team was last in the standings in what was then an eight-team league in 1945 (40-86) and also last in attendance (24,780).

Things initially improved after World War II, as the team gradually got better and would finish as high as third in the standings, though it usually lost in the postseason playoff series;[12] attendance also picked up to third or fourth in the league. But the team slipped in 1948, its last year with Brooklyn, as the Oilers fell to 60-66, seventh in the standings and also in attendance.[13]

The woeful St. Louis Browns (53-101) were the parent team in 1949 and the Oilers shared in the misery when they finished last at 39-86 (40½ games behind the Bradford Blue Wings[14]) and in attendance (40,264).[15] There were 56 players who suited up at one time or another for the Oilers in 1949. The independent team of 1950 had 28 players[16] and was managed by Len Schulte,[17] who also made the league all-star team at third base. Infielder Chuck Harmon,[18] infielder Gerald Maley and outfielder Milton Neal were the holdovers from '49. Right-handed pitcher Bill Gates also suited up for 18 games with the Oilers in 1949 and 12 with Lockport that season. Harmon led the team with a .374 batting average, and the league in hits (206) and RBIs (139); he was selected to the PONY League All-Star Team[19] as a second baseman. Left-hander Edwin Williams was Olean's best pitcher with a 12-3 record and a 3.41 ERA.

1950 POSTSEASON

The impressive turnaround from the '49 season was highlighted by a second-place finish (71-54), 10½ games behind the Hornell Dodgers (81-43). The playoff round had Olean face the third-place Hamilton Cardinals (St. Louis) with its 68-57 record, and top-seeded Hornell playing fourth-seed Bradford Phillies (Philadelphia) with their 63-62 record.

Hamilton had 1950 All-Star catcher Joseph Ossola[20] and right-handed pitcher Thomas Keating.[21] Olean countered with its own all-stars of Harmon, player-manager Schulte and lefty pitcher Williams to win the series that September, four games to two.

One of the more dramatic games was the very first one of the series, an 8-7 Olean win before 1,036 fans in Bradner Stadium. The Oilers, trailing 7-1, scored six runs in the seventh inning to tie the game. In the ninth inning, Olean's Carroll Anstaett singled and manager Schulte sent in Bill Gazdik to run for him. Johnny Gates' sacrifice moved Gazdik to second. Keating then faced the top of the order and he intentionally walked Bill "Bud" Dowling to face George Rodems, who struck out. Henry Redmond came to bat for the Oilers, and his grounder was mishandled by Hamilton shortstop Bob Rooney. As the ball rolled into center field, Gazdik scored to give Olean the win.[22]

Olean outscored the Cardinals in the series 45-35, clinching the series with a 3-1 win on September 11. Hornell had already swept Bradford in four games, so the *Olean Times Herald* on September 12 boasted with no shortage of civic pride:[23]

> Bring on the pennant winning Hornell Dodgers, their .400 batting champion,[24] and their 23-game winner.[25]
>
> The Olean Oilers are ready.

> Monday night they eliminated the Hamilton Cardinals in the semi-final series of the PONY League playoffs for the Governor's Cup as they turned back the Canadian club, 3-1, as Bill Gazdik[26] turned in the best pitching performance of the series for the Oilers.

Despite Olean's bravado, Hornell had won the regular season meetings, 13 games to 5, and entered the series with confidence. The feeling was that Hornell's pitching would stymie Olean's batting.

That proved to be misplaced optimism as Olean took the first game, but it wasn't easy. Olean had a 2-0 lead at the end of two innings on Stan Anderson's two-run homer to right. The Oilers added another run in the third but Hornell scored six in the bottom of the third off Williams to take a 6-3 lead. Cas Iasillo's three-run homer was enough for Schulte to put Gates on the mound in relief.

Hornell pitcher Ralph Butler was pulled in the fifth inning for Ed Moore after giving up three runs that tied the score at 6-6.

The Oilers pulled ahead in the seventh inning, 8-6, when Anderson hit a triple along the left-field foul line that scored Harmon and Gene Haering.

Gates may have been tiring by the eighth inning when he gave up two singles and a walk that loaded the bases with no outs. Gazdik was brought in and got pinch-hitter Ralph Cascella to pop up to third for the first out. Dominic "Muzzy" Bertocci walked, however, which brought in a run and made the score 8-7. But Gazdik left the bases loaded as Don Kattus popped up to first and infielder Don Zimmer swung and missed on a 3-and-2 pitch. Neither team scored in the ninth and Olean took the opener with eight runs on 12 hits.

Hornell took the second game, 12-3, to even the series. But the Oilers won the next two games, 4-3 and 6-3, thanks to its pitching, according to the September 18 *Olean Times Herald*, for a three-games-to-one series lead.

The *Warren Times Mirror* reported that Hornell won, 6-5, at home on September 18 for its second win of the series, when player/manager Andrew "Doc" Alexson hit a grand slam. The Dodgers evened the series at 3-3 on September 19 with a 9-3 win:[27]

> Hornell overhauled Olean in the Governor's Cup race with a 9-3 triumph at Olean last night. Murray McDermid's pitching and a six-run third inning splurge sewed up the Dodgers' third win. A home run by Doc Alexson and a two-run triple by Ralph Cascella, both in the eighth inning, aided the Hornell dividend.

The seventh and deciding game was never comfortable for either team. Olean scored the first two runs in the fifth inning, but Hornell came back to tie it up in the sixth off a deep single to center by Zimmer that scored Gil Shirk and Bertocci.

Olean took a 4-2 lead in the eighth when Henry Redmond walked and Neal went in to run for him. Harmon and Schulte then each reached base on errors by the Dodgers' Leo Tuite and Henry Franklin. With the bases loaded and no outs, Haering hit a deep fly to left field that scored Neal. Anderson forced Harmon at third, but Anstaett's single to left scored Schulte from second.[28] But there was more drama to come:[29]

> The Hornell ninth was a humdinger. Tuite led off with a single through the box and Iasillo struck out. Cascella then doubled with Tuite holding at third. Gates was lifted in favor of Gazdik. He hit the first man he faced, pinch hitter Matt Flythe and the bases were loaded.
>
> Gazdik walked Bertocci to force in Hornell's third run before Neal popped into the double play to [George] Rodems ending the game and the PONY League playoffs for 1950.
>
> The attempted squeeze play backfired and Olean won a title as an independent team, 4-3, the first team to do so in the PONY League.

CONCLUSION

As the *Olean Times Herald* put it, "The runner-up Olean Oilers, rated the darkest of horses in their independent venture before the season opened, reaped sweet revenge in copping the Governor's Cup."[30]

An independent Olean team would again meet Hornell (still with the Dodgers) in the 1951 title series, but this time Hornell won, four games to three.[31]

Olean found a parent club but lost its Oilers nickname in the 1952 and 1953 seasons. The Olean Yankees finished third and fifth respectively those seasons. The Olean Giants in 1954 did even worse, finishing seventh in an eight-team league.

By 1955 the team was independent again and finished last in the league. Things rebounded in 1956 when Olean reclaimed the Oilers name and finished in third place. That year the Oilers were affiliated with the Philadelphia Phillies and made it to the Governor's

Cup, but lost to the Wellsville Braves (Milwaukee), three games to two.

The PONY League became the New York-Penn League in 1957 and Olean would remain with the Phillies organization through 1958. Things changed again in 1959 when the Olean Athletics became a farm team of the Kansas City A's.

Olean didn't have a team in 1960, but in 1961 the Olean Red Sox beat the Batavia Pirates in two straight games in the championship series. It would be Olean's last title. In 1962, Olean's last year in the minors, the Auburn Mets beat the Olean Red Sox two games to none in the title series.

This article was edited by Marshall Adesman and fact-checked by Laura Peebles.

NOTES

1 The city was also slowly growing. Its population in 1940 was 21,506, by 1950 it hit its peak at 22,884. The 2022 population estimate is 13,764, https://www.census.gov/quickfacts/fact/table/oleancitynewyork/INC110221.

2 St. Bonaventure was a college until 1950 when the New York State Board of Regents granted it university status. The sports teams have been called the Bonnies since 1992, rather than the Brown Indians.

3 St. John's lost to Dayton in the semifinals and Dayton lost to Brigham Young in the finals.

4 Lloyd Johnson and Miles Wolff, eds., *The Encyclopedia of Minor League Baseball*, 2nd edition (Durham, North Carolina: Baseball America, Inc., 1997), 116. The New York-Pennsylvania League of 1891 should not be confused with the Class-B New York-Pennsylvania League of 1923-32, or the Class-A New York-Pennsylvania League of 1933-37, which was the predecessor of the Class A (1938-62) and Class AA (1963-present) Eastern League, according to *The Encyclopedia of Minor League Baseball*.

5 The team nickname comes from the region's oil wells and refineries. In 1865 "Job Moses No. 1" in Limestone (15 miles southwest of Olean) became New York's first successful oil well. A big strike at Rock City (about six miles south of Olean) in 1877 marked the start of New York's first major oil field.

6 Coudersport, Pennsylvania, is about 35 miles southeast of Olean.

7 *The Encyclopedia of Minor League Baseball*, 202.

8 *The Encyclopedia of Minor League Baseball*, 202.

9 *The Encyclopedia of Minor League Baseball*, 275, notes that few major-league teams had recognized farm teams prior to 1932. In 1932 the publication noted, every major-league team had at least one farm club. The St. Louis Cardinals, led by executive Branch Rickey, had the most with 11.

10 Batavia was unaffiliated from 1939 to 1941, but a farm team of the Cleveland Indians from 1942 to 1951, and the Pittsburgh Pirates in 1952-53. It disbanded for several years after that. Olean was unaffiliated in 1950-51 and in 1955. Other unaffiliated PONY League teams were the Niagara Falls Rainbows/Jamestown Falcons in 1940 (the team moved to Jamestown on July 13), the Lockport White Socks in 1945 and Lockport Cubs in 1946, the Hornell Maple Leafs in 1948, the Wellsville Nitros in 1949, the Wellsville Rockets in 1951, the Corning Independents in 1953, and the Hamilton Red Wings in 1956. The league changed its name to the New York-Penn League by the 1957 season, though it was still a Class-D league. Vince McNamara of Buffalo was still president, and most of the teams returned from the 1956 season, though the Hamilton Red Wings and Bradford Yankees had disbanded on May 18, 1956. New to the league for the 1957 season were the Batavia Indians (Cleveland) and Elmira Pioneers (Washington Senators). The Jamestown Falcons (Pirates) disbanded on June 25, 1957. And the Bradford Blue Sox disbanded on May 23 and were replaced by the Hornell Redlegs (Cincinnati Reds).

11 The Bradner family, which owned a department store in Olean, contributed $50,000 to help finance construction of the ballpark in 1926.

12 To Batavia, for instance, four games to three in the 1946 first round, and to Jamestown (four games to two) in the 1947 finals.

13 Olean drew 41,363 fans., Only Hornell drew fewer at 40,282.

14 Farm team of the Philadelphia Phillies.

15 The Browns had 18 minor-league affiliates in 1949, but dropped to 11 in 1950 and '51, and 12 in '52 and '53 before they moved to Baltimore in '54.

16 On a personal note, one of them was a cousin of the author of this article. Jack Ludtka played first base for the unaffiliated Niagara Falls Citizens of the Class-C Middle Atlantic League and then for the Oilers. After his playing career ended in 1951, he worked in private industry and then became a Buffalo police officer. He retired as a homicide detective after a 37-year career.

17 Schulte was an infielder for the Browns from 1944 to 1946. In 1951, after his stint with the Oilers, he played in 28 games with the Double-A Birmingham Barons (Boston Red Sox) of the Southern Association and also managed the Class-B Anderson Rebels (St. Louis Browns) of the Tri-State League. In 1952 he managed the Class-B Burlington Flints (Cincinnati Reds) of the Three-I League.

18 Harmon played for the Reds in 1954-56 (also called the Redlegs in the mid-1950s), the Cardinals in 1956-57, and also for the Phillies in 1957. He was Cincinnati's first African American player.

19 *The Encyclopedia of Minor League Baseball*, 396.

20 1950 was 21-year-old Ossola's rookie year. He played in 61 games and had 59 hits, including one home run, and batted .281. He didn't make it to the majors but played until 1953 with three other minor-league teams.

21 The 23-year-old Keating played for two teams in 1950. He started with the Double-A Texas League Houston Buffaloes (Cardinals), where he was 4-1, then went to Hamilton. His 13-1 record with Hamilton was his best season. Keating never pitched in the majors but he played for five other minor-league teams until 1954.

22 *Olean Times Herald*, September 7, 1950: 10.

23 *Olean Times Herald*, September 12, 1950: 14.

24 Outfielder Oscar "Chico" Sierra batted .421 with 21 home runs; Don Zimmer led the league with 23 homers and 146 runs.

25 Nineteen-year-old righty Ralph Butler was 23-7 and also led the league with 175 strikeouts. *The Encyclopedia of Minor League Baseball*, 396.

26 The right-handed Gazdik was 11-9 that season.

27 *Elmira Star-Gazette*, September 20, 1950: 17.

28 *Olean Times Herald*, September 21, 1950: 5.

29 *Olean Times Herald*, September 21, 1950: 5.

30 *Olean Times Herald*, September 21, 1950: 5.

31 *The Encyclopedia of Minor League Baseball*, 406.

MY EXPERIENCES AS A GENERAL MANAGER IN THE 1951 GEORGIA-ALABAMA LEAGUE

By Norman L. Macht

I arrived in Atlanta in the spring of 1948 to work as a statistician and gofer for Atlanta Crackers broadcaster Ernie Harwell and at the radio station that carried the Crackers' games. I was 18. Midway through the season, Harwell was traded to the Brooklyn Dodgers for a catcher, Cliff Dapper, who became the Crackers' manager in 1949 and lasted one season. I continued to work for Harwell's successors.

Atlanta was a favorite stop for teams traveling north from spring training in Florida. Part of my job was to go to the hotel where they were staying in the morning and get the day's starting lineup from the manager. You might be surprised – as I was – at how some managers looked when they were not in uniform. That was the first year Jackie Robinson was with the Dodgers when they traveled through the South and stopped in Atlanta, an exciting – and peaceful – historical event at Ponce de Leon Park.

Courtesy Norman Macht.

The Jury Box. Lanett had a vocal group of fans, who situated themselves along the third-base line, and supported the home team, by ragging on the umpires and opposing team's players.

The Crackers, owned by Coca-Cola, were a mainstay of the Double-A Southern Association, an independent team until 1950, when they began a working agreement with the Boston Braves. The front office included three men, a concessions manager, and one scout. Situated at the back of the grandstand behind home plate, their quarters consisted of a small reception area that led to three small offices.

In 1950 I asked the club president, Earl Mann, for a job so I could learn something about the business end of baseball. He hired me as a receptionist and kept me busy with paperwork and helping the concessions manager. I continued to work for broadcaster Jim Woods, who had replaced Harwell.

At the end of the season, Earl Mann told me a team in the Georgia-Alabama League was looking for a business manager. Was I interested? I went down to Lanett, Alabama, to interview for the job and began the following spring. I don't recall the salary; I would guess it was somewhere around $30 a week (at a time when the average weekly salary for a White male was about $60). It was enough for my wife and me to live on. The job would last until October.

The Georgia-Alabama League was a Class-D minor league, the lowest classification. It had been organized in 1946 and consisted of six teams located in southern Georgia and eastern Alabama. The Chattahoochee River served as the border. In 1951 the teams were located in Opelika, Lanett, and Alexander City in Alabama, and LaGrange, Rome, and Griffin in Georgia. My wife and I rented the entire second floor of a rambling house in West Point, Georgia, just across the river from Lanett.

The area was dominated by textile mills, by far the largest employers. The Valley consisted of a string of towns: West Point in Georgia and Fairfax, Langdale, River View, and Shawmut in Alabama, along the Chattahoochee River. West Point was the biggest town, with a population of about 7,500. The only team with a major-league affiliation was the LaGrange Yankees.

The team was owned by the West Point Manufacturing Company, whose president, Robert Rearden, was also the team president. Although operating at a break-even or profit was desirable, it was not the primary concern. Providing a source of entertainment for baseball fans among the mills' employees was the priority.

The ballpark, Jennings Field, was located in Lanett. It consisted of an all-wood grandstand behind home plate, and bleachers that ran beyond first base and third base. There were no outfield bleachers. I would guess our capacity was about 1,000; our average attendance was about 600. An employee of the textile mills was the sole groundskeeper, cutting the grass with a lawn mower. I was the only other full-time employee.

There were no overnight road trips, only home-and-home series. The team would ride in a bus that was used by the school district during the day, with a driver who took them out of town and returned after the game. I occasionally rode with them, which is how I saw our 19-year-old pitcher Gene Black throw a no-hitter in LaGrange.

My duties included dealing with the paperwork of contracts, giving talks at civic clubs, hiring ticket sellers and concessions stands personnel (my wife sold the scorecards at the entrance), selling ads for the fences and scorecards, buying supplies for the peanuts and popcorn and snow cones and drinks (no beer), checking the concessions and ticket sales receipts (putting the sticky dimes from the snow cone sales into wrappers for the night deposit bag), and mixing with the fans during the game.

I did not have to find players or a manager. They had already signed a manager: 29-year-old Perley Grant, a veteran minor-league catcher who had never gone higher than the Class-A South Atlantic League. The team was a mix of veterans and youngsters; about half of them were year-round mill employees in their 30s who had played for the Rebels since the league began in 1946, were good hitters, and local favorites. Others were friends of Grant's from the Sally League. None of them made it to the major leagues.

We had a good, hard-hitting team and finished 64-52, four games back of pennant-winning LaGrange.

As an admirer of Bill Veeck, I came up with promotions: a Miss Valley Rebel beauty contest; farmers' night, complete with a milking contest and greased-pig chase; and an Opening Day parade of players riding in convertibles through the Valley, while a pilot and I flew overhead in a Piper Cub and I dropped leaflets with free admission coupons from an open door (and turned green in the process).

I had an idea to try to set a Class-D single-game attendance record, but had a problem: I didn't know what the record was. So I wrote to *The Sporting News* and asked if they knew. They didn't, but they ran an item in the June 6 issue about our inquiry. You can look it up. We received no response.

There was a space near home plate along the third-base line where a group of rabid and vocal fans gathered, standing, at every game. I put some folding chairs there and hung a sign on the nearby light pole that said JURY BOX. One night during a trip through the South, George Trautman, the head of the minor leagues, came to a game and eagerly joined the Jury Box fans.

I learned a lesson in labor relations – literally. I had inherited a public-address announcer, a middle-aged man who I thought lacked the enthusiasm that the job required. I wanted to replace him, but wiser heads at the textile mill suggested I reconsider: The announcer was the club president's son-in-law. He stayed. None of the club's officers gave me any problems.

My job lasted until October. Three months later I started a new job, with the US Air Force, that lasted four years. Unrelated to my temporary departure from baseball, the Georgia-Alabama League also went out of business.

This article was edited by Marshall Adesman and fact-checked by Mike Huber.

HOW CITIZENS RESCUED THE WELCH MINERS FROM FINANCIAL RUIN AND BROUGHT BASEBALL TO MARION, VIRGINIA

By Chad Osborne

Not fireworks. Not a chance to win a boat. Not even sunny evenings in the valley watching an improving ball team go on a hot streak. Not even a home-run basher nicknamed Muscles coming to town.[1] None of those could bring folks out to Blakely Field to welcome and watch the Miners of Welch, West Virginia, play Appalachian League baseball in the middle of summer 1955.

"It looked like the handwriting on the wall," an unnamed Welch baseball club official said of the town's interest level in the Miners, a team that was suffering on and off the field.[2]

On July 13 the Welch Miners were playing the sluggers from Kingsport, Tennessee; the Cherokees, they were called. Almost immediately after lefty Leo Ghilardi's masterful four-hit performance in a 5-0 nightcap, Welch baseball's board of directors gathered in a room at the stone-built ballpark to discuss the future of the team. The daunting question facing the board was this: With all the debt on the Miners' books, and a lack of interest from local fans, could the team continue to exist in Welch?

Already, the Miners were about $4,500 in the red for the 1955 season, and they carried another $6,500 from the previous season.[3] This was a hard pill to swallow for team President H.E. "Gene" Mauck and others governing the club.

Over the past couple of seasons, the Class-D club's debt had increased while fan interest declined. In August 1954, Miners' general manager Quinto Bary shooed away rumors that the Welch team was on strike because of the financial difficulties; he blamed the *Welch Daily News* for fanning the flames of such talk.[4]

Later, in January 1955, four months before the season was to begin, Welch fans formed a group to support the team, raise money to settle its debt, and ultimately, the group hoped, keep the Miners playing in the small McDowell County coal town. The team had just signed an agreement to be an affiliate of the Kansas City Athletics.[5] More than 40 individuals, referred to as the "certificate holders," paid $100 each to be among the group that worked with and elected officials, including President Mauck, to govern the franchise throughout the 1955 campaign.[6]

On May 2, the same day the Miners played their first home game of the season, the *Welch Daily News*, knowing the dire financial situation facing the club, published an editorial urging fans to turn out to the hometown ballyard, no matter the quality of product displayed, printing, "All of us should back the Miners by our attendance and our moral support. ... Our observation of the conduct of the grandstand managers in past seasons is that there are too many perfectionists – persons who are all for the Miners when they are winning, but criticizing and denouncing them, and even heckling them, when they are losing. Remember, many of the boys are playing their first professional ball. And remember, too, that win, lose or draw, they are our Welch Miners. Support them."[7]

In the early and mid-1950s, Welch, the seat of McDowell County, boasted a population of about 6,600. In 1955 the town was yet to feel the population declines that would soon come as a result of coal-mining jobs slowly leaving the area.[8] And people had money to spend.

"Prosperity is on the march in Welch with families earning more and spending more than those in most sections of the United States," the *Welch Daily News* reported, citing a survey on nationwide buying power.[9]

The ballpark, however, was one place Welch citizens were not willing to spend their hard-earned dollars.

Before the season's first pitch was tossed on May 1, the Welch directors held fundraisers, sold advertising, box seats, and season tickets. It all helped, but not nearly enough.

When the season was in full swing, results were less than stellar on the field and at the turnstiles. The

Miners got off to a slow start and few people were paying to walk through the dark stone Blakely Field gates to watch a mediocre team play – certainly not enough to whittle down the club's debt. In fact, the Miners organization was falling deeper into a financial pit. Mauck claimed that for every dollar the club made, it spent $3.[10]

All of this was all part of the late-night discussion that began that Wednesday night after the Miners' doubleheader split with Kingsport.

The scene was set a few days earlier. The Miners were about to embark on a four-day, five-game home series; two games against the Johnson City Cardinals followed by three against Leo "Muscle" Shoals and his Kingsport mates, the "Fence-busters of the Appalachian League." According to the *Welch Daily News*, the certificate holders and board of directors had worked up a do-or-die plan that would put the decision in the hands of the fans. They simply asked fans "to demonstrate whether they wanted baseball by their attendance, or lack of it, at a four-game home series – one of the season's best home attractions."[11]

It was a test, Mauck said, "As to whether baseball stays or leaves."[12] Initially, the board and certificate holders were to offer their verdict on Monday, July 11, but soon delayed the decision to Wednesday.

Covering the story thoroughly, the *Welch Daily News* offered a dire assessment: "Drastic action is expected to result [from the meeting] including the bleak possibility that Welch may toss in the towel with many of the organization's bills past due." And with the team "flat broke," it was unlikely the Miners would make the fast-approaching July 15 payroll, especially when few fans were turning out to see the last-place Miners at the old ballpark on Stewart Street.[13]

To make ends meet, Mauck and the board said, the Miners must draw at least 1,000 spectators for each of the five games. As an enticement, Welch presented to its fans "Fireworks Night" after Monday's game against Johnson City, the second contest of the test stand. A player participation night, which allowed fans to interact with the Miners, was scheduled for Wednesday's doubleheader with Kingsport.[14]

None of these promotions, however, was promising. The Miners needed to make a significant amount of money in five games to keep the team in Welch. If the directors kept baseball alive, they stood to be more than $17,000 in the hole by the end of the 1955 season. However, if the Miners ceased operations at the end of the test stand on July 13, the debt would be only $11,740. Mauck expressed "extreme alarm" that the Miners could survive, prompting the July 13 meeting.[15]

On Wednesday night, the directors began a meeting that Mauck said "would determine the destiny of the Welch Miners."[16] "Numerous proposals were studied in a sincere attempt by the club officials to keep the Miners' operation going as long as possible, or as long as any hope remained that baseball could be kept alive here."[17] They discussed the $3,500 of debt just from this season alone. They talked about the decreasing gate attendance, even though player-manager Herb Mancini and his club had improved in the last few weeks. At one point in the meeting, the directors, passionate about saving baseball in McDowell County, spoke as if they were willing to take on personal debt to keep the club alive as they launched yet another fundraising campaign for the next couple of days as the Miners traveled to Salem, Virginia, for two games. But as they looked over the realities of the last few days, they realized the fans had spoken. Only 1,574 fans – a little more than 300 per game – turned out for the five-game test stand, well under the number needed. The meeting went on for hours, and as the clock hands approached 2 o'clock in the early morning of what was then Thursday, July 14, the verdict was declared.

Devoted Miners fans awaited the news. So did a baseball-starved group from 65 miles south of Welch in Marion, Virginia.

The Welch Miners' 1955 season could not have gotten off to a more promising start. Opening in Bluefield, West Virginia, before a crowd of 2,503 paid customers – the most in the Appalachian League that night – the Miners pounded rival Blue Grays' starting pitcher Danny Abbott for six runs in the top of the first inning. Abbott never made it past the opening frame. He was pulled before he could get a third out.

The lead seemed comfortable for a while, but Bluefield, the previous season's Appy League champions, slowly chipped away as the game wore on, scoring one run in the bottom of the first and a run each in the fifth and sixth innings. But as the walls appeared to be closing in on the Miners, Welch bats blasted open a little breathing room in the top of the seventh inning when second baseman Leo Pilibosian tripled and Ronald Glasgow drove him home for a 7-3 Miners lead. Player-manager Herb Mancini had a pair of doubles and an RBI in the contest. So did Welch's starting pitcher, John Shelbon, who threw for 7⅔ innings in the 7-5 triumph. It was a great way to open the season for the Miners, and the win made the hour-long bus ride through the curvy, mountainous roads of southern West Virginia a little easier to tolerate.

One win to start the season doesn't usually call for gloating, but tell that to Welch's daily newspaper, which wrote the next day:

Appy Champ Bluefield went to the post.
Cocky, Confident and Chock full of boast.
"We'll lower the pennant to Half-Mast," they said.
"In Respect to the Welch Miners, Long Since Dead."
The statement backfired, the BG's soon found,
It is they, not Welch, to the cellar are bound.[18]

To further taunt Bluefield's players and fans, the *Welch Daily News* wrote: "The Miners chopped the Blue Grays down to Class D size and quickly exploded the myth that the Windy Citizens are invincible."[19]

The next night, Welch welcomed the Blue Grays to their ballpark, Blakely Field, a rustic, not-yet-30-year-old place ensconced deep in a valley and surrounded by towering mountains. To welcome back their Miners and begin a fresh new season, Welch held a parade though its downtown before the game at 5 o'clock. The local high-school marching band led the way, with manager Mancini and his ballplayers following in open convertibles, tossing foam baseballs to the crowd lining the streets. The parade route traveled all the way to Blakely Field, where the players climbed out of the vehicles and began their pregame warmups. Representatives from the Air Force, Army, and Marines provided the color guard for a flag-raising ceremony on the field, and Welch Mayor Beno F. Harris tossed out the ceremonial first pitch before Miners starter Evans Killeen took the mound for the 7:30 P.M. first pitch.[20]

After all the hype and pregame festivities, Welch fans quickly felt the excitement drain all around Blakely Field. Killeen loaded the bases in the top of the first before walking home a run and allowing another to score. He gave up another run in the third. The Blue Grays picked up two more tallies in the fifth and one in the seventh in strolling to a 6-4 win over Welch. Bluefield lefty starter Tom Anglehart pitched the full nine innings and struck out five. The four runs he allowed came from six timely Miners' hits that took advantage of the six walks Anglehart allowed.[21]

The Miners dropped another game to the Blue Grays the next night, 9-3, at Blakely, but recovered the following evening for a decisive 12-2 pounding on Bluefield's home grounds.

The Miners split the next two games at Salem, Virginia, before traveling to Pulaski, Virginia, for a quick two-game set at Calfee Park. The hometown Phillies took Miners pitching to the woodshed that night. Pulaski totaled 17 hits in the contest, 12 for extra bases. Two home runs. Five doubles. Five triples. Five singles. Welch pitchers Bill George, Ray Giannelli, and Jerry Brehem walked 15 Phillies in the game, which lasted only seven innings because of a league curfew.[22]

The loss sparked a four-game losing streak in which Welch pitching gave up a total of 61 runs. The Miners continued to struggle, winning only two of their next seven games. Then they hit a modest three-game winning streak, winning two, 9-2 and 15-3, against the Twins in Bristol, Virginia, and a close 9-8 contest in Wytheville, Virginia.

Any good vibes the Miners and their few loyal fans might have been feeling quickly disappeared over the next two weeks. Welch won only two of its 14 games in that stretch, which included an eight-game losing streak in in Kingsport and Johnson City and back home in Welch against Pulaski. Those losses dropped the Miners to 10-21, giving little reason for Welch citizens to turn out to Blakely.

June was a terrible month on the field for the Miners. From June 1 to June 27, they were 8-18. Then the ballclub picked up the pace slightly. Their bats remained productive, and the pitching, it seemed, was beginning to take shape. From June 29 to July 2, Welch won six of seven games; with a five-game winning streak and doubleheader sweeps on consecutive days at Wytheville and at home against Bristol.

The winning didn't hold up, however, but the Miners were playing better and keeping games closer, picking up wins on a more consistent pace.

Still, many empty seats remained for games at Blakely Field, with just a few hundred people paying to get into the ballpark for each contest. Those dismal attendance numbers and the mounting, crushing debt led the board of directors and certificate holders to give fans the ultimatum: Fans had to show their support in a test run over four days and five home games against two of the better teams in the league, Johnson City and Kingsport, which had on its roster Leo "Muscle" Shoals, one of the most prolific home-run hitters in the Appalachian League.

But Muscle and fireworks and chances to win a boat and a car failed to draw enough fans to the ballpark. Only 405 came out on a pleasant Sunday summer evening for the first game against Johnson City – "the weather was A-1 for baseball"[23] – and only 460 attended the "gigantic display of pyrotechnics."[24]

"Several directors pointed out that the average draw of 300 during the season did not justify the unhealthy financial risk that less than a dozen men would have to face for the remainder of the season."[25] With all things considered, the board and the shareholders who provided financial support to the club came to a difficult but final decision inside that room at Blakely Field, just short of two hours past midnight on July 14, 1955. The Welch Miners called it quits.

Years later, Shoals said what many fans, and even opposing players, knew. "Welch just couldn't hack it. Nobody was coming to their games and the front office couldn't make ends meet."[26]

Although Welch couldn't hack it in the tough Class-D circuit, folks from Marion, Virginia, were willing to give it a shot.

When the Welch baseball organization folded, D.D. "Spud" Query and his contingent from Marion pounced on the opportunity to bring the struggling ballclub across the mountains south to the small southwest Virginia town. Query, a former semipro player who became an automobile dealer in Marion and was the president of the town's stadium corporation, was willing to settle the team's losses.[27]

For decades, Marion had lobbied to get a minor-league team, sending representatives to Appalachian League meetings only to be voted down. Marion had always been a baseball town, fielding popular semipro teams like the Bucks and Cuckoos (the latter a team that played in the 1930s and '40s on the grounds of the town's mental health institute). Appy League officials were skeptical about whether a minor-league team could compete with those squads made up mostly of homegrown ballplayers.

But Marion jumped at the chance to get the Miners, even though they were a subpar team and only a couple of months remained on the 1955 schedule. "Marion has taken over lock, stock and barrel," Welch Miners President Mauck told a reporter from the *Roanoke World-News*.[28]

From the Marion side, Query, a great promoter, assured the people in his town that they were getting a team, despite its record, worthy of turning out for at the ballpark. The major-league Athletics organization, which had just moved in 1955 from Philadelphia to Kansas City, wanted, Query astutely noted, to build a solid team for its new city. "Kansas City officials realize they must get the best possible youngsters in order to build up their team," he declared. "They will be seasoning many of these boys here in Marion, which will give us the cream of the crop."[29]

If Marionites weren't excited enough to see pro baseball in their town, Query's words offered further enticement to visit the ballpark for a chance to peek at future major leaguers.

The newly minted Marion Athletics played their first game on a Thursday night in Salem, Virginia, with results similar to those they had experienced in Welch. But there was plenty of fight in this team before it lost 6-5 to the front-running Rebels. Trailing 5-0 after six innings, Marion scored two runs in the top of the seventh and threatened more in the eighth and drove Salem starting pitcher Warren Rutledge out of the contest. Reliever Carmon Gugger squelched the rally but surrendered three runs in the top of the ninth to let Marion tie the game. Marion's hopes faded quickly, however, when Salem's Bob McKeirman dropped a blooper just over the outstretched glove of Marion third baseman-manager Herb Mancini in the bottom of the ninth for the Rebel victory.

The next night, Salem ripped into Marion starting pitcher Stephen Schuster, hitting three home runs off the righty. Two of those blasts popped off the bat of the Rebels' Charley Weatherspoon. He hit a solo shot in the second inning to tie the game at 1-1, and then broke a 4-4 tie with a two-run blast in the sixth inning. Both homers soared over the left-center field fence.

The Athletics were 0-2 and still in last place after having switched towns smack-dab in the middle of the season, but none of that mattered to people in Marion, who were starved to have a professional team to call their own.

Before the first game in their new town, the Athletics were treated to a welcome party near the lake at Marion's Hungry Mother State Park, about three miles from Marion Stadium, the town's new ballpark. Even though there was short notice of the team's official arrival, a group of women gathered Wednesday morning at the Marion Chamber of Commerce offices to plan the gathering. They spent that afternoon and Thursday morning spreading the word, mostly by telephone, hoping to get as many people as possible to the welcoming.[30]

"We want them to know they are now members of our community," an unidentified party organizer told the *Smyth County News*.[31] "We did not have time to plan a big welcome party, as Thursday night is their only night off in the immediate future. So we decided that a quick notice picnic would be our best way of welcoming them to town." About 100 people showed up for the picnic, and the players were delighted. "I've played a lot of baseball, but I've never seen a more wonderful town than this," one of the players told a reporter. "Just look at all that food."[3]

Though the Miners were cellar-dwellers in the eight-team Appalachian League, the skipper, Mancini, who was also one of the league's best fielding shortstops, promised to field a competitive and entertaining team. "We're just beginning to hit our stride," the Youngstown, Ohio, native said. "I hear the lights at Marion Stadium are as good as any in Class D baseball, and I'm sure the fans want us."[33] Mancini was right.

Marion, decked out in white and blue Kansas City A's hand-me-down uniforms, made its first appearance in the town's new ballpark and was greeted by 1,062 paying fans, roaring their approval for the new squad. Among them was Appalachian League President Chauncey DeVault, Miners' President Mauck, and a group of loyal supporters from Welch, who traveled more than two hours to cheer on their team in its new location.[34]

Mancini's team lived up to the hype, at least on this midsummer Sunday afternoon. Marion pitcher Leo Ghilardi gave up a run in the first that put his team behind early, but the A's leadoff hitter, Sid Smithdeal, got his team going in the bottom half. The Elizabethton, Tennessee, native smacked a single down the third-base line to further rev up the crowd and jump-start a three-run inning.[35] The Athletics tallied 13 hits against the Pulaski (Virginia) Phillies. The big hit came in the bottom of the fifth when second sacker Leo Pilibosian, a right-handed hitter from La Habana, Cuba, smacked a long drive over the center-field fence, just short of the railroad tracks, for a grand slam. The crowd roared louder as the scoreboard tallied up nine Marion runs against Pulaski's four.

The Phillies, however, didn't roll over, collecting timely hits to rally from behind. They got the tying run on second base in each of the last two innings, but the fresh-start A's refused to disappoint their new fans. Sid Smithdeal's single in the sixth, followed by a Glasgow sacrifice fly and an RBI double by Art Oody gave Marion enough runs to squeak out a 10-9 victory.[36] "Everything went all right, I reckon," Oody said on the phone nearly 67 years later from his home in Harriman, Tennessee.[37]

Despite a thrilling victory in their home debut, the Marion Athletics won only 14 more games, finishing 45-77 with a couple of ties, good for dead last in the Appalachian League, 39 games behind first-place Salem.

Still, Marion citizens were overjoyed with having a minor-league team playing in their hometown. On the final night of the season, the team held a player appreciation night. Fans were asked to leave donations and gifts for the ballplayers at the offices of the *Smyth County News* and a local radio station. Buckets were placed at the Marion Stadium ticket gates to give fans another donation option. Baseball comedian Max Patkin was there, too, to deliver smiles to the faces of fans and players alike after a long, strange season.

Soon, however, it was over. Not just the season, but the Marion franchise, too. The Appalachian League ceased operations after the season – but came back in 1957 without a team in Marion. It had been a tough year overall, DeVault, the league president, said. Welch wasn't the only town that struggled. Officials in Kingsport asked for league approval to move to Morristown, Tennessee, and the Pulaski franchise had to raise more than $1,800 to keep the team in town.[38]

Marion got a second chance at minor-league baseball 10 years later when the New York Mets placed a rookie-league affiliate in Marion Stadium. Townspeople were just as excited to see the Marion Mets – perhaps even more so knowing they had a full season to root for the club.

With the exception of Evans Killeen's four games with the Kansas City A's in 1959, the 1955 edition of the Welch Miners/Marion A's did not feature a future major-league player. The Marion Mets, however, did. During the team's 12-year existence (1965-1976), several future big-leaguers donned Marion uniforms, including Nolan Ryan, Jim Bibby, Mike Jorgensen, Ernie McAnally, Tim Foli, John Milner, Álex Treviño, and Jody Davis. Former major-league catcher and skipper Birdie Tebbetts managed Marion in 1967 – *Life* magazine sent a writer and photographer to feature the "big-leaguer big in the boondocks"[39] – and Whitey Herzog, before becoming the manager of the great St. Louis Cardinals teams in the '80s, spent many summers in Marion as New York's director of minor-league development. In 1971 Yogi Berra paid a visit to Marion to help raise money for the Baby Mets, as they were affectionately called, while his son, Larry, was a catcher on the squad.

Marion "was a small community that was very excited about the fact they had professional baseball," Nolan Ryan said in early 2021. "They made the players feel very welcome."[40]

This article was edited by David Siegel and fact-checked by Mike Huber.

NOTES

1 "Only 405 See Miners' Sunday Contest; First of Crucial Four-Day 'Test Stand,'" *Welch* (West Virginia) *Daily News*, July 11, 1955: 6.

2 "Only 405 See Miners' Sunday Contest; First of Crucial Four-Day 'Test Stand.'"

3 "Cherokees Split Twin Bill with Welch," *Kingsport* (Tennessee) *News*, July 14, 1955: 13.

4 "Highlights on Area Sports Scene During 1954," *Johnson City* (Tennessee) *Press*, January 2, 1955: C-2.

5 "Athletics Make Tie With Welch Miners," *Johnson City Press*, January 26, 1955: 10.

6 "Directors Elect H.E. Mauck President of Welch Miners," *Welch Daily News*, April 5, 1955: 6.

7 "Take Me Out to the Ballgame," *Welch Daily News*, May 2, 1955: 4.

8 "Revitalization in Welch, WV," Found online at https://seor.vse.gmu.edu/~klaskey/Capstone/MSSEORProjectsSpring18/Welch_Revitalization/index.html.

9 "Welch Families Earn, Spend More Than in Most of Country," *Welch Daily News*, July 14, 1955: 9.

10 "Miner Directors Delay Fold-Up Action Until Wednesday," *Welch Daily News*, July 9, 1955: 5.

11 "Debt-Ridden Miners Quit; Marion, Va., May Get Franchise," *Welch Daily News*, July 14, 1955: 6.

12 "Miner Directors Delay Fold-Up Action Until Wednesday."

13 "Welch Miners on Verge of Folding: Directors to Decide Fate Tonight," *Welch Daily News*, July 8, 1955: 6.

14 "Kingsport Moves In for What Looms as Last Miners Series," *Welch Daily News*, July 12, 1955: 6.

15 "Miner Directors Delay Fold-Up Action Until Wednesday," *Welch Daily News*, July 9, 1955, 5.

16 "Welch Miners on Verge of Folding: Directors to Decide Fate Tonight."

17 "Debt-Ridden Miners Quit; Marion, Va., May Get Franchise."

18 "Parade to Get '55 Appy Season Started Here," *Welch Daily News*, May 2, 1955: 6.

19 "Parade to Get '55 Appy Season Started Here."

20 "Parade to Get '55 Appy Season Started Here."

21 "Bluefield Bumps Welch," *Johnson City Press*, May 3, 1955: 6.

22 "Phils Wallop Welch Miners in 24-12 Tilt," *Kingsport News*, May 8, 1955: 20.

23 "Only 405 See Miners' Sunday Contest: First of Crucial Four-Day 'Test Stand.'"; "Miner Directors Delay Fold-Up Action Until Wednesday."

24 "Only 405 See Miners' Sunday Contest: First of Crucial Four-Day 'Test Stand.'"

25 "Debt-Ridden Miners Quit; Marion, Va., May Get Franchise," *Welch Daily News*, July 14, 1955: 6.

26 George Stone, *"Muscle": A Minor League Legend* (Conshohocken, Pennsylvania: Infinity Publishing Company, 2010), 295.

27 Bob Roemer, "Marion Getting Better Team Than Record Indicates," *Roanoke* (Virginia) *Times*, July 17, 1955: 22.

28 "Marion Takes Over Franchise," *Hagerstown* (Maryland) *Morning Herald*, July 15, 1955: 32.

29 "Pro Baseball Comes to Marion," *Smyth County News* (Marion Virginia), July 14, 1955: 1.

30 "Spontaneous Party for Newcomers in Is? Planned Tonight," *Smyth County News*, July 21, 1955: 1.***???? How should headline read?***

31 "Spontaneous Party for Newcomers in Is? Planned Tonight."

32 "Man, that's Eatin'," *Bristol* (Tennessee) *Herald Courier*, July 25, 1955: 6.

33 Roemer.

34 Alex Crockett, "Marion Athletics Win Home Debut 10-9 Before 1,062 Fans," *Bristol Herald Courier*, July 18, 1955: 6.

35 Crockett.

36 Crockett.

37 Art Oody, telephone interview, June 16, 2022.

38 "Pulaski to Stay in Appy Circuit," *Bristol Herald Courier*, July 10, 1955: 19.

39 "A Big-Leaguer Big in the Boondocks," *Life*, September 1, 1967: 28.

40 Nolan Ryan, telephone interview, January 15, 2021.

THE CUBAN CONNECTION THAT INTEGRATED THE LOUISVILLE COLONELS

By Chris Betsch

When Elijah "Pumpsie" Green made his debut for the Boston Red Sox in 1959, the American League team became the last of the original 16 major-league White clubs to cross the color line, 12 years after Jackie Robinson and the Dodgers broke the major-league color barrier. Thus, Green became forever the answer to a not-so-trivial trivia question. The Louisville Colonels of the American Association, a longtime Boston affiliate, integrated before the Red Sox, but the Colonels likewise finished well behind other teams in breaking through the color barrier. It took a new kind of ownership group, headed by baseball pioneer Joe Cambria, to push the Southern-based team through it.

Boston was actually presented with one of the earliest opportunities to cross the color line. In April 1945, a tryout was arranged with Boston for Jackie Robinson and two other Black players, Sam Jethroe and Marvin Williams, but the team didn't sign any of the players. The Red Sox were likely never fully invested in the tryout to begin with and said instead that the players would not want to be assigned to their farm team in Louisville "because of the racial feelings at the time."[1] But as Bill Nowlin pointed out in his biography of Red Sox owner Tom Yawkey, Boston had other affiliated minor-league teams in cities that would probably have been more welcoming. They had an affiliate in Scranton, Pennsylvania, and in 1946 they began agreements with teams in the North including Oneonta, New York, and Lynn, Massachusetts.

Tom Yawkey also was part-owner of the Louisville Colonels dating back to 1938. Yawkey and the Red Sox have been called out over the years for not wanting to bring Black players into the organization. Although the Louisville Colonels management went on record in 1952 as saying that they would welcome Black players,[2] Boston had yet to sign any to farm out to them. By then several major-league teams and their minor-league affiliates had already integrated.

The Red Sox ultimately signed Earl Wilson in 1953 and then Elijah "Pumpsie" Green in February 1956. Notably, Wilson was farmed out to the Montgomery Rebels in the Deep South South Atlantic League to play in 1955, and then was assigned to Albany in the Eastern League for 1956, as was Green. Both players likely would have been slated to play for the Colonels in 1957, but in November 1955 Yawkey parted ways with Louisville and purchased the San Francisco Seals, which became the new top Red Sox affiliate. The split with the Colonels seemed to be mutually agreeable: Louisville fans had tired of seeing the Red Sox pull the team's best players off their roster year after year,[3] and Yawkey saw a golden opportunity to get in on the ground floor of plans for major-league baseball in the Western US. As a result, Pumpsie Green suited up for the Seals in 1957. Wilson was drafted into military service for two years.

SABR: The Rucker Archive.

Pumpsie Green.

When the Colonels were put up for sale, there was immediate interest from Joe Cambria, the longtime baseball businessman, minor-league team owner, and renowned talent evaluator. After a short career as a player and manager in the lower minor leagues, Cambria progressed to running his own teams. In the 1930s Cambria reached a working agreement with the Washington Senators to sell players he signed and developed on his clubs. Players signed by Cambria who went on to play for the Senators included Mickey Vernon, George Case, and Eddie Yost. But Cambria was better known for being one of the earliest and most prolific scouts in Latin America. Cambria signed hundreds of ballplayers from Cuba, Venezuela, and other Latin American countries and funneled them into the Washington farm system. Hall of Famer Tony Oliva, Camilo Pascual, and Connie Marrero were some of his most successful Latin signees.

Since the 1930s, Cambria had focused his scouting on Cuba and spent several months each year living in the country. There he developed business ties, and on hearing the Colonels were up for sale, he assembled a team of Cuban businessmen to make a bid. His group included sugar broker Victor Menocal (nephew of former Cuban President Mario Menocal), sugar planter Louis Mendoza, and Mendoza's associate Gonzalo de la Vega. Two American businessmen living in Cuba were also part of the investment group: Arthur Rankin, a native of Kentucky, and Edward Wheeler, an employee of Western Union.

Like most Cubans, Cambria's business partners were enthusiastic baseball fans. With money to spend, they were eager for a chance to run a baseball organization. Given that no Cuban Winter League teams were available for purchase, the group sought ownership opportunities in the United States.[4] The Louisville Colonels seemed the ideal answer for all parties involved: The Cubans would get their own team to run, the Senators would improve their minor-league system by setting up their first agreement with a Triple-A team, and Cambria would have another location to stash more of his scouting finds. This would not be the first time Cambria and Cubans were involved with a team in Organized Baseball. Cambria co-owned the Havana Cubans of the Florida International league in the 1940s and 1950s. But Cubans running a baseball team based in the United States would be a new endeavor.

Initially there was no official announcement that the Colonels would be affiliated with a major-league club, but in case the Cambria connection wasn't enough evidence, Wheeler, the prospective ownership group's representative in the United States, was certified by a bank in Washington DC., supporting speculation that the Senators were tied into the purchase.[5] The Cuban consortium's acquisition of the Colonels was made official on January 6, 1956, and the agreement was made public. On the 9th, news followed that the Colonels would be integrated not only on the field but also in the stands at Louisville's Parkway Field.[6] The story made the front page of the Louisville papers as "custom-shattering,"[7] but the city should have expected these changes. Several teams farther south had already integrated heading into the 1956 season, and Louisville was the only club in the American Association that had not yet employed Black players.

Also announced was the official affiliation agreement with Washington, which would supply Louisville with players for the coming season. They would include several of Cambria's Latin signees. Ballplayers of Latin American descent were not new to the Colonels. As early as the 1910s, Louisville rosters had included Latin players considered light-skinned enough to be accepted as White, such as Cubans Dolf Luque from 1916 to 1918 and Merito Acosta from 1919 to 1928. But Louisville had not filled its rosters with Latin players to the degree that Cambria would. As many as 16 Latin players wore a Colonels uniform during the 1956 season,[8] and nearly all of them were Cambria signees. To help Louisville manager Red Marion and the coaching staff work with the Latin players and deal with the language barrier, Cambria brought in Oscar Rodriguez to be one of the Colonels' coaches. Rodriguez was a Cuban native who for several years had coached and managed teams in the minor leagues and the Cuban Winter League.

While the new ownership group did not bring in African American players, some of the Latin American players were dark skinned and were effectively the first players to integrate the team. Technically outfielder Dario Rubinstein was the first Black Colonel when he was obtained in February 1956. The speedy Venezuelan had been Rookie of the Year in the Venezuelan League in 1955 and was considered a promising hitter. Rubinstein, however, failed to arrive in the United States in time for the season opener. He joined the team a few days after the season began. Had he arrived earlier he would have taken part in spring training at Fernandina Beach, Florida, with the other Latin signees who were too dark-skinned to join the Colonels at their official spring-training site in Winter Garden, Florida.[9]

After the Colonels' Opening Day game on April 17, the *Louisville Courier-Journal* wrote with little fanfare that "Oleon" Castro became "the first Negro ever to wear Louisville livery."[10] (Though Louisville had employed Latin players over the years, foreign players were still very – for lack of a better word – foreign to Kentuckians in the 1950s. Cuban outfielder Julian Castro was misidentified in newspaper reports as Oleon throughout his time with the team.) Castro entered the Opening Day game in the ninth inning to pinch-hit for pitcher Tony Ponce and grounded out in his debut. The news in February that the Colonels had added Dario Rubinstein gained more attention in the press than the first official appearance of a Black player on the field for the Colonels, even in the Black newspapers. Castro's appearance was only briefly mentioned in the *Courier-Journal* game story, and not at all mentioned in editions sent outside the city.

Any *Courier-Journal* sportswriters present at the game on the especially frigid evening in mid-April failed to mention that the Colonels' starting first baseman, Julio Becquer, was also dark-skinned. Becquer had been a last-minute addition to the Colonels' roster after he was transferred from the Chattanooga Lookouts, another of Washington's minor-league affiliates. Becquer was moved off the Chattanooga team in the Southern Association since at the time "Negro players … are not being used in this league under present circumstances."[11] It was Becquer who broke the color barrier for the team.

A native of Havana, Becquer had been in Washington's minor-league system since 1952 and made his major-league debut in 1955, appearing in 10 games with the Senators. Most of the Latin players who suited up for Louisville in 1956 were reassigned to lower minor-league teams or released after short trials, but Becquer contributed to the Colonels as a left-handed power bat all season. He hit 15 home runs and led the team in games played, most of them at first base. When the team was in dire need of fielders on the other side of the infield, he was inserted as a left-handed-throwing third baseman.

The 1956 season was disastrous for the Colonels. It started with frigid conditions, and the weather didn't improve much over April, one of many factors blamed for keeping fans away from the ballpark all season long. The Colonels had not secured a contract with a local radio station to air their games, leaving the fans who were unable to attend games without a way to connect with the team, outside of newspaper coverage. Louisville also found itself in the same boat with

SABR: *The Rucker Archive.*

Tom Yawkey.

minor-league teams all over the country, competing for eyeballs with the new medium of television. And though not mentioned in newspapers, it is conceivable that some fans in Louisville simply turned their backs on the Latin-heavy team and the newly integrated park arrangements. After seeing attendance figures near 140,000 for the past two seasons, less than 80,000 fans showed up to see the Colonels in 1956.[12]

Given the slow start and disappointing crowds, the owners coerced general manager Fred Grimm into resigning in May. The ownership group accused Grimm of not doing enough to raise interest in the team and of failing to get Colonels games broadcast on the radio. Grimm blamed the lack of fan interest on the bad April weather and a scheduling conflict with the Kentucky Derby to start off May. Reporters in turn lashed out at the owners for not doing more to put together a winning ballclub. Toward the end of May, *Courier-Journal* columnist Earl Ruby speculated that the Cubans' unwillingness to take steps to draw larger crowds and strengthen the team's roster signaled that they had lost interest in the Colonels and that worse times lay ahead.[13] Ruby was proven correct. On June 1 the Colonels had a .500 record and sat in fourth place in the eight-team American Association. From there, the team's season went into a tailspin.

Tom Yawkey had been less concerned with losing money in Louisville if the team developed players for the Red Sox, but the new Cuban owners wanted to turn a profit, or at least break even.[14] As fans stayed away from Parkway Field, the team's debt started mounting. In response, the team sold off several top assets. Some players, like pitcher Bud Byerly and Cuban shortstop José Valdivielso, were sold to the Senators, but several players were sold to other minor-league teams. Catcher Ray Holton was traded to Miami, temporarily leaving Louisville with one catcher. A leading hitter, outfielder Roy Hawes, was also dealt to Miami, as were pitcher Tony Ponce and popular infielder Yo-Yo Davalillo. The Colonels continued to sell off talent, which resulted in more losses and less fan interest, sinking the team even further in debt. At the end of the season, Louisville found itself in last place in the American Association for the first time since 1948, with its lowest attendance in nearly 20 years.[15]

Despite the mounting financial problems, Cambria stated in August that the Colonels would remain in Louisville in 1957, though the Cubans would likely sell their stake in the team. Clearly the Latin group had turned away from their venture. Cambria claimed the loss of interest was due in part to the difficulty of traveling to Louisville. He said the group wanted a team closer to their home.[16] There was talk that the Cubans would sell the Colonels for the right price, but Cambria's statement also stirred speculation that the group might move the team. Cambria owned another team in Tampa, Florida, an ideal location to appease the Cuban investors. Although Cambria said he and the ownership group were looking into refinancing the team's debt to keep the club, it is doubtful that the Cubans were still involved at that point. The American Association took control of the team after the season, quashing the possibility of Cambria's relocating it. The Colonels were handed over to the city to be run as a nonprofit foundation.[17] With Cambria no longer in the mix, the team's agreement with Washington was discontinued, and the Colonels were left unaffiliated for 1957.

Though the arrangement between the Cubans, Joe Cambria, and the Colonels was short-lived and a failure financially, it pushed change that was long overdue in Louisville: Cambria signed dark-skinned players and Louisville integrated Parkway Field.

The next step was taken in 1957. While the Colonels no longer had Cambria and the Senators supplying players, they did finally add African Americans to the team. In the Colonels' home opener on April 18, outfielder Mitchell June became the first African American to play for Louisville.[18] The team's roster that year also included two veterans of the Negro Leagues and the minor leagues, Butch McCord and Dave Hoskins.[19] However, by the 1957 season, a decade had passed since Jackie Robinson could have played for Louisville and the Red Sox, and the top talent from the Negro Leagues had long since been signed away to other teams.

This article was edited by Cathy Kreyche and fact-checked by Laura Peebles.

SOURCES

In addition to the sources cited in the Notes, the author consulted the following:

Figueredo, Jorge S. *Who's Who in Cuban Baseball: 1878-1961* (Jefferson, North Carolina: McFarland), 2007.

Scimonelli, Paul. *Joe Cambria: International Super Scout of the Washington Senators* (Jefferson, North Carolina: McFarland), 2023.

NOTES

1 Bill Nowlin, *Tom Yawkey: Patriarch of the Red Sox* (Lincoln: University of Nebraska Press, 2018), 184.

2 "Louisville Colonels Would Welcome Race Players," Louisville Defender, February 16, 1952: 1.

3 Harold Kaese, "Too Many Talent Raids by Red Sox Blamed for Louisville Plight," *Boston Globe*, December 20, 1955: 18.

4 Tommy Fitzgerald, "Horse-Riding, Gun Shooting Menocal 'Grateful' To Buy Cols," *Louisville Courier-Journal*, January 27, 1956: 28.

5 Earl Ruby, "Ruby's Report," *Louisville Courier-Journal*, January 6, 1956: 26.

6 Tommy Fitzgerald, "Negroes to Play for the Colonels," *Louisville Courier-Journal*, January 9, 1956: 1.

7 Fitzgerald, "Negroes to Play for the Colonels."

8 Baseball-reference.com was used to identify some of the Latin players on the team; not all of the players on the team have birth locations listed in Baseball-Reference.

9 Johnny Carrico, "Lack of Games Hurts Colonels," *Louisville Courier-Journal*, April 5, 1956: 33.

10 Johnny Carrico, "Colonels Rally to Tip Saints 3-2 in the Ninth," *Louisville Courier-Journal*, April 18, 1956: 28.

11 Wirt Gammon, "Just Between Us Fans," *Chattanooga Daily Times*, April 17, 1956: 14.

12 Johnny Carrico, "Cols Have Proven to Be Gate Attraction," *Louisville Courier-Journal*, November 7, 1956: 25.

13 Earl Ruby, "Ruby's Report," *Louisville Courier-Journal*, May 29, 1956: 24.

14 Fitzgerald, "Negroes to Play for the Colonels."

15 "Colonels' Attendance Figures," *Louisville Courier-Journal*, November 7, 1956: 25.

16 Johnny Carrico, "Cubans Are in No Hurry to Sell: Colonels May Get John Herbert," *Louisville Courier-Journal*, August 17, 1956: 30.

17 Johnny Carrico, "Cols Survive Another Crisis," *Louisville Courier-Journal*, December 30, 1956: 15.

18 The leadoff batter for the game, Clarence Moore, was also dark-skinned, but he was a native of Panama.

19 Hoskins, who played parts of two seasons with the Cleveland Indians, had broken the color line in the Texas League.

THE 1955 KEOKUK KERNELS: THREE-I LEAGUE CHAMPIONS

By Steve Smith

The spring of 1955 found minor-league manager Pinky May walking around Indianville with a list of players in his pocket.[1] May, a journeyman third baseman who put in five years in the majors as a player with the Philadelphia Phillies, had been a manager in the Cleveland Indians farm system for the previous three years.[2] He was named manager of the team's Class-B farm team in Keokuk, Iowa, for 1955, succeeding Joyner "Jo-Jo" White, who had moved on to manage Class-A Reading. May was looking to staff his 1955 Keokuk team with players who could win and had identified 36 players to select from.[3] Competing with other Cleveland minor-league managers for the same players, May did such a great job identifying his players that 46 years later, in 2001, baseball historians Bill Weiss and Marshall Wright named the 1955 Keokuk Kernels the 30th best all-time minor-league team for the 100th anniversary of minor-league baseball.[4]

The 1955 Keokuk Kernels roared to a record of 92–34, a .730 winning percentage. They won the Three-I League by 22 games over second-place Waterloo.[5] The team breezed through the playoffs, defeating Peoria three games to none and Burlington three games to one. Led by Three-I League batting champion and future major-league catcher Russ Nixon, they hit for a .292 team batting average. Jim "Mudcat" Grant (19-3) headlined the pitching staff.

Of the 17 players assigned to Keokuk at the end of spring training, 11 had been on manager May's list. Four went on to play in the major leagues. A key to the team's success was that this core group stayed together virtually the entire campaign, as 13 of the players on the Opening Day roster spent the entire season with Keokuk. Of the 24 players who appeared on the Keokuk roster for 1955, 12 were identified in the first dispatch from Indianville.

The stability of the 1955 Kernels contrasted with an uncertain financial future. Professional baseball in Keokuk had always lived on the edge financially. Franchises had come and gone since Keokuk first fielded a team in 1875. In 1954 the franchise finished $20,000 in the red.[6] The current edition of the Kernels was operated by the Keokuk Baseball Association, a group of local businessmen headed by team president Roy Krueger. Prior to Opening Day, Keokuk vice president and business manager John Burress said, "This is the year Keokuk is on the spot. Unless it makes the grade at the box office Keokuk will not be able to hold onto its Class B franchise and playing independently would be impossible."[7]

THE SEASON

The team was scheduled to leave Indianville on Friday, April 22, stop overnight in Alabama, and arrive in Keokuk early Sunday morning. The team would

SABR: The Rucker Archive.

Jim "Mudcat" Grant.

sleep Sunday during the day, have an afternoon breakfast, and conduct an 8:00 P.M. workout at Joyce Park that would be open to the public.

Joyce Park was the home field of the Kernels. The wooden structure was built in the 1920s and named for local businessman Thomas Joyce, who donated the ballpark to the City of Keokuk. It was the smallest facility in the Three-I League, with a capacity of 2,500. Dick Hofleit of the 1955 Kernels said he didn't believe Joyce Park was as good as the other ballparks in the league.[8] The field itself was questionable. Future Boston Red Sox manager Joe Morgan, who played for Evansville of the Three-I League in 1953, was more blunt: "The field was terrible, worst I ever played on, rocks and pebbles in the field."[9]

The 1955 baseball season opened at Joyce Park on a chilly Monday night as the Kernels took on the Terre Haute Huts. A brief pregame ceremony began with short speeches by Krueger and Burress. Keokuk Mayor Hubert Schouten threw out the first ball to starting pitcher Wally Harr. The Keokuk Municipal Band played the national anthem, while the National Guard Company of Keokuk raised the flag and fired a series of flares into the sky.

With 1,176 fans looking on, Harr, a right-hander, struck out the Terre Haute leadoff batter, Sam Davis. Harr induced the next batter to ground out but then issued a walk, and Dick Camilli's double to the left-field fence scored the run. Three consecutive walks by Harr forced in the second run of the inning before Bob Newton fanned to end the inning.

The Kernels scored their first run of the season in the second inning on a single by Bob Stephens and an error by Terre Haute second baseman Sam Davis. Both teams scored runs in the fourth before the Kernels scored four in the bottom of the sixth for a 6-3 lead. Manny Fierro came on to pitch the final four innings, allowing only two runs while the Kernels added three for a final score of 9-5.

The following evening right-hander Bill Dailey pitched a five-hitter and struck out 11 in a 5-1 victory over Terre Haute. Enrique "Hank" Izquierdo led the offense with a home run, and shortstop Bob Pedigree had his second three-hit game. Attendance for game two of the series dropped to 329, an ominous sign for the season. Keokuk did not have another crowd that exceeded 1,000 until August.

Keokuk beat Terre Haute again the following night to sweep the opening series, then lost two of three to Evansville before embarking on its first road trip.

Keokuk was immediately hit by the injury bugaboo. Left fielder Gordy Coleman underwent an emergency appendectomy on May 2 and missed the next 27 games. Right fielder Mitchell June was in the hospital with an infection that developed after he slid during the Terre Haute series. Keokuk headed to Peoria tied for the league lead with Evansville, both with 7-2 records.

Catcher Russ Nixon suffered a shoulder separation in Peoria on May 7 and missed 23 games. The only other catcher on the roster was Armando Flores, the sole returnee from the 1954 Kernels. Flores, along with utilityman Izquierdo, handled the catching duties while Nixon was on the disabled list. Upon Nixon's return in early June, Flores was released to the Mexican League.

By the middle of May, the Kernels stood at 8-8 and in fourth place. The Indians sent Bob Truss from the Class-A Reading farm club as a short-term replacement for Coleman.[10] Then, on May 21, Dick Hofleit was sent to Keokuk from Spartanburg, South Carolina, a Class-B farm club of the Indians, returning Truss to Reading after he played 11 games for the Kernels. Hofleit, who had been released from the Army in April 1955, had played only a few games with Spartanburg. He would be the primary right fielder for the remainder of the season.

While the outfield was in flux, the infield was a constant for manager May.

- At first base was ex-GI Robert Stephens, who hit .331 for Class-C Sherbrooke in 1954. Stephens would start every game of the season at first base and hit .270 with 10 homers and 88 RBIs.
- Leroy Handcock, 24, of Caldwell, Arkansas, started the season at second base.[11] After the first week, Handcock was sent to Class-C Fargo and Steve Jankowski arrived from Double-A Tulsa. Jankowski would play 113 games at second base and bat .288 with an on-base percentage of .396.
- Bob Pedigree, in his second year of minor-league baseball, provided solid shortstop play while starting 122 games for the Kernels and batting .262.
- On third base was 19-year-old Larry Spinner of Pana, Illinois, who batted .286 for Class-D Tifton, Georgia, in 1954. Spinner was cited by the *Keokuk Daily Gate City* as "a real hustler who hit 19 homers and drove in 96 runs last season."[12] He played in 116 games for the Kernels in 1955.

Once Gordy Coleman recovered from the appendectomy, he was back in the lineup. Coleman would hit .349 with 16 homers and 77 RBIs. When Mitchell June returned, he took over center field from Billy Williams, who was sent to Fargo. With Dick Hofleit arriving from Spartanburg to take over right field, the trio of Coleman-June-Hofleit manned the outfield for the remainder of the season.

Beginning May 15, the Kernels went on a 10-4 run and climbed to second place by May 31. In June the team went 19-7, taking over first place for good on June 15. A 26-8 record in July left them 63-27 on July 31. The Kernels clinched the Three-I League pennant on August 21 with a 14-4 victory over the Burlington Bees before 541 fans at Joyce Park. In August they finished 29-7, ending with a 92-34 season record.

Since taking over first place on June 15, the Kernels had gone 65-18. Only twice during the season did Keokuk lose four consecutive games.

THE SUPER SUB

Hank Izquierdo, from Matanzas, Cuba, was in his fifth minor-league season. He had played the 1954 season with Winston-Salem of the Carolina League. A versatile player, Izquierdo was able to catch and play any of the infield or outfield positions. He played 119 games for the Kernels, filling in wherever he was needed. For the season, he batted .302 with 7 homers, 55 RBIs, and 22 stolen bases.

Izquierdo had played every position except first base and pitcher going into the September 2 game with Waterloo. Keokuk took a 10-0 lead into the top of the eighth when Izquierdo, who started the game at shortstop, traded places with first baseman Bob Stephens. In the top of the ninth, Waterloo's Deacon Jones homered over the right-field wall, ruining the shutout. Pitcher Bill Dailey walked to first base and traded mitts with Izquierdo. Izquierdo got three groundouts sandwiched around a walk and an error to end the game as the fans went wild.[13] Izquierdo had achieved his dream of playing every position during the season.

By a vote of the fans, he was named Keokuk's most popular player for the season and received a wristwatch. In 1999 Izquierdo recalled: "My year with the Kernels ended with our team being champions. When I left Keokuk I felt like a champion myself, not only because of the championship but because of the way the people made me feel, they were a very special group of fans."[14]

THE PITCHERS

The Kernels started the season with seven pitchers: Jim Grant, Wally Harr, Lev Spencer, Bill Dailey, Manny Fierro, Bob Yanen, and Dick Hemmerle.[15] They ended the season with seven. The only roster change on the pitching staff occurred on June 2 when Hemmerle was sent to Class-C Sherbrooke and Bobby Locke was sent to Keokuk from Class-A Reading. Hemmerle, the sole left-hander, had made three starts and five relief appearances for Keokuk. After his departure no left-hander threw a pitch for Keokuk for the remainder of the season.

Mudcat Grant, with a record of 19-3, was the ace of the staff. After losing his first start, on April 29, he won six in a row before losing his second game, on June 30. Grant won the next two before losing at Peoria when the Kernels were shut out 5-0. He then won 11 in a row to end the season and followed up with two wins in the playoffs.

On July 4, when Grant pitched a three-hitter against Cedar Rapids, he hit three home runs, in the sixth, seventh, and eighth innings.

Bill Dailey ended the season 17-4, nearly matching Grant's record. Dailey led the Three-I League with a 2.52 ERA. Bob Yanen and Lev Spencer provided solid starting pitching and the occasional relief effort for the Kernels. Yanen started 24 games and went 15-5, while Spencer started 19 games and finished 13-5. After arriving in Keokuk in late June, Bobby Locke went 8-4, starting 18 games. Steve Jankowski said of Locke: "Very funny and always complaining about his sore arm and would rub his elbow." Locke went on to pitch nine years in the major leagues.[19]

Manny Fierro and Wally Harr provided solid relief pitching as well as the occasional start. Harr, who had played in the minors from 1949 to 1952 but spent the next two seasons in the military, relieved in 25 games and started five. Fierro, a 24-year-old Californian who was in his sixth minor-league season, relieved in 25 games and started 12. The Kernels pitching staff had 68 complete games, so the bullpen was often well rested.

THE THREE-I LEAGUE ALL-STAR TEAM

The Three-I League all-star team was announced by league President Hal Totten on August 26. Hank Izquierdo, Keokuk's leading vote getter, was named to the first team as the utility player. Left fielder Gordy Coleman was the only other Kernel named to the first team.

Keokuk dominated the second team, with Larry Spinner at third base, Mitchell June in center field, and Russ Nixon as catcher. Bill Dailey and Mudcat Grant were named as right-handed pitchers. On the third team were Steve Jankowski at second base and right-handed pitcher Bob Yanen.

Pinky May was named the manager of the year. Steve Jankowski reflected on May's managerial style: "Pinky May was a very easygoing manager, but strict when it was necessary. He was a very smart baseball man. I felt very confident while playing with the '55 team. You could count on the guys to come up with the big play."[20]

Bob Stephens, Bob Pedigree, Dick Hofleit, Manny Fierro, Lev Spencer, and Bobby Locke were named honorable mention.

The only man on the roster not given all-star recognition was pitcher Wally Harr.

MAY HONORED

Pinky May was honored with a day at the end of the season. May recalled the day some years later: "The ballclub in a generous gesture presented me with a fine Hereford heifer and helped in the transportation of her to our farm in Indiana."[21]

Hank Izquierdo recalled: "On that day I was playing 3B. He was presented with a gift (the heifer). His gift decides to run towards third and relieve himself right on the base. Well, they tried cleaning up as much of the mess as possible, but some was still left with the very unpleasant smell to go with it. After the game started, a ball was hit towards third causing me to dive right smack in the mess that Pinky's gift left behind. Talk about a third baseman that smelled great for the rest of the game."[22]

THE PLAYOFFS

The season wrapped up with a 9-4 Labor Day victory over Burlington, which knocked the Bees into fourth place, allowing the Kernels to face Peoria in the first round of the Shaughnessy playoffs beginning on Wednesday, September 7. Tuesday was a day off for the Kernels on but not off the field. A championship banquet was held at the Knights of Columbus Hall.

C.R. "Doc" Logan, the master of ceremonies, welcomed Mike McNally, director of the Cleveland Indians farm system, Steve O'Neil, assistant to Cleveland general manager Hank Greenberg, and Laddie Placek, chief of the scouts for the organization.[23] All three remained in Keokuk to attend the opening game of the playoffs on Wednesday.[24]

Mudcat Grant's Experience with Racism in Keokuk

Recalling his time in Keokuk, Grant concluded: "From a baseball point of view, my time in Keokuk was very successful." He went on to describe the significant challenges faced by the African American players on the team:

> From a personal point of view, Keokuk was a little bit more prejudiced than Fargo, North Dakota. In Keokuk they didn't want you in some places if you were black. That year there were only two of us on the team, me and Mitchell June.[16] The Kernels' team office was in the Metropole Hotel, but they didn't want us there. They had a place for us to stay with a black lady that had been renting out rooms to ballplayers for a number of years, we stayed with her instead of staying at the hotel. And they didn't want us using cabs and public transportation used by the whites, so they gave us a station wagon to use for transportation to go to the ballpark come downtown, eat, etc. One place where they didn't want us to eat was the Wagon Wheel, a restaurant near the Metropole Hotel. … But, since we were paying to eat, we just didn't eat in there anymore. They won on that one but they lost because we were customers like everybody else. That's the way we looked at it.[17] …
>
> Believe me, the racial thing was a brutal psychological war between me and the people out to bury me. … From the time the Keokuk team photographer said, "You black boys do strange things to the lighting," I was ready to explode. I thought once I signed a pro contract I'd be able to eat where I wanted, or live peacefully like any other human being. It wasn't to be.[18]

Bill Dailey gave them something to see, as he pitched Keokuk to a 6-1 complete-game victory, allowing only four singles. The lone run for Peoria was unearned. In Game Two on Thursday, Mudcat Grant pitched Keokuk to a 12-3 complete-game victory, allowing all three runs in the seventh inning. (Only one run was earned.) Attendance for the first two games was 719 and 688.

The series moved to Peoria on Friday night, and the Kernels finished off the Chiefs with a 9-7 victory.

Keokuk bolted to a 9-3 lead after seven innings, only to see Peoria add four runs in the final two innings on three home runs.

After a day off on Saturday, Keokuk met the fourth-place Burlington Bees in the first game of the championship series on a chilly Sunday evening at Joyce Park. The Bees touched four Keokuk pitchers for 18 hits in a 16-6 Burlington victory. The *Daily Gate City* reported that more Burlington fans were on hand than Keokuk fans. The attendance was 580.

On a cold Monday night, the Kernels turned the tables. They walloped the Bees 14-1 as Bill Dailey pitched a complete-game victory. This was the final home game of the season at Joyce Park. The concession stands made things even more enjoyable for the 598 fans at the game. Beer was sold at 10 cents a bottle and the Swift Company gave all the ice cream left in the freezers to the children attending the game.

The series moved to Burlington, where the Kernels continued to hit. They finished the series with 18-9 and 13-9 wins to take the Three-I championship and the $1,250 that went with it. The $1,250 was split among the team members. Burlington, the runner-up, received $750 to divvy up.

THE LEGACY

The 1955 Keokuk Kernels tied a league record for most games won in a season with a 92-34 record.[25] Their winning percentage (.730) and their lead (22 games) were both league records. The team led the league in batting (.292), runs (813), hits (1,277), and fewest opponents' runs scored (531). Seven of the players went on to play in the major leagues.[26]

But the team was not successful at the box office. Keokuk finished seventh out of the eight teams in the league with a home attendance of 39,179.[27] Keokuk was able to field a Class-B franchise for the 1956 and 1957 seasons but dropped to the Class-D Midwest League for the 1958 season. Poor attendance continued to bedevil the franchise. In midseason of 1962 the Keokuk franchise folded and moved to Dubuque, Iowa. Professional baseball has never returned to Keokuk.

This article was edited by Cathy Kreyche and fact-checked by Ray Danner.

SOURCES

Sources for this chapter include the *Daily Gate City* of Keokuk, Baseball-Reference.com, and the players' correspondence with Shane Etter, a dedicated Keokuk baseball historian.

NOTES

1 Merrill "Pinky" May is the father of former major-league catcher Milt May; Indianville, located in Daytona Beach, Florida, was the spring-training base for the Cleveland Indians' minor-league players.

2 May joined the Navy after the 1943 season and never made it back to the big leagues.

3 "Spring Training Roster of Kernels Narrowed to 36 Players," *Daily Gate City* (Keokuk, Iowa), April 5, 1955.

4 "100 Best Minor League Teams," Baseball Reference, BR Bullpen, last edited August 4, 2012, https://www.baseball-reference.com/bullpen/100_Best_Minor_League_Baseball_Teams.

5 The Three-I League included teams from Illinois, Indiana, and Iowa.

6 *The Sporting News*, March 2, 1955.

7 "Lions Tell Burress Play Ball," *Daily Gate City*, April 20, 1955.

8 Dick Hofleit to Shane Etter, June 1, 2001.

9 Steve Smith, "An Encounter with Joe Morgan" (unpublished).

10 Robert Maley Truss, also referred to as Maley Truss.

11 Handcock had played in the Negro Leagues and was recommended to Cleveland by Larry Doby while barnstorming with Roy Campanella's all-stars.

12 "Club to Arrive in Keokuk Next Sunday; Season Opens Tuesday," *Daily Gate City*, April 16, 1955.

13 "Hank Pitches, Plays First in Circus Contest,"*Daily Gate City*, September 3, 1955.

14 Enrique Izquierdo correspondence with Shane Etter, July 12, 1999.

15 Richard Bruce Hemmerle, also referred to as Bruce Hemmerle.

16 African Americans Billy Williams and Leroy Handcock were with the team briefly early in the season.

17 Jim "Mudcat" Grant with Tom Sabellico and Pat O'Brien, *The Black Aces: Baseball's Only African-American Twenty-Game Winners* (Chula Vista, California: Aventine Press, 2007), 206-207.

18 Edward Kiersh, *Where Have You Gone Vince DiMaggio* (New York: Doubleday, 1983), 90.

19 Steve Jankowski to Shane Etter, June 6, 2001.

20 Jankowski to Etter, June 6, 2001.

21 Pinky May to Shane Etter, ca. 1999.

22 Enrique Izquierdo to Shane Etter, July 12, 1999.

23 Logan, a longtime Keokuk baseball booster, was a member of the Keokuk Baseball Association Board of Directors.

24 Greenberg was scheduled to attend the dinner and game but was called to New York for a meeting with Commissioner Ford Frick.

25 In 1912 Springfield won 92 games in a 137-game season.

26 Izquierdo, Nixon, Dailey, Williams, Grant, Coleman, and Locke all played in the major leagues.

27 Burlington led the league in attendance with 91,946. Keokuk finished seventh with an attendance of 39,179, edging Quincy with 39,081.

AL PINKSTON: FORGOTTEN COLOR LINE CASUALTY

By Will Christensen

Al Pinkston was one of hundreds of minor-league stars whose career accomplishments came to light decades later thanks to the efforts of SABR.

For the most part, Pinkston's numbers, outstanding though they might appear, seem a bit pedestrian compared with others in SABR's first volume of *Minor League Stars*: He doesn't have the highest batting average, the most homers, or the most hits of any minor leaguer.[1]

There's a reason for that, and it makes Pinkston's career all the more fascinating.

Pinkston, like many other players, broke into Organized Baseball in the low-level minors, with Farnham in the Class-C Provincial League in 1951. When he hung 'em up 15 years later, he had six batting titles to his name on his way to a .352 batting average over the course of 1,827 games.[2] His .372 mark after seven seasons in the Mexican League is the all-time high in that league for any player who has more than 2,400 at-bats.[3]

Courtesy Major League Baseball Players Alumni Association.

Al Pinkston.

Pinkston wasn't just a singles hitter. He led his league in home runs once, RBIs four times, and total bases five times. His career on-base percentage is .412; his career slugging average is .554.

That's pretty good. Now, here's where it gets really interesting. Pinkston's first season, in 1951, when he hit .301 with 15 homers and 21 steals, the kid was all of 33 years old, having been born in October 1917.

Thirty-three.

At age 33, Sandy Koufax had been retired for a year. Pinkston, who was known as Beartracks, among other nicknames, presumably for his huge feet and stride (he was listed at 6-feet-5½ with a size 14 shoe[4]), was just getting started.

The next year, Pinkston won the Provincial League triple crown while playing with St. Hyacinthe, thus beginning a career that finished with more than 2,300 hits, 1,300 RBIs, exactly 250 homers and the aforementioned .352 batting average.

As one might suspect, Pinkston ranks among the top five professionally in just about every category for players after age 33 and is at the top of the list in doubles (461), extra-base hits (786), total bases (3,729), and, most importantly, runs created (1,468).

Naturally, considering how good Pinkston was after an age when most players are either retired or winding down their career, the obvious question is: What the heck was he doing before 1951?

Well, he was doing a lot of things men his age were doing: working,[5] getting married,[6] starting a family,[7] fighting a world war[8] … and playing a little baseball. Of course, Pinkston's options to play professionally were limited severely, because he had committed Organized Baseball's cardinal sin of being born Black.

There's a perception that when Jackie Robinson broke the color barrier in 1946 before moving up to the White major leagues in 1947, Black players suddenly had equal opportunities to play in the minors and majors.

Not true, of course. The American and National Leagues weren't fully integrated, that is, with every team having at least one Black player, until 1959. The minor leagues weren't fully integrated, as in every league had at least one Black player (let alone team), until 1963.[9] Between 1946 and 1963, progress happened incrementally.

So Pinkston actually didn't have much opportunity to get into Organized Baseball any sooner than he did.

Pinkston played in the Negro Major Leagues, sort of. He got all of one at-bat with the Cleveland Buckeyes in 1948. He also played for the St. Louis Stars in 1936 when it was an independent team. All of 18 at the time, Pinkston played well enough to be mentioned as a candidate for the 1936 East-West Game (he didn't play in the game),[10] but no stats for the season exist.

In between those two stints, only an anecdotal record remains. From 1947 to 1950 Pinkston played with the New Orleans Creoles in the Negro Southern Association and Negro Texas League,[11] and only a few box scores from that period are generally available. By 1949 and 1950, certainly, Pinkston was drawing interest from Organized Baseball.[12]

Despite the late start, Pinkston still almost made the extant majors. Having been acquired by the Philadelphia A's organization before the 1952 season,[13] he raced up the ladder, and after a monster season in the Class-A Sally League, he got a spring-training invite with the big club, then from Kansas City, before the 1955 season.[14]

At the time Pinkston was trying to pass himself off as nine years younger,[15] which was why he got a shot at all. It later was suggested that in talking about his past, Pinkston let slip a few facts that messed with his known timeline,[16] but it's more likely that a .226 mark with no homers or RBIs during the exhibition season put him in Triple-A ball.[17]

An injury-riddled 1955 season[18] and a decline in 1956 then doomed him to the minor leagues, where he became a Hall of Famer (in Mexico)[19] and a legend. He played with Los Diablos Rojos del Mexico in 1959 and 1960 and with Los Rojos del Aguila de Veracruz from 1961 through 1965.[20]

For the record, this was Pinkston's "average" season for the next nine years after 1956, when he was 38 and playing on bad knees:[21]

G	AB	R	H	2B	3B	HR	RBI	BB	BA	SLG	RC
130	488	88	179	35	6	17	102	45	.367	.567	109

What could have been for Pinkston had baseball been a true meritocracy all along and he got to play in his 20s: 4,000 career professional hits? 500 homers? 2,000 RBIs? A run as a major-league All-Star? We can only wonder.

This article was edited by Thomas Rathkamp and fact-checked by Tony Escobedo.

NOTES

1 The first volume of *Minor League Stars* was published by SABR in 1978.

2 ² Roberto Hernandez, "Pinkston Second to Cop Six Swat Titles in Minors," *The Sporting News*, November 10, 1962: 23. Pinkston hit .360 in the Provincial League in 1952; .360 in the South Atlantic League in 1954; and .369, .397, .374, and .381 in the Mexican League in 1959 to 1962.

3 Pedro Treto Cisneros, *The Mexican League* (Jefferson, North Carolina: McFarland & Company, Inc., 2000), 53.

4 ³ Brad Willson, "Cullop Plans Heavy Workouts for Jets," *Columbus* (Ohio) *Dispatch*, February 28, 1955: 14.

5 US Census Bureau, Sixteenth Census of the United States, 1940. Pinkston was listed as still living at home in Newbern, Alabama, as a farm laborer.

6 Dr. Layton Revel and Luis Munoz, "Forgotten Heroes: Alfred Pinkston," Center for Negro League Baseball Research, 2013: 2. This otherwise excellent downloadable biography incorrectly listed Pinkston's new bride as Vera Lewis. It was Velma Lewis, but no date was mentioned or found.

7 "Vital Statistics," *New Orleans Item*, November 4, 1943: 2. This listing mentions the birth of a girl to a "Mesdames Alfred Pinkston." Another listing dated November 6, 1946, reports the birth of a boy to a "Mesdames Alfred C Pinkston." Pinkston's middle name was Charles, and Pinkston's first two children were a daughter and son in that order, so it's safe to assume these are his first two children.

8 US Department of Veteran Affairs, *BIRLS Death File*, 1850-2010. The file lists a prewar enlistment of August 7, 1941, and a discharge of January 24, 1946. Revel and Munoz report Pinkston was discharged in 1944 but cite no source to confirm. In any event, it appears Pinkston spent the entirety of his service in New Orleans.

9 Oscar Kahan, "22 Clubs, Only 20 Tieups, Add Up to Headache," *The Sporting News*, December 8, 1962: 8.

10 "Announce All Star Game," *Chicago Defender*, August 8, 1936: 14.

11 Revel and Munoz, "Forgotten Heroes: Alfred Pinkston": 4.

12 James LaFourche, "Scouts Trailing Three Negro Players," *Northwest Enterprise* (Seattle), September 7, 1950: 1.

13 "Importante transaction bâclée entre les clubs Farnham et S. Hyacinthe," *Le Clarion* (St. Hyacinthe, Québec), January 25, 1952: 7.

14 Walter L. Johns, "A's Put Finger on Pinky, 227-Pound Sally Slugger," *The Sporting News*, March 16, 1955: 15.

15 Sam Lacy, "Long Jump to Majors Fails to Dim Al Pinkston's Hopes," *Baltimore Afro-American*, April 9, 1955: 17.

16 John Schulian, *Twilight of the Long-Ball Gods* (Lincoln: University of Nebraska Press, 2005), 66-67.

17 "Averages," *Kansas City Times*, April 1, 1955: 40.

18 "Meet the Jets," *Columbus Dispatch*, April 13, 1956: B-23.

19 "Mexican League," *The Sporting News*, July 20, 1974: 36.

20 https://www.baseball-reference.com/register/player.fcgi?id=pinkst001alf.

21 Hernandez. An apparently unpublished feature by Bill Bryson from 1957 found in *The Sporting News* archives quoted Pinkston as saying, "I don't know how my knees are going to hold up. I got bad cartileges [*sic*] in both of 'em."

RON NECCIAI STRIKES OUT 27 BATTERS IN A NINE-INNING GAME

By Joel Rippel

After the 1952 season, the National Association of Professional Baseball Leagues published a history of minor-league baseball, beginning with the association's formation in 1901. The book included a list of the 50 most outstanding records for performances other than season records. The editors didn't have to do much research to find the number-one performance on the list. Details of the performance, which occurred early in the 1952 season, were likely still fresh for the editors.

Ron Necciai, a 19-year-old pitcher for the Bristol (Virginia) Twins of the Class-D Appalachian League, had set a record "not remotely approached in the history of baseball."[1]

More than 70 years later, Necciai's record of 27 strikeouts in a nine-inning minor-league game still stood.

Necciai was in his third season in the Pittsburgh Pirates farm system in 1952. He signed with the Pirates in June of 1950 right after his graduation from Monongahela (Pennsylvania) High School and days before his 18th birthday.

His professional career almost ended before it started. Necciai, who was signed as a first baseman, was made a pitcher after he reported to Salisbury of the Class-D North Carolina State League.

In his first two professional appearances, he walked six and allowed seven runs in three innings. The Pirates reassigned Necciai to Shelby of the Class-D Western Carolina League. After one appearance for Shelby – which saw him allow three runs without retiring a hitter – Necciai left the team and returned home to Pennsylvania.

"Baseball was never really a passion of mine," Necciai said. "To be honest, I never did have any passions. Baseball was just something to do. I was just an average kid drifting through, and it didn't seem to make much sense to stay."[2]

The Pirates didn't give up on Necciai. The team stayed in touch with him and persuaded him to give baseball another try in 1951.

After spring training in Deland, Florida, the Pirates again assigned Necciai to Salisbury. He struggled, with seven consecutive losses and he again considered quitting baseball. But he rebounded with four consecutive victories. With Salisbury, he struck out 111 batters in 106 innings, but walked 84 and surrendered 91 hits. Despite a 4-9 record with a 4.84 ERA, the Pirates promoted Necciai in July to New Orleans of the Double-A Southern League.

In his debut with New Orleans, on July 29, Necciai allowed just two runs and five hits in seven innings in a 2-0 loss to Mobile in New Orleans.[3] That outing was the highlight for Necciai in his time with New Orleans.

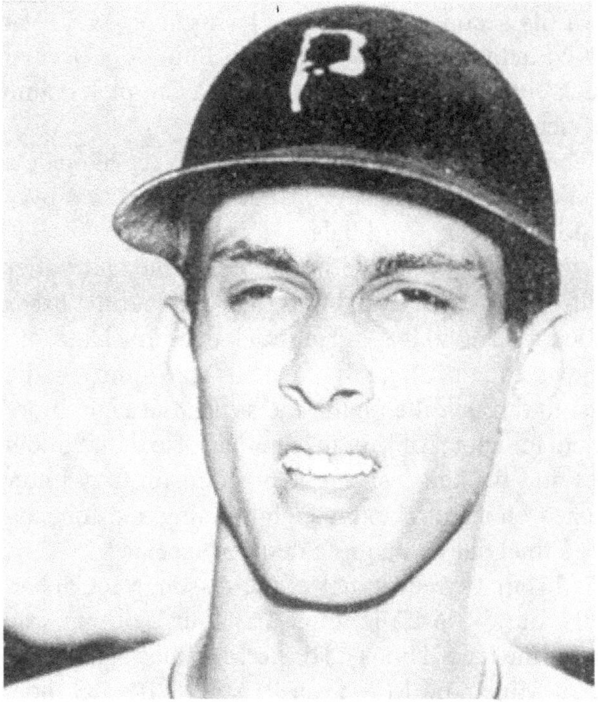

SABR: The Rucker Archive

Ron Necciai.

He finished 1-5 with an 8.45 ERA in eight appearances with the Pelicans. His season ended with a twisted ankle near the end of August.[4]

After the 1951 season, Necciai took part in the Pirates' fall instructional camp in Deland. He showed progress on the mound and the Pirates invited him to their big-league spring-training camp in San Bernardino, California.

On March 18 in San Bernardino, Necciai pitched five shutout innings against the defending National League champion New York Giants. He allowed just two hits – an infield single and a bloop single to short center field.

Late in 1952 spring training, Necciai was sidelined by an ulcer. After treatment, which included a brief hospital stay, he was assigned to Class-D Bristol. Necciai was nearly unhittable in his time with Bristol, allowing just 10 hits in 43 innings of work, during which time he struck out 109 opposing batters and recorded an 0.46 earned-run average.

On May 1, the Twins opened the season with a 9-3 loss to the Kingsport Cherokees at Kingsport. The next night the teams met at Shaw Stadium in Bristol for the Twins' home opener, and Necciai was Bristol's starting pitcher. He allowed just two hits and struck out a ballpark record 20 in the Twins' 4-0 victory. Necciai's 20 strikeouts were one shy of the Appalachian League record set by Bob Kuhlman in 1945.

In his second start for the Twins – on May 7 at Shaw Stadium against the Pulaski Phillies – Necciai struck out 19 and allowed six hits in a complete-game 7-4 victory.

Three days later at Shaw Stadium, Necciai made a relief appearance and saved Bristol's 5-4 victory over the Johnson City Cardinals.

He entered the game in the top of the sixth after Johnson City had scored two runs and had the bases loaded with nobody out. He struck out three batters in a row to end the threat. In the next three innings – the seventh through the ninth – he struck out eight more batters for a total of 11 in four innings. He didn't allow a hit and walked just one. One Johnson City hitter reached on an error in the eighth inning and Johnson City's final out was a groundout to Necciai.

In his first three outings of the season, Necciai had struck out 50 in 22 innings. His fourth outing was one for the record books. His performance against the Welch Miners on May 13 in Bristol "left 1,183 thoroughly chilled spectators practically speechless."[5]

On a damp Tuesday evening, a half-full Shaw Stadium gathered to watch the first-place Twins (8-3) take on the third-place Miners (6-4). Necciai was mesmerizing from the start. He struck out three in the first, with the third being thrown out at first after catcher Harry Dunlop dropped the third strike.

Necciai struck out two in the second inning with the middle out coming on a groundout to shortstop. After Welch's leadoff hitter in the third inning reached on an error, Necciai struck out the next three hitters.

In the fourth inning, Necciai hit the leadoff hitter but then struck out the next three hitters.

He struck out the side in the fifth and sixth innings and then opened the seventh with two strikeouts for his 11 consecutive strikeout. After walking the third hitter in the seventh, he recorded another strikeout for the third out.

When he took the mound for the eighth inning, the Twins had staked him to a 7-0 lead. He struck out the side in the eighth inning. The ninth inning had a little drama. The leadoff hitter hit a pop foul between home and first base, which wasn't caught. The official scorer gave catcher Dunlop an error but the hitter became strikeout victim number 24 after being called out on strikes.

The next hitter, a pinch-hitter, struck out for the second out in the inning. Necciai's 25th strikeout tied the professional baseball record for strikeouts in a nine-inning game set by Hooks Iott, who struck out 25 while pitching for Paragould of the Northeast Arkansas League in June 1946. Five years earlier, in July 1941, Iott had struck out 30 in a 16-inning game.

With two outs, Billy Hammond became strikeout number 26, but reached first base after the pitch got past Dunlop. Dunlop denied that he had let the pitch get by him to give Necciai a chance at number 27. Dunlop said, "He had a great curveball, an old-fashioned drop. A lot of them dropped in the dirt. He wasn't easy to handle."[6]

Bob Kendrick, Welch's cleanup hitter, struck out to end the game and finish off the no-hitter and the Twins' 7-0 victory. Necciai's 27 strikeouts in a no-hitter broke the previous record of 20 strikeouts in a no-hitter by Darrell "Cy" Blanton in 1933 while pitching for St. Joseph of the Western League.

Of the 31 hitters Necciai faced, four had reached base. Of the 27 strikeouts, 17 were swinging and 10 were called.

In an interview in 2022, Necciai said he didn't know how many he had struck out until his manager (George Detore) and Dunlop told him after the game.

"I've heard all kinds of things," Necciai said. "I've heard the fans in the stands were chanting 25, 26. I don't remember that. I don't pay attention to the fans. There's a guy down there between me and Dunlop with a bat."[7]

On May 21, in his final outing for Bristol, Necciai struck out 24 and allowed just two hits in Bristol's 7-1 victory over Kingsport. After that outing, the Pirates promoted him to Burlington-Graham of the Class-B Carolina League.

In six appearances with Bristol, Necciai was 4-0 with a 0.42 ERA. In 43 innings he had allowed just two earned runs and 10 hits. He had walked 20 and struck out 109.

Necciai's no-hitter was the first of five for the Bristol pitching staff in 1952 – three of them by one pitcher.

On May 22, five days after Necciai's gem, 18-year-old Bill Bell threw the first of back-to-back no-hitters, striking out 18 in a 1-0 victory over Kingsport. In his next start, on May 26, Bell struck out 20 while no-hitting the Bluefield Blue-Grays, 4-0.

On August 25, Bell no-hit Bluefield again. The next night Frank Ramsey also no-hit Bluefield.

In 18 appearances with Burlington, Necciai was 7-9 with a 1.57 ERA. He allowed 73 hits and struck out 172 in 126 innings.[8]

Both Necciai and Bell joined the Pirates in 1952.

Necciai made his major-league debut on August 10, when he allowed seven runs in six innings, striking out three against the Chicago Cubs in Pittsburgh. He made three more appearances before earning his only major-league victory on August 24. He allowed just two earned runs and seven hits in the Pirates' 4-3 victory over the Boston Braves in the first game of a doubleheader in Pittsburgh's Forbes Field.

In his final outing of the season, in the Pirates' season finale on September 28 in Cincinnati, Necciai allowed two runs in seven innings with a major-league career-high eight strikeouts in a no-decision in the Pirates' 3-2 loss to the Reds.

In his 12 appearances for the Pirates, who were 42-112 in 1952, Necciai was 1-6 with 31 strikeouts in 54⅔ innings.

After the season, Necciai was drafted into the US Army. He spent 65 days in the Army before receiving a medical discharge in March 1953 because of an ulcer. After the discharge, he began preparing for the 1953 season.

Back in Burlington, Necciai made his season debut in late May of 1953 but after several outings, he was sidelined because of a pinched nerve. He didn't pitch in 1954 and tried a comeback in 1955. He made five minor-league appearances before ending his career in May 1955 at the age of 23.

"Finally, one doctor at Johns Hopkins told me to quit baseball and go find a job in a gas station," Necciai said. "It was tough to accept at the time. You look around and you think, 'My God, can't they heal me?' Young people heal."[9]

Necciai eventually got over the initial disappointment of the premature end to his baseball career. He went on to a successful career in business as a manufacturer's representative selling fishing and hunting equipment. In retirement, Necciai was living in Belle Vernon, Pa., near his hometown of Monongahela.

"I gave baseball a nickel and got a million dollars back," said Necciai.[10]

This article was edited by Thomas Rathkamp and fact-checked by Mike Huber.

SOURCES

In addition to the sources cited in the Notes, the author consulted Baseball-Reference.com, Newspapers.com, Retrosheet.org, and SABR.org.

NOTES

1 L.H. Addington, Robert L. Finch, and Ben M. Morgan, eds, *The Story of Minor League Baseball, 1901-1952* (Columbus, Ohio: The Stoneman Press, 1952), 234.

2 Warren Corbett. "Ron Necciai," SABR Biography Project.

3 "White Sox Sell Rothblatt to Memphis," *Nashville Banner*, July 30, 1951: 10.

4 George K. Leonard, "Five Clubs Fight for 2-3-4 Spots," *The Sporting News*, September 5, 1951: 29. Baseball-Reference.com does not show Necciai as playing with New Orleans. Statistics from Necciai's time with the Pelicans come from Warren Corbett's biography of Necciai.

5 Jimmy Carson, "Necciai Fans 27, Hurls No-hitter," *Bristol Herald-Courier*, May 14, 1952: 1.

6 Corbett.

7 Jonathan Abrams, "His Night of Baseball Fame Has Lingered for 70 Years," *New York Times*, August 17, 2022. https://www.nytimes.com/2022/08/17/sports/baseball/fame-baseball-ron-necciai.html.

8 Necciai's statistics with Burlington are from James Selko, *Minor League All-Star Teams, 1922-62* (Jefferson, North Carolina: McFarland & Co., Publishers), 2007.

9 Corbett.

10 Corbett.

THE 1955 HAMILTON CARDINALS

Why Did the 1955 PONY League Champions Franchise Fold in May 1956?

By Allen Tait

INTRODUCTION

The Hamilton Cardinals of the Pennsylvania-Ontario-New York (PONY) League experienced a rapid rise and fall between 1955 and 1956. The team won the 1955 PONY League championship in September 1955, yet ceased operations in May 1956. The Hamilton team was the primary reason for the "O" in the PONY acronym; it had operated continuously since the league was founded in 1939 (excluding the war years 1943-1945 when the league operated exclusively in the United States). The only other Ontario-based PONY League team had been the London Pirates (1940-1941). The demise of the Hamilton Cardinals led to the league being renamed the New York-Pennsylvania League in 1957.

SABR: The Rucker Archive

Ken Boyer.

Hamilton made the postseason in three of its first four seasons prior to the wartime hiatus. Its return to the PONY League in 1946 was a challenge; Hamilton did not make the postseason again until 1948. That started a string of six consecutive playoff appearances before the team failed to make it in 1954.

Before the 1955 season, a total of 20 Hamilton players had made the major leagues with careers lasting from a few games to many seasons. The two most recognizable names played on the third-place Hamilton Cardinals in 1950:

Ken Boyer was primarily a third baseman and hit .342. He also pitched in 21 games for Hamilton, posting a record of 6-8 with a 4.39 ERA. Boyer was the starting third baseman for the St. Louis Cardinals from 1955 through 1965, compiling a batting average of .293 with 255 home runs and 1,001 RBIs over those 11 seasons. Boyer played four more seasons with the New York Mets, Chicago White Sox, and Los Angeles Dodgers before retiring in 1969. His final career statistics include a .287 batting average, 282 home runs, and 1,141 RBIs.

Stu Miller was the ace of the Hamilton staff, starting 27 games and compiling a 16-13 record with a 3.21 ERA. Miller went on to have a 16-year major-league career with the St. Louis Cardinals, Philadelphia Phillies, New York/San Francisco Giants, Baltimore Orioles, and Atlanta Braves, compiling a lifetime record of 105-103 with a 3.24 ERA, plus 153 saves.

THE 1955 CHAMPIONSHIP SEASON

Hamilton had only two holdover players from the 1954 team, outfielder Arthur Resma, who had provided respectable offensive production in 1954 (.285/9/76), and 1954 backup catcher Bill Brown (.252/0/15 in 42 games). The influx of new players appeared to mesh from the start as Hamilton led the league throughout the season.

On May 26, they had a 17-5 record and a 4½-game lead over Wellsville and Corning.[1] By the PONY League all-star break, *The Sporting News* reported, "The Hamilton Cardinals were running away with the race, leading by ten and one-half games."[2]

However, the league was facing financial challenges with two franchises.

"The Directors of Hornell (Pony), who had voted to drop out of the league, rescinded the decision, June 27, after a fund-raising campaign produced more than $3,500 to meet the Dodgers' operating deficit. The drive will continue in an effort to keep the club going for the remainder of the season. ... With Hornell's troubles apparently solved, the Pony League faced a new difficulty when General Manager Mike Cannavano of Erie announced the Senators 'were ready to call it quits.' However, Erie fans rallied to the support of the club, with donations and ticket purchases, and Cannavano said 'I think we can make out all right.' ... In an effort to aid tail-end clubs, the directors of the Pony League have voted to split the season."[3]

However, the split-season plan was not implemented. On July 8, National Association President George Trautman ruled that the plan's approval required a unanimous vote. Hamilton and seventh-place Jamestown opposed the split season. Also rejected was a proposal by Pony League President Vince McNamara to hold a six-team round-robin playoff in lieu of the four-team Governors Cup series. Corning (second place) and Wellsville (fourth place) opposed.[4]

On August 4, Hamilton had a 9½-game lead over second-place Bradford. However, despite being in playoff contention, Bradford was facing financial pressure:

"Fans at Bradford (Pony) burned more than 300 season tickets at home plate during a double-header with Jamestown, July 30, and pledged cash support of the club at $1 admission per game to enable the Phillies to finish the season. Mayor Hug Ryan proposed the 'waiving' of the season tickets, which were sold at the beginning of the year at a bargain $10 each. With all-cash admissions, at present average attendance of 800, it was believed the Phillies would raise sufficient funds at the box office to remain in operation."[5]

Late in the season, second-place Wellsville, 13½ games behind, achieved an accomplishment against Hamilton by ending its streak of 76 consecutive games without being shut out. Wellsville pitchers Don Nottebart and Bob Stoico pitched back-to-back five-hit shutouts, with Wellsville winning the games, 7-0 and 5-0.[6]

Hamilton finished the 1955 regular season in first place with an 82-43 record, leading the league in runs scored (836) and fewest runs allowed (572). This was a significant improvement over the 1954 team, which had scored 783 runs and allowed 792 runs.

The top four starters had a combined record of 61-24, led by Gary Geiger (20-7 with a 1.98 ERA). Geiger did make the major leagues in 1958, forging a 12-year career as an outfielder with a career batting average of .246. Reliever Paul Toth (three seasons) also reached the majors. The Hamilton hitting was led by 32-year-old second baseman Ed Lyons, who batted .350 and hit 17 home runs. Lyons was the only Hamilton player with previous major-league experience, having played for the 1947 Washington Senators and hitting .154 in 26 at-bats.

Hamilton defeated the fourth-place Wellsville Braves (68-58) two games to one in round one of the playoffs.[7] Wellsville was led by future major-league pitcher Don Nottebart (18-11, 2.57). Nottebart had a nine-year major-league career with a record of 36-51/3.65, including a 1963 no-hitter against the Phillies. Wellsville catcher Ron Henry (42 games) later reached the majors, and 38-year-old second baseman Alex Monchak had previous major-league experience, having appeared in 19 games for the Philadelphia Phillies in 1940.

The third-place Corning Red Sox (69-57) upset the second-place Bradford Phillies (74-51) two games to one in the other semifinal. Hamilton proceeded to sweep Corning in three games in the final to win the PONY League championship.[8] Corning starter Ken McBride (10-9, 3.81) later had a seven-year major-league career, primarily with the Angels, compiling a 40-50 record with a 3.79 ERA and three All-Star Game selections. The only other future major leaguer on the team was Bill Monbouquette. He appeared in only one game for Corning, a start that lasted two innings in which he yielded six hits and three earned runs in a no-decision. Monbouquette went on to have an 11-year major-league career, amassing a 114-112/3.68 record, and was chosen for four All-Star teams, including 1963, when he was a 20-game winner for the Red Sox.

PONY LEAGUE ATTENDANCE

PONY League attendance fluctuated over four seasons, with Hamilton being one of the stronger franchises.

Year	Total Attendance	Hamilton Attendance	Rank
1952	339,764	82,286	1st
1953	291,325	53,291	1st
1954	375,981	41,379	5th
1955	339,040	53,989	1st

As noted above, three of the eight PONY League teams (Hornell, Erie, Bradford) disclosed that they had experienced financial difficulties that required civic support to complete the season. The final standings for 1955, including attendance, were:

Hamilton Cardinals	82	43	53,989
Bradford Phillies	74	51	35,979
Corning Red Sox	69	57	42,919
Wellsville Braves	68	58	45,799
Erie Senators	66	60	53,151
Hornell Dodgers	50	76	27,314
Jamestown Falcons	48	78	32,700
Olean Oilers	46	80	47,189

1956 HAMILTON RED WINGS – THE FINAL SEASON

The 1955 success of the franchise on the field and at the box office did not provide a guarantee for a 1956 affiliation renewal with the parent St. Louis Cardinals. An indication that the future of the Hamilton Cardinals was in doubt appeared shortly after they won the 1955 championship. In an interview with August Busch, owner of the St. Louis Cardinals, the reporter noted that the Cardinals had 19 farm clubs in 1955, some of which were owned outright. Busch was asked if there would be any reduction in the farm system in 1956. Busch responded:

"We're going to take a serious look at our minor league setup. Our aim is a basically sound, well-balanced system rather than mere numbers."[9]

All of which led to the Cardinals dropping four minor-league affiliates, including Hamilton.

Hamilton was unable to replace the lost Cardinals affiliation and began the 1956 season rebranded as the independent Hamilton Red Wings. To make matters more challenging, Hamilton did not have any players return from the 1955 championship team. The efforts to operate as an independent franchise proved unsuccessful, and the Red Wings, as well as the New York Yankees-affiliated Bradford Yankees, folded on May 16, 1956. *The Sporting News* summarized the contributing factors: Bad weather in early May hurt the league; 25 of the first 40 scheduled games were postponed. This particularly hurt the finances of the independent Hamilton Red Wings. The league did consider assuming operation of the franchise; however, with the Bradford Yankees also experiencing financial problems, both franchises were folded on May 16.[10]

The final 1956 standings were:

Wellsville Braves	74	56	30,470
Corning Red Sox	68	55	33,450
Olean Oilers	68	58	27,281
Hornell Dodgers	57	58	20,334
Jamestown Falcons	52	62	19,757
Erie Senators	45	74	28,223
Hamilton Red Wings	6	8	1,200
Bradford Yankees	3	9	1,258
Total Attendance	161,973		

With the demise of the sole Canadian franchise and falling attendance, the league restructured as the New York-Pennsylvania League beginning in 1957. The original eight franchises included newcomers Batavia and Elmira, plus former PONY League cities Bradford, Corning, Erie, Jamestown, Olean, and Wellsville. Once again, however, there were difficulties with Bradford, now an independent team named the Blue Sox. They struggled with a 5-15 record, being outscored 130-75 and drawing only 1,700 fans. The franchise folded on May 23 and was relocated on May 28 to Hornell as the Redlegs, an affiliate of the Cincinnati Reds.

Despite the start-up challenges in 1957, the New York-Pennsylvania League operated continuously as a Class-A short-season league until 2019, when Major League Baseball initiated a radical overhaul of the minor-league system. Three franchises – Aberdeen, Brooklyn, and Hudson Valley – remained affiliated with major-league teams. The teams in Lowell, Massachusetts, and Staten Island, New York, were eliminated, while all the other clubs drifted over to a variety of independent or college summer leagues. After more than 60 years, the New York-Pennsylvania League ceased operations.

This article was edited by Marshall Adesman and fact-checked by Mark Richard.

SOURCES

Data regarding the teams and players is drawn from Baseball-Reference.com, except as noted.

NOTES

1 "How They Stand," *The Sporting News*, June 1, 1955: 40.

2 "Minor League Highlights Class D," *The Sporting News*, July 6, 1955: 36.

3 "Minor League Highlights Class D," *The Sporting News*, July 6, 1955: 36.

4 "Minor League Highlights Class D, " *The Sporting News*, July 20, 1955: 44.

5 "Minor League Notes Class D," *The Sporting News*, August 10, 1955: 37.

6 "Minor League Notes Class D," *The Sporting News*, August 3, 1955: 35.

7 "Playoff Standings," *The Sporting News*, September 21, 1955: 37.

8 "Playoff Standings," *The Sporting News*, September 21, 1955: 37.

9 Carl T. Felker, "Busch Would 'Do It Again' in Buying Cardinals," *The Sporting News,* October 12, 1955: 2.

10 "Jean and Carroll Jean Drop Pony Franchise at Hamilton," *The Sporting News*, May 23, 1956: 37.

DOUG HARVEY AND THE OTTAWA SENATORS

By Martin Lacoste

Professional baseball in Ottawa was sporadic in the early to mid-twentieth century. From 1912 to 1915, the Ottawa Senators played in the Class-C (later Class-B) Canadian League and finished first in three of the four seasons. The Senators resurfaced in the Class-B Eastern Canada League in 1922, finishing second to the Trois-Rivières Trios, and in 1923, renamed the Canadiens, they finished second again, this time behind the Montreal Royals. The Ottawa-Hull Senators were one of six teams in the ill-fated Québec-Ontario-Vermont League (which operated only for one season, 1924), finishing the season in fourth place. Over a decade passed before Ottawa joined the Class-C Canadian-American League in 1936. This was a less successful venture; after a strong rookie campaign in which they finished second, they ended up no higher than sixth for the following three years. Poor performance, combined with low attendance, "a lack of lights and the pressures of war [made it difficult] to continue."[1] Surprisingly, they managed for one more season by combining with Ogdensburg, and further stunned all by finishing first. This still did not prevent them from bowing out of the league after the season.

Courtesy La Patrie du Dimanche - *December 3, 1959.*

Doug Harvey.

In 1946 a new Border League (the original operated in 1912 and '13), a Class-C league with six teams from Canada and the United States, was formed. It included the Granby Red Sox, Kingston Ponies, and Sherbrooke Canadians, but Granby and Sherbrooke left after the 1946 season and were replaced by the Geneva Red Birds and another new professional team from Ottawa, this time called the Nationals. Ottawa's return to Organized Baseball was a great success right from the start, due to a "mix of young prospects and older guys nearing the end of their playing days."[2] They were managed by former St. Louis Cardinals pitcher Paul "Daffy" Dean, brother of Dizzy Dean. This eclectic assemblage enabled Ottawa to outdistance its competition handily and finish the season 12 games ahead of the Watertown Athletics. The Nationals went on to defeat the Ogdensburg Maples in the finals (aided by a triple play in the final game) to win the league championship in their rookie season.

Despite this great success, "Paul Dean had been a disappointment at the helm, and had left the club in the middle of the 1947 playoffs."[3] William Metzig, a Border League all-star who led the team in 1947 in home runs and RBIs and was a solid second baseman, "was better than Dean when it came to handling players,"[4] so took over as manager. With Metzig at the helm for 1948, Ottawa (which reverted to their Senators nickname) once again finished the season in first, 6½ games ahead of the Geneva Robins, though they lost the championship in the playoffs to the Ogdensburg Maples. The tables turned in 1949 when they finished 6½ games *behind* Geneva. The 1950 season was marked by the closest pennant race in Border League history. On September 1, with 10 games remaining, Ottawa (once again as the Nationals) held a slim one-game lead over their old foes, the Ogdensburg Maples.

The Maples won eight of their last 10 games, but the Nationals held them off with clutch wins of their own, including dominant victories in their last five games of the season (outscoring their opponents 33-9, highlighted by a no-hitter by Don Bryant on the next to last game of the season against Geneva).

But the pennant was still up for grabs on the final day of the season, and it took another strong pitching performance, this time by Ed Flanagan, who scattered five hits and allowed only one run, for Ottawa to clinch its third pennant in four years on the final day of the season. The Nationals came up short in the playoffs however, surrendering the league championship to Ogdensburg.

Ottawa did not return to the Border League for the 1951 season, but rather fielded a club in the Triple-A International League, the Ottawa Giants, who struggled to stay out of last place for most of the season. The Border League itself also struggled in 1951, with clubs disbanding at the end of June and into July before the entire league ceased operations on July 16, 1951. Overall, Ottawa was the most successful of all the clubs of the Border League, finishing with an overall record of 310-198.

During Ottawa's run in the Border League, the team featured five players who played in the major leagues. Three of these saw minimal action in the majors: player-manager William Metzig (with Ottawa from 1947 to 1950), who had played five games with the Chicago White Sox in 1944; pitcher Walt Masters, who pitched for Ottawa in 1947 at the age of 40 and had very brief stints with the Washington Senators in 1931, the Philadelphia Phillies in 1937, and the Philadelphia Athletics in 1939; Catcher Bo Wallace (with Ottawa in 1950) played briefly with the Newark Eagles of the Negro National League in 1948. The remaining two players enjoyed much greater success, ultimately becoming Hall of Famers. That is where the similarities end for these two elite athletes.

Willard Brown, who played 30 games with Ottawa in 1950, was, as celebrated on his plaque in Cooperstown, a "power-hitting center fielder who helped lead the Kansas City Monarchs to six pennants in 10 seasons from 1937-1946, including a Negro Leagues championship in 1942."[5] This was broken up by his service in the US Army for two years during World War II: "He was among those sailing on 5,000 ships that crossed the English Channel during the D-Day Invasion of 1944."[6] He returned to the Monarchs in 1946 (rejoining fellow Hall of Fame teammates Satchel Paige, Buck O'Neil, and Hilton Smith).

The next season, "Hank Thompson and Brown became the second and third Black players in American League history when they signed with the St. Louis Browns on July 17, 1947. The Browns, however, sent the duo straight to the majors. The adjustment proved difficult as Willard Brown played in just 21 games between July 19 and Aug. 21 before he was released."[7] He went on to win two Triple Crowns with the Puerto Rican Winter Leagues and was inducted to the Hall of Fame in 2006.

Ottawa's other Hall of Famer is not to be found in Cooperstown however, but rather in Toronto, home of the Hockey Hall of Fame. Regarded as one of the top defensemen in NHL history (listed third by *Sports Illustrated*, behind only Ray Bourque and Bobby Orr), Doug Harvey excelled in virtually every sport he played, and from 1947 to 1950, many wondered if he was destined to find fame on the diamond rather than in the hockey rink.

Douglas Norman Harvey was born on December 19, 1924, in Montreal, the second child of Alfred and Martha Harvey. Alfred was born in 1896 in Hammersmith, England, a borough of London, and joined the Canadian Army medical corps and served as a stretcher-bearer in France and Belgium during the First World War. He married Martha Evans in September 1921 in Kingston and worked mostly for a pharmaceuticals company in Montreal.

Growing up in the Notre-Dame-de-Grâce district of Montreal, author Brown writes, "there was never a problem finding a pick-up game of football, baseball, or hockey. And the parks in the area had hockey and softball leagues (the grounds were not yet big enough for baseball)."

"When Doug had arrived at West Hill [High School] for grade eight in September 1938, he wanted to play football but was told he was too small. He played soccer instead [and] made the school's senior soccer team, even though he was still a couple of months shy of his fourteenth birthday."[9] The following year he played on a newly created Bantam football team at West Hill.

A versatile and competitive athlete, Harvey tried badminton, track, lacrosse, and boxing during his high-school years. But it was football that Harvey excelled in during his time at West Hill, notably in his grade twelve year in 1942. *The Sporting News* declared that "he was one of the most promising running stars on Canadian gridirons."[10] He and team captain Don Loney helped lead the West Hill Red Raiders to the championship game against the team from Catholic

High, only to lose after a controversial call by the referees.

The football season over and World War II raging, Doug decided to enlist in the Royal Canadian Navy and, though a month shy of his 18th birthday, the Navy "found a spot for Doug right away – on its hockey team."[11] He yearned to see some action in the war and did join the war effort, but "he was kept close to home until the spring of 1944 so he could continue to play football and hockey for the Navy."[12]

Since he remained at home during the summer of 1943, Harvey was asked to play fast-pitch softball in the newly formed Snowdon Fastball League (founded by 17-year-old Sam Pollock, who would one day take over from Frank Selke at the helm of the NHL Montreal Canadiens). Harvey was a line-drive-hitting third baseman for the league's St. Augustine team, and one of the top players in the extremely competitive league. A teammate of Harvey's, Alex Smart, remembered how Harvey loved to catch someone with his head down: "The guy'd be running around second, never looking, and all of a sudden BINGO, he'd run into Doug, and Doug would have the ball. He was thinking all the time."[13]

In the fall of 1943, Harvey was assigned by the Navy to play for Donnacona in the Québec Rugby Football Union. This was common practice at the time, as quite a few "NHLers and top amateurs [also played] for military teams all over the country. It was thought the teams would be good for enlisted and civilian morale."[14] He continued to attract attention for his overall ability, notably his defense, and at the end of the season was named the league's Most Valuable Player. In 1944, he sailed across the Atlantic Ocean as a gunner on a merchant ship. After the war, he resumed his hockey career with the Navy as well as the junior Montreal Royals of the Québec Junior Hockey League.

Harvey's last football season was 1945 with the Montreal Hornets (forerunner of the Montreal Alouettes of the Canadian Football League). In 1946 he decided that since Canadian football was semiprofessional, his best bet was hockey. He was moved up to the Royals' senior squad, and helped the team win the Québec Senior Hockey League Championship in 1946. The following year, he starred on defense with the Royals as they went on to repeat, and then defeated Calgary to win the Allan Cup, awarded to Canada's amateur hockey champions.

In between hockey and football seasons, Harvey continued to play softball, and in the summer of 1947, as he prepared to play again with St. Augustine, a new opportunity arose. "Thomas Gorman (one of the founders of the NHL), now back in Ottawa, having recently retired as GM of the Montreal Canadiens, approached him about playing baseball for a new franchise he had landed in the Class 'C' Border League. Gorman was looking for players and thought of Harvey – he had grown fond of him while he was playing for the Royals, and he had given him summer jobs around the Forum."[15]

"Harvey is probably the only athlete who has been signed to play baseball on his ability as a hockey player,"[16] but Gorman admired Doug's durability and determination. So while he had never seen Harvey play baseball, "he offered him a contract and never regretted it."[17]

But Harvey was very green when it came to baseball. American players "made fun of Harvey because his beat-up glove looked like it came from a dime store."[18] They were even more amused when they saw the way he gripped a bat, with his hands several inches apart. Manager Metzig "got Harvey a proper glove and some baseball cleats, and he persuaded him to put his hands closer together on the bat. Although Harvey didn't crack the starting lineup and didn't even get into a game until mid-August, he showed he could hit, run, and handle himself in the outfield."[19] In his very first game, he came off the bench and got two hits, helping the Nationals defeat the Auburn Cayugas, 9-5.

That season Harvey made it into only 10 games but made the most of it as he went 6-for-15, "an amazing performance for someone facing professional baseball pitching for the first time."[20] As the Canadiens training camp had opened, Harvey missed the playoffs; he had to focus on making the Canadiens. Though he tried to manage both sports for a time, "jumping into his car after a ballgame and driving the more than 250 kilometers to the training camp, but he could only keep that up for a week or so."[21]

After his first NHL training camp, Harvey made the Canadiens team, but had limited ice time and did not often impress with the opportunities he was given. He was sent down to Buffalo of the AHL in mid-December, and though not spectacular while there, was recalled to Montreal about a month later and remained with the Canadiens until season's end. The 1947-48 campaign proved a major disappointment for the Canadiens, who after finishing first the last four seasons, ended up next to last and failed to make the playoffs. Some of the criticism fell on Harvey, who himself was unspectacular in his rookie season and failed to live up to the expectations made of him by the fans and the media. The only saving grace of missing the playoffs was that it allowed Harvey to be on the diamond from the start of the 1948 baseball season.

Back in the Border League, the Nationals had many players back from the previous season and there were only a few openings in the starting lineup. One of them was in right field, where Harvey had played briefly in 1947. He showed up for spring training leaner than he had been the summer before and was obviously determined to make the team. He hit the ball hard during exhibition games, picking up where he had left off the previous fall. On the eve of the season opener, manager Metzig announced that Harvey would be his starting right fielder. "Harvey's a steady fielder, covers a lot of ground, and in our game Thursday he hit two drives to center field that would have been out of the park on our diamond," the manager said.[22]

The season started well for Harvey and the Nationals, as they "walloped the Ogdensburg Maples 15-3 in front of more than 4,000 Ottawa fans. Harvey, wearing number seventeen, managed a base hit and a walk. He batted sixth at first, but gradually moved up in the order. By August, he was the team's cleanup hitter and was contending for the Border League batting title. He was also named as a starter in the league's mid-season All-Star game."[23]

Helping the Nationals win the pennant in 1948, Harvey finished sixth in batting (.340), second in hits (144), and second in runs scored (107). This caught the attention of major-league scouts: "They'd say, 'Who the hell is this guy?'"[24] In the playoffs, Harvey batted .357 with two home runs and five RBIs in the first four games against Ogdensburg. He missed the final game because he had to report to the Canadiens training camp. "Harvey, it seems, was in no hurry to emerge from the baseball boonies to rejoin the cushy ranks of the NHL."[25]

Many scouts later commented that Harvey had "all the skills to become a star on the diamond, but unfortunately was a bit too old when he started playing Organized Baseball. He was 22 years old when he accepted an offer from Ottawa. ... Normally, in the US where baseball is considered as the national sport, an athlete makes the jump into Class C when he is 18 or 19 years old, at most."[26]

In early May of 1949, as the Nationals began spring workouts, Metzig telephoned Harvey to ask him when he would be reporting to camp. Harvey was vague, saying he had to wait until doctors examined the knee he'd injured during the hockey season. But he left Metzig with the impression that he wanted to play baseball and would eventually report to the team. A few days later, word came out that Harvey was getting married and might not play baseball at all.

Harvey would eventually report to the team, although he missed spring training. His return did not go unnoticed; the *Ottawa Journal* reported: "Metzig is relieved by the arrival of Doug Harvey, who should bolster the hitting department."[27] This proved an understatement, as Harvey improved upon his impressive 1948 season. He continued to terrorize Border League pitchers, winning the batting title with a .351 average and leading the league in runs (121) and RBIs (109). He also demonstrated increased power with 14 home runs and continued to display impressive speed, stealing 30 bases and hitting 10 triples. "And the fact that he struck out only 28 times proves that he had a very precise eye to make the distinction between a ball and a strike."[28] He was once again named to the all-star team and "to Metzig's satisfaction, he also became a team leader."[29]

In the semifinals, as headlined in the *Ottawa Journal,* Harvey was "... in Hero's Role When Nats Triumph."[30] In the ninth inning of a 1-1 game against the Auburn Cayugas, he hit a triple and tried for home, where the "charging Ottawa runner brushed the ball out of [catcher] Bruss's outstretched hand."[31] Auburn nevertheless sent Ottawa packing by winning the series in seven games. For Harvey, this was likely fortuitous; he would not have been able to play in the finals, for he once again had to report to the Canadiens training camp.

Now with two outstanding baseball seasons under Harvey's belt, more major-league scouts began to take notice. Harvey "was drafted by the National League's Boston Braves and offered a spot on their Class B team in Pawtucket, Rhode Island. And some reports said the Boston Red Sox were interested as well. In addition, Harvey later told friends that he had received a letter from the St. Louis Cardinals but had put it aside unopened. He found out later that the letter contained a minor league contract."[32] Much like when he was tempted with offers to play professional football, he ultimately had to decline.

This was never an easy choice for Harvey. In later years he often commented on the joy he found on the diamond. "He would never really say which sport was his favorite, but it was clear that he believed hockey provided the best career path."[33] "Harvey said he must concentrate on hockey because "that is where the money is." His hockey salary as a big leaguer was roughly three times what he made playing Class C baseball. Since the hockey playoffs sometimes ran well into April, through most of the baseball training season, this would seem to preclude any immediate possibility of Harvey reaching higher minors in the diamond sport."[34] Years later, he was quoted as saying, "[M]aybe I would have been interested in reporting to spring training if I could have gotten the chance to make a Double-A team. But as they weren't really interested in giving me a serious try, I preferred to stay in Canada."[35]

The team that had drafted him hadn't heard this news however, as "sometime during the 1950 NHL semifinals, the phone rang on Harvard Avenue. It was someone from the Boston Braves wanting to know why Doug Harvey had failed to report to spring training. [...] Harvey had never told the Braves he was passing up their offer. When he failed to report to [the Braves], Tommy Gorman re-acquired his contract and asked him to play for the Nationals again. Harvey agreed to play on an occasional basis, depending on his commitments in Montreal. Ursula had given birth to their first child, Doug Jr., in February 1950. [...] In the end, Harvey was too busy for baseball that summer and played only ten games for the Nationals. [...] It was now time for him to concentrate on hockey and his life in Montreal."[36]

But Harvey's career as a baseball player was not immediately over. After leaving Ottawa, he batted .449 to lead the Valleyfield Chiefs (which featured a 17-year-old pitcher named Johnny Podres) to the pennant of the Laurentian Senior Baseball League, a semipro league in Québec. And in 1951 he was player-manager-co-owner of the Lachine Canucks, also of the Laurentian League, and brought along several other hockey players to play on the team on occasion, including fellow Hockey Hall of Famer Maurice "Rocket" Richard. Harvey managed Lachine into the 1952 season but left partway during the season as Lachine floundered at the bottom of the standings.

Harvey was a natural both at the plate and on the basepaths, though defensively, he admitted, "I was no Mickey Mantle in terms of covering ground in the outfield, but, he added with modesty, I did well enough."[37] We can never know if he indeed would have made it to the major leagues, let alone be anywhere near the success that he was in the NHL, but baseball, he noted, "is a sport that I always loved to play and still, today, when I have the opportunity, I make my way to the De Lorimier stadium to see the Montreal Royals at work. If I chose hockey over baseball, it was that my chances of progress within the organization with the Canadiens were better than they were with the Boston Braves. Personally, I think I made a wise decision to abandon baseball."[38] He "would later claim, during moments of nostalgia, to regret not having pursued baseball more seriously."[39]

What is known is the result of Harvey's decision to commit to hockey. As part of the great Montreal hockey dynasty along with fellow Hall of Famers Maurice "Rocket" Richard, Jean Beliveau, Dickie Moore, and Jacques Plante, under coach Toe Blake, Harvey helped Montreal win the Stanley Cup six times, including a record five in a row from 1956 to 1960. He then played for three seasons with the New York Rangers and briefly with Detroit and St. Louis before retiring in 1969. He was named to the NHL All-Star Game 13 times and won the Norris Trophy as the league's top defenseman seven times from 1955 to 1962, losing only to teammate Tom Johnson in 1959. Only Bobby Orr won more Norris Trophies in his career (eight). Doug Harvey was inducted into the Hockey Hall of Fame in 1973. The Canadiens retired Harvey's number 2 in 1985, a few years before his death on December 26, 1989, in Montreal at the age of 65.

This article was edited by David Siegel and fact-checked by Kevin Larkin.

SOURCES

In addition to the sources cited in the Notes, the author consulted a number of newspapers and other sources including:

Baseball-reference.com

Costello, Rory. "Willard Brown," SABR Baseball Biography Project, https://sabr.org/bioproj/person/Willard-Brown/, accessed January 11, 2023.

"Douglas Harvey," The Sporting News Player Contract Cards, https://digital.la84.org/digital/collection/p17103coll3/id/69118/rec/5, accessed December 23, 2022.

"How Doug Harvey Loafed His Way to Fame," http://archive.macleans.ca/article/1958/2/15/how-doug-harvey-loafed-his-way-to-fame, accessed December 5, 2022.

"Top 25 NHL Defensemen of All Time," https://www.si.com/nhl/2015/01/16/top-25-nhl-defensemen-all-time#gid=ci02554d8260052580&pid=2-ray-bourque, accessed December 8, 2022.

"Willard Brown," Hall of Fame Explorer, https://baseballhall.org/hall-of-famers/brown-willard, accessed January 11, 2023.

Christian Trudeau files and research

NOTES

1 David Pietrusza, *Baseball's Canadian-American League* (Jefferson, North Carolina: McFarland & Co., Inc., 1990), 43.

2 William Brown, *Doug: The Doug Harvey Story* (Montreal: Véhicule Press, 2002), 29.

3 Brown, 43.

4 Brown, 43.

5 Hall of Fame Plaque, "Willard Brown," National Baseball Hall of Fame, https://baseballhall.org/hall-of-famers/brown-willard, accessed January 5, 2023.

6 "Willard Brown."

7 "Willard Brown."

8 William Brown, 68.

9 Brown, 71.

10 Lloyd McGowan, "Canadiens' Doug Harvey Border League Slugger," *The Sporting News*, February 23, 1949: 2, 5.

11 Brown, 78.

12 Brown, 82.

13 Brown, 82.

14 Brown, 83-84.

15 Brown, 29.

16 McGowan.

17 McGowan.

18 Brown, 31.

19 Brown, 29-30.

20 Brown, 31.

21 Brown, 31

22 Brown, 43.

23 Brown, 43.

24 Brown, 44.

25 Brown, 45.

26 Bert Souliere, "Harvey aurait pu se créer une carrière au baseball," *La Patrie du Dimanche*, December 3, 1959: Section Spéciale, 4.

27 Brown, 54.

28 Souliere.

29 Brown, 56.

30 Gordon Ryan, "Harvey in Hero's Role When Nats Triumph," *Ottawa Journal*, September 10, 1949: 35.

31 Ryan.

32 Brown, 57.

33 Brown, 58.

34 McGowan.

35 Souliere.

36 Brown, 57.

37 Souliere.

38 Souliere.

39 Brown, 58.

THE COLUMBUS JETS: TAKEOFF FOR THE LUMBER COMPANY

By Thomas Kern

The state of Ohio has a rich baseball history. The city of Columbus has played a major role in that history, even though, unlike its sister cities Cincinnati and Cleveland, it has never hosted an American or National League team. It has been the home of an array of minor-league teams as well as several Negro League teams, namely the Buckeyes (1921), the Turfs (1932), the Blue Birds (1933), and the Elite Giants (1935).[1] This story is about the Columbus Jets and their Pittsburgh Pirates connection as an International League Triple-A franchise from 1957 to 1970.

Minor-league baseball in Columbus dates from an independent team named the Buckeyes that joined as charter members of the International Association of Baseball in 1877. The Buckeyes were part of the expanding "major league" American Association in 1883, dropped out for a time, and then rejoined in 1889. The team was not included when the American Association merged with the National League in 1891 and for a time moved itinerantly between the minor-league-level Inter-State and Western Leagues. In 1902 Columbus, under the name of the Senators, joined the inaugural season of a reformed American Association and was a continuous presence until 1954. The American Association of those days was an independent minor league, but as American and National League teams established farm systems, Columbus became a St. Louis Cardinals affiliate in 1931 and became the Redbirds.[2]

Columbus Jets logo.

At the end of the 1954 season, the Cardinals opted to move their American Association entry to Omaha. The team won the Junior World Series in 1950, but otherwise had routinely finished in the second division and attendance suffered as a result. Fortunately for Columbus, "local business enthusiasts put up $10,000 each to re-establish pro ball in the city the following year. The Ottawa franchise of the International League was purchased [and relocated to Columbus] for $50,000."[3]

The reconstituted franchise became known as the Jets, in honor of Columbus's wartime role in the aviation industry.[4] Curtiss-Wright Corporation, the largest US aircraft manufacturer, built a plant in Columbus in 1941 to build naval aircraft for the war in the Pacific. Its Curtiss SB2C Helldiver was a major contributor to the war effort.[5]

The Columbus Jets' first parent club was the Kansas City Athletics for the 1955 and 1956 seasons. In 1957 the Pittsburgh Pirates established their Triple-A presence in Columbus, where they would remain for the next 14 years. Columbus and Pittsburgh are only 185 miles apart, making it relatively easy to move players back and forth as needed. The Jets' early years were not promising, but in 1959, managed by Cal Ermer, the team finished second in the regular season to Buffalo, though it was swept by the eventual league champion Havana in the playoffs.[6] Columbus won the regular season in 1961 under new manager Larry Shepard, and this time lost to Buffalo in the playoffs. Shepard helmed the team for six years before joining the Phillies as their pitching coach in 1967 and then managing the Pirates in 1968 and 1969.[7] In Shepard's next to last year at the helm, 1965, the Jets made it to the finals, but were defeated by Toronto, four games to one. This was the first of six successive playoff appearances for the Jets, through 1970, their final year in the International League.[8]

In 1965 the beginnings of the eventual Pirates roster for the late 1960s and 1970s began arriving in Columbus. Steve Blass had already surfaced, but Dock Ellis, Jerry May, José Pagán, and Luke Walker were now developing their skills at the Triple-A level. In 1966, when the Jets tied for second in the IL but lost to Toronto in the first round of the four-team playoffs,[9] Manny Sanguillén appeared on the scene. Discovered by Herb Raybourn in Panama and then signed by him and Pirates superscout Howie Haak,[10] Sanguillén started his play in Organized Baseball with the Batavia Pirates (New York-Penn League) in 1965. His potential was clear, and he spent time at both Raleigh (Carolina League) and Columbus in 1966. He played well overall, but in his brief time in Columbus hit only .231. (He batted .328 for Raleigh.) Sanguillén spent all or parts of the next two seasons in Columbus[11] before being called up to Pittsburgh in 1969. Emerging prospects notwithstanding, the 1966 Jets were carried by their veterans; Gene Michael, 28 years old, George Spriggs, 29, and Dave Roberts, 33, provided the offense. They were aided by double-digit wins from Wilbur Wood, John Gelnar, Luke Walker, Jim Shellenback, and Ed Hobaugh to produce an 82-65 record.

The following year, 1967, after Shepard's departure to the Phillies, Pete Peterson managed the team to fourth place and a sub-.500 regular-season finish. As the fourth-place team, they still made the playoffs and defeated Rochester before losing in the finals to Toledo, four games to one.[12] That year, two new faces appeared, Bob Moose and Bob Robertson – key pieces for the Pirates of the coming years. The 19-year-old Moose went 4-1 with a 3.38 ERA. Fellow moundsman Dock Ellis, at the ripe old age of 22, was 5-7, leading the team in walks allowed, even though four other pitchers threw more innings. However, Ellis's upside exceeded any concerns about his lack of control of the strike zone. Robertson showed the promise that would steer him to the majors. At the age of only 20, in 108 games he hit .256 with 14 doubles, 19 home runs, and 63 RBIs to go with an OPS of .810. At the end of the season, Peterson, more of a fill-in for Shepard than a long-term managerial solution, moved to the Pirates front office, where his subsequent career flourished, first as the team's farm director, then as general manager.

Former Red Sox player and manager Johnny Pesky took over the team in 1968, having most recently served as Pirates manager Harry Walker's first-base coach from 1965 to 1967. The 1968 season marked the arrival of Richie Hebner and Al Oliver, two more key pieces in the parent club's future offense. The Jets finished second and made their fourth straight appearance in the IL playoffs, making it to the finals only to lose to Jacksonville, the New York Mets affiliate.[13] Hebner (a first-round draft choice in 1966[14]), at 20 managed 420 plate appearances and had a workmanlike year, batting .276 with 51 RBIs and a slugging percentage of .402. Oliver, a year older, did what he became known for in the majors: hit! He played in 132 games and had 149 hits, 14 home runs, and 74 RBIs. His batting average of .315 tied Manny Jiménez and Sanguillén had a breakout season, hitting .316. The future Lumber Company was beginning to come together.

The now revolving door of Columbus managers saw Don Hoak take over the reins in 1969. Hoak's 11-year career in the majors was followed with a brief stint as a Pirates broadcaster and then as a manager in the Pittsburgh farm system. By the beginning of the season, Ellis, Moose, Walker, Hebner, Oliver, Robertson (who split time between Columbus and Pittsburgh), and Sanguillén were now in Pittsburgh. Dave Cash and Johnny Jeter were emerging, but the pipeline was beginning to dry up. The team finished fourth at 74-66 and made it to the playoff finals, which they lost to Syracuse, four games to one.[15]

Columbus's final year as the Jets yielded one more postseason appearance. Under yet another new manager, Joe Morgan, the Jets compiled an 81-59 record, good enough for second place. Morgan, a journeyman in the majors, began coaching in the Pirates' minor-league system in Columbus in 1966 and went on to manage the successor Charleston Charlies, with a one-year coaching stint with the Pirates in 1972 sandwiched in. He later managed the IL's Pawtucket Red Sox and then the Boston Red Sox.

The Jets' second-place finish in 1970 guaranteed a playoff spot, but after beating Rochester in a hard-fought first round, three games to two, they lost to Syracuse in the finals, three games to one.[16] At this time, one more piece of the Lumber Company appeared, Rennie Stennett. Signed by Herb Raybourne, the Pirates' talent scout in Panama, he was only briefly on the Jets roster. He gained further playing time in the minors with Charleston before making it to the Steel City.

Despite a run of six straight playoff appearances and five trips to the finals, the franchise struggled at the gate. An old ballpark and poor marketing both contributed to a 40 percent decline in attendance from its second highest of 197,680 in 1965 to a low of 140,700, its second worst as a franchise, in 1970. Columbus's competitiveness in the mid- to late1960s spoke to the promising talent in the Pittsburgh farm system that, once promoted, fueled the Pirates' competitiveness and regular appearance in the National League playoffs in the early 1970s.[17]

Columbus never won the International League crown in any of the years as the Pirates' Trip le-A team. In its four trips to the finals – 1965, 1967, 1968, and 1969 – Toronto, Toledo, Jacksonville, and Syracuse bested Columbus, indicative of their own promising stars who would move to their parent teams (the Red Sox, Tigers, Mets, and Yankees respectively).

The Columbus-Pittsburgh tie was severed after the 1970 season. According to author O'Neal, "Although Columbus fielded consistent winners, attendance was disappointing, and spiraling costs triggered a franchise transfer to Charleston after the 1970 season."[18] The Pirates purchased the club from the Columbus Baseball Club, Inc. to move the team to West Virginia.

However, the Pittsburgh-Columbus connection was resurrected in 1977 when Harold Cooper, the long-standing general manager of the Jets, facilitated the move of the Memphis IL club to Columbus. Alas, this final connection lasted only one year before the franchise was moved again, this time to Portland in the Pacific Coast League.[19] However, the reconstituted Clippers did not skip a beat. They were affiliated with the Yankees from 1979 to 2006, the Washington Nationals in 2007 and 2008, and the Cleveland Guardians (previously the Indians) ever since.

It might have been the Pirates' iconic announcer Bob Prince who gave the offensive juggernaut that was the Pirates in the 1970s its name. The nascent Lumber Company (without being explicitly labeled so at the time) first surfaced in 1971, when Roberston, Hebner, Oliver, Sanguillén, and Stennett were fixtures. Willie Stargell, not quite yet the Pirates elder stateman (that moniker would be more appropriate in 1979 when Pittsburgh ended the decade with its second World Series win) was the veteran presence.

In August of 1971, Roy Blount wrote in *Sports Illustrated*, "The main difference between the Pirates who eked out a division title last year and the Pirates who are outmuscling all of baseball now is that not only are the line-drive hitters like Clemente, Cash, Sanguillen, Al Oliver and Clines still flourishing, but Stargell is heading toward 50-plus homers. Third Baseman Richie Hebner and First Baseman Bob Robertson (who reached Three Rivers' left-field upper deck) have good shots at 30 and almost anyone in the lineup is a feasible threat to hit one out. Three Rivers' fences are at nice, standard 340-, 385- and 410-foot distances."[20]

In 1973 Dave Parker added his bat and glove to the team and was an obvious addition to the Lumber Company; the turn of phrase now became the norm for the team. The Pirates, better known for their hitting than pitching, nonetheless benefited from Doc Ellis, Bruce Kison, Bob Moose, Luke Walker, and John Lamb – all home-grown talent to go along with the pitchers they traded for to fill out their rotation and bullpen. Solid hitting and serviceable or better pitching made them a force to be reckoned with, and perhaps – if there had been no Big Red Machine – a multiple World Series winner in the mid-1970s to go with their trophies in 1971 and 1979.

Willie Stargell later wrote in his autobiography, co-authored with Tom Bird, "We were a confident, cocky group of hitters ... who loved to bang the ball. We had built a name for ourselves as the Lumber Company. Posters featured Sangy [Sanguillén], Rennie Stennett, Richie Hebner, Scoop [Al Oliver], [Richie] Zisk,[21] David [Parker], and me were printed and distributed everywhere in Pittsburgh. We loved our reputation. We wanted opposing pitchers to dread us."[22]

There was no dearth of talent on the Jets teams of the late 1960s as evinced by the players named in this essay. But there were even more who made it to the majors, among them Bruce Dal Canton, Woodie Fryman, Gene Garber, José Martínez, Freddie Patek, Bob Priddy, and the aforementioned Gene Michael and George Spriggs. For many a Pirates fan, the Pittsburgh-Columbus connection is fondly remembered as the point of takeoff for the Lumber Company. It is the wish of any major-league club to have had such a good run of home-grown talent.

This article was edited by David Siegel and fact-checked by Mike Huber.

SOURCES

All statistical and biographical references are from Baseball-Reference.com, unless noted otherwise.

NOTES

1 All but the Turfs (a short-lived appearance in the Negro Southern League) were in either of the two Negro National Leagues.

2 Bill O'Neal, *The American Association: A Baseball History-1902-1991* (Austin, Texas: Eakin Press, 1991), 206-208.

3 O'Neal, 206-208.

4 Richard Worth, *Baseball Team Names: A Worldwide Directory 1869-2011*, (Jefferson, North Carolina: McFarland & Co, 2013), 82.

5 Columbus's storied wartime aviation history is captured in part in these references: Table of U.S. Airplane Factories in WW2 - Grumman, Curtiss-Wright, Bell, etc. (acepilots.com) and Curtiss-Wright Corporation, Airplane Division - Ohio History Connection Selections - (ohiomemory.org).

6 O'Neal, 408.

7 These details on Shepard and the careers of the Jets managers who followed him are from Baseball Reference.

8 O'Neal, 409.

9 O'Neal, 409.

10 Bob Hurt, "Manny Sanguillen," SABR Biography Project.

11 Sanguillén appeared in 30 games (with 23 starts) for the Pittsburgh Pirates in 1967, batting .271.

12 O'Neal, 409.

13 O'Neal, 409.

14 Allan Simpson, *The Baseball Draft: The First 25 Years, 1965-1969* (Durham, North Carolina: American Sports Publishing, 1990), 32.

15 O'Neal, 409.

16 O'Neal, 409.

17 O'Neal, 264-267.

18 O'Neal, 265.

19 O'Neal, 265.

20 Roy Blount, "On the Lam with the Three Rivers Gang," *Sports Illustrated*, August 2, 1971, found online at https://vault.si.com/vault/1971/08/02/on-the-lam-with-the-three-rivers-gang.

21 Zisk's Triple-A stint was with Charleston a year after the Pirates moved from Columbus.

22 Willie Stargell and Tom Bird, *Willie Stargell: An Autobiography* (New York: Harper & Row, Publishers, 1984), 173. Fairly nor not, Bob Robertson did not officially figure in the Lumber Company lineup. He played for the Pirates until 1976, but suffered recurring knee problems, leading to operations on both. He did not play in 1977, was signed as a free agent by Seattle in 1978, and then played briefly for Toronto in 1979 before retiring from the game. Pirates fans will nonetheless remember him fondly for his contributions to the team's World Series run in 1971 and for over 100 home runs in a Pittsburgh uniform.

THE 1959 JUNIOR WORLD SERIES

By Matt Clever

The 1959 season was the 44th in which the Junior World Series (called the Little World Series until 1932) represented the pinnacle of Triple-A ball, pitting the winners of the International League (which covered the East Coast from Canada to the Caribbean) against the best that the American Association (spanning the Midwest and Rocky Mountains) had to offer.

The Minneapolis Millers emerged as the American Association champs for the second straight year under manager Gene Mauch. Though they finished two games behind Louisville in the regular season, the Millers caught fire in the playoffs thanks to the red-hot bat of 20-year-old second baseman Carl Yastrzemski. The Boston Red Sox had promoted Yastrzemski to Triple A just in time for the playoffs, after a regular season that saw him hit .377 in the Carolina League.

The Havana Sugar Kings likewise did not finish in first place during the International League season. But they swept the Columbus Jets in the first round and then won four one-run games over the Richmond Virginians to clinch the IL crown (known as the Governors' Cup). A farm club of the Cincinnati Reds, the Sugar Kings featured notable Cubans including Leo Cardenas, Tony Gonzalez, Mike Cuellar, and Cookie Rojas, as well as manager Preston Gomez.

SABR: The Rucker Archive.

Minneapolis Millers manager Gene Mauch is shown, front and center, with Fidel Castro, president of Cuba, during the 1959 Little World Series in. Havana, Cuba. The series pitted the International League champion, the Havana SugarKings, against the American Association Millers.

Cuba for much of the 1950s was a popular vacation destination for Americans. Its capital city, Havana, was described by the travel magazine *Cabaret Quarterly* in 1956 as "a mistress of pleasure, the lush and opulent goddess of delights." In other words: "Havana then was what Las Vegas has become."[1] But by 1959 a communist revolution led by Fidel Castro had unseated the country's president/dictator, Fulgencio Batista.

The situation improved from all-out guerrilla warfare to a nonviolent but combustible tension after Castro named himself prime minister in February. Armed revolutionaries still patrolled Havana's streets. On July 26 two bullets, fired in celebration of the six-year anniversary of the revolution's beginning, flew into the ballpark (which in 2024 was still standing, renamed Estadio Latinoamericano) during a Sugar Kings home game, hitting Cardenas and Rochester Red Wings coach Frank Verdi. Neither was seriously wounded, but the incident made other IL clubs reluctant to come to the island. The Sugar Kings survived largely because of the intervention of Castro, a huge fan of the game and promoter of the team.[2]

The series opened at the Millers' home ballpark, Metropolitan Stadium in Bloomington, Minnesota, on Sunday, September 27. A chilly drizzle kept all but 2,486 of the hardiest fans at home, and many of those who showed up were Cuban-Americans who brought flags and maracas to loudly root for the visitors. Havana rode a four-run third inning to a 5-2 victory.

The next morning brought a wintry freeze, so barely 1,000 were in attendance for Game Two. They saw the Millers erase a 2-0 deficit on a two-run homer off the bat of Roy Smalley (the brother-in-law of manager Mauch, and the father of Roy Smalley who later played in the same stadium as a Minnesota Twin).[3] The Sugar Kings took a 5-2 lead; the Millers erased it again on homers by Lou Clinton and Red Robbins. It was still knotted 5-5 when Millers catcher Ed Sadowski led off the bottom of the ninth with a home run to win the game and even up the series.

The biggest story of the first two days was the cold. The Sugar Kings especially were not accustomed to it, and sought to combat it by consuming large quantities of coffee. During Game Two they built a fire in a trash can in their dugout to provide some heat.[4] Game Three was scheduled to be played in Minnesota too, but as the mercury in the thermometers continued to drop, the decision was made (by the commission that governed the minor leagues) to shift the rest of the Series to Havana, where the weather would be more hospitable.[5]

Upon arrival both teams enjoyed a splendid parade from the airport to Havana's city hall. A sellout crowd of 25,000 jammed Estadio Latinoamericano for Game Three, including Castro and many of his lieutenants. After landing on the field in a military helicopter, Castro addressed the handkerchief-waving fans, telling them (in Spanish): "I come here not as prime minister but as a lover of baseball. I want to see our club win. After the triumph of the revolution, we should win the Little World Series also."[6]

Castro's bearded soldiers made themselves a visible presence throughout the game, occasionally taking seats right next to the players in the dugouts. Teenage soldiers barely even old enough to grow beards were "waving their guns around like toys," said Millers pitcher Ted Bowsfield.[7] His teammate Tom Umphlett remembered returning to the bench after catching the final out of an inning, and being greeted by a soldier who made a threatening slicing motion across his throat.[8]

Yastrzemski, who homered to give Minneapolis an early lead in Game Three, would later write in his autobiography: "We were warned not to leave the [Havana Hilton] hotel between games… with the guns and the noise, it was scary."[9]

"Our players were truly fearful of what might happen if we won," said Mauch.[10]This was the atmosphere in which the Millers blew a late lead and lost 3-2 in 10 innings.

Game Four followed a similar script. Havana native Daniel Morejon of the Sugar Kings ripped an RBI single in the bottom of the ninth to tie the game, then did the same thing in the 11th ~~to~~ put the Sugar Kings one win away from the championship. But the Millers took their cues from Mauch, who snarled, "We still tried our hardest, figuring we'd take our chances if we did win."[11] They took Game Five 4-2, and Game Six 5-3, setting the stage for a decisive Game Seven on Sunday, October 4 – the same day the Los Angeles Dodgers hosted the first World Series game in California, and a Soviet spacecraft's camera gave humanity its first look at the dark side of the moon.

Displaying a revolver on his hip, Castro strolled through the Minneapolis bullpen before Game Seven and said to the pitchers, "Tonight we win."[12] The Millers made Castro sweat in the 90-degree heat, as they jumped in front 1-0 on a home run by utility infielder Joe Macko.[13] Lou Clinton's second homer of the series, leading off the sixth, made it 2-0, Minneapolis. But just as they had done several times before, the Sugar Kings came back. Elio Chacon singled to open the bottom of the eighth. With one out, Morejon dropped a ground-rule double just inside the right-field line, putting runners on second and third. With two out, pinch-hitter Larry Novak came through with a two-run single to tie the score. And so the 1959 Junior World Series would go right down to the wire. Apparently, Morejon was destined to be the hero. His clean single up the middle with two out in the ninth knocked in the series-winning run for Havana. Pitcher Raul Sanchez slid safely into home plate a half-second before Umphlett's throw. A short, grainy video of the moment still exists.[14]

All of Cuba celebrated the Sugar Kings' victory. Many guns were fired into the air. As for the Millers? They were "happy to get it over with and get out of there with [their] hides," according to Bowsfield.[15]

Sadly, affiliated baseball would not survive in communist Cuba. Partway through the 1960 season, the Sugar Kings were compelled to relocate to Jersey City, New Jersey. For the remainder of the twentieth century, baseball-crazed Cubans had to get their fix from afar (or by watching their poorly paid countrymen play on teams approved by Castro's government). The Millers would play one more year at Metropolitan Stadium (during which Yastrzemski learned to be an outfielder) before the big-league Twins came to town in 1961. Both clubs are remembered for their roles in the 1959 Junior World Series – a truly unique episode in baseball history.

SOURCES

In addition to the sources cited in the Notes, the author also consulted baseball-reference.com and the following:

Briere, Tom. "Millers Win 6-5, Tie Havana Series," *Minneapolis Tribune*, September 29, 1959: S1.

Thornley, Stew. *On to Nicollet: The Glory and Fame of the Minneapolis Millers* (Minneapolis: Nodin Press, 1988).

NOTES

1 Natasha Geiling. "Before the Revolution," *Smithsonian*, July 31, 2007, https://www.smithsonianmag.com/history/before-the-revolution-159682020/

2 Tyler Maun. "The Minor Leagues' Last Nights in Havana," milb.com, March 26, 2020, https://www.milb.com/news/minor-league-baseball-left-cuba-after-revolutionary-uncertainty-219279574

3 The elder Smalley was the brother-in-law of manager Mauch, and father of the Roy Smalley, Jr., who later played in the same stadium as a Minnesota Twin, from June of 1976 through the 1981 season.

4 "Chilled Cubans Thaw on Java," *The Sporting News*, October 7, 1959: 30.

5 Bob Beebe, "Junior Series Moved to Havana Because of Weather," *Minneapolis Star,* September 29, 1959: 11B.

6 Bill Madden, "Orioles' Cuba Trip Opens Old Wounds," *New York Daily News,* March 28, 1999: 92.

7 Stew Thornley, "Minneapolis Millers – 1959 Junior World Series vs. Havana," at http://www.stewthornley.net/millers_havana.html

8 Thornley.

9 Carl Yastrzemski and Gerald Eskenazi, *Yaz: Baseball, The Wall, and Me* (New York: Doubleday Books, 1990), 51.

10 Thornley.

11 Thornley.

12 Letter from Millers pitcher Stu "Lefty" Locklin to Stew Thornley, March 1984.

13 Thornley.

14 "Junior World Series 1959.mp4." YouTube.com, uploaded by cbrioso23. https://www.youtube.com/watch?v=WJAehLwu2aw.

15 Thornley.

THE 1960 TORONTO MAPLE LEAFS

By David Siegel

This is the story of the 1960 Toronto Maple Leafs baseball team. It is a story that is worth telling because this team has been adjudged by Bill Weiss and Marshall Wright to be the 87th best minor-league team of the twentieth century,[1] and because it illustrates how the minor leagues changed from 1946 to 1963, the period covered in this book.

Celebrating the 87th best anything might not seem particularly noteworthy. The authors of the book that awarded that ranking did not disclose how many teams they considered, but a conservative estimate would suggest that at least 12,000 teams had played during the twentieth century,[2] so the 87th best team falls well within the first percentile. As will be discussed, this was truly a very strong team.

The Toronto Maple Leafs was a proud franchise. It had been a part of the Triple-A International League (and its predecessor Eastern League) since 1895,[3] which made it one of the oldest continuously operated franchises in the league. It had won league championships in 1902, 1907, 1912, 1917, 1918, 1926, 1943, 1954, 1956, and 1957,[4] but recently had fallen on hard

Top Row- Bill Smith-Trainer, Wynn Hawkins, Don Dillard, Pat Scantlebury, Ron Negray, Bob Chakales, Tim Thompson, Al Cicotte, Stan Kucway- Clubhouse boy.
Middle Row - John Bukowski, Frank Funk, Herb Plewes, Steve Demeter, George Anderson, Bob Wilson, Steve Ridzik, Rip Coleman.
Bottom Row - Allan Jones, Earl Hersh, Bob Smith, Archie Wilson-Playing Coach, Mel McGaha- Manager, Jack Waters, Russ Heman, Bill Moran, Jim King.

Courtesy Canadian Baseball Hall of Fame and Museum.

times. The Leafs had finished the 1959 season in the cellar in the eight-team league, 20½ games behind the regular-season champion Buffalo Bisons.[5]

We must begin with a discussion of the team owner, because the story of the 1960 Leafs cannot be told without also telling the story of the team's activist, colorful (he rejected the description "flamboyant") owner, Jack Kent Cooke. Some owners are quiet observers; Cooke was neither quiet nor a mere observer. The next two sections focus on the team; the second section discusses how the team was put together before the season started, and the third focuses on how the team performed during the season. The final section introduces the ballpark in which the team played. Maple Leaf Stadium is an important part of Toronto history.

JACK KENT COOKE: CANADIAN BUSINESS MOGUL WARMS UP FOR THE WORLD STAGE[6]

Jack Kent Cooke (he always liked the full three names) was a Canadian who made it big in business, first in Canada, then in the United States. He purchased the Maple Leafs franchise during the 1951 season and owned it until after the 1963 season. Under his active leadership, the Leafs became a successful franchise on the field, if not as a business venture.

Cooke was the classic self-made man. He was born in Hamilton, Ontario in October 1912. His family moved to Toronto shortly thereafter. His father, Ralph Ercil Cooke, was a salesman, first of picture frames and later of encyclopedias. His mother, Nancy Marion Jacobs Cooke, was a homemaker who looked after Jack and his three younger siblings.

Jack's time in high school was spent more on the athletic fields and playing in and managing his various bands than in academic pursuits. There is some ambiguity about the credential he received when he left Malvern Collegiate, but it was not adequate to allow him to take up the hockey scholarship that was offered by the University of Michigan.

He married Barbara Jean Carnegie shortly after leaving school and, feeling some obligation to provide support to his parents and siblings, he followed in his father's footsteps and became a salesman. He began selling soap in northern Ontario, where he met Roy Thomson, who would become the wealthy media mogul Lord Thomson of Fleet. Thomson hired him to manage his money-losing radio station in Stratford, Ontario, which Cooke quickly turned around. At first, Thomson was his mentor, but later they became partners in various business ventures. Eventually they

Courtesy Canadian Baseball Hall of Fame and Museum.

1960 Toronto Maple Leaf Baseball Club Maple Leaf Stadium, Toronto..

parted ways amicably as Thomson cast his lot mainly with print media, while Cooke explored the relatively new field of electronic media.

Cooke's first major venture was the 1944 purchase of an undistinguished Toronto radio station. Changing its call letters to CKEY, he revised its format in ways that revolutionized radio in Canada and turned it into one of the most popular stations in Toronto. He moved the station to 24-hour operation, introduced a lively, singing jingle, and switched from 15-minute programming segments to one- or two-hour musical programs. Apparently, listeners were so happy about these changes that they didn't notice that time devoted to commercials was increasing beyond the limit imposed by the regulatory agency.[7] This and some other investments put him well on the way to becoming a wealthy businessman.

Cooke's biographer, Adrian Havill, speculates that he was drawn to sports because being rich did not make him famous, but being in the world of sports could make him both rich and famous.[8]

When Cooke purchased the Leafs, he focused the same promoter's eye on his new baseball team that he had earlier applied to his radio station. He instituted all sorts of promotions: carnation nights, black-cat nights, hot-dog nights, and family days, when women received reduced admission and children were admitted free. Other promotions involved children receiving comic books, entertainment provided by opera stars, classical pianists, choral groups, or comedians. Seniors were given free passes, and the proceeds from a game were donated to a local charity, Variety Village. Cooke partnered with a used-car salesman to employ the classic "hit the ball through a hole in the wall and win a used car" promotion. Fireworks were set off when the home team scored. One of his giveaway promotions drew a charge of operating an illegal lottery, which cost him a $250 fine.[9] "Maple Leaf Stadium became the place to be on a summer's night," his biographer Havill observed.[10]

Further evidence of Cooke's promotional skills can be seen in the programs sold to those coming through the turnstiles. Much more space was devoted to paid advertising than to baseball information of interest to fans.[11]

Writer Louis Cauz sums up the Jack Kent Cooke years very well: "The Cooke era in Toronto's baseball history was as flamboyant, exciting and entertaining as the man himself. Cooke made Toronto the greatest city in the minor leagues. To do this, he ran what sometimes looked like a three-ring circus."[12]

Cooke also understood the value of vertical integration. His radio station, CKEY, broadcast all the games with popular commentators Joe Crysdale and Hal Kelley.[13] They called road games by re-creating them through teletype (although sometimes the feed from Havana suffered glitches).

In another move toward vertical integration, Cooke offered to buy the Maple Leafs' home ballpark, Maple Leaf Stadium. This would have given him control over his team's operating venue, as well as ownership of a valuable piece of harborfront property. The Toronto Harbour Commission declined the offer, citing the need for a traffic study[14] – a useful bureaucratic evasion. It might well have been the case that the Harbour Commission saw the same long-term value in the property that Cooke did.

Initially, Cooke had some success at the gate. As indicated in Figure 1, attendance jumped by about 50 percent, from under 300,000 in 1951, when he bought the team, to almost 450,000 in 1952, his first full year of ownership. After the 1952 peak, attendance followed the general minor-league trend in that it steadily declined, uninterrupted by the on-field triumph of 1960.

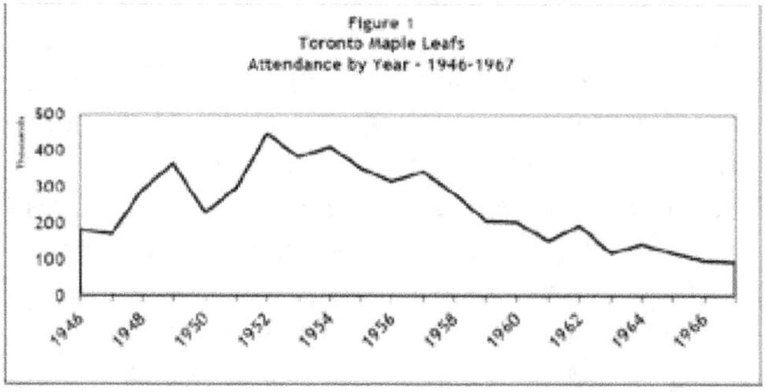

Source: baseball-reference.com; statscrew.com (Accessed, July 30, 2022).

As the 1960 season approached, two aspects of Cooke's world were converging; that had an immediate impact on the 1960 Leafs and a much broader impact on Cooke personally.

First, there was the real possibility that Cooke could realize his long-held desire to own a major-league baseball team in Toronto. However, to make this happen, Cooke had to prove his mettle as an owner, and he had to have at least a commitment that a major-league-quality ballpark would be built in Toronto.

There were two possibilities for obtaining the franchise. In 1959 Cooke became involved in an attempt by Branch Rickey to form a third major league, to be called the Continental League. Rickey had been a highly successful general manager of several major-league teams, but now in his late 70s, he had been put out to pasture. He had, however, not lost his enthusiasm.[15] Cooke was one of the members of a core group of presumptive owners who met regularly to discuss the new league.[16]

At the same time, expansion of the existing major leagues seemed clearly on the horizon. The US Congress was beginning to take an interest in major-league baseball's antitrust exemption, although this could be headed off if new teams were strategically located. Also, with the recent move of the Brooklyn Dodgers and New York Giants to the West Coast, New York City now had only one team, providing an opportunity for an expansion franchise.

Surely one of these two possibilities would come through for Cooke if he could prove his skill as an owner.

The commitment to a new ballpark seemed more difficult. Proponents had prepared some solid plans for a 60,000-seat stadium that could be built on existing parklands close to the Rosedale subway station.[17] However, Cooke and the other proponents had difficulty stimulating the interest of civic politicians.[18]

The fact that Cooke's desire to enter the major leagues seemed to have arrived at a dead end had an impact on the second aspect of his life that was unfolding at this time.

Cooke had come to realize that his ambition was of sufficient size that it could no longer be contained within Canadian borders.[19] His brother had moved to California some years earlier, and Cooke was interested in following him and practicing his entrepreneurial skills on a broader canvas.

The confluence of these two factors had an impact on the 1960 Maple Leafs. It would assist Cooke's aspiration for elevation to major-league status if he could demonstrate his baseball acumen, and his skill as an owner, by assembling a strong team.

Cooke began the 1960 season on a positive, hopeful note, but by the end of the season, all this had come crashing to earth. The plans for the Continental League were demolished by a combination of major-league expansion[20] and some unfavorable legislation passed by the US Congress.[21] Major-league expansion would definitely occur, but it had passed Cooke by, in part because he could not convince Toronto's civic leaders that the city needed a major-league-quality baseball stadium. This provided further proof that Cooke needed to find a larger canvas for his ambition than Canada provided.

Ever the astute businessman, Cooke had seen this coming, and by May 1960 his plan to move to the United States was well underway. The immediate reaction in Toronto to his conversion to Uncle Sam was a backlash against a turncoat. Attendance had been declining for some time; this was in line with what was happening across the minor leagues. The changing affection for Cooke personally was sometimes cited as an additional reason for this decline in Toronto.[22]

The 1960 team was a mixed success for Cooke. He could take pride in the fact that he had put together a very strong team. This certainly polished his reputation with other owners that could have helped him obtain a major-league franchise. At the same time, his personal actions hurt his reputation with Toronto locals, and this likely had an impact on attendance. The winning team that Cooke had put together so brilliantly was a success on the field, but not in his pocketbook. At the end of the season, he disassembled the team, reportedly selling several of the players for a profit. Three years later he would sell the team to local investors. Three years after that, more red ink would accumulate and the franchise that had represented Toronto since 1895 would be sold to an investor who moved it to Louisville, Kentucky, after the 1967 season.

ASSEMBLING THE TEAM

Relationships between minor- and major-league teams were different in those days from what we are familiar with today. The Leafs had played without an agreement with a major-league team through most of the 1950s, but Cooke was able to sign a working agreement with the Cleveland Indians for the 1960 season. Working agreements at this point were not exclusive as they would become later. The Indians provided a manager, and they could provide some players to the farm team, but the major-league team might also ship players to other farm teams. It was expected that minor-league teams would purchase, sell, or trade their own players independent of what the major-league team might be doing. Therefore, executives of minor-league teams could build their own teams in ways that would not be available to them in later years.

The Indians provided Mel McGaha to manage the Maple Leafs. He came with a very positive reputation, having managed the Mobile Bears to a second-place finish in the regular season topped with a win in the playoffs in the Double-A Southern League in 1959.[23] He seemed to be ticketed to move upward in the Cleveland organization, and he ultimately did become a major-league manager for a relatively short period (Cleveland for all but two games in 1962, and Kansas City for parts of the 1964 and 1965 seasons).[24]

The Indians also provided several players who had a real impact on the Leafs' success,[25] but it was clear that the major architect of the team's success was its owner, Jack Kent Cooke.

The Leafs presented a substantially new face for 1960, with a new general manager, Danny Menendez, joining new field manager McGaha.[26] This new management team went about assembling a team that was substantially different from the previous season's doormat, putting together one of the strongest pitching corps ever seen in the minor leagues.

The Leafs purchased major-league journeyman pitchers Al Cicotte from the Indians for $12,500[27] and Steve Ridzik from the Cubs for $15,000,[28] as well as several other key pitchers.[29] The team also spent $25,000 on a relatively unknown second baseman named Sparky Anderson.[30] In total, Cooke was said to have spent over $100,000 on purchasing players,[31] which raised some eyebrows among owners of other teams.[32] In fact, if this were a Sunday-morning beer-league team, some might use the word "ringers." The transformation of the team was so complete that none of the Opening Day starters on the 1960 team had played a similar role on the 1959 team.[33]

One of the transitions that was happening at this time was an increase in the number of Black players throughout Organized Baseball. One of Cooke's first acts after buying the team in 1951 was bringing the first Black players to Toronto, Charlie White and Leon Day.[34] The 1960 team photo shows two Black players (Pat Scantlebury and Bob Wilson). Other players could have joined the team later in the season. Three players seem to be Hispanic based on their birthplaces (Miguel de la Hoz [Havana], Clyde Parris [Panama City, Panama], and Scantlebury [Gatun, Panama]). By today's standards, this does not seem outstanding, but for the time, and in a lily-white Toronto, it might have been considered ground-breaking.

THE SEASON

The Leafs started the season battling the Buffalo Bisons for first place, but by May 26, Toronto had inched ahead in terms of winning percentage, but were actually a half-game behind the leaders.[35] They stayed in the lead for the remainder of the season, building to a 17-game bulge by the end of the season. (The gap between the second- and eighth-place teams was 21 games.) This was the largest winning margin since 1946.[36] The team finished with a 100-54 record.[37]

Tables 1 and 2 make it very clear that the team's success was based on an outstanding pitching corps supported by a fairly weak cadre of hitters.

The team's league-leading ERA of 2.82 was 0.45 runs better than the next lowest in the league.[38] The pitching corps threw an amazing 67 complete games, including 32 shutouts, eclipsing the previous IL and major-league records, both of which stood at 30.[39]

Al Cicotte, who had previously pitched in the majors for three seasons, was the star pitcher among an outstanding group. He won the Topps (Chewing Gum, Inc.) Minor League Player-of-the-Year Award by a vote of the National Association of Baseball Writers.[40] He also finished the season by pitching 56 consecutive innings without allowing an earned run.[41] On September 3 he pitched an 11-inning no-hitter.[42] His heroic effort in that game was necessitated by the anemic support that he received from hitters, who scored one run on 10 hits, and left 12 runners on base.

The overall strength of the pitching corps is indicated by the fact that five pitchers had ERAs of less than 3.00, and the 32 shutouts were divided among nine pitchers. Add to this a good balance between righties and lefties, and seeing the Leafs must have been a nightmare for hitters.

Table 1
1960 Toronto Maple Leafs
Selected Pitching Statistics

Name	Throws	Innings Pitched	Complete Games	Shutouts	W-L	ERA
Al Cicotte	R	201	12	8	16-7	1.79
Frank Funk	R	90	4	3	6-3	2.10
Pat Scantlebury	L	106	2	1	7-5	2.63
Rip Coleman	L	153	7	4	9-8	2.71
Russ Heman	R	76	0	0	8-2	2.72
Bob "Riverboat" Smith	R	166	10	3	14-6	3.04
Wynn Hawkins	L	77	5	2	7-3	3.04
Steve Ridzik	R	184	13	4	14-10	3.13
Ron Negray	R	158	8	2	10-6	3.19
Bob Chakales	R	113	6	2	9-3	3.74
Total*		1341	67	32	100-54	2.82

*- Figures do not add because some players are not included in listing
Source: https://www.baseball-reference.com/register/team.cgi?id=d1da423c
(Accessed July 25, 2022).

It was good that the pitchers were so dominant because the hitters contributed little to the team's success. The team batting average of .246 placed it fifth in the league.[43] The best hitters were Don Dillard and Jim King; while King was a strong power hitter, neither of them broke the .300 barrier. The team was obviously no stolen-base threat. Sparky Anderson led the team with 12 SBs, but he was caught stealing 14 times, leading to questions about his judgment.

Table 2
1960 Toronto Maple Leafs
Selected Batting Statistics

Name	Bats	Position	Games	BA	HR	Stolen Bases
Don Dillard	L	OF	133	.294	9	0
Jim King	L	OF	139	.287	24	4
Herb Plews#	R	Sub-IF	81	.278	0	2
Earl Hersh	L	1B	134	.262	12	4
Steve Demeter	R	3B	121	.261	11	1
Tim Thompson	L	C	103	.256	10	2
Allen Jones#	R	Sub-C	82	.249	10	0
Billy Moran	R	SS	121	.242	4	3
Jack Waters	R	OF	150	.236	7	8
Sparky Anderson	R	2B	148	.227	5	12
Archie Wilson#	R	Sub-OF, PH	52	.223	2	0
Total*				.246	116	39

*- Figures do not add because some players are not included in listing
- Players who were not regular starters, but had more than 100 ABs
Source: https://www.baseball-reference.com/register/team.cgi?id=d1da423c (Accessed July 25, 2022).

There was some strong fielding. Center fielder Jackie Waters was voted the best defensive outfielder in the International League. Anderson won awards for the league's best defensive infielder, smartest player, and best hustler.[44]

Outfielder Jim King's 24 home runs helped him win the league's Most Valuable Player Award.[45] Anderson, Cicotte, King, and Bob "Riverboat" Smith were selected to the International League All-Star Team.[46] Given Anderson's hitting skills, this must have been a tribute to his work in the field.

In the postseason playoff, the Maple Leafs beat the fourth-place Buffalo Bisons four games to none in the semifinal, and Rochester four games to two in the final series. The Maple Leaf juggernaut finally met its match in the Junior World Series, when the Louisville Colonels of the American Association beat them four games to two.[47]

Several members of this team went on to play in the major leagues, some for several years, but no player became a star as a player. However, two players went on to make big names for themselves as managers.[48] Sparky Anderson came back to manage the Leafs in 1964 and went on to be elected to the Baseball Hall of Fame because of his success managing the Reds and Tigers. Chuck Tanner, who played 28 games for the Leafs at the end of the season, went on to considerable managerial success with the White Sox, Pirates, Athletics, and Braves.

Given what was on the horizon for relations between major- and minor-league baseball, Cooke was one of the last minor-league owners who had the freedom and the skill to build his own winning team. And he did that in the classic manner – strength up the middle. He assembled an excellent pitching corps, supported by two good, experienced catchers (Tim Thompson and Allen Jones), backed up by an award-winning defensive second baseman and center fielder. This was the textbook way of building strength up the middle.

MAPLE LEAF STADIUM

The Leafs played in Maple Leaf Stadium, which was an older, but adequate, facility. It was built in 1926 by Lol Solman, an entrepreneur and owner of the team.[49] He covered the full $750,000 construction cost by selling some of his other properties.[50] It was standard procedure at the time for the team owner to build and own the baseball park as a part of operating the team, so there seems to have been no consideration of financial assistance from government. In the case of the Taylor family, which built Fenway Park, for instance, the real estate deal seemed to take precedence over the baseball team.[51]

To this day, Canadian governments at all levels have traditionally been much more reluctant to spend taxpayers' dollars to subsidize professional sport than their counterparts in the United States. This attitude on the part of governments has been reinforced by the fact that public involvement has not always produced a positive result. Olympic Stadium in Montreal is recognized as a terrible facility built at a hugely inflated cost.[52]

Maple Leaf Stadium was built in the steel and concrete style that was common at that time.[53] Its row of arches was reminiscent of Philadelphia's Shibe Park, without the ornate French Renaissance extravagance.[54] The arch motif would reappear later in Cooke's life when he built the Forum in Los Angeles – the iconic facility that would be home to the Los Angeles Lakers, Los Angeles Kings hockey team, and many special events.

Its seating capacity was originally advertised as 23,500, but this figure was later changed to 19,000. The higher figure was similar to those of several major-league ballparks built at this time.[55] The ballpark generated enough excitement that W.A. Hewitt, the sporting editor of the *Toronto Daily Star,* wrote: "Toronto baseball fans will be amazed when they get their first look at the new Maple Leaf Stadium

– from the inside. It is the last word in modern baseball construction."[56]

Anecdotal evidence from fans indicates that Hewitt was correct to be so excited. From the fans' perspective, the ballpark provided a sense of intimacy and easy sightlines that added to the enjoyment of the games.

It was located at the foot of Bathurst Street, very close to the harbor. This also fit the idea of the time of being close to downtown but avoiding the high cost of land right in the downtown area.[57] The new ballpark also happened to be just across the water and within sight of Hanlan's Point Stadium, which had been the team's home for most of the period from 1897 to 1925.

By the time Cooke bought the team in 1951, the ballpark was owned by the Toronto Harbour Commission, which seems logical given its location. However, the commission had no interest in operating a ballpark, so all operating expenses were borne by the operator of the team. Cooke reportedly spent $57,000 to improve the facility.[58] As mentioned earlier, Cooke attempted to buy the ballpark from the Harbour Commission, but was rebuffed.

The Leafs would continue to play in the adequate but antiquated ballpark until the team moved to Louisville after the 1967 season. Maple Leaf Stadium was demolished shortly after, to be replaced by a residential condominium development.

CONCLUSION

The 1960 Toronto Maple Leafs team illustrates several characteristics of how minor-league baseball operated in the 1946-1963 period. It had a working agreement with a major-league team, but this was rather loose. It did not limit the ability of an ambitious, entrepreneurial owner to build a team in the way that he wanted in hopes of making money both at the turnstiles and through buying and selling players.

Jack Kent Cooke was not shy about using his autonomy as an owner in ways that helped him prove his mettle and accomplish other goals. He was one of the last owners in minor-league baseball who had both the freedom and the competence to build his own very strong team. As an enlightened owner, he could also move tentatively to support the movement toward racial integration that was occurring at the major-league level.

Cooke owned the team until 1964, but he seems to have lost interest after 1960, when he moved to California.[59] He made his fortune by obtaining franchises for the new innovation of cable television in

SABR: The Rucker Archive.

Dixie Walker with Jack Kent Cooke, 1959.

small towns across the United States. Eventually he moved into a variety of investments; at one time, he owned the iconic Chrysler Building in Manhattan. Sports fans will recognize hm as the owner of the Los Angeles Kings hockey team, the Los Angeles Lakers, and the Super Bowl champion Washington Redskins.

A marketing-oriented owner could use his skills to build attendance as Cooke did in the early years of his ownership, but even a highly skilled marketer was unable to counter the broader trend of declining interest in minor-league baseball. The 1960 Toronto Maple Leafs embodied both the height of minor-league baseball, in terms of the quality of the team that Cooke assembled, and the coming depth: even an excellent team with an accomplished marketer in charge could not offset the impending crisis facing the minors.

The 1960 Toronto Maple Leafs was not only a great team, but it also illustrated the ways in which minor-league baseball was changing in the 1946-1963 period.

ACKNOWLEDGMENTS

The author would like to thank Michael Fenn and Robert J. Williams for their helpful comments, and Christi Hudson and Andrew North of the Canadian Baseball Hall of Fame & Museum for their assistance in gathering material.

This article was edited by Marshall Adesman and fact-checked by Carl Riechers.

NOTES

1 Bill Weiss and Marshall Wright, *The 100 Greatest Minor League Baseball Teams in the 20th Century* (Denver: Outskirts Press, Inc., 2006), 44-6.

2 In the latter part of the century, when minor-league baseball was highly structured, there were 120 teams each year. In the earlier years, there were

almost always considerably more than that. The low estimate of 120 teams each year times 100 years equals 12,000.

3 David Siegel, "Professional Baseball Comes to Toronto to Stay: The Toronto Baseball Club in the Eastern League, 1895," in Andrew North et al., eds., *Our Game, Too: Influential Figures and Milestones in Canadian Baseball* (Phoenix: Society for American Baseball Research, 2022), 184-93.

4 International League, *White Book No. 3* (1959), n.p.

5 https://www.baseball-reference.com/register/league.cgi?id=2dece84d (accessed July 25, 2022).

6 Most of the material in this section comes from three sources: Adrian Kinnane, *Jack Kent Cooke: A Career Biography* (Lansdowne, Virginia: Jack Kent Cooke Foundation, 2004); Adrian Havill, *The Last Mogul: The Unauthorized Biography of Jack Kent Cooke* (New York: St. Martin's Press, 1992); and Kevin Plummer, "Historicist: The Best Minor League City in the World," https://torontoist.com/2009/04/historicist_the_best_minor_league_c/ (accessed August 28, 2022). Not surprisingly, the authorized and unauthorized biographies differ in some significant areas. But they do not differ in any substantial manner in the presentation of the facts related to the narrow slice of Cooke's life discussed here.

7 Havill, 55-61.

8 Havill, 87.

9 Havill, 93.

10 Havill, 89.

11 Several are held in the archives of the Canadian Baseball Hall of Fame and Museum.

12 Louis Cauz, *Baseball's Back in Town* (Toronto: Controlled Media Corporation, n.d.), 101.

13 "Minor League Air Log," *The Sporting News,* April 13, 1960: 31.

14 Havill, 92.

15 Murray Polner, *Branch Rickey: A Biography* (New York: Atheneum, 1982), 255-62; Russell C. Buhite. *The Continental League: A Personal History* (Lincoln: University of Nebraska Press, 2014).

16 Milt Dunnell, "No Beer in the Ball Park, Though," *Toronto Daily Star*, January 6, 1960: 20; Milt Dunnell, "The Source of Baseball Supply," *Toronto Daily Star,* March 4, 1960: 12; Dick Gordon, "Player Pool Plan Aired by B.R. in Twin-City Visit," *The Sporting News,* January 13, 1960: 9; Clark Nealon, "Cullinan Group, Owners of Buff Work on Merger," *The Sporting News,* February 24, 1960: 24.

17 "60,000-Seat Ball Park Plan," *Toronto Daily Star,* January 11, 1960: 1, 9.

18 Kinnane, 25.

19 Kinnane, 29.

20 Ed Prell, "Majors to Increase to 10 Each In '62," *The Sporting News,* July 20, 1960: 1.

21 Dave Brady, "Changes in Kefauver's Bill Jolt Continental's Chances," *The Sporting News,* June 1, 1960:13; Buhite, *The Continental League,* 103, 131, and passim.

22 "Leafs, Thumping I.L., Show 5,000 Drop in Attendance," *The Sporting News,* July 27, 1960: 29.

23 https://www.baseball-reference.com/register/league.cgi?id=2864d5ab (accessed July 25, 2022); Neil MacCarl, "Tribe Tie-Up, Free Spending by Cooke Bring Toronto Flag," *The Sporting News,* September 7, 1960: 29.

24 https://www.baseball-reference.com/managers/mcgahme99.shtml (accessed October 23, 2023).

25 David F. Chrisman, *The History of the International League (1919-1960) Part III* (self-published, 1983), 129.

26 "Leafs Seeking Marshall, Pisoni," *Toronto Daily Star,* February 23, 1960: 13.

27 Neil MacCarl, "Parris Adds Bat to Bolster Leaf Hopes," *Toronto Daily Star,* April 1, 1960: 33.

28 Neil MacCarl, "Leafs Pay Cubs 15 Grand for Pitcher Steve Ridzik," *Toronto Daily Star,* April 1, 1960: 14; https://www.baseball-reference.com/players/r/ridzist01.shtml (accessed July 25, 2022).

29 Neil MacCarl, "Rebuilt Leafs Loaded With Slab Whizzes," *The Sporting News,* June 8, 1960: 43.

30 Neil, MacCarl, "Leafs Plug Leak Buy Anderson From Phillies," *Toronto Daily Star,* April 11, 1960: 11.

31 Neil MacCarl, "Tribe Tie-Up, Free Spending by Cooke Bring Toronto Flag," *The Sporting News,* September 7, 1960: 29.

32 Earl Flora, "Int's Race Too Hot for Bucs' Castoffs," *The Sporting News,* August 3, 1960: 33.

33 Neil MacCarl, "Not a Repeater From '59 Opener," *Toronto Daily Star,* April 18, 1960: 19.

34 Kinnane, 20.

35 *The Sporting News,* June 1, 1960: 29.

36 Chrisman, 128.

37 Weiss and Wright, *The 100 Greatest Minor League Baseball Teams of the 20th Century*, 45.

38 https://www.baseball-reference.com/register/league.cgi?id=56716f8b (accessed August 15, 2022).

39 "Chakales, Coleman Extend Toronto Zero Mark to 32," *The Sporting News,* September 14, 1960: 38.

40 *The Sporting News*, October 19, 1960: 25.

41 "Cicotte Finished in Grand Style – No ER in 56 Innings," *The Sporting News,* September 21, 1960: 35.

42 Lloyd McGowan, "Leafs' Cicotte Hurls 11-Inning No-Hitter," *The Sporting News,* September 14, 1960: 37.

43 https://www.baseball-reference.com/register/league.cgi?id=56716f8b (accessed August 15, 2022).

44 Neil MacCarl, "Leaf Glove Guys Nab Top Honors in Skippers' Poll," *The Sporting News,* September 14, 1960: 37.

45 Cauz, 123.

46 "Caught on the Fly," *The Sporting News*, October 12, 1960: 38.

47 Weiss and Wright, 44.

48 A good summary of the players' careers is found in Weiss and Wright, 45.

49 William Humber, *Diamonds of the North: A Concise History of Baseball in Canada* (Toronto: Oxford University Press, 1995), 151, 155.

50 Humber, 151, 155.

51 Paul Goldberger, *Ballpark: Baseball in the American City* (New York: Alfred A. Knopf, Publishers, 2019), 85.

52 Jonah Keri, *Up, Up, and Away: The Kid, the Hawk, Rock, Vladi, Pedro, le Grand Orange, Youppi!, the Crazy Business of Baseball, and the Ill-fated but Unforgettable Montreal Expos* (Toronto: Random House Canada, 2014).

53 Goldberger, 76.

54 Philip J. Lowry, *Green Cathedrals: The Ultimate Celebration of Major League and Negro League Ballparks* (New York: Walker & Company, 2006), 177.

55 Goldberger, Chapter 5.

56 W.A. Hewitt, "Sporting News and Reviews," *Toronto Daily Star*, April 20, 1926: 10.

57 Goldberger, 64-5.

58 Doug Taylor, "The history of Maple Leaf Stadium in Toronto," blogTO (https://www.blogto.com/sports_play/2021/03/history-maple-leaf-stadium-toronto/ (accessed July 30, 2022).

59 Chrisman, 138.

THE 1962 SAN DIEGO PADRES: A PCL PENNANT ... WITH AN EYE ON THE MAJOR LEAGUES

By Tom Larwin

The San Diego Padres' first season in the Pacific Coast League was 1936. The team's last The run up to the 2005 seasonseason in the PCL was 1968. In only four of those 33 years did the Padres finish in first place.

This story is about one of those four teams, 1962, when they ran away with the pennant and had wrapped up first place by the end of August.

The 1962 PCL season was the fifth year that followed the end of the league's "Golden Age," the period from 1903 to 1957, before the National League's Giants and Dodgers franchises took up residency in San Francisco and Los Angeles respectively.[1]

The move of two teams to the West Coast in 1958 was followed by the major-league owners' actions in 1960 to expand each league by two teams, the American League in 1961 and the National League in 1962. More expansion of the two leagues was anticipated in the future and in 1962 it was a hot topic, particularly in cities in the South and West, like San Diego, that were experiencing high population growth.

Back: Chico Ruiz, Ron Samford, Zach Monroe, Rogelio Alvarez, Jim Pisoni, Sammy Ellis, Howie Nunn, Jesse Gonder, Bobby Klaus
Middle: Brian McGiveron, Bucky Peralta, Hal Bevan, John Tsitouris, Marv Schultz, John Flavin, Ken Walters, Tommy Harper, Les Cook, Danny Ledford
Front: Bob Risenhoover, George McWilliams, Harry Anderson, Ray Rippelmeyer, Don Heffner (manager), Whitey Wietelmann, Greg Jancich, Carl Thomas

Courtesy of Tom Larwin.

1962 San Diego Padres.

With the above as background, here is the story of the 1962 San Diego Padres.

OCTOBER 1961-MARCH 1962: AN ACTIVE OFFSEASON

The 1961 baseball season in San Diego was a "downer." The Padres finished in fourth place, 25 games off the lead, with a record of 72-82 (.468). They were out of contention early in the season.

After the 1961 season, there was disappointment and there was disenchantment – within the Padres organization as well as with the fans and with the San Diego business community. The collective frustration was summarized by *San Diego Union* beat writer Johnny McDonald in his October 25, 1961, column: "Pained by last year's experience when veteran ball players failed to live up to past season credentials, the San Diego Padres management will experiment with a younger crop next season."[2]

Padres Seek Affiliation with New Club. Within a few weeks of the end of the season, the Padres' general manager, Eddie Leishman, was pursuing change. Leishman, a career minor leaguer as player and manager, managed teams to pennants in the Pioneer and International Leagues, and then one as general manager of the PCL's Salt Lake City team in 1959. For the 1960 and 1961 seasons, San Diego's affiliation was with the Chicago White Sox, and both years the Padres finished in the middle of the eight-team league. Leishman had made it known that he was not pleased with the quality of players being assigned to San Diego by the White Sox.

Barely a month after the end of the 1961 season Leishman made his first significant move, entering into a full working agreement with the Cincinnati Reds, the National League's 1961 pennant-winner. Padres' management had strongly bought into the notion that "a tie up with Cincinnati would be a big boost for the Padres and afford them a better chance in obtaining a title contender."[3]

Leishman's belief was that the Chicago farm system had "been going to pieces in recent years," while Cincinnati's talent was believed to be so bountiful that the Padres "will have to choose among eight second base candidates when the Padres open camp."[4]

New Manager Hired. The next big move came in November 1961with the hiring of Don Heffner as the 1962 team's manager. Heffner had three decades of professional baseball experience, having played 11 seasons in the major leagues, and managed for nine years in various minor-league levels. Leading up to 1962 he had spent the prior four seasons as a major-league coach with the Kansas City Athletics (1958-60) and Detroit Tigers (1961). Reports were that he was a "good teaching coach" and had the "respect and affection of just about everybody in baseball."[5]

San Diego Business Leaders Push for a Major-League Team. For the business community the interest in the 1962 Padres seemingly had three objectives:

- To have a winning team.
- To draw bigger crowds.
- To provide the foundation for a future major-league franchise in San Diego.

With major-league baseball coming west in 1958, and the later expansion in 1961, there was a strong belief in the business community that more expansion was likely and that San Diego should be an attractive candidate.

The business community decided to organize around a strong, clear message, one that would leave no doubt that the city was ready. The result was creation of the Greater San Diego Sports Association to officially launch a "Push the Padres" campaign. One of the objectives was to sell 1962 Padres season tickets, but the other was not at all subtle: getting major-league baseball for the city. This objective was reinforced at the Sports Association's January 31, 1962, banquet when Buzzie Bavasi, the Los Angeles Dodgers' general manager, told the crowd, "You'll have major league baseball here. You have the ideal man here to get it for you – Eddie Leishman."[6]

The association was aligned with two other business groups. The Chamber of Commerce had a Sports Committee, which was coordinating San Diego's sports future for major-league baseball, while the San Diego Hot Stove League was "pushing the Padres boosting ALL baseball."[7]

At about the same time, Charlie Finley, owner of the Kansas City Athletics, weighed in with his opinion that San Diego was destined to become a major-league city.[8]

Lobbying efforts for a major-league franchise continued in mid-March as a delegation of 21 members of the Chamber of Commerce traveled to Phoenix to meet with executives from six major-league clubs. The group's message rallied around four points:

- Financing was at hand for an "adequate ball park as early as 1963."
- San Diego's interests are open to the best proposal from either the American or National League.

- Evidence of local support for major-league sports has been demonstrated through the first two seasons of the San Diego Chargers professional football team, which began play in 1960.
- There continues to be major growth in the San Diego region, with 4.0 million people living within 90 minutes of San Diego's current ballpark.[9]

As the season proceeded, the subject of expansion was placed on the back burner. Later in the year, at the major leagues' December Winter Meeting, the owners "agreed that no further expansion would occur without 'full discussions between both leagues in a joint executive session.'"[10] It would take another six years for further expansion to become a reality.

JANUARY 1962-APRIL 1962: BUILDING A ROSTER

The move from the White Sox to the Reds meant a complete turnover in player personnel. Coming off a pennant-winning 1961 campaign, the Reds did not have many holes to plug. Plus, their farm system was in good shape:

- Four of their 1961 minor-league teams finished in first place.
- They had two Triple-A clubs in 1961 (Indianapolis and Jersey City) but only one in 1962, the Padres.

This depth would bode well for San Diego's 1962 roster.

The makeover for 1962 had its kick-start with the signing of new manager Don Heffner in November 1961.

Based on the quality and depth of the Reds' minor-league system, the Padres' primary effort to build a 1962 roster was to evaluate the talent existing in the system.

One example of the depth of the talent: Leishman and Heffner had to choose among eight second-base candidates when the Padres opened spring camp at Tampa, Florida, on March 12.[11] One of the candidates was Pete Rose, who would turn 21 in 1962. He had already played two seasons at Class D and had demonstrated that he was a potential .300-plus hitter. Rose did not make the Triple-A club even though he played in a Padres uniform for nine spring games between March 26 and April 3. It wasn't good enough and he ended up being assigned to the Reds' Class-A team in Macon (South Atlantic League).

The Padres did add four players in the off-season. One was catcher Jesse Gonder, whom the Reds acquired in a trade with the New York Yankees on December 14, 1961.[12] Gonder, a former Reds farmhand, was with the big-league team most of the spring before being sent to San Diego on April 3. The other three players were outfielders: Dan Dobbek, acquired in a trade for Jerry Zimmerman of the Minnesota Twins (January 30); Ken Walters, purchased from the Philadelphia Phillies (February 9); and former big-leaguer Jim Pisoni, obtained by the Reds from the Yankees on February 15 in a multi-player trade.[13]

A key late-spring acquisition for the Padres came on April 9, a week before the start of the season, when right-handed pitcher Jim Maloney was sent down to San Diego by the Reds.

APRIL 17-SEPTEMBER 9: THE 1962 SEASON - 21 WEEKS AND 154 GAMES

The 1962 Pacific Coast League scheduled 154 games to be played between April 17 and September 9. That totals almost 21 weeks of play and an average of 7.33 games per week. A relief of sorts was provided by a league rule that called for one game of double-headers to be seven innings rather than nine.

The Padres' season of 21 weeks resulted in 18 dates without a game – either due to rain or a game not being scheduled. This was an intense schedule especially considering that one team was in Canada, another in Hawaii, and the other six were scattered in four states. San Diego was the only PCL team in California.

Padres Opening Day Lineup	
Chico Ruiz	SS
Teolindo Acosta	CF
Jim Pisoni	LF
Rogelio Alvarez	3B
Ken Walters	RF
Hal Bevan	C
Harry Anderson	1B
Bobby Klaus	2B
Jim Maloney	SP

April 17: Opening Day in San Diego. Opening Day was Tuesday, April 17, at the Padres' home field, Westgate Park. The Padres Opening Day lineup is shown to the right. There were a record 7,152 fans in attendance to witness the 2-1 defeat. Jim Maloney took the loss when the Tacoma Giants scored the go-ahead run in the ninth inning.

April 17-July 1: Weeks 1-11, Reaching the Season's Halfway Mark. The Padres got off to a slow start. On April 26, with a 10-4 loss to Salt Lake, they finished the 10-game opening homestand with a 4-6 record.

Over the next three weeks it was more of the same mediocrity. On May 15 the Padres lost at Salt Lake City to the Bees, 6-5, and their record plunged to a season low of three games under .500, at 12-15. They occupied fifth place and were nine games out of first place.

A positive break occurred on May 10 when Sammy Ellis arrived after the Reds sent him down. Two days later Ellis pitched a shutout in a 3-0 home win over Portland.

After the May 15 loss, the Padres went on a five-game win streak, with four of them coming against Hawaii at Westgate Park. That win streak left the Padres two games over .500, at 17-15, on May 21.

Wednesday, May 16 Snapshot of the PCL Standings		
Padres Position	Record	Games Ahead/ Behind
5th Place	12-15	9 GB

In late May the Padres were aided with two pitching acquisitions. First, on May 20 it was reported that veteran Joe Nuxhall was released by the Angels and signed by San Diego.[14] This news was followed a week later, on May 27, by John Flavin's joining the team from Class-A Macon.

The team followed that short win streak with two losses to the Vancouver Mounties and were 17-17 on May 25. That day the Padres played at Spokane and Maloney won his second game of the season, 41. This began a run during which the Padres won 12 of 14 games in 13 days through June 6. Maloney won three of the games, with Nuxhall and John Tsitouris each winning two. Nuxhall had an impressive start with a 3-0 shutout in his first game, on May 30. Also during this period, Flavin won his first start as a Padre, a 9-2 victory at Hawaii on June 3.

As of June 7, the Padres had turned things around and had a record of 29-18. They had moved into third place and were only two games out of first place. However, spoiling things a bit was news on this day that the Reds had recalled Jim Maloney (who was 4-1 with a 2.16 ERA) and replaced him with Howie Nunn.

The team's progress then slowed over the next two weeks, June 7-17, during which they went 5-8. The losses were bad enough, but the last one, on June 17, really stung. On the road against first-place Salt Lake City, the Padres were blown away, 21-7, despite having held a 7-0 lead going into the bottom of the sixth inning. Yet, the Padres were still in the race with a 34-27 record on June 18 that left them three games out of first place.

After losing four in a row to the Bees, on Monday, June 18, the Padres had one last game to play in the teams' five-game series. After the big 14-run loss on Sunday, the Padres needed a confidence-restoring victory. They got it with a 10-inning win, 11-9, behind Joe Nuxhall.

With confidence seemingly restored after their June 18 win, the Padres went on to win six straight before losing the second game of a doubleheader on June 24 against Portland at home. They ended the day in first place, a half-game ahead of Salt Lake City.

Monday, June 18 Snapshot of the PCL Standings		
Padres Position	Record	Games Ahead/ Behind
3rd Place	34-27	3 GB

The Padres were on a roll and the next week (June 25-July 1) they won six of eight on the road at Vancouver and Tacoma. With their 12-4 win on June 28 against the last-place Mounties, the Padres took sole possession of first place.

Joe Nuxhall kept things going with a one-hitter on June 30 against the Giants. A scratch hit by Tacoma's Bob Perry in the top of the eighth inning broke up his attempt for a no-hitter in a 3-0 win.

The next day, July 1, Bobby Klaus hit for the cycle with a single, two doubles, a triple, and a home run.

After a successful month of June, during which the Padres won 23 of 35 games, at the season's halfway mark on July 2 they were in first place – barely.

Monday, July 2 Snapshot of the PCL Standings		
Padres Position	Record	Games Ahead/ Behind
1st Place	47-30	2 GA

July 2-September 9: Weeks 12-21, Can the Padres Hold First Place to the Finish? The Padres began the second half of the season just as they had the first half … with a loss, this time to the Seattle Rainiers, 3-2. But unlike the first half's slow start, the team won 10 of its next 12 games.

A key player in the Padres' rise was third baseman Tommy Harper. His play was getting noticed during the first half and it increased in early July when he hit five home runs over a five-game stretch (July 6-10) leading into the July 11 PCL All-Star Game in Portland.

Harper and four other Padres players were selected to the all-star team: Alvarez, Ellis, Gonder, and Walters … plus, Heffner was to be the squad's manager.

None of these All-Star picks were surprising. However, it was Tommy Harper receiving most of the attention. With a batting average of .343 and 20 home runs, Harper was off to a great start with the Padres and was selected to start at third base. There was some anxious anticipation in the Padres' front office that Harper could be called up to the Reds at any time, especially with the call-up deadline date of July 31 being just 20 days away. Pete Seghi, the Reds farm director, commented on whether Macon's Pete Rose would be Harper's replacement should the big-league club call up Harper. Seghi responded that Rose was doing a fine job there but might be still a year away from Triple-A competition.[15] A day earlier, Seghi was quoted as saying that Rose and Tommy Helms should help the Padres in 1963.[16]

As for the pitching, on July 12 Nuxhall was at it again, but this time it was because of a home run that he hit in the 10th inning to win his own game, 2-1, at Westgate Park. Catcher Jesse Gonder led the offense in mid-July with six home runs in 13 games, 10 of which were won by San Diego (July 17-28).

Parent Cincinnati was paying attention to the Padres, too, and on July 18 the Reds recalled Nuxhall, who departed with a 9-2 record. The Reds replaced him with Ray Rippelmeyer, who was purchased from the Washington Senators for $12,500.[17]

In the meantime, two other Padres pitchers were getting hot, Ellis and Tsitouris. On July 27 Ellis won his eighth game against three losses when he struck out 13 as the Padres blanked Vancouver, 2-0, at Westgate Park. That win was followed the next day by another whitewashing as Tsitouris won 6-0, upping his record to 8-6.

With a record of 23-11 in July the wins were not only piling up but so was the team's first-place lead, which had widened to 7½ games going into August.

Wednesday, Augsust 1 Snapshot of the PCL Standings		
Padres Position	Record	Games Ahead/ Behind
1st Place	69-40	7½ GA

On the last day of July, the Padres lost a doubleheader to the Seattle Rainiers. The July wins were in the rear-view mirror as the Padres lost six of their next nine games through August 9. Their first-place lead had been reduced to six games, with the Padres set to face off against their second-place challenger, the Bees, in a five-game home series. It was billed as a "crucial" series: "This home stand could determine whether San Diego will have to struggle the rest of the way in the pennant chase or have enough cushion to claim its first title since 1954. The defending champion Tacoma Giants, currently in third spot, will follow the Bees into town."[18]

SABR: The Rucker Archive.

Don Heffner.

Behind the pitching of Ellis, the Padres took the first game on August 10, 2-1. Then, leaving little doubt as to the pennant chase, the Padres won the next four games. The Padres' first-place lead had increased to 11 games on August 14 as the Tacoma Giants arrived in town for a three-game series.

Ellis was the Padres' starting pitcher in game one of the series. He came into the game with a 9-5 record and came through with a dramatic 4-0 victory. Ellis's performance was described this way in the next day's newspaper:

> "Wow! The flame-thrower was hot last night.
>
> "Blazing-fast Sammy Ellis, a 21-year-old Birmingham, Ala., righthander, thrilled a huge,

overflow crowd of 9,124 at Westgate Park by throwing a no-hit, no-run game to give the San Diego Padres a 4-0 victory over third-place Tacoma."[19]

The team won seven of its next nine (August 15-22), but then slumped a bit, winning only two of seven games on the road (August 23-29).

However, as they started play on August 30 in Vancouver, and with 14 games left in the season, the Padres needed only one win or one Salt Lake loss to clinch the PCL pennant.

Next up was a doubleheader on August 31 vs. the Mounties.

Padres August 31 (Game 1) Lineup	
Chico Ruiz	SS
Rogelio Alvarez	1B
Tommy Harper	3B
Jesse Gonder	C
Ken Walters	RF
Harry Anderson	LF
Bobby Klaus	2B
Jim Pisoni	CF
John Tsitouris	SP

The Padres' game-one lineup is shown to the right. John Tsitouris started and bagged the win, 3-2. He was backed by a two-run home run by Alvarez and a run-scoring double by Gonder in the second inning. Tsitouris had been a dependable pitcher for the Padres all season and was lauded in the next day's news:

"The crafty, 26-year-old righthander, who has been the most consistent pitcher on the squad, hurled the Padres into the league lead at this same stadium on June 28 with a 12-4 victory.

"Last night, the Monroe, N.C., athlete fanned six hitters and bore down in the trouble spots to check the dangerous Mounties. This was his 14th complete game in 22 starts and gave him a 13-7 record."[20]

The Padres finished their season with a lackluster final two weeks but won the pennant with a 12-game cushion over the two second-place teams. (The Pacific Coast League did not have postseason playoffs.)

SPORTS The San Diego Union SPORTS

Padres Clinch Pennant, Beat Vancouver Twice

August 31, 1962, San Diego Union, *p.32.*

The 1962 Pacific Coast League's final standings are shown in Table 1.

Table 1

PACIFIC COAST LEAGUE 1962 FINAL				
	W	L	Pct.	GB
SAN DIEGO	**93**	**61**	**.604**	--
Salt Lake City	81	73	.526	12
Tacoma	81	73	.526	12
Seattle	76	74	.507	15
Hawaii	77	76	.503	15½
Portland	74	80	.481	19
Vancouver	72	79	.477	19½
Spokane	58	96	.377	35

THE 1962 PADRES' CORE PLAYERS

During the season, the Padres used 30 players. Sixteen were pitchers and the other 14 were position players. A team photo of the 1962 Padres is shown in Figure 1.

Over the course of the 154-game season there were nine core position players who each played in 100 or more games for the team. The nine players are listed in Table 2 with the number of games they played shown, both by their total, and by games played at their primary position.

Table 2

GAMES PLAYED BY CORE POSITION PLAYERS			
		Games	
Pos.	Player	Total	At Pos.
C	Jesse Gonder	136	113
1B	Rogelio Alvarez	132	121
2B	Bobby Klaus	150	148
SS	Chico Ruiz	144	140
3B	Tommy Harper	144	132
OF	Harry Anderson	115	91
OF	Jim Pisoni	132	130
OF	Ken Walters	152	151
Util	Hal Bevan	102	47-C

Table 3 provides the season's batting statistics for the core nine. Also shown on the table for each player are the number of major-league seasons played, prior to 1962, and for 1962 and after. Finally, Cincinnati's influence on building the roster is exemplified by noting whether the player was in the organization in 1961.

The key offensive leaders on the team were:

Jesse Gonder	.342 batting average	
	116 RBIs	
Tommy Harper	1.020	OPS (on-base+batting +slugging pcts.)
	120 runs	
	26 home runs	

Table 3

1962 SAN DIEGO PADRES BATTING STATISTICS FOR NINE KEY POSITION PLAYERS (100G+)														
MLB Seasons: Career		CIN Org												
Prior	1962+	in 1961?	Pos.	Player	G	AB	R	H	2B	3B	HR	RBI	BA	OPS
2	6	No-NYY	C	Jesse Gonder	136	491	76	168	31	1	21	116	.342	.927
0	15	Yes	3B	Tommy Harper	144	499	120	166	24	8	26	84	.333	1.020
1	1	Yes	1B	Rogelio Alvarez	132	481	88	153	27	5	18	73	.318	.834
3	0	Yes	Util	Hal Bevan	102	280	33	86	13	0	12	52	.307	.846
2	1	No-PHI	OF	Ken Walters	152	583	87	175	43	6	22	96	.300	.846
0	8	Yes	SS	Chico Ruiz	144	621	108	176	29	6	5	43	.283	.667
5	0	Yes	OF	Harry Anderson	113	348	46	90	19	0	14	61	.259	.760
0	2	Yes	2B	Bobby Klaus	150	508	78	130	24	3	13	73	.256	.736
5	0	No-NYY	OF	Jim Pisoni	132	442	55	104	16	3	17	69	.235	.686

Note: Listed in order by batting averages, high to low

Table 4 shows the pitching statistics for eight core pitchers, defined to be those who pitched at least 20 games for the Padres. However, two pitchers with fewer than 20 games – Joe Nuxhall and Jim Maloney – were added to the core group due to their immense contributions during their relatively short stays with the team.

The team's pitching leaders were:

John Tsitouris	13	wins
	16	complete games
	200	innings pitched
Greg Jancich	2.58	ERA
John Flavin	.857	won-lost pct.

Table 4

1962 SAN DIEGO PADRES PITCHING STATISTICS FOR EIGHT KEY PITCHERS (20G+)														
MLB Seasons: Career		CIN Org in												
Prior	1962+	1961?	Pitcher	W	L	W-L%	ERA	G	GS	CG	Sho	IP	SO
0	0	Yes	Greg Jancich	6	6	.500	2.58	28	16	4	2	122	85
4	7	Yes	John Tsitouris	13	8	.619	2.93	29	25	16	3	200	107
0	1	Yes	John Flavin	12	2	.857	3.45	22	19	8	0	141	75
0	7	Yes	Sammy Ellis	12	6	.667	3.53	27	25	10	4	171	162
0	0	Yes	George McWilliams	12	7	.632	3.59	48	5	1	0	123	87
2	1	Yes	Howie Nunn	5	5	.500	4.74	25	9	1	0	76	37
0	0	Yes	Bobby Rasenhoover	3	5	.375	4.80	27	5	2	0	60	25
2	0	Yes	Zach Monroe	8	6	.571	5.51	41	5	1	0	98	41
Note: Listed in order by earned run averages, low to high													
TWO IMPORTANT CONTRIBUTORS (Less than 20 G)													
11	5	No-KCA	Joe Nuxhall	9	2	.818	3.21	15	11	7	3	84	71
2	10	Yes	Jim Maloney	4	1	.800	2.30	7	7	2	0	45	37

At a ceremony held before the last game of the season, on September 9, Jesse Gonder received the team's Most Valuable Player trophy, and John Tsitouris was named the most valuable pitcher.[21]

RETROSPECTIVE

The Team's Position Players Were a Talented Core Group Who Played the Entire Season. The article's headlines in *The Sporting News* said it well:

"Champion Padres Toss Posies to Reds for No-Shuffling Tieup
"Cincy Called Up Only Single Key Player, Nuxhall, and Sent Quick Replacement"[22]

From the opening game to game number 154, manager Heffner was able to count on nine position players to play in a majority of the games. Offensively, they offered a balanced attack game after game with the same core players being in the lineup. There were no major disruptions due to injuries or to shuffling back and forth with the parent Reds.

As a testament to the team's talent, at the end of the season six Padres were selected to the PCL All-Star team as the best at their position:

1B-Rogelio Alvarez	3B-Tommy Harper	SS-Chico Ruiz
OF-Ken Walters	C-Jesse Gonder	RHP-John Tsitouris

Padres' management also was recognized, with Eddie Leishman being voted as the PCL's General Manager of the Year.

Gonder received more, and bigger, laurels when he was named the PCL's 1962 MVP and won the Topps-J.G. Taylor Spink Minor League Player of the Year Award.[23]

Padres' Offensive Leaders Were League Leaders. The 1962 Padres had four players who led the Pacific Coast League in these key offensive categories:

batting average	Jesse Gonder	.342 (second was Tommy Harper, .333)
RBIs	Gonder	116
OPS	Harper	1.020
runs scored-	Harper	120
stolen bases-	Chico Ruiz	40[4]
doubles-	Ken Walters	43
walks-	Harper	105

Cincinnati's Talented Farm System Provided the Foundation for a Winning Team. Of the 1962 Padres' 19 core players, 15 were with the Cincinnati organization, at one level or another, in 1961.

The Majority of the Core Players were, or Would Be, Major-League Players. Further underscoring the excellent talent on the 1962 Padres was the high number of players who would play in the major leagues. All nine of the core field position players played two or more years at that highest level. Of the 10 core pitchers, seven played in the major leagues. After the 1962 season, five of the core 19 would go on to play five or more seasons in the major leagues. Tommy Harper led the way with 15 seasons, followed by Jim Maloney with 10 and Chico Ruiz with 8.

Guarded Optimism Regarding Having a Major-League Team. Early in 1962 the business community was convinced that San Diego was ready for a major-league team. The emotion died down a bit during the season. However, in September team President Jim Mulvaney said, "I think we must hold on until the major leagues expand to 12 teams. I would think this will be in about two to three years."[25] That hope was optimistic as it took seven more years before the National League Padres took the field.

NOTES

1. The Pacific Coast League's history has been characterized as having four eras: The "Golden Age" from 1903-1957, the "Silver Age" from 1958-1968, the "Modern Age" from 1969-1997, and the "Platinum Age" from 1998 on. (Source: Mark Macrae, "Welcome to the 'New' Potpourri!," Pacific Coast League Potpourri, April 2017 (Pacific Coast League Historical Society): 1.
2. Johnny McDonald, "Padres Sign With Cincinnati," San Diego Union, October 25, 1961: 29.
3. McDonald, "Padres Sign With Cincinnati."
4. Jack Murphy, "Only One Restriction on Padre Boss: Stay Away from the Ducks," San Diego Union, February 18, 1962: 105.
5. Jack Murphy, "Heffner Appears Likely Choice to Pilot Padres Next Season," San Diego Union, November 29, 1961: 31.
6. Gene Gregston, "Padres' Ticket Drive Aimed at Future Big-Time Ranking," The Sporting News, February 14, 1962: 25.
7. Advertisement, 1962 San Diego Padres Official Program and Scorecard: 20.
8. Phil Collier, "Finley OKs San Diego," San Diego Union, March 11, 1962: 109.
9. Bob Williams, "Baseball Boosters to Woo Majors," San Diego Union, March 17, 1962: 19.
10. Chris Jones, "1962, Addition by Subtraction" in Steve Weingarten and Bill Nowlin, eds., Baseball's Business: The Winter Meetings, Vol. 2, 1958-2016 (Phoenix: SABR, 2017), 31-35.
11. Jack Murphy, "Only One Restriction on Padre Boss: Stay Away from the Ducks," San Diego Union, February 18, 1962: 108.
12. The trade involved pitcher Marshall Bridges being sent to the Yankees.
13. "Asaro Glad to Be Here," San Diego Union, February 15, 1962: 11, 13; Laurence Leonard, "Sports," Richmond (Virginia) News Leader, February 15, 1962: 47.
14. Nuxhall was purchased from the Orioles before the start of the season and then released by the Angels. The San Diego signing gave him a new lease toward a successful major-league career.
15. Johnny McDonald, "Countdown for Harper in Padres' Camp," San Diego Union, July 12, 1962: 11.
16. Seghi was correct about Helms, who played three years with the Padres (1963-65) before having an excellent major-league career. He was wrong with regard to Rose, who was good enough to play for the Reds in 1963 and be voted National League Rookie of the Year, beginning a career in which he set the major-league record for total hits with 4,256.
17. Rippelmeyer was drafted by the Senators from the Reds in a Rule 5 draft, then returned to Cincinnati.
18. "Pads Host Bees Tonight," San Diego Union, August 10, 1962: 11.
19. Johnny McDonald, "9,124 See Padres' Ellis Hurl No-Hit 4-0 Victory," San Diego Union, August 15, 1962: 27.
20. Johnny McDonald, "San Diego Wins 3-2, 6-3: First Title in 8 Years," San Diego Union, August 31, 1962: 32.
21. Johnny McDonald, "Padres Split With Seattle to Close '62 PCL Campaign," San Diego Union, September 10, 1962: 25.
22. Earl Keller, "Champion Padres Toss Posies to Reds for No-Shuffling Tieup," The Sporting News, September 15, 1962: 39.
23. Advertisement, Topps Chewing Gum Co., "Meet the Winner of the Topps-J.G. Taylor Spink Minor League Player-of-the-Year Award," The Sporting News, October 20, 1962: 39.
24. Harper had 22 stolen bases for the season and the Padres as a team had 78. Together, Ruiz and Harper accounted for almost 80 percent of the team's stolen bases.
25. Johnny McDonald, "Padre-Red Pact Renewal Due," San Diego Union, September 11, 1962: 22.

THE POWER OF ONE

By Will Christensen

It looks like a misprint on the page.

In the league stats for the 1952 Class-D Georgia-Florida League, under home runs, for Cordele it says "1." Not 101, not 51, not even 21. Just 1.

It isn't a misprint. The Cordele Athletics, a farm team of the Philadelphia A's, hit exactly one home run in 1952.

It also isn't a record. The Wilmington Sailors, playing in what almost certainly was the greatest pitchers' league ever – the 1910 East Carolina League – were shut out in 88 games, and perhaps there were other teams during the Deadball Era that somehow avoided hitting a homer. That said, Cordele's feat, in 139 games and at a time when homers were common, is notable.

Cordele's lone homer was struck on July 3, which was the team's 73rd game of the season,[1] during a 14-2 blowout of Brunswick.[2] The hitter was one Ralph "Froggie" Betcher, who connected off the unfortunately named Joe Super in the fourth inning.[3]

The game story out of Brunswick didn't note the significance of the blast. In fact, it gave far more ink to the legitimately crazy play that preceded it. When Betcher stepped to the plate, the bases were loaded, yet his home run was a solo shot, because all three baserunners scored after a wild pitch by Super, an overthrow by the catcher to Super covering home and another throwing error to try to catch a runner at third. On the next pitch, Betcher homered.[4]

According to a story decades later, Betcher said it was a legitimate over-the-wall shot to center field,[5] and the Brunswick account neither confirms nor refutes the location, although it did say the ball cleared the fence. In the later story, however, it was said to be during a home game, but the game in question actually was at Brunswick.[6]

Often, when you see this singular event mentioned, the author will note that the Georgia-Florida League wasn't a homer haven. That's true, and Cordele's home park, named City Park back then,[7] certainly seemed to curtail the long ball even though its center-field fence was only a reported 372 feet from home plate.[8] Cordele's teams finished last in homers four times in the nine years the city fielded a team after World War II.

But that 1952 season was just plain fluky. You almost have to *try* to not hit home runs to hit only one. The year before, Cordele hit 20 homers; the year after, 16. (It ranked seventh in the league in homers each year.) Interestingly, in 1955, now under the livery of the Baltimore Orioles, Richard Lubinski of Cordele led the league with 20 homers, and the team finished fourth overall in homers.

That 1952 team wasn't a terrible team. In fact, the Cordele A's finished 66-73 and in fifth place, which was the best finish for a team from Cordele after World War II. And it wasn't just pitching that saved the day. The almost completely powerless offense finished fifth in the league in runs, because its OBP was a league-leading .361.

Manager Norman Wilson did a fantastic job of cobbling together a good offense consisting of guys who could barely hit the ball *to* the wall, let alone over it.

The 1952 Cordele team just didn't have any power. Although it led the league in triples, the A's hit only 133 doubles, which was last in the league by 20. This, plus the homer outage, led to the team's .310 slugging average, which has to be among the lowest of any team after the introduction of the cork-center ball in 1910. Three pitchers in the league hit at least as many homers as the entire Cordele roster – or more – in 1952.[9]

And, in the end, it wasn't just the league or the park. Of the 22 players who made the league stats in 1952 (at least 10 games played), only eight ever hit even a single home run during their minor-league career. Here are the homer hitters in chart form:

Name	Seasons	HR	AB
Froggie Betcher	4	8	1,824
John Colflesh	4	6	1,197
Bob Davidson	3	1	802
Donovan Day	2	5	964
Paul Demont	8	2	2,627
Jerry Schypinski	4	2	1,515
Carl Watson	5	8	423
Norm Wilson	8	11	3,040

All told, players on the 1952 Cordele A's hit 36 career homers in 14,947 career at-bats. Only Betcher and Day hit as many as five in a single season. Day, in fact, hit five in 1951 playing for Cordele. Schypinski actually made the majors, getting a cup of coffee with the Kansas City A's in 1955. Unsurprisingly, he didn't homer.

This article was edited by Thomas Rathkamp and fact-checked by Tony Escobedo.

NOTES

1 "Minor League Class D Highlights," *The Sporting News*, July 16, 1952: 39.

2 Associated Press, "Cards, Bears Lose Two in Georgia-Fla.," *Thomasville* (Georgia) *Times-Enterprise*, July 4, 1952: 6.

3 "Pirates Defeated by Albany Cardinals, 4-1," *Brunswick* (Georgia) *News*, July 5, 1952: 5. The July 3 game account was added to the bottom of the report of the July 4 Albany game.

4 "Pirates Defeated by Albany Cardinals, 4-1."

5 Kevin T. Czerwinski, "Recalling a Once-in-a-Season Blast," MILB.com, January 24, 2007, https://www.milb.com/news/gcs-151006.

6 "Pirates Defeated by Albany Cardinals, 4-1."

7 "Cordele Fans Buy $10,000 in Tickets in 24-Hour Drive," *The Sporting News*, November 30, 1955: 21.

8 Tim Hagerty, "Solo Homer: The Team That Hit Only One Home Run," *The Sporting News*, November 9, 2014, https://www.sportingnews.com/us/mlb/news/solo-homer-the-team-that-hit-only-one-home-run-cordele-as/1kyydopj76eux1skw4mpwklhlz.

9 The homer-hitting pitchers were Fred Green (2), Don Robinson (2), and Fred Volk, although Robinson played as many games in the outfield as he pitched.

MR. SEPTEMBER

By Will Christensen

It can't be said with absolute certainty, but it would seem almost certain that no one in the history of professional baseball had a better postseason than Bill Serena had in 1947.

Actually, no player on any level probably had a better 1947, relatively speaking, than Serena.

That year, Serena, in his second year of pro ball, had one of the greatest seasons of any minor leaguer ever. After a solid rookie season in Class-B ball in 1946, Serena had a brief tryout in 1947 with the Dallas Rebels in the Texas League before being shipped to Lubbock in the Class-C West Texas-New Mexico League.[1]

Yes, the WTNM is a legendary pinball league, but no one lit up the table that year quite like Serena. When the dust settled at the end of the year, he had a .374 batting average with 140 walks (a .514 on-base percentage). He had 109 extra-base hits, including 57 home runs (an .832 slugging average). He drove in 190 runs and scored 183. The extra-base hits, homers, runs, RBIs, and slugging average led the league. It's estimated that Serena created 197 runs in his 137 games.

That's not bad for a first basemen, except that Serena was a shortstop, not a good one but one who had a fielding percentage above league average.[2] Even still … a shortstop. The only shortstop who ever hit more home runs in a season than Serena did – Tony Lazzeri in 1925 – needed 60 more games to hit just three more.[3]

With Serena leading the way, the Lubbock Hubbers fashioned a sterling 99-41 record, behind the league's leading offense (1,247 runs) while also allowing the fewest runs in the league (794). They took first place in a stroll, 14 games ahead of the runner-up Gold Sox of Amarillo.

Serena had a huge series in the semifinals, which started September 9:[4]

AB	R	H	2B	HR	RBI	BB	BA	OBP	SLG	RC
19	8	10	1	4	8	1	.526	.550	1.211	9

He homered in Games Two, Three (twice), and Four as Lubbock routed fourth-place Lamesa in four straight, outscoring the Lobos 56-16.

The championship series against Amarillo wasn't quite as good:

AB	R	H	2B	HR	RBI	BB	BA	OBP	SLG	RC
27	9	11	4	5	10	2	.407	.448	1.111	11

That Serena underperformed might explain why it took six games for the Hubbers to dispense with the Gold Sox. Heck, Serena even took an oh-fer in the first game![5]

Serena started slow, 1-for-8 through the first two games, before having a five-hit Game Three that included three doubles and a homer.[6] But it was Game Five when he really made his mark. With the Hubbers one out away from falling into a 3-2 hole, Serena hammered a homer to right to tie the game at 7-7.[7]

SABR: *The Rucker Archive.*

Bill Serena.

Then he drilled a two-run dinger as part of a nine-run 11th inning that salted away the game.[8] (He also homered in the Game Six clincher as well as in Game Two – he homered in all four of the Hubbers' wins.)

Now West Texas-New Mexico League champion, the Hubbers turned to what was known as the Class-C Championship of Texas, or the Little Dixie Series, against Kilgore, the champion of the Class-C Lone Star League. Serena did all right:

AB	R	H	2B	HR	RBI	BB	BA	OBP	SLG	RC
22	8	10	2	4	10	1	.455	.478	1.091	9

The Hubbers won in five games (ending the season on September 30), and, again, Serena homered in all four of his team's victories.[9] His biggest game was the first one, when he went 3-for-5 and drove in six runs to pace his team to a 14-1 win.[10]

When you put it all together, this is what Bill Serena did in the 1947 postseason:

G	AB	R	H	2B	HR	RBI	BB	BA	OBP	SLG	RC
15	68	26	31	7	13	28	4	.456	.486	1.132	29

It turns out that as good as he was during the regular season, Serena was even better during the postseason – against the best opposition.

To give you some perspective, the major-league record for home runs in a single postseason is 10 by Randy Arozarena, in 20 games in 2020. Further perspective: Just add a zero to the end of each above number to see what a full season of this sort of performance would look like. Sure, the 40 walks aren't much, but I think most seamheads could live with the 130 homers.

Other players have put up better slash percentages over a shorter postseason, but it seems doubtful anyone has had that brilliant a performance over such a sustained period when it counted the most. (It wasn't perfect; Serena made eight errors to fashion a .905 fielding percentage during the postseason, and his error rate in the Class-C title series was brutal, although it didn't seem to cost his team much overall.)[11]

Overall, Serena was a pretty good player. He never really had a bad year in the minors – finishing with 182 home runs in seven seasons – and he did all right in five-plus seasons in the majors.

But he never came close to scaling the great heights he achieved in 1947.

This article was edited by Thomas Rathkamp and fact-checked by Tony Escobedo.

NOTES

1 "Rebs Send Five Men to Lower Loops," *Dallas Morning News*, April 23, 1947: 5.

2 The *1948 Sporting News Baseball Guide* carried fielding averages for West Texas-New Mexico League players who played at least 10 games at shortstop. Shortstops who played at least 10 games fielded .902; Serena fielded .911.

3 Lazzeri hit 60 homers with the Salt Lake City Bees in 197 games. Álex Rodríguez hit 57 homers with the Texas Rangers in 2002, the major-league record for a shortstop.

4 Bill Chick, "Hinrichs Hurls Three-Hitter as Hubbers Win First Series Tilt," *Lubbock* (Texas) *Morning Avalanche*, September 10, 1947: 8.

5 Harry Gilstrap, "Lonergan's Four-Hitter Whitewashes Hubbers, 7-0," *Amarillo Daily News*, September 17, 1947: 4. Serena would get his revenge later in the series.

6 Bill Chick, "Hubbers Batter Gold Sox 21 to 11, to Go One Ahead in Final Playoff Series," *Lubbock Morning Avalanche*, September Sept. 19, 1947: 10.

7 Frank A. Godsoe Jr., "Hubbers Rout Sox, 16-7," *Amarillo Sunday News-Globe*, September 21, 1947: 15.

8 Godsoe, "Hubbers Rout Sox, 16-7." Both homers were off Lonergan, who had blanked Lubbock and gave Serena his only oh-fer of the postseason four days earlier.

9 "Hubbers Drub Kilgore, 8 to 1, in Finale," *Lubbock Morning Avalanche*, October 1, 1947: 7. The subhead noted Serena's 70th homer of the season, including 57 in the regular season and 13 in the postseason.

10 Choc Hutcheson, "Heavy Hitting and Stingy Pitching Give Hubs Victory," *Lubbock Morning Avalanche*, September 27, 1947: 8.

11 "Hubbers Are Humbled by Kilgore Drillers, 10 to 2, in Fourth Game of Class C Series," *Lubbock Morning Avalanche*, September 30, 1947: 8. In the series against Kilgore, Serena made six errors in 35 chances, for an .829 fielding percentage. Nevertheless, four of the errors came during Lubbock victories.

STARS AMONG STARS

By Will Christensen

All-Star games had been an annual event in most minor leagues since their origin in 1934,[1] but two games only eight days apart in 1955 stand alone in the annals of professional baseball history.

On July 11, 1955, Bill Drummond, Bob Wiltse, and Bob Shipman combined to pitch the only no-hitter in an all-star game. The trio blanked the El Dorado Oilers, who were leading the Class-C Cotton States League, disappointing 1,588 hometown fans in a 2-0 victory.[2]

Actually, it was a heck of a pitchers' duel. The all-stars' first baserunner didn't come until the fourth inning, and through seven innings, the all-stars had the only two hits of the scoreless game.[3] In the eighth inning, the all-stars broke through for two runs on three hits, including a leadoff home run by Marshall Gilbert, who was named the game's MVP.[4] He had two of the all-stars' five hits and drove in what turned out to be the winning run. But how do you not give it to all three all-star pitchers?

Drummond and Shipman walked a batter apiece, and two more El Dorado batters made it to first on errors, but neither advanced farther than the initial sack.[5] Shipman in particular shut the door in getting the victory, striking out the side in the seventh and then whiffing the next two batters after walking the leadoff batter in the ninth.[6]

Wiltse, of Greenville, retired at the end of the season, while Shipman of Monroe played two more seasons. Drummond, however, was just getting started. After he and Shipman led Monroe to the 1955 Cotton States League championship, finishing second and fifth in ERA, respectively, Drummond pitched another nine years, most as a pretty effective reliever, going up as high as Triple-A ball before retiring after the 1964 season. Their three-man no-hitter was the only one each was involved in during his professional career.

Eight days later, down the road in Birmingham, Alabama, the hitters got their revenge, well, one hitter anyway. On July 19 Jim Lemon, right fielder for the Chattanooga Lookouts, racked up the only four-homer game in an all-star game. Once again, the fans for the league-leading team watched their team lose to a collection of all-stars. This time, however, it was 19,830 disappointed Barons fans.[7]

What's particularly notable about Lemon's feat is that Rickwood Field, site of the Southern Association all-star game, wasn't anything like a hitter's haven. It was 405 feet to left field and 334 to right, so none of Lemon's dingers was a cheapie.[8] Lemon, a right-handed batter, hit two to left-center and two to right during the game.

He hit them off four different pitchers and got the cannonade rolling early with a three-run homer in the first. A two-run shot that made the score 5-2 came in the third. Then Dave Benedict retired Lemon in the fourth, getting him to line out to short.[9]

At this point, history could have been averted, because all-star manager Cal Ermer, of Chattanooga, said later that he originally planned to take Lemon out after the fourth or fifth inning, but after the two homers decided to leave Lemon in, to see what he could do. Solo shots in the seventh and ninth, the last one making the final score of a 10-5 game, were the answer.[10]

Lemon went 4-for-5 with seven RBIs. The unanimous vote for him as the game's MVP was a foregone conclusion.[11]

Lemon, who was tied for the league lead in homers before the game, slowed up considerably, finishing with 24, good for fourth overall.[12] After bouncing up and down for a few years, he made it to the big leagues to stay in 1956 and finished with 164 major-league homers, including back-to-back 30-homer seasons in Washington in 1959 and 1960, when he played in his only other All-Star Game.

He didn't homer that day, apparently having used up all his good fortune five years earlier.

This article was edited by Thomas Rathkamp and fact-checked by Tony Escobedo.

NOTES

1 "Another All Star Game," *The Sporting News*, December 21, 1933: 4. The announcement of a second major-league All-Star Game after the success of the first one in 1933 was followed by a notice that the American Association also would hold one the following summer. However, the Class-A New York-Pennsylvania League snuck in and beat the American Association by 16 days, July 3 to July 19, for the first minor-league all-star game.

2 Charles S. Kerg, "Cotton States Stars Down Oilers 2–0," *Delta Democrat Times* (Greenville, Mississippi), July 12, 1955: 5. The Cotton States League's all-star game, as was the case for many minor-league all-star games, was set up as a team of all-stars taking on the league-leading team, in this case, the El Dorado Oilers.

3 Ray Stephens, "No Hitter for League All Stars," *Camden* (Arkansas) *News*, July 12, 1955: 6.

4 Stephens.

5 Stephens.

6 Stephens.

7 George K. Leonard, "Stars Win on Four Homers by Lemon," *The Sporting News*, July 27, 1955: 35.

8 Philip J. Lowry, *Green Cathedrals* (Manhattan, Kansas: AG Press, 1986), 92.

9 Leonard.

10 Leonard.

11 Leonard.

12 Leonard. Lemon finished behind Bob Hazle (29), Jim Gentile (28), and Earl Hersh (25).

I DON'T CARE IF I EVER GET BACK ...

By Will Christensen

On May 9, 1950, Bill Sisler finally ended his baseball odyssey with a record that makes any other player look like a homebody.[1] Sisler played for at least 44 different teams during his 23 active years in the minors between 1923 and 1950.[2] Forty-four. It can't be said with absolute certainty that it's a record, but ... it has to be.

Further, Sisler signed contracts with eight other teams for which he didn't play (two as a manager), and God only knows how many more teams gave him a tryout.[3] Sisler played in 27 leagues[4] (likely another record) as far north as Canada, as far south as Florida and as far west as Texas.[5] He finished a season with a team only once – Syracuse in 1944 – and played for the same team twice only once: Clarksburg in the Mid-Atlantic League in 1928 and in 1931 – each stint totaling a single game.

Sisler was small (5-feet-6, 150 pounds) and didn't throw hard, which certainly held him back to a degree. Although it's unknown whether he used it his entire career, by 1943 at least, Sisler had developed a delivery that was described at various times as "tricky,"[6] "confusing,"[7] and "freakish."[8] The *Syracuse Herald-Journal* said he "swings his left hand around with the ball to his right hip before delivery."[9] Apparently, he did this repeatedly before making the pitch, to the point where opposing fans would call out "one, two, three ..."[10]

More important, however, Sisler wasn't much of a pitcher. Because he frequently pitched only a handful of games in most of his stops – 12 of his stints consisted of just one game – his record is far from complete. What information we have tells the story, though.

Research has determined that, with a few stints missing from the record, Sisler went at least 47-72 during his career and had a 6.64 run average in 1,024 innings of work in which we can measure.

But where Sisler's record really stands out is in the strikeout category. Sisler struck out 204 batters in 981⅓ innings for which a record can be assembled, or a strikeout ratio of 1.87 per nine innings. It isn't the lowest figure ever, but it probably is for someone whose career started after World War I.

In short, Sisler might have had difficulty throwing the ball through a plate-glass window. As a result, he was very easy to hit, allowing an average of 11.79 hits per nine innings for innings that we have a record for.

Every once in a while, it all worked. On May 11, 1944, Sisler pitched his only complete game on the Double-A level (then one step below the majors), lasting 10 innings and allowing only eight hits and two runs in a 3-2 victory over the Montreal Royals.[11] It doesn't appear that he ever threw a professional shutout. The best game found was a three-hitter with one run allowed in Sisler's only victory for Drummondville in 1939.[12]

Obviously, Sisler won 47 actual professional games, so he had some ability, but really, how was he able to get so many chances to prove he didn't really belong?

Several writers profiled Sisler over the years, although the definitive source is Ed Brooks, who was able to track down Sisler late in life and interview him about his singular career. Surprisingly, Sisler didn't have much good to say, even that he wanted to "forget it."[13]

Almost every profile portrays Sisler as ... well, not heroic, but a player worthy of admiration, a model of perseverance. For example, Andrew Hendriks on the Canadian Baseball Network website wrote this about Sisler:

"A cynical man would call him a con artist. But to those passionate about the game, his story is one of tenacity, endurance and sheer dedication to a game in which he held so dear to his heart."[14]

There's no doubt Sisler loved baseball,[15] but that's beside the point. The truth is Sisler *was* a con artist, or at least a prevaricator, which might explain why he didn't want to talk about his baseball career later in life. Because deceit was his modus operandi, on and off the mound, perhaps, later in life, it brought him some shame.

Clearly, Sisler was a master self-promoter and marketer, taking advantage of the difficulty and effort required at the time to check out stories. For example, for years it was reported, even as late as 1941, that Sisler played with the Cleveland Indians in 1932.[16]

Of course, he didn't. In fact, no record exists that he even got a tryout with the team. In February 1932, *The Sporting News* ran an Indians spring-training roster that listed 16 pitchers.[17] Sisler's name wasn't on it. By 1944, when Sisler pitched for Syracuse, which was a good-sized city with a decent following, no mention was made of his association with The Show.

Nor did it come up again when, late in his career, Sisler was hired to manage various teams and when managers, naturally, drew most of the ink in small towns. One would think fans in, say, Rehoboth Beach, Maryland, would want to know that their team's skipper had a brush with the bigs, but nothing was written about it.

Maybe Sisler was invited to train in 1932 with the New Orleans Pelicans – where the Indians trained that year.[18] Perhaps that later became conflated with "a trial with the Indians" by writers who wanted to puff up a new player's credentials or by a certain left-handed pitcher. Who knows? You can draw your own conclusions.

All too frequently, the Sisler story played out the same: Sisler would arrive in town, typically a small town that had a losing team looking for anyone who might be able to pitch,[19] on the recommendation of a scout or even, sometimes, a well-known major leaguer. (Rabbit Maranville, in St, Joseph, Michigan, was the most prominent name dropped.[20]) Then Sisler would take the mound, sometimes to initial success, more often to not, and soon after reality set in, would be sent on his way.

No one called him on it, until he got to Nyack, New York, in 1947. The local paper said this after Sisler's release (after five games):

"Bill hooked on with the team through misrepresentation by calling the Rockies' office and saying he was a Boston scout. According to a well-founded report, he then proceeded to sell the team on Sisler (himself) and also wrote a letter to the Nyack club. When Bill, old and way past 34 [he was 46] arrived in Nyack, the surprise on the part of the owners and manager of the team must have been great and probably would rival any comedy ever made."[21]

Maybe, in fairness, all Sisler really was was the ultimate guy who could get the job, through manipulation and exaggeration if not outright untruths, but couldn't do the job. (Today, through social media, Sisler probably would be a millionaire or in prison for fraud – or both.)

Heck, his name wasn't even Sisler. It was Seeler.[22] Adopting the surname of one of baseball's biggest superstars at the time his career began in 1923 – although familial ties weren't always claimed – couldn't have hurt the faux Sisler's chances.[23]

Regardless, it still was a heck of a run.

This article was edited by Thomas Rathkamp and fact-checked by Tony Escobedo.

NOTES

1 "Sisler Quits His Post as Team Pilot," *Syracuse Herald-Journal*, May 11, 1950: 69. There's no evidence Sisler played that year for Auburn in the Class-C Border League or the previous year when he managed in Rehoboth Beach in the Class-D Eastern Shore League, so his playing career seems to have ended in 1948.

2 Baseball-Reference.com lists Sisler playing for 41 teams, but playing records have been found for him in Ottumwa in 1925, Drummondville in 1939, and Granby in 1946. It's possible more might be found.

3 Ed Brooks, "Bill Sisler: Career Minor Leaguer," *Baseball Research Journal* 17 (1988): 10-12. The teams identified as having signed Sisler but for whom he seemingly didn't play were Shamokin in 1927, Dayton in 1932, Muskegon in 1934, Terre Haute in 1935, Portsmouth (Virginia) in 1938, Fort Pierce in 1942, Rehoboth Beach in 1949, and Auburn in 1950. In the final two cases, he was signed as a player-manager. In addition, research found mentions of his getting a tryout or playing in Saginaw and Amarillo as well as with the House of David.

4 This counts the New-York Pennsylvania League, which took the Eastern League name in 1938, as the same league. Sisler had five stints in this league: 1923, 1930, 1933, 1943, and 1945.

5 The corners based on his known playing record are Québec City; Daytona Beach, Florida; and Gainesville, Texas.

6 Howard Pierce, "Along the Sidelines," *Elmira* (New York) *Star-Gazette*, July 28, 1943: 11.

7 "Sports from the Sidelines," *Nyack* (New York) *Journal News*, July 29, 1947: 5.

8 Jack Durkin, "Down the Line," *Syracuse Herald-Journal*, May 19, 1944: 31.

9 Durkin.

10 "Highlanders Win 10-1, 6-2; Lose, 5-2," *Peekskill* (New York) *Evening Star*, July 28, 1947.

11 United Press, "Bill Sisler Hurls Chiefs to 3-2 Win," *Rochester Times-Union*, May 12, 1943: 16.

12 "Local Nine Is Second in Provincial League," *Sherbrooke* (Québec) *Daily Record*, May 22, 1939: 10.

13 Brooks, *Baseball Research Journal:* 17.

14 Andrew Hendriks, "William Sisler a Minor Leaguer Who Made 48 Different Stops," *Canadian Baseball Network*, November 16, 2015, https://www.canadianbaseballnetwork.com/canadian-baseball-network-articles/2015/11/16/william-sisler-a-minor-leaguer-who-made-48-different-stops?format=amp. Note that the title is incorrect.

15 "Kiwanis Clinic Hopes to Move Outdoors," *Lockport* (New York) *Union Sun & Journal*, May 17, 1961: 16. Several stories after his retirement from the pro game mention Sisler conducting baseball clinics and camps for area youth in upstate New York.

16 "Puerto Ricans Meet Trojans Tomorrow at 3," *Berkshire Evening Eagle* (Pittsfield, Massachusetts), June 14, 1941: 16.

17 "Roster of the Cleveland Indians," *The Sporting News*, February 4, 1932: 6.

18 "Players on 14 Major League Teams Swinging Into Hard Work at Camps," *The Sporting News*, February 25, 1932: 6.

19 Eleven of the 44 teams Sisler seemed to have played for finished with a winning record, including two who were right at .500. Conversely, 12 of the teams finished last in their league.

20 "Vet Southpaw Hurler Joins Autos Lineup," *Benton Harbor* (Michigan) *News-Palladium,* August 2, 1940: 9. Other prominent names mentioned over the years included major leaguers Fred Merkle, George Selkirk, and Ripper Collins, an impressive network for a player who only made it to Double-A ball during World War II.

21 "Sports from the Sidelines," *Nyack Journal News,* August 11, 1947: 5.

22 Brooks, *Baseball Research Journal:* 17.

23 "Jimmy Shelton Named Pilot of South Boston Ball Team," *Danville* (Virginia) *Bee,* March 12, 1937: B7. In this story, which named Selkirk as the link to the job, Sisler was called "a cousin of the famous George."

CONTRIBUTORS

Because he couldn't hit the curveball, **Marshall Adesman** moved from the outfield to the mound. Because the curveballs he threw were all landing beyond outfield walls, he moved to the business side of the game, serving as an assistant general manager, general manager, and business manager for minor-league teams located in Florida, Texas, Iowa, New York, Virginia, and North Carolina. He co-authored one book about baseball, contributed to two others, served as an associate editor on a third, and is now the author of the novel, *The Mountain Empire League* (Arkett Publishing; visit mountainempireleague.com for more information). After 21 years at Duke University, he is now happily retired in Northeast Tennessee, though he remains a professional curmudgeon.

John Bauer resides with his wife and two children (although one is now at college) in Bedford, New Hampshire. By day, he is general counsel of an insurance group headquartered in Manchester, New Hampshire, with specialties in corporate and regulatory law. By night, he spends many spring and summer evenings staying up too late to watch the San Francisco Giants, and he is a year-round avid reader of baseball, history, and baseball history. He is a past and ongoing contributor to various SABR projects.

Chris Betsch has been a SABR member since 2019. He lives in New Albany, Indiana, and is a member of the Pee Wee Reese Chapter (Louisville, Kentucky). Chris has written a number of SABR bios and Games Project articles, as well as articles for newsletters of the Minor Leagues and Deadball Era committees.

Kurt Blumenau grew up in the Rochester, New York, area, following the Mets and the Triple-A Rochester Red Wings. After a dozen years as a journalist, he now works in corporate communications in the Boston area. He has a strong interest in the minor leagues, particularly the New York-Penn League, and also enjoys watching college games.

Matt Clever retired from the Air Force to become a land surveyor in his native Pennsylvania. A member of SABR since the 1990s, he has contributed to publications including *The Glorious Beaneaters* (2019); *Whales, Terriers, and Terrapins* (2020); *The Pride of Smoketown* (2020); and *Baltimore Baseball* (2021). Matt lives with his teenage son, Trey (who, sadly, cannot understand his father's obsession), and two old cats named Utley and Rollins.

Will Christensen is a former journalist, avid researcher, and certified minor-league baseball nut. He has been a member of SABR since 1986 and has been interested in minor-league baseball most of the time since then. His first game to watch was the Columbus Jets during the team's final season in 1970.

Alan Cohen has been a SABR member since 2011. He chairs the BioProject fact-checking committee, serves as vice president-treasurer of the Connecticut Smoky Joe Wood Chapter, and is a datacaster (MiLB stringer) with the Eastern League Hartford Yard Goats, the Double-A affiliate of the Colorado Rockies. He also works with the Retrosheet Negro Leagues project and serves on SABR's Negro League Committee. His biographies, game stories, and essays have appeared in more than 70 baseball-related publications. He has four children, nine grandchildren, and one great-grandchild, and resides in Connecticut with wife Frances, their cats, Zoe and Ava, and their dog, Buddy.

Robert Cvornyek is professor emeritus of history at Rhode Island College and currently serves as a teaching professor at Florida State University. He received his Ph.D. in History from Columbia University in 1993. He has written extensively on the history of baseball in Newark, New Jersey, with emphasis on the city's premier teams, the Bears and Eagles.

Ray Danner lives in Cleveland Heights, Ohio, where he is a local real estate investor specializing in the area's beautiful century homes. When he is not fixing toilets, he can be found underwater at the Greater Cleveland Aquarium as part of the dive team. He was on the sports beat for *The Cauldron* at Cleveland State University while completing his MBA and was a contributing writer at "It's Pronounced Lajaway" and a member of the ESPN SweetSpot Network. Ray also plays rover on a vintage base ball club, the Whiskey Island Shamrocks. A SABR member since 2012, he is a lifelong Strat-O-Matic fan and enjoys contributing to SABR's Games Project and BioProject.

Anthony Escobedo has been a SABR member since 2018. A native of Belleville, Illinois, he is a lifelong Cardinals fan. He is also an avid collector who specializes in St. Louis sports memorabilia. Now retired after 40 years with the federal government, he resides in Springfield, Virginia.

Vince Guerrieri is a journalist and author in the Cleveland area. He's the secretary/treasurer of the Jack Graney SABR Chapter, and has contributed to the SABR BioProject, the SABR Games Project, and several SABR anthologies. He's written about baseball history for a variety of publications, including *Ohio Magazine*, *Cleveland Magazine*, *Smithsonian*, and *Defector.* He can be reached at vaguerrieri@gmail.com or found on Twitter @vinceguerrieri.

A SABR member since 1996, **Mike Huber** is a professor of mathematics at Muhlenberg College. He routinely offers a course titled "Reasoning with Sabermetrics" and has mentored several undergraduates in research projects involving statistics and sports. He has written close to 350 articles for SABR's Games Project since its inception in 2014, concentrating on rare events in baseball, such as hitting for the cycle.

Thomas Kern was born and raised in Southwest Pennsylvania. Listening to the mellifluous voices of Bob Prince and Jim Woods in his youth, how could he not become a lifelong Pirates fan? He now lives in Silver Spring, Maryland, and sees the Pirates, Nationals, and Orioles as often as possible. He is a SABR member dating back to the mid-1980s. With a love and appreciation for Negro League baseball in addition to the Pirates, he has written SABR bios for the 1979 Pirates and Clemente books and has completed bios for Leon Day, John Henry Lloyd, Willie Foster, Judy Johnson, Turkey Stearnes, Hilton Smith, Louis Santop, Andy Cooper, Double Duty Radcliffe, and others.

Cathy Kreyche is an independent editor and writer who lives in Hopewell, New Jersey. She has edited and contributed to popular nonfiction as well as prize-winning academic and trade publications, and served on the executive board of Rutgers University Writers Conference. Cathy recently co-edited a memoir of Marty Devlin, an eight-year minor-league player and manager with the Dodgers during the 1950s (*Ol' Buddy Marty: With Average Ability and Supreme Effort, All Things Are Possible*). She has participated in MLB's Take the Field program and realized her dream of playing baseball with the Eastern Women's Baseball Conference in Sacramento and the 2003 24-Hour benefit game played in Tucson, Arizona. She is a lifelong fan of the Kansas City/Oakland/Las Vegas[?] Athletics.

Martin Lacoste recently retired as a high-school music educator and is excited to have more time to devote to some of his interests, including baseball. Once an avid Montreal Expos fan, since their relocation he has refocused his passion for the sport toward its history, notably nineteenth-century Canadian baseball. He has presented papers at the Canadian Baseball History Conference, written biographies for SABR, and contributed articles for the 2022 SABR publication on the development of Canadian baseball entitled *Our Game, Too*. When not poring through microfilm or digital newspaper files, he continues to engage in his musical interests, either as a performer or director, and enjoys keeping active by playing squash, hockey, slo-pitch, and cycling.

Kevin Larkin was a police officer for over 20 years and has been going to baseball games since he was 5 years old. After retiring, he continued his love for the sport by writing about the game. He joined SABR in 2015 and began to fact-check articles and then write stories for the Games Project and BioProject. He has a monthly show on a local radio station. He has a keen interest in the Civil War and has written about that period of United States history as well. According to Mr. Larkin, "Baseball is a great way to learn and I am honored to be able to do this."

Tom Larwin, a retired transportation engineer, grew up in Chicago as a Cubs fan. After a move to San Diego in 1976, he gradually shifted allegiance to the hometown Padres. His first SABR essay was about Walter Johnson and the 1907 San Diego Pickwicks, published in *The National Pastime* (1999). His baseball research passion is pursuing the history of baseball in San Diego from 1870 to 1936.

Len Levin is a longtime newspaper editor in New England, now retired. He lives in Providence with his wife, Linda, and an overachieving orange cat. He now (Len, not the cat) is the grammarian for the Rhode Island Supreme Court and edits its decisions. He also copy-edits many SABR books, including this one. He is just down the interstate from Fenway Park, where he has spent many happy (and some unhappy) hours.

Norman L. Macht is the author of 36 books including a three-volume biography of Connie Mack. His most recent book, *They Played the Game*, was published in 2019. He is currently writing for the baseball history website peanutsandcrackerjack.com.

Joe Marren is an emeritus professor and former chair of the Communication Department at SUNY Buffalo State University, as well as former chair of the College Senate. He also teaches religious studies classes in the Philosophy Department. He has been teaching at Buff State for 27 years. Prior to his academic career, he was a newspaper reporter for seven years and an editor for another 11 at various community newspapers in Western New York, winning several state and national awards. During his newspaper career he was a general-assignment reporter, sports editor, and business editor.

Bill Nowlin hasn't gone far in life. He still lives about five or six miles from where he was born in Boston, and less than five miles from Fenway Park. Counting bios and Games Project articles, he's written more than 1,000 articles for SABR and helped edit many of SABR's books. His professional career was in the music business as a co-founder of the Rounder Records label, and more recently Down the Road Records.

Chad Osborne is a media relations specialist at Radford University in Virginia and has worked in higher education communications for more than 20 years. He researches and writes a Substack newsletter about the Marion Mets, a now-defunct rookie league affiliate of the New York Mets that played in the small Virginia town from 1965 to 1976 and was Nolan Ryan's first professional team. You can find Chad's newsletter at https://marionmets.substack.com/.

Len Pasculli is a retired lawyer and adjunct professor born in one of baseball's alleged birthplaces, Hoboken, New Jersey. He has been a SABR member since 2001 and writes for SABR's BioProject. Besides playing pickleball and pulling out what's left of his curly hair while managing his Rotisserie League baseball teams, Len enjoys cooking, as well as traveling with his wife, Jan, and their children and grandchildren.

George Pawlush grew up in Wilkes-Barre, Pennsylvania. In his career, he spent 43 years as a senior public-relations practitioner in health care and higher education institutions, first at his alma mater, Wilkes University, and then at Geisinger-Wyoming Valley Medical Center and other hospitals in Connecticut, including Yale-New Haven Hospital. Pawlush has published two books – *Dawn and Dusk of the Colonial League*, a post-World War II minor-league circuit that operated in Connecticut and New York, and *Zeus and His Boys,* about coach Rollie Schmidt and his Wilkes College football teams of the late 1960s that produced a 32-game winning streak. Pawlush, who joined SABR in 1992, is chairman of the Minor Leagues Committee.

Laura Peebles is a retired CPA, now an associate editor for the SABR Baseball Games Project. Besides writing and fact-checking stories, she puts her rhyming ability to work summarizing games and writing baseball parodies of holiday songs. She grew up with the Oakland A's, but has been a Washington Nationals fan since 2010. She lives in Arlington Virginia, with her wife, two cats, and an extensive collection of baseballs.

The founding president of SABR's Pacific Northwest chapter, **Jim Price** has been a SABR member since 1979. He received the Macmillan-SABR Award for "A Half Century of Pain," marking the Spokane accident's 50th anniversary, which appeared in the *Spokane Spokesman-Review* on June 24, 1996. A former beat writer, official scorer, and public-address announcer in three professional leagues, he got his first paid daily newspaper byline in 1952. A longtime Spokane resident, he has been a Spokane Indians publicist and play-by-play announcer, the track announcer and publicist at several thoroughbred racetracks, and the sports information director at Eastern Washington University. He retired from the *Spokesman-Review* in 2003. He has contributed to several books, including *Rain Check*, the 2006 SABR convention publication, and *Drama and Pride in the Gateway City*, the story of the 1964 St. Louis Cardinals, and to popular-music biographies.

Bill Pruden has been a teacher of American history and government for more than 40 years. A SABR member for over two decades, he has contributed to SABR's BioProject and Games Project as well as a number of book projects. He has also written on a range of American history subjects, an interest undoubtedly fueled by the fact that as a seven-year-old he was at Yankee Stadium to witness Roger Maris's historic 61st home run.

Thomas Rathkamp, a senior technical writer, is the author of *Happy Felsch: Banished Black Sox Center Fielder* and is pondering his next book. Thomas has also written for three SABR ballpark books (*From the Braves to the Brewers*, *Dome Sweet Dome*, and *Ebbets Field*). He also writes a monthly baseball column for the Ken Keltner Chapter newsletter. Thomas used to cover high-school sports for local newspapers. He lives in Cedarburg, Wisconsin, and has a wife and three children.

Mark Richard has been volunteering with the SABR BioProject since late 2022, though he first became a SABR member several years prior during college. He's fascinated by the community around baseball research, and enjoys using his degree in mathematics to explore statistics and modeling in his free time. He currently works for a math education company, where he has held roles in curriculum development and operations.

Carl Riechers retired from United Parcel Service in 2012 after 35 years of service. With more free time, he became a SABR member that same year. Born and raised in the suburbs of St. Louis, he became a big fan of the Cardinals. He and his wife, Janet, have three children and are the proud grandparents of two.

Michael Rinehart Jr. is a parks and recreation professional by day and an avid baseball historian by night. He was born into a family of Red Sox fans and pledges their allegiance for life but grew up in Arizona and adopted the Diamondbacks as another team to root for. He now lives in California. It was the minor-league scene that ignited his passion for the history of America's pastime. His main areas of expertise and focus of historical research are on the California League and nineteenth-century baseball in California. Michael has been a member of SABR since 2015 and enjoys spending time with his wife, daughter, and two cats.

Joel Rippel, a Minnesota native and graduate of the University of Minnesota, is the author or co-author of 12 books on Minnesota sports history and has contributed as a writer or editor to 26 published by SABR.

C. Paul Rogers III is co-author or co-editor of several baseball books including *The Whiz Kids and the 1950 Pennant Race* (Temple University Press, 1996) with boyhood hero Robin Roberts and *Lucky Me: My 65 Years in Baseball* (SMU Press, 2011) with Eddie Robinson. Paul is president of the Ernie Banks-Bobby Bragan DFW Chapter of SABR and a frequent contributor to the SABR BioProject, but his real job is as a law professor at the SMU Dedman School of Law, where he served as dean for nine years. He has also served as SMU's faculty athletic representative for 37 years and counting.

David Siegel has been a member of SABR since 2006. After 40 years as a professor of political science and administrator at Brock University in St. Catharines, Ontario, Canada, he has now turned his attention to writing about baseball.

Steve Smith is a retired CPA who has been a SABR member since 2000. His primary passion is researching the baseball history of his hometown, Keokuk, Iowa, where in his youth he attended many minor-league games. He spends his winters in Englewood, Florida, near the Tampa Bay Rays' spring-training site in Port Charlotte.

Douglas Stark served as museum director at the International Tennis Hall of Fame in Newport, Rhode Island. He has also held positions at the United States Golf Association Museum in Far Hills, New Jersey, and Naismith Memorial Basketball Hall of Fame in Springfield, Massachusetts. He has written several books about basketball history and is working on a multivolume series about race and sports in Boston.

Allen Tait is a longtime SABR member and retired fraud investigator residing in Grimsby, Ontario. Allen is currently chapter leader for the Hanlan's Point (Toronto/Southwestern Ontario) Chapter of SABR. Allen now applies his investigative skills to baseball research and has contributed to the SABR books *Our Game Too: Influential Figures and Milestones in Canadian Baseball* and *We Are, We Can, We Will: The 1992 World Champion Toronto Blue Jays*. Allen also wrote the Toronto Blue Jays section for the SABR BioProject's Team Ownership Histories.

Christian Trudeau is a professor of economics at the University of Windsor (Ontario). He is a game theory specialist by day, and a historian of Québec baseball by night. He is a co-editor of the *Journal of Canadian Baseball / Revue du baseball canadien.*

Brian Williams began writing as a high-school sports stringer before launching a broadcast, writing, and voice-over career at age 15. He has performed radio play-by-play for PIAA state championship baseball and football as well as some minor-league baseball. After he built a new FM radio station with three partners, added an AM station, and sold both in 2001, Brian switched gears to a career in medical equipment software, where he authored several articles for national trade magazines. Brian still writes and voices projects (brianwilliamscreative.com), and currently works with a middle-school emotional support team and coaches high-school baseball in Harrisburg, Pennsylvania.

The Stars Shone on Philadelphia: The 1934 Phila. Stars

ISBN 978-1-960819-04-8 $9.99 ebook

ISBN 978-1-960819-05-5 $29.95 paperback

Biographies of Ed Bolden's 1934 Negro National League champions, including Biz Mackie and Jud Wilson.

Yankee Stadium: America's First Modern Ballpark

ISBN 978-1-960819-16-8 $9.99 ebook

ISBN 978-1-960819-21-5 $39.95 paperback

Essays about the history of Yankee Stadium and recaps of over 50 historic games and other events there, including papal visits, football, and more.

Ebbets Field: Great, Historic, and Memorable Games at Brooklyn's Lost Ballpark

ISBN 978-1-960819-16-1 $9.99 ebook

ISBN 978-1-960819-17-8 $39.95 paperback

Relive Jackie Robinson's and Sandy Koufax's debuts, and over 90 other heartbreaks and triumphs in Brooklyn, plus essays on the ballpark.

Nichibei Yakyu: Volume II: 1960-2019

ISBN 978-1-960819-14-7 $9.99 ebook

ISBN 978-1-960819-15-4 $34.95 paperback

Fascinating recaps of the exhibition tours and MLB games by US baseball teams in Japan.

Sox Bid Curse Farewell: The 2004 Boston Red Sox

ISBN 978-1-960819-18-5 $9.99 ebook

ISBN 978-1-960819-19-2 $34.95 paperback

Biographies of every player and coach on the 2004 World Championship team, as well as essays about the season, effects of the win on fans, and more.

Dodger Stadium: Blue Heaven on Earth

ISBN 978-1-960819-20-8 $9.99 ebook

ISBN 978-1-960819-21-5 $29.95 paperback

Essays about the history of Dodger Stadium and recaps of over 50 historic games there, from Fernandomania to Vin Scully's bow.

One-Win Wonders

ISBN 978-1-960819-13-0 $39.95 paperback

ISBN 978-1-960819-12-3 $9.99 ebook

Biographies of 78 players whose entire major league pitching record consisted of just one win, from the tragic, like Nick Adenhart, to the improbable, like catcher Brent Mayne.

Willie Mays: Five Tools

ISBN 978-1-960819-02-4 $9.99 ebook

ISBN 978-1-960819-03-1 $29.95 paperback

Twenty essays on Mays' life and career, plus recaps of 30 historic games.

Society for American Baseball Research

Become a SABR member today!

If you're interested in baseball — writing about it, reading about it, talking about it — there's a place for you in the Society for American Baseball Research.

SABR members include everyone from academics to professional sportswriters to amateur historians and statisticians to students and casual fans who merely enjoy reading about baseball history and gathering online or in person with other members to talk baseball.

We hope you'll join the most passionate international community of baseball fans!

Check us out online at SABR.org/join

SABR Membership Benefits

- Receive two e-book editions (spring and fall) of the Baseball Research Journal, our flagship publication
- Receive e-book edition of The National Pastime, our annual convention journal
- New e-books published by the SABR Digital Library, FREE to all members
- "This Week in SABR" e-newsletter, sent every Friday
- Regional chapter meetings, which can include guest speakers, presentations, and trips to ballgames
- Participate in research committees and online discussion groups
- Contribute to books, the Baseball Biography Project, and the SABR Games Project
- Collaborate with SABR researchers and experts
- Publish your research in peer-reviewed SABR journals
- Discount on registration to our annual conferences and National Convention
- FREE online access to Historical Black Newspapers Collection via ProQuest, the Newspapers.com World Collection, and The Sporting News via Paper of Record
- Discounts with other partners in the baseball community

SABR MEMBERSHIP FORM

Name ______________________

Email ______________________

Address ______________________

City __________ **State** _____ **Zip** _____

Phone ______________________

If you wish to pay by credit card, please contact the SABR office at (602) 496-1460 or sign up securely online at SABR.org/join.

We accept Visa, Mastercard & Discover.

	Standard	Young Pro.	Student
Annual:	❑**$80**	❑**$55**	❑**$25**
3 Year:	❑$215		
Monthly:	❑$7.95	❑$5.95	

Members who wish to be mailed a printed copy of the Baseball Research Journal should add $7 per issue (U.S.) or $11 per issue (international). Two (2) issues of the BRJ are delivered each year.

SABR memberships are available on an annual, multi-year, or monthly subscription basis. Memberships auto-renew for your convenience. Young Professional memberships are for ages 30 and under. Student memberships are available to currently enrolled middle/high school or full-time college/university students. Monthly subscription members are eligible for SABR event discounts after 12 months.

Mail to: SABR, PO Box 1715, Milwaukee, WI 53201

www.ingramcontent.com/pod-product-compliance
Lightning Source LLC
Chambersburg PA
CBHW080751120626
46557CB00005B/1225